King Baggot

KING BAGGOT

A Biography and Filmography of the First King of the Movies

Sally A. Dumaux

McFarland & Company, Inc., Publishers
Jefferson, North Carolina, and London

The present work is a reprint of the illustrated case bound edition of King Baggot: A Biography and Filmography of the First King of the Movies, *first published in 2002 by McFarland.*

LIBRARY OF CONGRESS CATALOGUING-IN-PUBLICATION DATA

Dumaux, Sally.
King Baggot : a biography and filmography
of the first king of the movies / by Sally A. Dumaux.
p. cm.
Filmography: p.
Includes bibliographical references and index.

ISBN 978-0-7864-4496-0
softcover : 50# alkaline paper

1. Baggot, King, 1879–1948. 2. Motion picture actors and actresses—
United States—Biography. 3. Motion picture producers
and directors—United States—Biography. I. Title.
PN2287.B137D86   2010   791.43′028′092—dc21   2002007812

British Library cataloguing data are available

©2002 Sally A. Dumaux. All rights reserved

No part of this book may be reproduced or transmitted in any form or by any means, electronic or mechanical, including photocopying or recording, or by any information storage and retrieval system, without permission in writing from the publisher.

Cover photograph: King Baggot circa 1923. Photo by Jack Freulich, a gifted Universal still photographer. Collection of the author.

Manufactured in the United States of America

*McFarland & Company, Inc., Publishers
Box 611, Jefferson, North Carolina 28640
www.mcfarlandpub.com*

To my beautiful daughter Holly.
Her father Bill would be so proud of her, and so am I.

Acknowledgments

When a work of this kind takes five years to produce, it is inevitable that a great many people become involved. First and foremost, my love and thanks go out to Annette D'Agostino Lloyd. Long before I had faith in myself, she had faith in me. Ages before I thought this would be a book, she knew it would be one. She has mentored, encouraged and occasionally corrected me and has given of herself without reservation. She is an inspiration to all who attempt this early kind of work in film history because she believes in it so passionately herself. Special thanks also to Kevin Brownlow, one of the finest film historians of our time. From the beginning, he opened his heart and his files to me. He not only cares deeply about silent films but, more importantly, he cares about the people who made them. He allowed me to see this period in a way I never could have without his help. Special acknowledgment to genealogist David Stielow, for without his knowledge and skill I never could have found all that I did. My heartfelt thanks as well to Mimi Baggot Landberg, who, through good times and bad, provided me with so much love, enthusiasm and encouragement that it kept me going.

So many professional film historians and people with very special film knowledge have consistently and continually supported me that they, too, deserve special thanks: Bob Birchard, Kelly Brown, Diana Serra Cary, John Cocchi, Susan Dalton, Sam Gill, Mike Hawks, John Hillman, Chris Horak, J.B. Kaufman, Bob King, Miles Kreuger, Betty Lasky, Philip Leibfried, Jack Lodge, Bruce Long, Madeline Matz, Lisa Mitchell, David Pierce, Richard Roberts, Michael Schlesinger, David Shepard, Anthony Slide, Marc Wanamaker and Valerie Yaros.

Longtime friends and associates as well as those I met along the way have my gratitude: Jerry Anker, the entire Baggot family, especially Bruce, King, Tom and Mary, Evelyn Fenton, Rose Keegel, Arthur and Burdell Kilz, Andy Lee, Mary Madill, Lillian and Harold Michelson, Helene Mochedlover, Melody Prichard and Arlene Witt.

Archivists and librarians are the very soul of film research and so many of them have helped me. They need to be thanked: The entire staff of the Academy of Motion Picture Arts and Sciences, Margaret Herrick Library; American Film Institute Catalog Project (Pat Hanson); Biblioteca Nacional Jose Marti (Mirtha Diaz Dominguez);

Boise State University, Hemingway Center (Tom Trusky); British Film Institute (Olwen Terris and Matthew Ker); Catalina Island Museum (Jennie Pederson); Chicago Public Library (Lauren Bufford); Christian Brothers Archives (Brother Robert Werle, FSC); Cleveland Public Library, Literature Department (Evelyn Ward); Fort Lee Film Commission (Tom Meyers and Lou Azzollini); George Eastman House (Ed. Stratmann); Georgetown University, Quigley Collection (Lynn Conway); Kentucky Derby Museum (Chris Goodlette); Library of Congress Motion Picture, Broadcasting, and Recorded Sound Division (Madeline Matz and Rosemary Hanes); Los Angeles County Museum of Natural History (John Cahoon, Seaver Center); Los Angeles Public Library (Literature, History, Art and Music, and International Languages Departments); Missouri Historical Society (Dennis Northcott); Museum of Modern Art Department of Film and Video (Ron Magliozzi); Nederlands Filmmuseum (P. Westervoorde); New York Public Library for the Performing Arts, Robinson-Locke Collection (David Bartholomew); St. Louis Public Library, Special Collections (Jean Gosebrink); San Juan Capistrano Mission (Father Bill Krekelberg); Shubert Theatre Collection (Regan Fletcher); State Historical Society of St. Louis; State University of New York Purchase College (Rosalind Smith); UCLA Film and Television Archive (Bob Gitt and Rob Stone); USC Cinema and Television Library (Steve Hanson and Ned Comstock); Wichita State University Special Collections (Mary Nelson); and Wisconsin Center for Film and Theatre Research (Susannah Benedetti and Maxine Ducey).

Three important people in the evolution of this work did not live to see it realized. In grateful celebration of these fine contributors to the film world who deserve to be held in universal memory: Richard Braff, 1924–2001, Roddy McDowall, 1928–1998, and Gene Vazzana, 1940–2001.

Sally Dumaux

Contents

Acknowledgments vii
Preface 1
Prologue: Welcome Home 5

1 St. Louis — The Beginnings 7
2 Curtain Calls 10
3 New Directions 13
4 IMP's First Year 17
5 The Stars Are Coming 21
6 Union Station, St. Louis 25
7 IMP — Growing, Growing, Growing 28
8 Cuba 32
9 Home Again 40
10 A Star at Last 45
11 The Screen Club and Wedding Bells 51
12 Higher and Higher 56
13 Assault on England 60
14 On to Paris 65
15 Triumphant Return 70
16 The Good Life 74
17 Fame and Change 81
18 The Parade Moves On 89

19	Cast Adrift	95
20	New Hope	99
21	A Slippery Slope	104
22	Troubled Times	109
23	California, Here I Am	112
24	Crossroads	119
25	Settling Down in Hollywood	126
26	Ups and Downs	132
27	Winds of Change	138
28	Tumbling Around	144
29	Trouble Ahead	149
30	Beginning of the End	155
31	The End of an Era	159
32	The Last Days	165

Coda 173
Filmography 175
Appendix 261
Notes 263
Bibliography 275
Index 279

Preface

This book came about as the result of an accident. It was born out of the kind of serendipity and synchronicity that defies logical explanation. Its genesis was a simple question asked by a Baggot family member of a reference librarian from the Hollywood Library in California some years ago. I was that librarian. The question was in two parts: "Would you be able to put together a list of my grandfather's films?" and "The family does not know much about him—could you find out more about his life?"

Reference librarians love challenges, but this was a challenge that might test the mettle of the best film historians alive today. It was a good thing I did not know that at the time. What drew me to King Baggot was his very elusiveness. Here he was, the first publicized leading man in America, and yet almost nothing had been written about him. When the early digging for him turned up so little, it felt as though I had embarked on an archaeological expedition. The only way to find Baggot would be with tweezers and a jar—quite literally.

At the outset, I had no idea why those very early film pioneers were not well documented in the annals of film history, but there are some very good reasons, all of which I had to learn. For one thing, almost all their films are gone — scrapped for their silver content, destroyed by fire, left to rot from nitrate damage, or simply dumped by an industry that neither knew nor cared about their value to the future. For another thing, Baggot's early films were made in a time so long ago that it was not a practice in that infant industry to name the actors in them. Over a period of some 90 years, he had become at worst "lost," at best, just a shadowy memory.

As I began to follow his dusty footprints, it became more personal than just answering a reference question. I experienced puzzlement, surprise, wonder, anger and downright indignation. The story of this man's life was fascinating and his many accomplishments needed to see the light of day once more. One discovery led to the next. The chase was on. What a marvelously rich and interesting time he lived in. Somewhere along the way, the talented and handsome Irishman hooked me. Whatever research skills I possessed, I turned to the task of revealing his life and times so that he could be appreciated anew by whole new generations. He deserves that.

The research was conducted on two fronts—the films and the life—often simultaneously, but at other times, one aspect at a time in different directions. It seemed obvious to go to St. Louis where he was born. I spent a week there looking for him and trying to find those footprints. The house where he lived for most of his early life was still there. City directories gave valuable information about his whereabouts, year by year, and revealed his various occupations. Theater programs showed a handful of the stage productions in which he appeared and the roles he played in the early years of the twentieth century. Local newspapers were of some small help, but not much. I had hoped for more. A visit to Calvary Cemetery revealed where some of his family was buried and the startling fact that his father had committed suicide, which led to a visit to the St. Louis Coroner's Office one rainy afternoon. But there were only bits and pieces. I gathered up what I could and forged ahead.

The Library of Congress in Washington, D.C., was the next logical stop. Contained here are quite a few, but not all, of the copyright entries on microfilm for his early films. Unfortunately, IMP, his first film company, failed to file copyright records consistently. They began to do so in mid–1911, then stopped abruptly in August 1912 during the company's reorganization, and resumed again in March 1915. Most all of the hundreds of films that Baggot made no longer exist, but the Motion Picture, Broadcasting and Recorded Sound Division has the best collection in the world of what is left of them, including nine of his one- and two-reelers. It was here that I learned the mysteries of the Steenbeck viewing table. Day after day I pored over the images of King Baggot, the silent film actor. I could manipulate the speed, slowing to catch the nuances of his gestures, stopping to capture his expressions, furiously writing the contents of the intertitles. At last I was beginning to understand his enormous popularity as an early silent screen star. Call it a subjective judgment if you will, but he had a kind of magnetism and a screen presence that made it difficult to focus on any other actors in a scene. When he appeared, it was difficult to take my eyes from him. Although it was frustrating that there was so little left to see, I came away with a better sense of who he was—and why.

One day during the early stages of the work, I shared my rather natural frustration with film historian Marc Wanamaker over the difficulty I was having trying to find anything at all about Baggot in secondary sources. He had been down the same road himself many times and he gave me perhaps the best advice any early silent film researcher could have. He said, "Sally, you are just going to have to sit down in front of a microfilm machine and go through the trade papers day by day and week by week to find out what old King was up to." How right he was. I went again and again to the Academy of Motion Picture Arts and Sciences Library over such an extended period of time that the staff would jokingly say, "Good morning, Sally. Are you *still* working on Baggot?" Well, yes, I was. I sat in that cool, dark little microfilm viewing room countless numbers of times, an exercise which was by turns either maddening or exhilarating. At the end of the day I might walk out with a fat stack of photocopies. But on other days, I would have only two or three pages or, worse, none. However, Marc was right—there were no short cuts to reconstructing a life like Baggot's.

New York was another important resource. The Museum of Modern Art was the place to see a tiny sample of his work as both an actor and a director. The Museum has a print of Herbert Brenon's magnificent 1913 *Ivanhoe*, the vehicle that made Baggot an international star. And it was here that I first saw his great directorial effort, *The Tornado*, from 1925. It was that film that allowed me to understand what a skillful director he was. If only we could see more of the films he directed—but we cannot, because they are mostly gone. And if only he had been given better films to direct, his reputation might have endured. Sadly, he was seldom given the chances (like *The Tornado*) he needed to prove just how good he could be.

I admit to being both proud and at the same time a bit ashamed that the hunt for Baggot took over five years, just to find this much. However, for most of that time I was not unlike a "working mother" who had to earn a living. Until recently I was the special collections librarian for the Frances Howard Goldwyn Hollywood Regional Library. Time had to be snatched and stolen from days off, vacations and those odd moments I could spare. There were phone calls made, letters composed, leads followed up. But slowly it all began to come together. There is no denying the fact that there will always be areas within his life that will forever remain a mystery. Yet, as in the field of archaeology, the future may still hold new clues. Perhaps somewhere in the world, in basements, attics, landfills or in long-forgotten depositories, more of his films will be found; more industry records will come to light; and the film history record will become more complete. Let the reader understand that what we have should be considered only the beginning.

I think of this as a beginning—not only because there is so much more room for further research on Baggot—but also because there are many, many other deserving film pioneers out there like King Baggot who need our rediscovery and serious attention. If this work demonstrates anything, it is how frustrating and tedious this kind of investigation can be. Yet, I hope it also demonstrates the satisfaction that can be found in doing it—the pleasure and rewards that film archaeology can bring not only to the writer, but also to the reader seeking a better understanding of the formative years of our early film heritage. If what is found here inspires others to undertake and improve upon what I have managed to do so far, that will be ample reward.

It has been a long and joyous personal journey for me. This book is the result.

Prologue: Welcome Home

Tugboat horns blared. Flags and banners waved in the late afternoon breeze. A band played and people cheered. The New York harbor was alive with the sounds of celebration. King Baggot was back from Europe after four months of moviemaking in England and France.

It was September 13, 1913, a sparkling Saturday afternoon. At about 4:30, the S.S. *St. Paul* of the American Line slowly made her way into the harbor, where a large delegation of well-wishers had chartered the tugboat *Robert Palmer* of the Barrett Towing Company. When the tug pulled off the 24th Street dock, it was equipped with an orchestra which to the delight of the crowd played "The Star-Spangled Banner," "America" and "Dixie." It flew the official banner of the Universal Film Manufacturing Company, as well as "Old Glory" and the green flag of Ireland.

The *St. Paul* reached Quarantine about 6 P.M. When it came within earshot of the ship, the *Robert Palmer* began to circle her. The orchestra struck up "Hail to the Chief," while a 40-foot banner was unfurled on the starboard side bearing the legend "Welcome King Baggot. King of the Movies."

By this time the sun was low in the sky, but King, with his wife Ruth beside him, climbed to the topmost deck and acknowledged the enthusiastic cheers from the hundreds there to greet him. In pantomime, he expressed his pleasure at being home again and it was reported that unrestrained tears demonstrated his appreciation of the glorious welcome.

When the *St. Paul* finally cleared Quarantine, the *Palmer* followed in her wake and landed the tug's passengers back at the 24th Street wharf. After King and Ruth disembarked and passed through customs, they became the subject of another large demonstration, terminated only when the couple was whisked away in producer Mark Dintenfass' automobile.[1]

It had been quite a journey for 33-year-old King. He had struggled so long and hard trying to become a matinee idol of the stage, but fate had another role for him. He became, instead, the first publicized leading man of the screen. His New York welcome home was an acknowledgment of the glittering fame he had achieved. For the moment, at least, he had it all — the recognition of his peers, the woman he loved at his side, the public's adulation and a limitless future in the exciting new medium called the "moving pictures." At that moment, he was indeed "King of the Movies."

1

St. Louis—The Beginnings

There were enough Irish people in St. Louis as early as 1819 to organize a local Hibernian Society. But in 1845, the first year of the Irish potato famine, they began to arrive in larger numbers. Those early arrivals were poor, Catholic, malnourished and fiercely communal. By 1870, they numbered over 32,000 out of a total population of 310,000.[1]

The Baggot family can be traced to the city by 1855. King Baggot's father William arrived in St. Louis from County Limerick at about age seven with his brothers Edward and Patrick. William attended public school and by 1870 was a grocery clerk in his brothers' store, Baggot & Brothers. The spelling of the family name went through a number of changes between the 1870 and 1880 Censuses, but by 1900 they had settled on the spelling "Baggot."[2] William became a deputy sheriff in 1875 and not long after that was appointed to be first marshal of the St. Louis Court of Appeals. It was around this time that he met Harriet (Hattie) King, the daughter of John King, a local St. Louis contractor, and his wife Mary O'Brian King. John King, like William Baggot, was born in Ireland, but Hattie was born in Missouri in 1859. She was 13 years younger than William when they married in 1879.

They started their family right away. King William Baggot was born on November 7, 1879. He was named King for his mother's family. By this time, St. Louis had transformed itself from a fur-trading riverboat town, well known as a supply center for Union troops during the Civil War, into a bustling metropolis with a population second only to Chicago. Rail transport had taken over from the Mississippi riverboats and the town was a vital hub for shipping goods to every place in the country that the rails would run.

As would be expected of a traditional Irish Catholic family, it was not long before more children began to arrive. Their second son, Amos Taylor Baggot, was born in December 1881, followed by Arthur Lee in March 1885. William was active in state and local Democratic Party politics and was appointed a state oil inspector by Governor John Marmaduke about 1885. He continued at this post under two succeeding Democratic governors—A.P. Morehouse, whose term ran from 1887 to 1889, and David R. Francis, Missouri's governor from 1889 to 1893. As the family grew and William's prospects improved, the family moved from their small home on Finney Avenue to more substantial quarters—a large brick house at 1463 Union Boulevard. Hattie's two maiden sisters, Margaret and Ella King, moved in with them. Here Thomas Gantt, named for a judge who had been a St. Louis attorney and later a U.S. district attorney during President James Polk's administration, was born in March 1889, then John Marmaduke in April 1892. Marmaduke was named for the former governor.

King attended public school until 1890. When he was ten years old, his father enrolled him in Christian Brothers College, a venerable St. Louis Catholic institution of learning. He attended CBC until he was 15.[3] There is no way to know what kind of student he was, for a deadly fire in October 1916 destroyed the school's records and killed ten people. However, he was a good athlete. He excelled in sports and became captain of the soccer team. It could have been at this time that he acquired a taste for fame. Sprinting down the soccer field with the sound of the cheering crowds ringing in his ears most assuredly made him feel special. St. Louis was always a sports-loving city and its star athletes received a good deal of public acclaim.

After graduating from high school in 1895, King left St. Louis for almost three years. He moved to Chicago and worked as a clerk for his uncle Edward Baggot in the family business, which dealt in plumbing, gas and electric fixtures. Edward was considered a pioneer Chicago businessman. He had started his plumbing and gas fitting enterprise in 1861 and survived the Great Fire of Chicago in October 1871. He belonged to the Volunteer Fire Department and during the Civil War he served with the Board of Trade Battery of Chicago. His firm installed the electric lighting fixtures for the Manufacturing Building constructed for the Chicago World's Columbian Exposition in 1893, which may have been the largest building at that time — 80 acres — illuminated by electricity.[4]

The Baggot family home in Chicago was located at the southwest corner of Racine and Taylor streets. Edward had four sons. His wife died while still quite young and her sister, Miss Kelly, came and took charge of the household. King most probably lived with the family. He had moved from a big city to an even bigger one. Chicago in the 1890s had a population of a little over a million people, second only to New York. It is possible that it was in Chicago where King first became attracted to the theater. By the time he was living there, the town was a teeming and vital theatrical venue. A glance at the *Chicago Tribune* in the late 1890s shows dozens of theaters of all kinds attracting a clientele from many diverse walks of life. One could visit Kohl and Middleton's Clark Street Dime Museum, where the Yankee Whittler whittled, bagpipers played, a petrified woman was on view, or Pearlie the midget vocalist was singing. The more discerning theatergoer could find Henry C. de Mille and David Belasco presenting *The Wife* at the Lincoln Theatre. They could see E.H. Sothern in *Prisoner of Zenda* at Hooleys, Ada Rehan performing Shakespeare in repertory at the Columbia, or thrill to a performance of *Trilby* by Wilton Lackaye at the Schiller. Perhaps it was one of these that caught the attention of an impressionable 16-year-old boy and made him crave a theatrical career for himself.

King returned to St. Louis in 1897. By then his father was well into a new career as a real estate agent. He and a partner, William M. Haley, had opened an office at 815 Chestnut Street. Back at his old home on Union Boulevard, the family continued to grow. King's little sister Marion Loretta was born that year. It is not certain why King returned home, but an interesting coincidence appeared in the St. Louis City directories for that time period. In the 1897 directory, there was a new listing for an Edward Baggot, manager of F.A. Lavercombs, a wholesale and retail dealer in electric, gas and combustion. W. King Baggot was listed as a collector for Edward Baggot. It is possible that this Edward Baggot was one of the sons of the Chicago Edward Baggot and therefore King's cousin. However, in 1898 and 1899, King was no longer working for Edward Baggot. He was listed as a clerk for Merchants' Life Association of the U.S.

While it can only be guessed why King returned to St. Louis and there are only faint inklings of what he did for a living, it is certainly known what he did for recreation: He was once again playing soccer for the Christian Brothers College team and he was their captain. A report on the Association Football (soccer) League in the *St. Louis Dispatch* of November 9, 1899, when he had just turned 20, noted that King had come to the newspaper's office and advocated that the teams take turns playing on each others' fields:

> We will play next Sunday's game with the Shamrocks at Athletic Park ... and the Cycling Club and the West Ends will play their game out on the college campus. This will be CBC's first game on foreign ground. I think the move to play our games away from home the same as the rest of the clubs is a good one, for it will add novelty to the contest and give the downtown folks a chance to see just what sort of team we have.[5]

The following year, in 1900, Tom W. Cahill, founder and first secretary of the U.S. Soccer Football Association, signed King to play for his professional team, the Shamrocks.[6]

William Baggot, like most fathers, wanted his first son to follow in his footsteps. He fervently hoped that King would join him in the real estate business, but King wanted something more. In interviews in later years, King often mentioned his father's aspirations for him; however, he also said that real estate was not a career avenue he ever wished to pursue. William did get his way for a time. In 1900, King joined his father's firm and he was listed in the city directories as working for his father for the next three years. However, the events of this time period were pivotal in setting him on the road to his no-doubt-destined profession.

2

Curtain Calls

Soon after his return to St. Louis, King found acting — or perhaps acting found him. He joined a now unknown amateur Catholic theatrical group and it was not long before he fell in love with the stage. The theater can sometimes be an intoxicating mistress and St. Louis was a good place to pursue a theatrical career. All the important touring companies played in its many theaters — the Garrick, the Olympic, the Grand, Havlin's and the Imperial. The richness of stage life in the city carried enough weight for the *New York Dramatic Mirror* to provide weekly news of events there in a separate "St. Louis" column.

For a time, King had to balance working for his father, playing for the Shamrocks and doing amateur theatricals, but the theater would win out. He remembered this period in his life with all the longing of a young man in love. He told Hugh Hoffman, then a reporter working for *Picture-Play Weekly*, "I used to hang around the theaters hoping that some actor might recognize me as a future star, but no actor ever did. I had to get right down on the ground and work my way up."[1] It was at this time that he developed another skill — he found he could organize people — which led to his founding of the Players Club of St. Louis. He was the club's first president.[2]

He landed his first professional role playing Horatio in *Hamlet* with the Beulah Kimball–Will Rising Stock Company. In 1902 and 1903, he worked with a number of such companies in and around St. Louis and beyond. In the same interview for *Picture-Play Weekly,* he also recalled:

After a lot of wasted time I left St. Louis one day with a very shaky repertoire company, playing very small parts and doing lots of hard work besides. My salary at that time was so small that even a sweatshop proprietor would be ashamed to offer it to anyone. As might be expected, the company went on the rocks before many weeks, and I was stranded in a Western town. By rare fortune, I had noticed that there was a better-known company that would be playing there in a few days in the last town where our show had been. I walked back to that town and waited there for the show to come in. When it came, I found the manager and convinced him that he needed me, and that was a very hard thing to do in those days when repertoire actors were all supposed to double in brass. That was the beginning of my career. I finished out the season with that company. The following season I got work in my home city of St.

Louis at a theatre doing small parts in a stock company."[3]

In an article a year earlier for *Moving Picture World*, another on-the-road adventure was related:

> The first place he played was Kansas City, and it was there that he had his first thrill. In one of the scenes Mr. Baggot was to battle with coyotes, which he supposed were to be represented by "Property" heads made to cause the effect of many of these animals dashing about, the bodies of which were to be indistinctly seen by the audience. All went well until the moment for the fight, when Baggot discovered, much to his chagrin, that they were live coyotes. Less acting but real fighting occurred for a few moments.[4]

No perfect understanding of King's early theater days can ever be gained, because he was not playing leading roles and because he so often played with road companies which came and went with great rapidity. However, it *is* possible to get some small glimpses into the past from a handful of playbills which can be found both in the theater collections of performing arts archives and from interviews he gave later in life. In the summer of 1903, he performed in his hometown with the Lawrence Hanley Stock Company at Koerner's Garden, located at Kingshighway and Arsenel streets, a popular outdoor summer theater in its day. Two theater programs are in the collection of St. Louis' Missouri Historical Society for that year. Hanley must have had a company of very young actors, or perhaps he felt King was good at character roles, for during the week of May 3, Baggot played the role of Baptista, the father of Katherine and Bianca, in *The Taming of the Shrew*. He was only 23 at the time. However, during the week of July 12, he was the more youthful Antonio in *The Merchant of Venice*.

Following that summer stock season, Baggot toured with a production of *Queen of the Highway*, written by Charles Taylor in 1902. Charlotte Severson and Helen McGowan played the leads and King was billed as a supporting player. It must have been a grueling experience. They played St. Louis at the Imperial Theatre the week of September 13, 1903, then crisscrossed the East and Midwest playing Sioux Falls, South Dakota, Massilton, Ohio, and New Castle, Pennsylvania. In the depth of winter, they found themselves in Canada in places like Toronto, Ottawa, Kingston and Hamilton. Between September 1903 and May 1904, they covered 51 cities in just about as many weeks.[5] But during that tour, he played New York City for the first time. In a 1914 interview in *Moving Picture World*, he recalled seeing the lights of the city, then visiting the Waldorf, where he wrote a letter to his mother from the writing room.[6] In New York, the company had played the Star Theatre, located at Lexington Avenue and 107th Street on the week of March 14, 1904. The tour finally ended in Pittsburgh, May 20, 1904.

Throughout the summer of 1904, King probably played stock in St. Louis, but he was soon on the road again that fall. The play was titled *More to Be Pitied Than Scorned*, a melodrama written and produced by showman and theater owner Charles E. Blaney. It opened in New York at Proctor's 58th Street Theatre on August 15 and ran there for a week before going on tour. When the play first opened, the part of hero Julian Loraine was played by J. Frank Burk, while the villain, who was shot and killed in the fifth act, was played by King. It ran at least 16 weeks all over the East Coast in cities like Boston, Pittsburgh, Philadelphia and Washington, D.C. However, some time after January 1905, there were a number of cast changes. Beginning with the week of February 13, 1905, when it opened at the Cleveland Theatre, Burk had disappeared from the cast and King had the role of Julian Loraine. It ran another ten weeks, playing Chicago, Detroit, St. Paul and St. Louis, and finally ended in Louisville, Kentucky on May 3.[7]

By this time King considered himself a seasoned veteran of the stage. He had come a long way from amateur theatricals and local stock companies. He had not yet reached Broadway — every actor's dream — but at least he had now played the lead in a large national touring company. His father's will could no longer hold him in St. Louis, nor could the razzle dazzle of hometown professional soccer. It was at this point that he dedicated his life to the stage and felt sure enough about his decision that in the 1905 St. Louis City directory, he listed his occupation as "actor."

The chance he had been waiting for came in the fall of 1906 when he was cast in the role of Mr. Bob by the Liebler Organization in a Broadway production of *Mrs. Wiggs of the Cabbage Patch*.[8] This was Broadway's second look at *Mrs. Wiggs*, which was first produced in 1904. A sprightly comedy with broad audience appeal, it was dramatized by Anne Crawford Flexner from two famous stories by Alice Hegan Rice, *Mrs. Wiggs* and *Lovey Mary*. The 1906 production had fresh new sets and "Mrs. Wiggs" was played by Maude Carr Cook for a second time. The role of Mr. Bob could be considered a secondary love interest. The character is a big city reporter who visits "The Cabbage Patch," where he meets Lucy, a Southern girl. They fall in love, marry and leave for the North. It did not do badly by Broadway standards, playing a respectable 24 performances at the New York Theatre in New York City from September 17 to October 10. The company then moved on to other theaters in the New York area, New Jersey and Brooklyn. The production completed its tour on November 17.[9]

In the early months of 1907, the Liebler Organization sent *Mrs. Wiggs* on a lengthy western tour and King reprised his role as Mr. Bob with them. It began in Los Angeles the week of March 11 at the Mason Opera House, then proceeded up the coast to San Francisco, Portland, Oregon, Tacoma, Washington and as far north as Vancouver, British Columbia. From there, the tour took them back through Washington and Oregon again, then east through Idaho, Montana and Utah; it finally ended in Denver, Colorado, the week of May 13. Those hard-working actors covered 22 cities in a little less than three months and many of the places they played were literally whistle stops and one-night stands.[10]

After the western road trip in 1907, King most probably played summer stock again in St. Louis. However, the fall of that year and all of 1908 are a tantalizing blur. No specific records can be found for this time period, but there are clues. In some of the interviews he gave after he became a film star, he described working for a number of companies run by well-known producers — names like James H. Wallick, Charles Frohman and the Shuberts. Plays such as *Salomy Jane* and *In the Bishop's Carriage* were mentioned, and also that he had worked with some very popular stars of that time (Wilton Lackaye, Virginia Harned and Amelia Bingham). Many of these vehicles were probably touring productions and his roles were, no doubt, less than stellar. But one name was to stand out above all others: Marguerite Clark.

3

New Directions

From the city directories, it can be seen that King was still living in St. Louis in 1909. No matter where he toured, he always came home. He was listed at the family home on Union Boulevard for every year between 1900 and 1909, but this year was going to be special. It would encompass hardship, joy, losses and a new direction.

A great mystery and tragedy befell the family at the beginning of 1909. King's father William disappeared from their home on February 13. When no trace of him was found by March 27, the family petitioned the Probate Court to have him declared legally dead. The final decree was issued by the Court on April 23, but on that day his body was found floating in the Mississippi River at the foot of Gratiot Street. The newspaper account said that his body was so decomposed that his features were not recognizable. The contents of his pockets were reported in the *St. Louis Globe-Democrat* on Saturday, April 24 as follows:

> In his clothing were found a card of his daughter, Miss Marion Loretta Baggot, a letter, a pair of eyeglasses, the keys to a safe deposit box and a few cents in change.... The letter, which is dated January 20, 1908, reads: "I sold all my rights and interests in the firm of Baggot and Haley to William Baggot, who assumed all liabilities and obligations of said firm. WILLIAM M. HALEY. An original copy of this was delivered to Judge O'Neill Ryan. WILLIAM BAGGOT." The time for the funeral had not been set by the family last night. Edwin H. Meyer of 3215 Dodier Street, who had succeeded Baggot in his real estate firm, died suddenly of heart disease Monday night.[1]

An inquest was held at the Coroner's Office on the twenty-fourth. King was there and testified for the family. After a few preliminary questions, the deputy coroner, T.L. Carrier, M.D., asked King, "Do you know anything of the circumstances of his death?" King replied, "I know he was under a doctor's care for seven or eight days before this and his mind was unbalanced and he had threatened suicide. He called my mother up and told her where she would find his insurance policy and he had some property that was condemned and that seemed to worry him and the doctor and all the folks at home thought if he didn't recover, they would have to send him away." Others to testify at the inquest included the police officer who was summoned to the scene and the two laborers in a skiff who pulled

Baggot's body out of the water. The coroner's verdict was "drowning while mentally deranged."[2]

One has to wonder — at what point did William call his wife? If he was missing since February 13 and had already been declared legally dead, as the newspaper report stated, that could have been quite a shock to the family. King's testimony that his father was under a doctor's care just seven or eight days before he was found is also puzzling. The deputy coroner did not question King more closely about his father's disappearance in February. Since it was never determined exactly when William went into the water, the actual sequence of events cannot be truly known. Sometimes the truth is untidy. However, the fact that William was thought to be "not of sound mind" was extremely important to a Catholic family. Since he did not commit suicide with a sound mind, he could be buried in good conscience in a Catholic cemetery — which he was — that same day at Calvary Cemetery in St Louis.

It was the week of May 16, 1909, when King began what would be his last season as a summer stock player. The plays were performed at the Suburban Garden Theatre, Koerner's Garden having burned down in 1904. The season started with *Salomy Jane*, that old theatrical favorite based on the short story *Salomy Jane's Kiss* by Bret Harte. It starred Julia Herne as Salomy Jane while King played her father, Madison Clay. He had parts in all of the plays that season; unfortunately, they were not large ones.[3] The stars were actors like Amelia Bingham, Wilton Lackaye and Countess Venturini (Lea Siria). But on the week of July 25, the Shuberts brought Marguerite Clark to town to star in a production of *Peter Pan*. Although Maude Adams had become synonymous with that role, Clark did very well, indeed. This was Clark's first dramatic role and an important change in her career. After this, she would never again be confined to musical comedies and light opera. On opening night, the *St. Louis Star* reported:

> There were so many bouquets that one could not see the tiny star. (And she was tiny — only four feet, ten inches tall and weighed 90 pounds.) Two huge bouquets were of American Beauty roses taller than Miss Clark — one from Lee and Sam Shubert and the other from De Wolfe Hopper. Floral tributes also came from Jefferson de Angelis, Ralph J. Cohn, Eugene Barrington, Wilton Lackaye and others.[4]

King did not have a substantial part. In fact, he played one of the pirates — Cecco. *Peter Pan* was held over into a second week, then on the week of August 8, Clark starred in a production of *The Golden Garter* as Zaidee, a young and innocent Turkish girl who was adept at disregarding conventions. King played a supporting role as Capt. Kadek, a young Turkish officer. In the two weeks that remained of the season, he had small parts in *Frou Frou* and *Jenny*, both starring Countess Venturini.

When the season closed, another fateful event occurred. He was cast by the Shuberts (in a supporting role to Marguerite Clark) in a touring production of *The Wishing Ring*, a play by Owen Davis, founded on a short story by Dorothea Deakin. Why the Shuberts cast him is not known. They could have chosen any actor from their vast stable of young men with greater experience. But cast him they did. Perhaps Marguerite Clark liked him. Perhaps, because he was then "at liberty," he was readily available and probably would not have demanded a large salary or intricate negotiations. His looks may also have influenced their decision. He had not yet reached his thirtieth birthday. Physically, he was six feet tall with an athlete's build. He was a handsome man with piercing blue eyes and brown hair, which even then had a distinctive shock of white running through it. Whatever the reason, he surely must have been grateful to be employed for that winter season, even if it did mean being on the road once again.

Although *The Wishing Ring* was not high drama, it was a charming story. It also provided an appropriate vehicle for Clark's first legitimate role with no connection to the musical stage, although reviews indicated that she did sing one song. It was a sort of "Cinderella" tale with an English setting. She played the part of Sally, the daughter of an absent-minded and improvident parson. The Shuberts cast Cecil De Mille as the father; De Mille also staged the piece. (At this time, he had not yet officially added the "B." to his name.) Sally's lover Giles was played by Robert Dempster, another handsome young man who, unfortunately, would never achieve great theatrical fame. In the play, he pretended to be a gardener when in actuality he was the heir of a wealthy landed Squire who would eventually rescue Sally from poverty and the care and feeding of ducks and chickens. King played William, who really is of humble origins and who is fated to win the heart of Grace Goodhall, who had the part of "The Goddess Girl," a disillusioned and rich American who supposed William to be the Squire's son disguised as the gardener. As the curtain fell on the last act, both pair of lovers became the beneficiaries of the power of the "wishing ring."

The play opened at the Princess Theatre in Montreal on Tuesday evening, October 19, to a packed house and excellent reviews. The last stop on the tour was the Great Northern Theatre in Chicago, where it opened on November 7. Originally slated for a two-week run, it was held over for a third week and closed November 27.[5] According to local reviews, and reported in *The New York Clipper* of November 20, 1909, this play was "beautifully staged and costumed"; however, Clark was quoted in *The New York Telegram*, November 25, as saying that she and *The Wishing Ring* were an established success in spite of handicaps such as, "shop worn scenery, cheap actors, no printing, nor a frame of pictures and a canine member of the cast for which the management paid sixty-five cents."[6] Quite an indictment considering the play was still running at that time.

Now that the tour was over, King was once again "at liberty." Later accounts of exactly what happened next vary. One account suggests that King went back to New York to audition for a role in a production of *Seven Days*.[7] Mary Roberts Rinehart and Avery Hopwood wrote this play, a drama. Their literary agent was Matilda Beatrice DeMille — William and Cecil's mother.[8] Since Cecil and King appeared together in *The Wishing Ring*, it might be a likely supposition that King had a chance to try for a role because of his association with Cecil. The only problem with this scenario was that *Seven Days* had already opened at the Astor Theatre in New York on November 10, 1909, where it played 397 performances, while King and the cast of *The Wishing Ring* was still engaged in their extended run in Chicago.

John Drinkwater, in *The Life and Adventures of Carl Laemmle*, wrote:

> ...an upstanding young man of good looks, visiting the IMP studio was persuaded to put on grease paint and try a small part as a screen test. This proving satisfactory, he was invited to join the company. William De Mille, also impressed by the novice's possibilities, stepped in with an offer of a hundred dollars a week in the theatre from which he had not yet extended his activities to the screen, but with no guarantee as to its duration. Laemmle offered seventy-five, but on a fifty-two week contract and King signed up as the first IMP leading man.[9]

The problem with this explanation of Baggot's entry into the film business is that, as far as can be known, William De-Mille was not involved in any theatrical production at this time. He had written *The Royal Mounted*, with Cecil in 1908, and it played only 32 performances. His next known work was *The Woman*, which did not open until September 1911 and was staged by David Belasco.[10] If William DeMille had a part in mind for King, that fact must be deeply buried in theater annals.

King's own recollections, even if reported some time later, must be considered the most reliable. In *Motion Picture Supplement*, October 1915, he told the story this way:

> I owe my start to Harry Solter, the motion picture director and husband of Florence Lawrence. I was playing with Marguerite Clark in *The Wishing Ring*, in Chicago. The show closed and I came over to New York again to join another company. One morning I entered a Greek shine parlor, when someone called to me and turning, I found it was Harry Solter, with whom I had appeared on the stage several seasons previous. "What brought you to New York?" he asked. I explained, asking him what he was doing. "Oh, I'm in moving pictures," he replied. We both laughed, for he seemed just a little ashamed, and I did not take motion pictures very seriously in those days. Solter asked me to go to the studio with him, which was the first IMP studio opened in New York City, and one of the first of the "Independent" plants. I was amused at the violent gestures and jumping about of the players, and mentally characterized the industry as a fad. I did not become a picture player immediately, going back on the road for twelve weeks. Upon returning to New York, I hunted up Solter and told him I was ready to turn picture player.[11]

While probably closer to the truth, this account does not exactly fit the facts either. Since *The Wishing Ring* did not close until November 27 and it is fairly certain that King's first film for IMP, as he said himself, was *The Awakening of Bess*, released December 27, 1909, there would have been no time for him to do another 12 weeks on the road. Somehow, too, the meeting at a Greek shoeshine parlor in the depth of a New York winter does not quite ring true. But another possibility does present itself. Suppose King went back to New York after the close of the summer stock season. The Suburban Garden Theatre's last production of that season was *Jenny*, in which he played the role of "The Honorable Evelyn Farquhar." It closed September 4. He may have had to audition for his role as William in *The Wishing Ring* for the Shuberts before actually getting the part. He could have met Harry Solter at that time, then gone on the road with *The Wishing Ring*. By the end of November when he came back, it may have been too late to get a spot in a Broadway play or even with a touring company. It could have been at that time that he looked up Harry and "turned picture player."

4
IMP's First Year

Carl Laemmle was the founder of IMP, which stood for "Independent Moving Pictures Company of America." He was born in Lauphein, Germany, in 1867. Although small in stature, he had in-born capacity for hard work and an indomitable spirit when faced with adversity. He was the tenth of 13 children born to a middle-class Jewish family. Seeking his fortune, he left Germany at age 17 and arrived in New York, a poor but enterprising immigrant. He swept floors in a drug store for a time; moved to Chicago where he worked at a number of jobs, including bookkeeping; tried farming in South Dakota; then moved to Oshkosh, Wisconsin, where he worked his way up to become the manager of the Continental Clothing Store. After a salary disagreement with the store's owner, Sam Stern, he moved back to Chicago, taking with him Sam's niece, Recha, as his wife.[1] Casting about for a new enterprise, he noted that nickelodeons were becoming popular with working class people. He had some savings and became an owner of a theater, the White Front.[2]

He soon bought another, the Family Theatre, but encountered great difficulties obtaining first-rate films from the local film exchanges. He solved the problem for a time by opening his own film exchange, the Laemmle Film Exchange, in 1906.[3] He started exchanges in other cities and before long became one of the leading distributors in the business. However, more trouble came in the form of the Motion Picture Patents Company, which formed in January 1909: a blatant trust which was beginning to put other independent distributors out of business. Laemmle was not one to be cowed or threatened. He decided to start his own production company and go into direct competition with the powerful Trust. As it turned out, he had formidable skills to help him. He had been a bookkeeper, a profitable retail store manager, an exhibitor, a distributor, and he had enormous faith in himself. By then he knew a great deal about the film business and had made many friends and allies who knew him to be a good and fair man.

He refused to join the MPPC and on April 12, 1909, he fired the first salvo by announcing in *Moving Picture World* that he would not pay a license fee to the Trust, but would began producing his own pictures: "the best pictures a man's skill can execute. And no cheating on the measurements."[4] Laemmle also had a secret weapon in the form of an extremely talented advertising man — Robert H. Cochrane — who had worked with him from the time he managed the Continental Clothing Store in Oshkosh.[5] These two men were on the verge of helping to change the complexion of the motion picture business radically and forever.

Laemmle opened his first IMP studio at 111 East 14th Street in New York in June 1909. The business office was on the ground floor with the "factory" on the floors above.[6] Although there are a number of versions of the story, his first film was probably not shot in New York or Minnesota, but around Coytesville and Fort Lee, New Jersey, with stock footage edited into the film from locales around the "falls of Minnehaha," presumably outside of Minneapolis.[7] His first director was William V. Ranous, who had gained experience working for Biograph and Vitagraph. The initial IMP film was called *Hiawatha*, and starred Gladys Hulette, but she received no credit since stars were not yet being named. The film was 985 feet in length, or about one reel, standard for the times. It was released October 25 and reviewed in *Moving Picture World* where, rather surprisingly, it was lavishly praised, considering it was Laemmle's first production. The fledgling company went on to make eight more films between November 1 and December 27. That meant that this newly launched company was producing a new film almost every week.[8]

Starting a new film company from scratch must have been quite a challenge, even for Carl Laemmle in those early days. In addition to dodging the Trust, finding and outfitting a studio, hiring competent technical staff and producers, and obtaining cameras and film stock, they also had to find experienced actors who would keep the public coming back to see their films. The Trust was trying to strangle any independent producer foolish enough to defy them. The Eastman Company, at that time a willing participant of the Trust, held the major patents for raw film stock and refused to sell to any company not part of the Trust. Thomas Edison and his partners in the Trust controlled the patents to all the U.S.–made cameras and refused to allow an independent to have them. The experienced film actors had to think long and hard about leaving a Trust film producer and going over to an independent, for they were told that to do so would mean they would never be hired by one of the licensed companies again. Looking for stage actors was not any easier. Theater managers, already painfully aware that this new medium was beginning to eat into their business, also threatened that any actor who worked in film would never work on the stage again.

But, the company began to come together in spite of all the threats and uncertainties. IMP's first real leading lady was Florence Lawrence, whose film debut preceded King's by at least two years. As so many actresses of her day had done, she began her career in the theater at a very young age. She began in film with the Edison Company in a one-reeler called *Daniel Boone* (1907), but soon after was engaged by Vitagraph. It was there that she met her husband, Harry Solter. In August 1908, they were both working for Biograph where, with her strong acting ability and lovely, recognizable face, she climbed her way up through the ranks to become a star — the original "Biograph Girl."

Mary Pickford was to follow her and become the second "Biograph Girl," although the public was not yet allowed to know their names. It continues to be written that Laemmle "lured" Florence and her husband Harry away from Biograph. However, the real facts were known as early as 1923 when she gave an interview to a *Photoplay* reporter. She stated that she and Solter wrote to Essanay hoping to get a joint contract, but Essanay officials

IMP's first open-air studio on Dychman Street, The Bronx, New York, 1909. Photograph courtesy of Bison Archives.

reported the letter back to Biograph and the Solters were dismissed.[9] William V. Ranous knew the Solters from his days as a director with Vitagraph and hired them — Harry as a director and Florence as their leading lady. Her first film for IMP and IMP's second film ever was *Love's Stratagem*, released on November 1, 1909.

King came on board with the IMP Company sometime between the week of December 13 or December 20. His first film was *The Awakening of Bess*[10] with Florence as "Bess." He was taking a big chance, and he knew it. He later said, "When I jumped from the stage into motion pictures I committed professional suicide, according to my friends who tried to keep me from it."[11] There were enormous technical difficulties making films in those early years, and stage actors had to adapt themselves to this new medium. King said, "In those days we had a lot of trouble producing a picture, and I recall Mr. William V. Ranous, who was directing the play, was considerably put out because I couldn't do the things he asked of me. We had to learn."[12]

Although *The Awakening of Bess* no longer exists, an enthusiastic quote survives from a theater owner, Mr. Rosenquest, of the Fourteenth Street Theatre. *Moving Picture World* reported that "it was so popular amongst the Independent theaters that within a few hours of its release we [motion picture reviewers] were unable to see a copy of it in New York City. So that without warning, we sought the opinion of Mr. Rosenquest, who was good enough to tell us that it was the best picture they ever had." The founder and publisher of *Moving Picture World*, James Petrie Chalmers, added:

> We have all along taken a very great interest in the progress of the "Imp"

pictures because the Independent Moving Pictures Company of America, of which Carl Laemmle is president, have to our mind established a record. Though only working for a few months, they have gotten down to the production of the moving pictures in its best technical aspects. They are making good photographs, which many of their Independent competitors are not. Hence, they earn the approbation of The Moving Picture World.... It is really wonderful to reflect that a year ago there was no such company as the "Imp" in existence, and that now the company is a strong factor in the American moving picture field.[13]

IMP had an auspicious future, but in spite of Laemmle's well wishers and supporters, there would be bumpy times ahead.

5

The Stars Are Coming

On January 15, 1910, an article appeared in *Moving Picture World* titled, "Photographs of Moving Picture Actors; a new method of lobby advertising." It reported that exhibitors and the public had been imploring both the editors of the trade papers and film manufacturers for photographs either to own or for lobby display. *Moving Picture World* cited the Kalem Stock Company as being the first to address this need by preparing a handsome lobby display card. With a half-page illustration, *Moving Picture World* showed the card that included Kalem's distinctive logo and photographs of 11 of their players. The only element missing was the names of these players. The thrust of this article was that even if film producers could ignore requests from love-stricken fans, they should not ignore pleas of theater managers who were beginning to recognize the large advertising advantages involved in bringing paying customers into their theaters. However, the article goes on at great length to discuss the objections of the players to being named:

> In former days, when amateurs were principally employed for the parts, it would have been a very easy matter to secure photographs of them for the purpose now in view. At the present time the characters portrayed by the pictures are enacted by professionals. These people are only too glad to play the parts and do their work ... but all of them try to shield their identity. They have an undisguised impression that the step from the regular productions to the scenes before the camera is a backward one.

The article went on to say:

> The speaking parts are cut out, so far as the audience is concerned, and in spite of the fact that some remarkably clever and effective work is done these days, the fact that it is in reality pantomimic work makes the people playing the parts feel that their artistic reputations would suffer should it become known that they were playing parts in moving picture studios.

The piece ends on a practical but hopeful note:

> Quite frequently the best people — recognized leaders in their respective lines [this meant theatrical actors] — are engaged to play leading parts in picture productions, and recently the names of these people have been used in connection with the announcements, but always with a well displayed notice that the particular actress or actor was specially engaged for the

production owing to particular adaptability to the part. At no distant day the stock company will be inaugurated in the moving picture studios and it will then be an easy matter to put the photographic display idea into more general operation. Many of the studios already have stock companies to a certain extent, but they are not sufficiently established to induce players to allow general publicity in connection with their part in the pictures.... Conditions will eventually change and the performers will not feel that they have so much at stake as they do now; then the patrons of the picture houses will be able to feast to their heart's content upon the photographic features of their favorites....[1]

It has often been written that the failure to depict the very early stars in advertising or name them as individuals was the direct doing of the film producers, reluctant to bill their "stars" for fear they would want more money. Certainly there had to be some truth to that assertion. No businessmen, and that is what the producers were, would want to incur more costs than they absolutely had to. Yet, every rule has its exceptions. There were several actors whose names were attached to their films in that very early time — John Bunny, Gilbert M. (Broncho Billy) Anderson and Ben Turpin; two were comedians, the other a Western star, but none could be considered a true "leading man."[2] Even a "leading man" like Maurice Costello, whose film career preceded Baggot's by about two years, was billed by Biograph only as "The Man with the Dimple." However, it can be seen from the early part of 1910 that the film community was beginning to question their own marketing tactics. To see this kind of discussion in early 1910 shows that this business, like any other, evolved over a period of time — that both actors and film producers had good reason for wanting to maintain the status quo. Just the same, it is evident that pressure was now starting to be exerted by the exhibitors and the fans upon the producers to be more forthcoming about identifying individual film performers.

Since change was now in the air, it should come as no surprise that men like Carl Laemmle and Robert Cochrane, who were already taking a number of risks, should be the first to recognize the need and desirability of finding a better way to publicize their films. After all, Laemmle had been both a distributor and an exhibitor — in other words, a showman. He was most certainly aware that the patrons of his theaters wanted to know as much as they could about their favorite actors and actresses. As an exhibitor, he also knew what is was like to try to attract crowds to his theaters over the competition of other theaters in the neighborhood. When he became a distributor, he, with Cochrane's help, recognized the power of publicity and made sure that the name of his company, the Laemmle Film Exchange, was advertised as boldly as possible. That was one of the reasons he was so successful. He knew that certain companies and particular players registered better with the public than others. As for Cochrane, beating the competition was most likely born in his blood. It seems obvious to us today, but someone had to start naming and publicizing those players, not just within the industry, but also to the general public — and these were the two men who first did it.

Between January and March of 1910, a great deal happened. First, a number of newspapers around the country were said to have been informed that Florence Lawrence had been struck by a streetcar/motor car in New York and had been killed on February 17.[3] On March 5, IMP published an ad for her film, *Mother Love*, in the *Moving Picture World* with her name attached. On that same day, *Billboard* published a report with a dateline out of Chicago from February 26, coyly calling attention to the story of her supposed death supplied only by "Dame Rumor" then debunking the story, "which was smuggled into newspapers from we know not where."[4] That same day, a very complimentary article appeared in *Moving Picture World*, titled "St. Louis to the Fore." It congratulated 16 exhibitors in that city for buying space in local newspapers to advertise their films. The article pointed out that, in St. Louis alone, there were 200 motion picture houses with over a million dollars invested in them and employing about 1,500 people. Again, it should be obvious that they should all have been actively advertising, but the evolutionary aspects of the film business were at work here. "This shows enterprise on the part of the newspapers and on the part of the exhibitors. It is an example to be followed by the exhibitors in other cities.... We have not the slightest doubt that the other great newspapers of the country would cooperate with them in having the moving picture theater more prominently brought to the notice of the public. Other cities, please imitate St. Louis as soon as possible!"[5] It is quite possible that St. Louis exhibitors were singled out for special praise at this precise time specifically because negotiations were already underway for what would be the next event.

On March 12, IMP took out a full-page in *Moving Picture World* which boldly stated, "We Nail the Lie." Almost half the page is taken up with a photograph of Florence Lawrence looking somewhat dolorous. Holding up the photo was the Imp himself, with his horns, hoofs and pointy tail. The copy read:

> The blackest and at the same time the silliest lie yet circulated by enemies of the "Imp" was the story foisted on the public of St. Louis last week to the effect that Miss Lawrence the "Imp" girl, formerly known as the "Biograph" girl had been killed by a street car. It was a black lie because so cowardly. It was a silly lie because so easily disproved. Miss Lawrence was not even in a street car accident, is in the best of health, will continue to appear in "Imp" films, and very shortly some of the best work of her career is to be released.[6]

Keep in mind that this announcement was made to a trade paper, not to the general press, but only a week later they were ready to go in an entirely new direction.

The *St. Louis Post-Dispatch*, in their Sunday supplement for the week of March 20, began the section with a large spread on Florence Lawrence. It read:

> The Girl of a Thousand Faces. Florence Lawrence, three times reported dead but still very much alive is the highest paid moving picture actress— an adept in pantomime, she rehearses 300 rolls [sic] a year, or one for each working day. An actress whose face is known to millions of people in the United States, but whose name is known to few, if any, is the girl whose lissome figure flashes through the comedies and dramas that are exposed on the screen in the thousands of moving-picture theaters in this country controlled by the independent film manufactures.[7]

The article contained a long interview with Florence about the intricacies of shooting her films, her frequent attendance at theaters, seeing her own films and listening to the applause and comments, and her delight at receiving fan mail. The first page had a full-length photograph and seven inserts showing her facial expressions while acting out the emotions of piety, coquetry, horror, determination, sadness, concentration and hilarity. The interview, unsigned, almost certainly took place in New York. At one point she took out a bundle of fan letters to show the interviewer. The stills were surely provided by IMP and it is significant to note that the interview stressed the fact that she worked for an "independent film company," but without mentioning the company's name.

It went on to say that millions of people were in theaters watching independent films and that such a company valued her so highly that she was reported to be the highest paid moving picture actress in the business. After that kind of build-up, it is not too surprising to see what would came next.

6

Union Station, St. Louis

The stage was now set. All that was needed was to bring on the players. On Friday, March 25, the *St. Louis Star* announced that Florence Lawrence would be appearing at a reception on Saturday at Union Station; King Baggot was named in association with this unprecedented event. "Accompanying Miss Lawrence will be King Baggott [sic], the St. Louis actor, who recently deserted the dramatic field and has accepted a position with the Imp Company and has appeared as Miss Lawrence's leading man in many of her pictures..."[1] Offering something free, even as early as 1910, was already an ancient advertising gimmick, and publicity-savvy men like Laemmle and Cochrane used it to good effect. In the want ads section of the *St. Louis Times* that day appeared this notice:

> March 25, 1910, Miss Florence Lawrence, Twentieth Street Entrance, Terminal Station, St. Louis, Mo., Dear Miss Lawrence — Kindly give me an order on the *St. Louis Times* entitling me to one of your autographed photographs, taken by their staff photographer, Burton. Wishing you and your company great success, I remain AN ADMIRER.[2]

It was an old ploy which usually worked and, indeed, it did this time.

The main event took place on Saturday afternoon, March 26. It was unprecedented insofar as it was the first time such an elaborate publicity scheme had been devised by a motion picture studio for the benefit of the film industry and the general public as well, by using the regular press. Years after the fact, an even more sensational spin was put on this historical first, but the actual facts were impressive enough as reported in the *St. Louis Times*, which appeared to have an "exclusive" on the story, and the give-away of photographs through their staff photographer known only as "Burton." The article was well positioned on page three and featured a large photograph of Florence with a thoughtful, almost reverent expression on her face, holding a large bouquet of lilies. It was captioned, "Miss Florence Lawrence in an Easter Pose for the Times. By staff photographer Burton." The headline read, "Ovation for Film Star at Union Station. Miss Florence Lawrence Nearly Swept From Feet by Admirers." The article went on to say:

> As early as 5 o'clock groups of women holding in their hands the letter clipped from The Times, and addressed to Miss Lawrence, began gathering at the Twentieth

Street entrance to the Station. The crowd continued to grow, and as might have been expected, women made up the huge bulk of the crowd.... Shortly before the train was due, several automobiles, containing Frank L. Talbot, the manager of the Gem and Grand theatres, where Miss Lawrence and her leading man, King Baggott [sic], the St. Louis actor will appear Saturday and Sunday, arrived accompanied by Carl Laemmele [sic], president of the Imp Film Company, which has a life contract with the famous actress, and Frank Daeheel and Fred Wehrenberg, president and secretary of the Moving Picture Men's Association.

The train, scheduled for 5:35 was seven minutes ahead of time, and hundreds of women and men succeeded in passing the gatemen and lined the platform leading to Miss Lawrence's car.

Talbot invaded the car, and introduced the newspaper men and the moving picture officials to the little woman who had made her name famous in every land, and that without her voice ever having been heard by the public.... Surrounded by her managers and with her leading man at her side, the actress whose features are shown to millions nightly, shrank from the crowd that gathered around her. At this point she gave a short speech: "I had no idea that so many people were interested in me," blushingly said Miss Lawrence, "and I so dread this ordeal of seeing so many people. But there is no alternative and I am so wearied by my long trip that I am anxious to get to the hotel and enjoy a nice long rest. But, indeed, I appreciate this honor, and it seems so strange that so many people would gather at the train to welcome one they had never seen only in pictures."

However, having a long rest was easier said than done.

The party tarried in the observation car but a few minutes, and the start was made for the automobile that was waiting to convey her to the Planters. If the crowd was embarrassing to the silent actress within the gates, it was many fold more so when she, between the huge forms of Talbot and King Baggott, attempted to make her way through the crowds that had assembled in the Midway.

Despite the fact that the large bulk of the crowd was made up of women and girls, the police had great difficulty in clearing a passageway. And no sooner had Miss Lawrence and her escorts passed the gates leading from the train sheds than there were enthusiastic shouts from female voices, and a rush of well-dressed women to get a closer view of the little woman in a close-fitting blue dress, whom they instantly recognized as Miss Lawrence, their heroine.

The flood of femininity that swept toward her was like an avalanche, and but for the strong men who supported her, she would have been swept from her feet. She tried to appear indifferent at first, and began bowing acknowledgments, but when the crowd pressed her so closely that it appeared she would be trampled underfoot she became frightened and her escorts had difficulty in making their way through the dense crowds.... Even after she had been placed in her automobile, the crowd so surrounded it that it was moved with great difficulty and the women who had barely obtained a glimpse of her, but had procured the coveted order for one of her autographed photographs, which cannot be duplicated, felt repaid for the journey to the Station, and for the exertion they had been compelled to put forth for the mere privilege of seeing for a fleeting moment the form of one they felt so familiar with.[3]

Many years later, in 1931, John Drinkwater, in his Carl Laemmle biography *The Life and Adventures of Carl Laemmle*, embellished the story by saying that when the stars were approaching the theater where they were to make their first personal appearance, the crowd "demonstrated their affection [for Miss Lawrence] by tearing the buttons from her coat, the trimmings from her hat, and the hat from her head."[4] Nothing in contemporary accounts of that time suggests that this was true, but the actual facts speak for themselves. A near riot at the train station did take place. Police had to be used to control the crowds, and it was certainly the first time known in film history that such an event was so carefully orchestrated by a film studio, where the general public was invited to see film stars at a personal appearance set up just for them.

Obviously, King Baggot's role was secondary to that of Florence. No St. Louis newspaper article can be found containing a separate interview with him, or even a home-town-boy-makes-good type of article that weekend. However, his name was well known to the locals, and there is little doubt that St. Louis was chosen not only because it was a big "motion picture" town, but also because he was Florence's leading man and apt to draw a larger crowd. Fate put him in a position to be the first publicized leading man in America. Because this was a "first," it is probable that no one — not Laemmle, nor Cochrane, nor anyone else — expected such a large demonstration. But there it was, and there would be no putting the genie back in the bottle. It had now been successfully shown that the exploitation of the stars was just what the public really craved. From now on, with the exception of Biograph, studios would begin to gear up to publicize their leading players.

J. Stuart Blackton and Albert A. Smith, the founders of Vitagraph, were quick to pick up on this promising new publicity trend. Less than a month later, in mid–April, they featured their "Vitagraph Girl," Florence Turner, at the Saratoga Park Moving Picture Parlor in Brooklyn in her first personal appearance using her name. In early December, she appeared at another event billed as "A Vitagraph Girl Night," where her public could see her in the flesh — not just on the screen.[5]

On Saturday and Sunday, Florence and King fulfilled their personal appearance obligations by doing turns in two different theaters — both at the time were being managed by Frank Talbot. He owned the Gem, but had leased the Grand Opera House, which was still undergoing renovation. A large advertisement in the entertainment section of the Saturday *St. Louis Post-Dispatch* announced, "First and only appearance in St. Louis. You've seen them on the 'screen,' come see them in person — Miss Florence Lawrence and King Baggott [sic] — different programs at each theater…. No advance in prices, admission ten cents."[6] As far as is known, their films were not shown at the two theaters, they were there to give little talks on how films were made — a topic which continues to fascinate the public today, as apparently it did in 1910. But they were far from the only show in town. The ad immediately above Talbot's was for Havlin's Theatre where Al W. Martin's $30,000 production of *Uncle Tom's Cabin* was offered. There were 50 people in the cast with their own orchestra, as well as ten Cuban and Russian bloodhounds. Admission price was 10, 20, or 30 cents, with a few seats available at 50 cents. There were also dogs in the ad below. The Mississippi Valley Kennel Club was sponsoring their fifth annual dog show. The admission price was 50 cents. So ten cents to see moving picture stars for the first time in person was a real bargain for St. Louisans.

And then it was over. Florence and King boarded a train and returned to New York.

7

IMP — Growing, Growing, Growing

The exact place of the film actor in this growing new medium was still very much up in the air in 1910. The independent film companies were likewise on rather shaky ground. Throughout this time, the Trust continued to try to keep exhibitors from showing independently produced films and to keep independent producers from making them. They did this by threatening to withhold product from the exhibitors who might buy independent films, to fine them, and to try to buy up or destroy their businesses. With regard to the independent producers, they faced a barrage of subpoenas and law suits. The Trust even occasionally hired strong-arm toughs to harass the actors and seize or break their "illegal" cameras. IMP and Laemmle, for example, were the target of no fewer than 89 lawsuits between 1910 and 1913.[1] No doubt many people in the business at times thought the Trust had a chance of winning—but not Carl Laemmle. Week after week, his advertisements in the trade papers told everyone to fight the Trust and have faith in this still young industry. In their advertising, Laemmle and Cochrane did the most brilliant thing that could be done to a tyrant or an adversary and that was to poke fun at him. Rhetoric alone would not work, but making jokes and showing cartoons of a pudgy "General Filmco" (The General Film Company) in a ludicrous light did much to dispel fear and put their threats in proper perspective.

In spite of the fact that Florence Lawrence and King Baggot were given an unprecedented early publicity rush, the practice of billing them on a regular basis, even in the trades, was still a long way off. Other producers, licensed or independent, did not immediately and consistently begin to attach the names of the public's favorites to the names of their films, either—even in the trades where the exhibitors could see them. The debate was still going on in 1911 when, in August, F.H. Richardson in *Moving Picture World* suggested that "a cast should be supplied with every film" sent to *MPW*. Richardson was still insisting in November, somewhat snappishly, "It is hardly up to them [the producers] to dismiss the matter with a curt, 'We don't wish to…'"[2] For this reason, it cannot be known exactly how many films Baggot participated in from 1909 to about 1912, although it is known that IMP produced 104 films in 1910 alone.[3]

IMP was growing despite having to engage in the lawsuits, worry about having sufficient capital, and provide enough films to satisfy those exhibitors brave enough to defy the Trust and buy from IMP. Drinkwater noted that in 1910, three companies were now employed and directors were, at least in theory, allowed a week to shoot a picture (at that time, a one-reel film of about 1000 feet was the industry standard[4]). By June of that year, the company needed more space. A full-page ad in the June 25 *Moving Picture World* boasted they were "Growing. Growing, Growing. Enormous factory for the 'IMP'. Negotiations closed and work of equipping new place now in progress — A sensational business success." The new "factory" would be located at One Hundred First Street and Columbus Avenue. It would have ten times the capacity of the present plant. This facility would be used for developing, drying and printing the film; the studios would remain at 111 East 14th Street. In this piece, Laemmle boasted with good reason:

> Eight months ago there was no such thing as an "Imp" Film. In that time it has grown so enormously popular through sheer force of quality and merit, that our present factory which we thought large enough for at least five years is already insufficient and cramped! In eight months we have accomplished the very thing which required as many as eight YEARS for other brands of moving pictures.... We owe this astonishing growth to loyal exhibitors and loyal exchanges as much as to our own efforts. We have spent money like water to better our product, but it would be barren of results without your loyal backing....[5]

Growth can also mean change. It was at this time that Harry Solter and Florence Lawrence decided to leave IMP. In August, Florence took some time off to visit her mother in Toronto. The break may have been more Harry's idea than Florence's, for in a letter to her, Harry told her:

> Am tired out with this job. Cochrane [Thomas D. Cochrane, general manager of IMP] has got on my nerves and I am going to have it out with him. I am going to tell him we will quit the first of Sept[ember]. We will take a chance and go somewhere else. We can go to England and get a job as they want us over there. We can try Lubin first and if there is any trouble, we can do the other. What do you say to a trip to Europe. This strain is too much with the I.M.P. If I had some assistance it wouldn't be so bad, but this continually bucking Cochrane is too much.[6]

They broke their contract in September and sailed for Europe, but Carl Laemmle did not let them off lightly. He sued them for breach of contract. However, after a bit of negotiation they were able to sign with Siegmund Lubin and move, for a time, to Philadelphia.[7] Florence would return to the Universal fold in 1912, working for the Victor Company. But, with the exception of bit parts they both played in *The Great Universal Mystery* (1914), and in Mary Pickford's production of *Secrets* (1933), King and Florence never starred together in another film. They did see each other often socially at large balls and other gatherings of the film community, and many years later, in Hollywood, they were neighbors, often living just a few blocks from one another.

At this juncture of King's career, it is difficult to know just how many films he made, or with whom he made them, due to the extremely spotty nature of announcing actor's credits. But this was not a fault of IMP's; it was still an industry-wide practice at this time. The last film he and Florence Lawrence made together was probably *The Count of Montebello*, released October 24, 1910. His next known film was *The Double*, released November 14. This was a novel production for two reasons. First, the scenario was written by a St. Louis doctor's wife, Katherine Boland Clemens, who won $100 in a scenario writing contest sponsored by the *St. Louis Times.* This certainly shows that the field of scenario writing was open to all comers and that at least some film producers were willing to use story material wherever they could find it. Secondly, it featured a dual role for King. He plays a soldier who goes off to war in Cuba and leaves his sweetheart behind. The soldier, it seems, has an exact double, whom the sweetheart mistakes for him. The double falls in love with her and complications arise when the soldier is killed in action. It is difficult to pronounce about "firsts" in film history for no sooner is a "first" proclaimed than an alert film historian comes forward with an earlier example. Yet, this was a very early example of the dual role, which would become so popular about 1912 as more experiments were made with superimposing film images.

On October 25, exactly one year after the release of their first picture, Laemmle and the IMP Company held a birthday party at the Imperial Hotel for the entire staff as well as representatives of the press, which included *Moving Picture World, Film Reports, Billboard* and *Motion Picture News.* The report of this event in *Moving Picture World* named many of the executives and representatives of the press, but did not single out any of the actors or actresses—except one. Many speeches were given that night, but only toward the close of the evening was one actor called upon to speak. He replied that it was unusual for a moving picture actor to make a speech, so he acted out his speech in "dumb show" instead of speaking, which reportedly brought down the house. The actor was identified as "Robert Miles."[8]

With the departure of Florence Lawrence, the company was in need of a new "IMP Girl." Laemmle by this time would do almost anything to disconcert the Trust; he struck a cruel blow by inviting Biograph's latest "Biograph Girl," Mary Pickford, to come to work for IMP. In Pickford's three-part biography, published by *Ladies' Home Journal* in 1923, she related how she envied Florence's position as "The Biograph Girl," especially with regard to their dressing room. About 25 women were assigned to a large room divided down the center by a shelf-like dressing table. The "regular" women of the company made up on one side, but the other side was reserved for the "stars." Mary was fiercely competitive from her earliest days. She said, "It was from the first day my ambition to get on the other side, the side where the supposed stars dressed. I wanted, too, one of those dressing tables. In succession I moved to 'the star side' and when Florence Lawrence left the company, I got that coveted dressing table." She proceeded to become a star in her own right, but at that time she was still only "The Biograph Girl," or "The Girl with the Curls," not Mary Pickford, and she was not making the money that Florence had been making at IMP.

Mary Pickford came to IMP in December 1910. According to Mary, negotiations were carried out by her mother Charlotte, who had learned how to bargain shrewdly. She was a tough lady, but she had to be. She had three children to raise. She had chosen for them to make their living in the hardscrabble world of the theater and they had endured many difficulties. At times the family could not all work in the same company and were split up. Their hours were grueling. Sometimes there was little or no work and she had to struggle to house, feed and clothe the family. When Mary began to get steady work at Biograph, it eased their burden considerably. IMP's offer was another step up for the whole family. She would be paid $175 a week and the opportunity to be a "star" in name as well as position. She would be billed in the tradition that Florence Lawrence had established—first as the "IMP Girl," but then as "Mary Pickford."

There may have been another reason she was willing to leave what had become a real home to her at Biograph, and his name was Owen Moore. They had been working together, and Mary had said later that she already had a crush on this handsome young man. It has often been assumed that Owen just came to IMP as part of a "package" which included Mary, Charlotte, brother Jack, and sister Lottie. That may be partially true, but it is now known that Owen had, at least for a time, already been working for IMP. An IMP film called *The Time-Lock Safe*, released in March 1910, was discovered at UCLA Film Archives in 2000. Although the credits are missing, Florence Lawrence, King Baggot and Owen Moore are clearly seen in it. Paul Spehr's *American Film Personnel and Company Credits, 1908–1920*, which is a name index to the earlier Einar Lauritzen-Gunnar Lundquist work *American Film-Index*, lists Owen Moore in its credits for two IMP films, *A Game for Two*, released June 30, 1910, and *The Irony of Fate*, released August 1 of the same year. One Pickford biographer, Eileen Whitfield (*Pickford, the Woman Who Made Hollywood*), has rightly suggested that at that juncture "Owen had been working for the troupe [IMP] for months."[9] Yet Moore must have returned to Biograph in the fall or winter of 1910 because Spehr's work shows that Owen Moore played in as many as nine more films released by Biograph between September and December of that year. Furthermore, he filed a lawsuit against IMP in 1914 claiming that he was hired in December 1910 on a one-year contract, but fired in June 1911 and was out of work for 14 weeks before he was hired by Reliance.[10] If Owen was kindly disposed toward IMP, it may have been one further incentive for Mary to take Carl Laemmle up on his offer.

Pickford's switch from Biograph to IMP was announced with great fanfare, which Laemmle undoubtedly relished. Both *Billboard* and *Moving Picture World* on December 24 gave significant space to the event. *Moving Picture World* called her "a real artist of the silent screen." In order to clear up any confusion about what happened to Florence Lawrence, *MPW* printed a brief explanation on January 7, 1911, saying that she was enjoying "a lengthy and well-earned rest and would appear back on the screen in about three months," which, of course, she had no intention of doing just then, at least at IMP. Directly below this announcement, they explained that although Mary Pickford's face may appear in a few more Biograph films that had not yet been released, she was, indeed, the same "little lady" profiled in their December 24 article.[11] Her stay at IMP was not a long one—less time than Florence Lawrence—but the company passed a few milestones during her time with them.

8
Cuba

In January 1911, Laemmle decided to take most of the IMP Company and move the bulk of their production efforts to Cuba. This was not an unprecedented act. Film companies, even in these early times, were already filming in many far-flung locations. Actually, one of their nemeses, the Edison Company, had sent a stock company to Cuba the previous year. Lubin, also in 1910, sent a unit to film in Florida, and that same year Essanay shot some background footage on the Isthmus of Panama and in Mexico.[1] D.W. Griffith, too, had taken a unit to film in California from January to April of 1910 for Biograph. What was unusual about this trip was that the IMP Company put almost all of its eggs in one basket. They sent two units and planned to have most of their output produced there.

Some of the reasons might seem obvious. Outdoor filmmaking in the winter months in New York and New Jersey, where so many companies were working at that time, could be cold, cruel and uncertain. Then, too, filming exotic locales, especially those with palm trees, added visual novelty for moviegoers despite the added costs. But there were other concerns. The Trust forces were becoming more of a threat to the day-to-day operations of the independents and it was not just the lawsuits. More equipment was being seized or broken, more actors and technical personnel were being bullied and threatened to the point where many wanted to escape to places where it was harder for the Trust to reach them and interfere with production. Mary Pickford's observations about the reasons for going to Cuba were most specific concerning the threats to the safety and well-being of the production units. She said, "Often when we were working on the streets a guard was provided so that no one could come up and smash the camera."[2] In *Sunshine and Shadow,* she remarked, "A battle royal was then going on between two bitterly opposed camps over the use of the camera. It reached such a bitter pitch at one point that hoodlums were hired to stone the cameras, and even the actors, at IMP. Pending decision of the courts, IMP decided to remove us from the danger areas and ship us to Cuba for three months."[3] This strategy was not 100 percent successful, as will be seen, but at the time IMP considered it a prudent option.

Cuba was certainly a long way from New York, but the IMP Company did not exactly sneak out of town hoping to hide from the Trust. They announced their intentions so that the entire industry would know. *Moving Picture World*, on January 21, carried an article about the trip and the IMP Company took out a full page ad. The article pointed out that this was yet another indication of the industry's expansion, mentioning that Selig, Biograph and the Revier Companies were all out seeking "local color"; to them, the editors, this was just one more proof of the stability of the moving picture business. "Shrewd business men have satisfied themselves that the demand for the picture instead of diminishing is likely to expand with the growth of the population.... Nearly the entire personnel of the company's staff goes to Cuba, where the negatives will be made and probably sent on to New York..." IMP's ad copy read, "IMPS in Cuba! Both Imp stock companies are now in Cuba producing films that will once more clinch the fact that the Imp is the most energetic and enterprising film-maker in the business. Watch for the Cuban Imps, the Florida Imps, the Mexican Imps..."[4]

By this time, the concept of a "stock company" (in other words, a theatrical style repertory company) had gained acceptance in the industry, but already they were moving toward the recognition of a stock company consisting of regular "players," and also "stars." This can be seen in what is thought to be IMP Company's first family portrait. It was published in *Moving Picture World*, February 11, 1911, on page 290, shortly after they had embarked for Cuba. At last there is some idea of who was working there at that point in time. In the center of the photograph sat Mary Pickford with King Baggot on her left and Owen Moore on her right. They were the stars. Altogether, there were 19 people in this photograph, some of whom would be looked back upon in later years as true film pioneers. In addition to Mary, Owen and King, there were Charlotte Smith, identified as "Mrs. Pickford," Lottie and Jack Pickford, both still children, Thomas Ince, who had just become a director, George Loane Tucker, Hayward Mack, William E. Shay, William R. Daly, Joseph Smiley, IMP's senior director, and the company's chief cameraman, Tony Gaudio. A later account, published in 1926, expanded the list of names of those who made the Cuban trip to include Murdock MacQuarrie, Joe Daly, David Miles, Edith Bostwick, and Leo White.[5]

According to John Drinkwater, a cast and crew numbering 72 people went to Cuba.[6] He indicated that they sailed aboard the S.S. *Havana* of the Ward Line, but it is now known that they did not all go at the same time. When Kevin Brownlow interviewed Irvin Willat in 1969, he mentioned that he and his brother, C.A. "Doc" Willat, were sent ahead to find quarters and scout locations.[7] Most probably other technical personnel went with them. The first mention of the company's arrival in Cuba was noted in *Dario de la Marina* on January 16th:

> A Movie Company. Numerous American artists from a company that devotes itself to filming arrived yesterday in Havana on the steamship "Hamburg." The movie company director's name is Thomas Ince and eleven artists of both sexes came with him. Twenty more artists to follow. He brings with him every apparatus and tool proposing to show various movies having clearly native Cuban themes. This company is called "Independent Moving Pictures."[8]

Havana's *El Mundo* reported:

> A steamship with eleven artists of the American movie company "Independent Moving Pictures" has arrived. They will take up residence in the Palacio De Carneado in the Vedado area under the direction of Mr. Thomas Ince. They will film movies taking as models Cuban topics and landscapes.[9]

The IMP Stock Company players' first known photograph, published in *Moving Picture World,* February 11, 1911. Collection of the author.

Ince, it seems from the Havana newspaper reports, was the lead director. He and the principals probably sailed on the same ship, but their journey did not start out auspiciously. According to Mary Pickford and several other sources, it was only then that she and Owen Moore announced that they had been secretly married in a civil ceremony on January 7th. This undoubtedly was not a complete surprise to everyone aboard, but it certainly did upset the Pickford family. Mary had not yet reached her 18th birthday; also Owen even then had a bad reputation as a heavy drinker and a Beau Brummel. Mary later related, "Mother cried for three days and nights when I told her, and for the entire voyage Lottie and Jack did not speak to me at all. I still have a vivid picture of Johnny standing at the rail, his cap pulled down over his eyes, his arm around his little dog, and tears streaming down his face."[10]

When they arrived, they had to deal with a whole range of discomforts and adjustments. According to Terry Ramsaye's account of the Cuban expedition, "Doc" Willat had leased a forbidding stone structure as quarters and studio for the company. The place seemed chilling and inhospitable to the actors. They were vastly reassured, however, when it was explained that this was nothing less than the "Palacio del Carneado of Vedado." Joseph Smiley and King, however, did some inquiring on their own account and found that, in spite of its sumptuous name, the Palacio was in fact an abandoned jail. They moved.[11] King, in a 1921 L. A. Express interview, did not seem to remember the abandoned jail incident but he did hint that their accommodations were less than palatial. "Upon our arrival in Cuba, Mr. Willat arranged for a camp for his company, and with the exception of a few of us who preferred the hotel life, everyone went into the camp."[12]

It was urgent that production begin immediately because Laemmle's announced goal for IMP was an output of two films a week. Their first undertaking was a one-reel effort called *Pictureland*, released February 20. It is a pity that this is a lost film because both units of the company were used to produce it and it may have had a considerable amount of charm. According to the reviews, it had a love story, great scenery and told a story within a story. It opened with the IMP Company arriving at a hotel in a motor car, dressed in their traveling clothes, and being warmly greeted by the staff. In the next scene, the director set up the cameras and prepared for action. The "story" featured Pickford as the beautiful Cuban maiden Rosita and Baggot as the humble Pablo, who loves her. The villain of the piece is Crawford (probably played by Owen Moore), an American tourist who flirts with Rosita until she begins to care more for him than for Pablo. When Pablo next calls on her, he plays his guitar, and sitting beside him she is lulled into sleep. Her dream is depicted on screen. In it, Crawford comes to her and tempts her with jewels. She is won over and willingly goes away with him. In her innocence, she leads him to a church, but Crawford does not have marriage in mind. Pablo comes to her rescue. A terrific fight ensues and Pablo bests the evil Crawford, whose life is saved by the intervention of a priest. Rosita awakes to find it was all a dream and the drama closes with Rosita and Pablo being united by the priest in marriage. In the final scene, the IMP Company returns to the hotel, changes into street clothes and is last seen driving away into a "rare tropical scene peculiar to Cuba."[13]

Hardship and downright danger lay ahead, but at times their experiences were merely mildly unpleasant comic relief. Almost all of the sources that documented the trip referred to the "cold cream incident." As Terry Ramsaye told it:

> The company had been at work but for a few days when everyone became mysteriously and desperately ill. The situation was doubly critical. Imp in New York was dependent for its very existence on the uninterrupted output of the company in Cuba. Ince, recovering, first made a searching investigation. He found that Charlie Weston, the property man, with an eye to business and personal profits, had taken to Cuba with him a very large wholesale tin of cold cream. Weston calculated that there would be no drug stores in Cuba and that he would make a fortune out of selling his cold cream to the actors for nightly removal of their makeup. So far so good. But he stored his drum of cold cream in the kitchen ice box. The Cuban cook decided it was just a fancy perfumed American lard and proceeded accordingly.[14]

Ramsaye may have embellished the story a bit. King, in 1921, and Drinkwater, ten years later, cover the same ground but without describing the company's plight as "desperately ill," or accusing Charlie of having larcenous intentions.

Drinkwater, quite a colorful storyteller, dealt at some length with the Trust's attempts to disrupt filmmaking. He described a "mysterious figure" who suddenly appeared, claiming he had patent rights to companies filming in Cuba, but would relinquish them for a five figure sum. His threats were more or less ignored, but the harassment continued. He described another incident where "Ingenuous looking travelers with early Kodaks lingered curiously by the wayside of IMP activities. What surprising luck to come upon great film stars in action. Might they be allowed —? Just a little snap, such a souvenir to take back to the home town. And then Tony Gaudio observed that one of the tourists was taking pictures not of Miss Pickford or King Baggot, but of his, Tony Gaudio's camera."[15] Apparently the ingenuous traveler tried to interest the American consul in signing an injunction against the company for illegal use of the motion picture camera, but the consul refused to become involved. Yet, the spying continued:

> Another enquiring soul met with ruder treatment. While King Baggot was directing a picture, the men of the company laid off to dig a deep trench required for the scene. The ground was tough and the weather hot. A stranger with innocent eyes loitered to watch proceedings. King Baggot, upon reflection, was not so sure that the eyes were so innocent. He opened conversation, which the stranger encountered somewhat shyly. Baggot said Trust, then he said detective, then he said dirty spy. Having no coat on, there was no necessity to remove it, and he invited the dirty spy to prepare for a thrashing that would teach him not to interfere with honest people trying to make an honest living. Baggot was known to millions for his physical attractions, but at that moment the deputy of the Trust hated the sight of him. Deputy explained that he didn't want to fight, that he was no sort of hand at fighting. Baggot retorted that he was not required to fight, but to get a hiding. Deputy pleaded that he couldn't bear a hiding, that it was not in his contract, that he was a poor fish anyway. Baggot relented. Terms were offered; the eavesdropper could either be beaten, or dig the ditch. He dug the ditch and returned to New York with an unfavorable report on the manners of Mr. Laemmle's employees.[16]

The danger and uncertainty of filming with the Trust seemingly breathing down their necks was also confirmed by Irvin Willat, Doc Willat's brother. In his 1969 interview with Kevin Brownlow, he said, "I was sent down there with film when I was with the IMP company. They sent me down there ... and they laid a gun on the camera and they started to shoot. They just laid a .45 on top of the camera and anybody who came round was ready to get it. They did that in New York, too, but I wasn't a cameraman at that time. I was still working with my brother in the laboratory."[17]

There was one last unpleasant incident that finally brought a close to IMP's Cuban sojourn. The story is told by a number of sources and in a number of ways, but in terms of a first hand account, Mary Pickford's has the most detail:

> To make the situation even more intolerable, the director Tom Ince and Owen took an immediate and violent dislike to each other, and Ince's assistant, a man named North, never missed a chance to insult us both. One night North said something rude to me and Owen struck him. North claimed that Owen had kicked him, and called the police with the avowed intention of having Owen put in Morro Castle prison.
>
> It was then that my resourceful mother took over. Before the police arrived Mother gave some quick orders.
>
> "Go to one of the actors you can trust and ask him if he can hide Owen until the police have gone. There is a boat sailing for home tomorrow morning, and we'll put him aboard secretly tonight. And you, Mary, must go with him."
>
> Mother's maneuver worked. When the officers came to take Owen she started a long and heated argument in the course of which two of the men sneaked off with Owen and delivered him safely on board the ship. The next morning, at dawn I joined Owen on the boat in Havana Harbor, and sailed back to the United States."[18]

The Company stayed in Cuba about three months. It is certain that they produced 14 films, mostly one-reelers. Those in this category were either clearly described as "Cuban IMPs" in the weekly trade papers, or their storylines strongly suggested Cuban backgrounds such as a tobacco plantation or a fruit company. These were released in the following order, although not necessarily produced in the same sequence:

Pictureland, 2/20

Artful Kate, 2/23

A Manly Man, 2/27

Army Maneuvers in Cuba, a documentary, 3/2

Tracked, 3/6

The Message in the Bottle, 3/9

The Secret of the Palm, 3/13

The Fisher-Maid, 3/16

In Old Madrid, 3/20

The Penniless Prince, 3/23

Sweet Memories, 3/27

The Lover's Signal, 4/3

A Good Cigar, half-reel documentary, 4/10

Behind the Stockade, 6/10

There is a possibility that at least five others were filmed there as well, even though they have no specific Cuban-like story line or tropical settings:

Thomas Ince, 1882–1924, producer, actor, and writer. He directed many IMP films, including some of those made in Cuba in 1911. Photograph courtesy of Frances Howard Goldwyn Hollywood Regional Library, Special Collections.

Second Sight, 5/1

The Temptress, 5/4

The Fair Dentist, 5/8

The Master and the Man, 5/15

Back to the Soil, 6/8

To lend some credence to this assumption, Isabel Rea, a member of the expedition, was quoted in the March 1926 *Motion Picture Directors* as saying, "We were there three months and made I don't know how many one reel pictures [some of which had] American settings such as we were accustomed to making in New York City."[19] King Baggot's participation is fairly well established in six of the first category

Mary Pickford and King Baggot in a tense moment from *The Master and the Man*, IMP, 1911, directed by Thomas Ince. Photograph courtesy of the Academy of Motion Picture Arts and Sciences.

and five of the second. It was originally decided that there would be two separate production units—one starring Mary Pickford and presumably Owen Moore and directed by Thomas Ince, the other for King and directed by Joseph Smiley. However, in actual production King and Mary starred together in at least four of the first category and three in the second. In *The Fair Dentist*, Mary played the dentist, while King, George Loane Tucker and Moore played the trio of romantically inclined gentlemen who got some of their teeth yanked out.

Most of the films IMP made in Cuba no longer exist, but there are a few. The Library of Congress holds both *The Secret of the Palm* and *The Penniless Prince*. From films like these, a bit can be learned about what they may have been like, but they are almost impossible to judge by today's standards. They had to be produced at breakneck speed to fill IMP's program. It is also quite probable that the directors Smiley and Ince, working under fairly primitive conditions, might not have seen them or had a chance to do any editing before they were shipped. Jack Cohn, then IMP's chief film editor back in New York, may not even have had time to do much with them. The reviews tell us a bit about how they were received by audiences, but even then the results are uneven.

The Secret of the Palm is a case in point. In one scene, the wicked Don Alvarez is jealous of ranch foreman Cecil Abbott, played by King, because he has the love of the ranch owner's daughter, Edna. He steals the ranch's mailbag and proceeds to climb a very tall palm tree in order to hide it. The blame for the lost bag will fall on Cecil, who Don Alvarez hopes will be fired. Don Alvarez is seen starting to climb the tree. He gets about a foot or two off the ground until we can only see his boots, then in the next shot, the top of the palm tree is seen and he is supposed to be up there, but he is being shot against a white background. Not very believable. One response might be that this is pretty lame stuff, but lo and behold, the review in *Motion Picture News* praises the backgrounds as splendid and singled out the climbing as "very effective." All of the scenes were shot outdoors, but the lighting is so poor in some places that it is difficult to distinguish the actors. This may be caused by print deterioration because there were no complaints about the lighting in the original review.

The print of *The Penniless Prince* is quite different. Again, most of the scenes were taken outdoors, but in this case the effect was all clarity and light at the tobacco plantation. For a one-reel film, the plot was fairly complicated and required numerous intertitles and close-up shots of "letters" being read to move the action along. The reviewer for *Moving Picture World* seems to have been totally bewildered by the plot, but he does concede that the photography was excellent. Perhaps he saw it right after lunch, or perhaps without the intertitles, which was not all that unusual a practice at that time. There is one particularly memorable scene in which the penniless prince Gustav, played by King, cannot go to the German embassy looking for word from his family because his clothes are too shabby and worn from working in the tobacco fields. Dolores (Isabel Rea), the girl who loves him, visits a dealer in hair and sacrifices her beautiful tresses so that he can buy clothes. They meet in a field and are sitting side by side when she gently and tenderly offers him the money. His reaction is a touching mixture of surprise, hurt and gratitude. In all, it is a sensitive and beautiful scene and shows that King, in a little more than a year, had developed into a very fine silent film actor.

9

Home Again

The Trust wars had not abated, but the arena of conflict was shifting from the streets to the courts. Litigation flew in all directions between the independents and the Trust forces that were desperately trying to monopolize the industry and put them out of business. The money thus expended on both sides was enormous and wearing on all concerned, but the independents were gaining ground. The lawsuits would continue for four more long years; however, it was now apparent that the moving picture business was not just a fad. The number of theaters all over the country continued to increase. The public, instead of turning to other forms of entertainment, was fascinated by this still new medium, and demand for product, whether from licensed or independent production companies, at times almost outstripped supply. With all that money to be made, the industry as a whole and most of the companies within it began to do everything possible to capture their fair share of this burgeoning market. Volume alone would not do it; now the notion of class and quality were being used to grab the attention of exhibitors and the filmgoers as well.

The power of advertising as a tool began to emerge as never before. It was no longer enough to put a banner out in front of a theater that announced "Vitagraph" or "Biograph" or "IMP." The public now demanded to know what the stories were about and, more importantly, who the stars were. IMP, for example, was well positioned to exploit this trend, no doubt in part to the advertising acumen of Robert Cochrane. In the May 13, 1911, issue of *Moving Picture World*, IMP offered the exhibitors "The New IMP Lobby Frame and 10 fine photos for five dollars." The frames were of "beautifully grained wide oak containing ten heavily glassed openings for the photos.... You'll be tickled to pieces when you see what a rich looking ornament it will make for your 'front.'"[1] All the major IMP players were depicted, including King, Mary Pickford and Owen Moore. There was, however, one missing component—their names. It would take another six months or so before naming the major players would become a more integral part of the game. As if to underscore the fact that even IMP was still more inclined to push the company before the actors, their other big advertising gambit that year was "The IMP Book." It was such a novelty for its time that *MPW* covered it as a three-quarter-page news item before the book was actually ready for the exhibitors. Billed as a "business booster," for exhibitors to either sell or give away as souvenirs on special matinee days, it was a book of ABCs described as appealing to both adults and children and printed on "splendid quality paper stock in rich green, red, orange and black." Jolly little imps danced around the front and back covers doing acrobatic stunts and showing off their diminutive hoofs, horns and tails. One example went:

> M is for music the orchestra plays
> As pictures are shown on the screen.
> Piano and fiddle and drum-i-tum-tum
> Add pleasure and fun to the scene.[2]

A few of these novel little books still exist today and turn up from time to time for sale as movie memorabilia.

When the two IMP companies returned from Cuba, the former threats of bodily harm for the actors and crew as they produced a picture had greatly decreased. They could now focus more on quality and interesting storylines that they hoped would capture the public's attention. In mid–June they released *A Piece of String*, based on a story by Guy de Maupassant. King was paired with Lucille Younge instead of Pickford. Younge had her first break as a leading lady with IMP, but would later go on to work for Kalem, Majestic, Lubin and other companies. Herbert Brenon wrote the scenario. He had recently been hired by IMP's then studio manager, Julius Stern, Laemmle's brother-in-law. As was the case with so many filmmakers in those early years, Brenon's previous experience as a scenarist was non–existent. He had been an actor in stock companies, then bought a theater in Johnstown, Pennsylvania, where he and his wife, Helen Oberg, produced plays, showed movies between the acts and finally incorporated the theater into a skating rink, alternating between skating and films.[3] In time he would become a world famous director, but that was yet to come.

A Piece of String was a somber story. King, as a good young man of thrifty habits, has a rival for his sweetheart's affection — the village blacksmith. He is falsely accused of stealing the purse of a local hunter, when it was actually the hunter's dog that found the purse and hid it among the rocks. He tries to explain to the villagers and his sweetheart that he had not picked up the purse, but only a "piece of string," but no one believes him. The accusations drive him to raving madness and he drops dead from anguish and grief. That seems to have been the kind of story that many film companies aimed for at that time. It was based on the work of a world-renowned author and actually went for a dramatic and tragic ending rather than the tried and true "happily ever after" standard. It also gave King a chance to "go mad," an opportunity that few dramatic leading men can ever resist. The director was George Loane Tucker, previously an IMP Company actor, and he probably co-directed it with the stalwart senior director, Joseph Smiley. Other actors known to have been in the cast were Robert Z. Leonard and J. Farrell MacDonald, both of whom would soon be directors in their own right. And the dog in the piece was no walk-on. She was a regular member of the company; a part collie named Lassie, who made the trip to Cuba, and later that month, according to the reviews, upstaged both Baggot and Pickford in a film titled *Science*, based on a story by Mark Twain, supporting the anti-vivisection cause.[4]

King's permanent place as the star of the IMP Company was still evolving from the time of his return from Cuba in March or April, until about the end of July 1911. While Pickford and Moore were still with IMP, he was clearly the leading man in a number of films both with Pickford or, increasingly, with Lucille Younge. But in three others, *In the Sultan's Garden, For the Queen's Honor* and *A Gasoline Engagement*, he played supporting roles. Because not all the films produced at this time were credited, there may have been more. When Pickford and Moore left for Majestic in October, it was quite a major defection for Laemmle. Thomas Cochrane, then IMP's general manager, also left, taking George Loane Tucker, Herbert Prior, Anita Herndon and David Miles with him.[5] But for King, from then on he was IMP's undisputed male star. That same month he received his first known credit as a scenarist for *The Rose's Story*. It was a poignant little tale of a dissolute young man who falls in love with a pure and simple woman whose gift of a rose makes him give up his former life. He may have written others before this, but since credits were still so sketchy at this time, this is the first one that is certain. At that stage, collaborative efforts were quite normal throughout the industry among all the companies to write, direct, produce, act and even dig ditches, as has already been seen.

Playing a dashing hero who performs feats of derring-do and who ends up with the love of the lady in hundreds of films can eventually pale on any actor after a time. As King's position and degree of control over his films increased, so did his need to do more creative and interesting work. His first known attempt in this direction was with *King, the Detective*, released November 2, 1911. Although uncredited as either the director or writer, he probably did have considerable artistic leeway. As the title indicates, he plays a skillful detective who solves the crime by collecting the fingerprints of the murderer from the victim's celluloid collar, then tricking the murderer into leaving his prints where they can be compared. This was by no means the first "detective film" on record, but King would become well known for such roles as time went on. He made four others in this series between 1911 and 1914: *King, the Detective and the Opium Smugglers* (1912), and *King, the Detective in the Jarvis Case* (1913). These were followed by *King, the Detective in Formula 879*, and *King, the Detective in the Marine Mystery*, both 1914. The following week's release (November 7, 1911) was *Tony and the Stork*. Here he played an Italian immigrant, most likely dressed and made up to closely resemble the stereotypical Italian of the day. But his Tony is a hard-working and lovable fellow who must go to work with a railroad crew far from home to earn money because his wife is expecting their first child. He finally receives notice that his wife has given birth and, drawing his pay, he heads for home, stopping first to buy a baby carriage and toys. However, when he arrives at the hospital, he is told that his wife is dead. When the sheet is pulled aside, he sees that it is not his wife. Grief gives way to joy and he is reunited with his wife and twins. The little film ends as he sets out to exchange the carriage for a larger one. By today's standards, they may seem like simple fare, but there was some scope to these roles that he had never had a chance to play before now.

On a cold Saturday, December 30, 1911, a contingent from the IMP Company boarded a train bound for California. As they said their farewells at the station that day, neither King, nor Laemmle, nor anyone else totally envisioned what an impact would ultimately result from this seemingly simple excursion. In a few short years, the output of film production would shift to the west and change many destinies. The "Western IMP Company," as they were first called, was being sent there "with the purpose of making a series of romantic photoplays against the background of the magnificent scenery for which California is noted throughout the world."[6] By February, their first film, *The Rose of California*, was ready for release.[7]

By no means were they the first. One of Selig's companies, directed by Francis Boggs, was shooting on location in the Los Angeles area as early as 1907, and by 1909 had set up "permanent facilities" on Olive Street in downtown Los Angeles.[8] Fred J. Balshofer, founder of the Crescent and Bison Companies, and also one of the founders of the New York Motion Picture Company, was filming in Los Angeles in November 1909. By that time many companies, including Biograph, were doing location shooting in California and other warmer places during the winter seasons in 1910 and 1911.

IMP's first West Coast offices and studios were in a section of the city then called Brooklyn Heights, now known as Boyle Heights, at 651 Fairview Avenue, just across the Los Angeles River from downtown.[9] Julius Stern, IMP's general manager, made a trip to Los Angeles in March of 1912 to help the new company get set up. Some of the players in this first group were E.J. La Saint, Margarita Fischer, Harry Pollard, Edward (Eddie) Lyons, Louise Crolius, Ben Horning and Eugene Kelly.[10] By mid June, Universal's presence became more pronounced. Fred Balshofer's Bison Company had joined Universal, and in addition to heading Bison, he now became Western Manager of IMP and Nestor as well. The original intention was for IMP to move from Brooklyn Heights to Edendale, where Bison already had a studio, so the two companies could work side by side, but by May 20, IMP had moved to the Nestor site in Hollywood. The Nestor Company,

First known publicity photograph of Baggot which appeared in *Motion Picture News*, 12/18/1911. Collection of the author.

headed by David Horsley, had set up their studios in Hollywood at Sunset and Gower the previous year, and Nestor, too, had became part of Universal in 1912. Nestor is credited with being the first motion picture studio physically located in Hollywood. Within another week it was announced that Fred Mace, who had come to California with the Biograph Company for their second annual winter season, would not be returning with them. Instead, he was tapped to be an IMP producer and head a second IMP company mainly made up of Biograph players who did not wish to return to New York. Mace's company would produce comedies, while Edward J. LaSaint was appointed director of IMP's dramatic films.[11]

As December drew to a close, IMP's growth and expansion continued. During that month, IMP began to release four films a week — one-reel features on Monday and Thursday, and two split reels on Saturday. IMP changed its corporate name from "Independent Moving Pictures Company of America" to "The IMP Films Company."[12]

10

A Star at Last

Nineteen twelve would be a watershed year for King. IMP launched its own trade publication on January 20, *The Implet*.[1] It was edited by Thomas Bedding, former editor of *Moving Picture World*, and was a handsomely printed large format newspaper containing a mix of studio news, comments from exhibitors, synopses of up coming films with release dates, and photographs of their productions and of the IMP players. On page four of volume one, number one, a half-page feature proclaimed:

IMP Players: No. 1. King Baggot.

If a vote were taken as to who was the most popular moving picture actor in the world, I do not hesitate to say that King Baggot would be the winner. On the screen he is, of course, known to millions, admired by millions, appreciated by millions. And if ever a man deserved his popularity, Baggot is that man. He has worked hard and loyally in the Imp pictures for two years — and the splendid quality of his work as an impersonator of a long list of widely diversified types of characters is universally admired. As a manly hero, with the bearing of a chivalrous gentleman, Baggot is unsurpassed in the moving picture field today.

Before he joined the Imp Company Baggot had had considerable stage experience, and carries the technique of the theatre at his finger tips. But he is essentially a product of the moving picture stage; he is untheatrical, he is natural, he is spontaneous in all that he undertakes.

Now, what is Baggot like in real life? ...Well, he is just as nice in real life as he looks on the screen. He has a most lovable disposition, a generous Celtic temperament, the manners of a well-bred gentleman — in short, he is a prince of good fellows, modest and good natured.

We of the Imperies just love Baggot; and when this publication was decided upon it was unanimously resolved that Baggot should be the first to figure in our Gallery of Players.... And so "King" as he is familiarly termed deserves to be. T.B.[2]

The accompanying publicity photo is probably the best known and most widely reproduced of all his portraits. He appears in a high-buttoned dark wool jacket and vest, and a snug-fitting collar. Lit mainly from his right, the left side of his face is shadowed and puffy looking. His hair is severely slicked back and his expression is closed, guarded — almost apprehensive. No smile. He looks at least ten years older than his actual age — 33. There is a solidity and dignity to the pose, but when one sees how he actually appeared on screen, it is evident that the motion picture camera was far more kind to him. He actually had a mobile, handsome face, expressive eyes, and there was a fluid grace to his movements that no still camera could possibly capture. It is difficult to believe this is the same man. It will remain a mystery whether this photograph was his own personal choice or whether it was chosen by the studio, but when one sees stills of some of his contemporaries like Francis X. Bushman, Maurice Costello or Arthur Johnson, one cannot help but wonder why this image was selected to represent him. It does not say "dashing leading man," and perhaps that explains in part, why, if one had never seen any of his films, that today he is so totally forgotten.

Otis Turner joined the IMP Company either late in 1911 or early in 1912. He was another film pioneer who had worked for William Selig as early as 1908, both as a director and as a scenario writer. By 1912, he had a fine reputation as a director of wide-ranging talent. At that time, King was occasionally working with Thomas Ince, with whom he made *The Kid and the Sleuth* and *Through the Flames*. In *Through the Flames*, he drove a real train through a forest fire. He was also directing some of his own films in the early months of that year, but now he was teamed with Turner. During that time, he undoubtedly did some of his best work—considering these were mainly one- and two-reel films. Most of them are now "lost" and it is difficult to determine their over all quality, but it is known from the reviews that most of them were well-received and roundly praised at that time. Perhaps the best known of these was *Lady Audley's Secret*. Turner also directed King in the 1912 production *Human Hearts*, and also *Shamus O'Brien*— King's first two-reel film. In all, there were 14 known to have been made between January and August of 1912.

Prints of *Shamus O'Brien* still exist at the British Film Institute in London and at the Library of Congress. The film was based on a stirring ballad about Ireland's struggle with the British for "Home Rule" in 1789. Shamus was its hero, an Irish patriot who continued to fight for his country even through he had a price on his head. Herbert Brenon wrote the scenario. Brenon was an Irishman himself, born near Kingstown (now Dun Laoghaire) near Dublin. There were some fine and very experienced actors in this film, including William E. Shay, William R. Daly, Rolinda Bainbridge as Shamus' mother, and Agustus Balfour as the priest, Father Malone. It was a picture with plenty of action; the barn dance sequence, the British bursting in looking for Shamus, the soldiers chasing him, his explosive leap from the hayloft to the dance floor to rescue his sweetheart, and his capture and imprisonment. The industry at that time had fallen in love with dramatic lighting effects and several were used in *Shamus*, most notably in a tender scene where Shamus is being hidden from the British by his mother. They are seated by the fireplace, both knowing he cannot stay without putting her life in danger. The firelight plays on their faces, underscoring their sadness and despair.

Lady Audley's Secret, his second two-reeler, was another important film for King. Unfortunately, all that seems to remain of this one is a still of Baggot as George Talboys and two frames of paper print fragments held by the Library of Congress. The reviews were most enthusiastic. This was a picture with "class," as the trades were fond of saying in those times. It was based on a best-selling novel first published in 1862 by the British author Mary Ellen Braddon, depicting English high society life and mores about 1840, shortly after Queen Victoria ascended to the throne. IMP went all-out to replicate this time period with authentic costumes and furniture. King, as the wicked Lady Audley's first husband, had the distinction of being thrown down a well and left for dead, and later almost being burned to a crisp in a fire at the Manor as Lady Audley tries to cover her tracks. Jane Fearnley, who was just becoming a dramatic film actress of note, played Lady Audley. Although Baggot got first billing, her role received much praise from the critics. This time it was she who went mad in the end.

In mid-year, June 8, 1912, IMP went through an important transition. Earlier, in 1910, a number of the independent producers had banded together to form the Motion Picture Distributing and Sales Company. It was comprised of many of the larger independent companies and its purpose was to take over the marketing of all independent production. The Sales Company contracted with the companies and serviced the exchanges. Naturally, not all of the independent companies joined — by their very nature, they were fiercely independent, and there were some major clashes within the Sales Company as well. However, with the strength of their numbers they began to give real competition to the Patents Company Group. IMP was among them and Carl Laemmle had become the president. Now, in June 1912, there were more squabbles and important defections, which led the Sales Company to regroup as the Universal Film Manufacturing Company.³ There would be a number of shifts

Often used publicity still of Baggot circa 1912. His expression reflects solidity and dignity, but does not shout, "dashing leading man." Collection of the author.

within this organization almost immediately, but the original members were IMP, Crystal, Frontier, Mecca, Victor, Yankee, Champion, Nestor, Eclair, Powers, Rex, Ambrosio, Italia and the New York Motion Picture Company. Henceforth IMP would be only one of the companies under the Universal banner and Carl Laemmle emerged, after a brief struggle, as president of the new, broader and more powerful Universal.⁴ Joining forces in this way was a good business decision for all concerned, but down the road each company would now be more directly in competition, not only with the Trust companies, but with each other as well. Some would find niches specializing in comedies, documentaries, serials or Westerns, but others would be going head to head with each other for their share of the market as all-purpose film companies. By October, the Universal program was able to offer 28 reels a week.[5] Laemmle would no longer be able to focus all his energy and attention on IMP and that shift in emphasis would slowly but surely erode the forward thrust that IMP was beginning to enjoy as a stand-alone enterprise. It would also eventually have a direct effect on King's position as the star of an up-and-coming company.

The third "heavy hitting" dramatic film for King that year was *Human Hearts*, released on September 12. Again, it was in two reels, befitting its importance both for Otis Turner, as a director, and King, as IMP's big star. In between these, he was making little one-reel and half-reel offerings almost every week. In most cases they were lighter fare, to be sure, but the work was demanding and probably somewhat grueling at the same time. IMP was getting full measure for what he was being paid. *Human Hearts* was a bit of a warhorse even by 1912. Originally it was a play by the celebrated playwright Hal Reid, first produced as *Logan's Luck* in 1895, but all subsequent productions were titled *Human Hearts*. In that first production, Reid played the lead as well as having written it, and his wife Bertha Belle Westbrook played opposite him. By 1912, Reid had become a scenarist for Universal. And Bertha and Hal were the parents of future star Wallace Reid.[6] This was not the first time it was produced as a film. Selig had done a one-reel version in 1910; however, this one was to be a "big picture" in which the plot was more developed and the characters better delineated. That it enjoyed such wide appeal for many years was undoubtedly because the themes were so familiar to audiences. It dealt with simple people caught up in events of a tragic nature, and often beyond their control. The hero was Tom Logan, a village blacksmith who must summon up manliness and courage in adversity, and face overwhelming emotional obstacles before the denouement. The reviews for Baggot were more than gratifying. *Moving Picture World* said:

> Human Hearts has been splendidly done as a picture by Producer Otis Turner. King Baggot plays the leading part. With an actor like him in the leading role, the play is given a vigor that might be expected of Mr. Baggot in the part of an honest country blacksmith. His work is better, if possible, than anything he has done in some time.[7]

Universal Weekly, which had replaced *The Implet* in June 1912, had good words to say about King's ability, of course, but those words ring with quite a bit of sincerity:

> If there is another reason why the picture should appeal to the exhibitor.... It is this: that King Baggot, who is probably the most admired motion picture actor in the world today, finds in the leading character in the play one of those sympathetic roles which brings out his fine powers of portraying manliness, heroism, and a conflict of emotions. It is in that latter regard that Baggot's art is gradually broadening and deepening. He has got to the stage of his career when his intellectual side is manifesting itself. Actors are of several kinds; mostly they are superficial. They act their parts physically—but not mentally. Baggot has passed through the first stage, and now he is reaching the second, and most important stage of his art. He is thinking and feeling his part so thoroughly that the result is apparent on the screen, and it is apparent in this picture....[8]

Otis Turner, without doubt, was having an important influence on the kinds of films IMP was now producing in terms of length and story quality. He also may have been instrumental in King's development as an actor. He and King were poised to take IMP films even further when it was announced that King was slated to play *Othello*. The first announcement appeared in *Universal Weekly* on August 31, but with no release date. Then, a few pages later in the same issue, there appeared a half-page feature announcing that Turner was leaving New York for California, where he would direct "mammoth" Universal Western pictures for the Bison brand.[9] Yet, for a time, production seems to have been going forward. A publicity still of Baggot in the costume of the Moor appeared in *Moving Picture World*, and in *Universal Weekly*, September 25, there was a promotion which declared, "…Just fancy, Mr. Exhibitor, 'Othello' with King Baggot playing the Moor. Can you imagine the thoroughly determined way in which Baggot goes about the hideous work of killing the hapless Desdemona?"[10] Then, that was all. The film disappeared from the production lineup with no further explanation. At that time, IMP was not exactly cutting back on "quality" films, however. They were also in production at almost the same time for *Leah, the Forsaken*, written and directed by Herbert Brenon and starring Vivian Prescott and William E. Shay. It was released on November 7 after several production setbacks. This was a big break for Brenon as a director. It was IMP's first three-reel film. It had an excellent cast and was well received. Yet, there is no doubt that both IMP and King had lost an important director in Otis Turner.

Now that it had become more firmly established that stars were to be publicized, King began to get that "star" treatment. Although quite a bit of it was engineered by the production companies, by mid–1912 there was a virtual flood of interviews and short pieces about individual players appearing in the trades and the emerging fan publications. One such blurb was published in a late August *Moving Picture World, and* mentioned that he indeed had written some of his own films. Calling him an "author-actor," it mentioned three: *The Breakdown*, *His Other Self* and *In Old Tennessee*. It also gave credit to William Robert Daly as a collaborator on some of these. This article repeated (then quickly discredited) a rumor to the effect that "Mr. Baggot was to leave the IMP Company, but from reliable sources it seems to have proven false."[11] Perhaps this sheds some light on what happened to the production of *Othello*, but that can only be conjecture.

King was selected to be on the cover of *Moving Picture News* for the October 26 issue. The photograph was a slightly different pose, but from his clothing it can seen that it was from the same sitting as the publicity still published by *Universal Weekly* in January. His demeanor is still guarded — almost baleful. He was interviewed by M.I. MacDonald for the column "Personalities of the Players." This was his first interview in a trade publication that is known. M.I. MacDonald is worth quoting here in order to get the flavor of her style and also to illustrate that New York City, in some respects, did not differ much from our present times:

> If first impressions are true King Baggot belongs to the category of human curiosities called gentlemen. Curiosities because in New York City where I live and have my being, they are few and far between. Judging from a ten minute interview with this popular actor (in pictures and otherwise) he has the true instincts of a gentleman, he feels himself a gentleman, and therefore he is a gentleman…. All that day on which the said interview occurred I had been from time to time consoling people who were in trouble, and glad to do so. All that day people who

were sick or hungry, or without means of support, seemed to gravitate toward me. Sometimes we haven't much to give but kind words, and our hearts bleed because we cannot do more. And then on that very day I went to the interview from talking to a man who was not a gentleman — one who was rude and had not one respectful thought for a woman. Therefore it was that King Baggot, with his wholesome personality and respectful manner impressed me just as a big burst of sunshine from the sky of dark clouds would have done.[12]

Several paragraphs dealt sketchily with King's theatrical career. It was mentioned that he had been in roughly 160 films, that he swam, rode and knew how to crank a camera. When he was asked to tell a little bit about himself, King replied, "Oh, just say we had a nice little chat." Obviously, he had a lot to learn about being interviewed. However, as time went on, interviewers invariably mentioned his modesty and his gentlemanly qualities. This seemed to be part of his nature.

Two more interviews followed in rapid succession. The October issue of *Photoplay* had an unsigned one-page feature titled simply "King Baggot," and the November *Motion Picture Magazine* had a page titled "King Baggot Of the Imp Company," written by Gladys Roosevelt. There were a number of similarities here. Both were written by women, with his fans in mind. Both used that unflattering publicity still. Both mentioned a bit about his early life and stage career. They each noted that he was living at the King Edward Hotel and tied that into puns on his name. The King Edward Hotel was located at 155 West 47 Street, while the IMP Studios were at 102 West 101st Street — quite a distance to commute. This was his second known residence in New York. In New York City directories for that period, his name appears for the first time the previous year at 16 104th Street. The articles also touched upon the upcoming but never released *Othello*. And although they both did some breathless gushing over his good looks and gentlemanly qualities, Gladys Roosevelt's was the one that managed to get some interesting quotes from him that showed how seriously he took his film acting:

> "The Silent Drama is an art," he declares. "In it no bad actor can ever succeed, and many a good one may fail — fail because he lacks repose, or because he is a type actor and cannot be photographed.... Motion picture work is no longer mere pantomime.... It is acting. Everything must be done naturally, and that requires thought and study. The audience must be told everything in the most direct, simple way, and yet it must be effective. I am a great believer in turning the back to the audience. It seems to me that there are times when it is most expressive."[13]

And finally, they both mention the fact that he had just recently founded the Screen Club, which would become, next to his best films, one of his finest achievements.

11

The Screen Club and Wedding Bells

On Labor Day, September 2, 1912, King and a few of his friends had an idea that would do much to change the social fabric of the motion picture industry in the second decade of the twentieth century. According to all accounts, it was his idea and it blossomed in a cafe on Broadway that evening. His friends included William R. Daly, an IMP actor and recent director, Dell Henderson and Edward Dillon, both actors (and soon- to-be directors at Biograph) and Owen Moore, who at that time was with the Victor Company.[1] The exact circumstances are not really known, but a story told later — possibly apocryphal — suggested that a waiter at the cafe gave King a counterfeit half-dollar in change. The proprietor would not take it back and he and his friends walked out in indignation. Supposedly, as he was striding down the street, he took out his knife and cut the counterfeit piece in half, flinging it into the gutter. "That was a pretty small thing to make us dislike the only congenial meeting place in New York. Why not start a club?"[2]

So enthusiastic were they that on Thursday of that week, the group held another meeting where about 16 of their fellows convened for further discussion. Among them were Lawrence B. McGill, Dell Henderson, George F. Blaisdell, Calder Johnstone, Pierce Kingsley, C.A. (Doc) Willat, Herbert Brenon, William E. Shay, William Camp, Frank Russell, H.C. Judson, Thomas Malloy, J.P. Carroll and Frank Powell. It was Powell who proposed the name for the club. They represented an interesting cross section of the industry. Some were actors, some directors, but some were also members of the industry press, and a few were producers. Things moved very quickly after that. The first membership meeting was held on September 11, and another meeting on September 21 produced a constitution and by-laws. On September 28, with over 200 present, the first officers were elected. They were:

King Baggot — President, by acclaim

John Bunny — First Vice-President

Gilbert M. (Broncho Billy) Anderson — Second Vice-President

Arthur Johnson — Third Vice-President

Calder Johnstone — Corresponding Secretary

Harry R. Raver — Recording Secretary

C.A. Willat — Treasurer

The Board of Governors included:

William R. Daly and Lawrence B. McGill — both for two-year terms

Herbert Brenon, A. Victor Smith, Tefft Johnson, Pierce Kingsley, Oscar C. Apfel, and C. Jay Williams — all for one-year terms[3]

By the first of October, their charter had been granted from Albany. They appointed a ways and means committee to find a clubhouse and set the dues structure to raise the needed cash. Charter membership dues would be $20, annual resident dues were $12, non-resident dues $6, and a life membership $100.

In one month's time, they had secured and furnished their first club house, and on Saturday, November 9, at 7:30 P.M., the Screen Club had its official opening. It was located at 163 West 45th Street and Broadway. King had a great deal to do with the Club's decoration. He chose their colors — green and gold — and personally helped select the furnishings, the wallpaper and the many potted plants and palms, and helped decide the Club's layout. There was a library, a smoking room, a music room, a grill, a café and a meeting hall. Photographs still exist. They are contained in a bound volume published in April 1913, on the occasion of their first annual ball held at the Terrace Garden in New York. A copy is owned by the Academy of Motion Picture Arts and Sciences in Beverly Hills, California. No club of its day would be complete without an official anthem, and the Screeners had one composed by William R. Daly.

The Anthem:

Members of the Screen Club we
Linked in true fraternity
Brothers marching hand in hand
A loyal and faithful band.
For we are members of the Screen Club we
Standing side by side
'Neath our good Club's standard
Which is our joy and pride
Members of the Screen Club we
And we will always be.

Today this kind of sentiment and rather bad verse might make one smile, considering our modern sophisticated film world gatherings, but it must be remembered that 1912 was a simpler and gentler time. For its day, this was a very important social club for a group that was only beginning to have any real professional or social standing. The two notable clubs before this were the Lambs and the Friars Clubs — both traditionally theatrical in nature. Before the Screen Club was created, the only other social occasions open to this diverse new group were industry oriented, and usually occurred once a year, (like the New York Exhibitors ball). This new club opened its arms to virtually every branch of the film industry — managers, actors, scenario writers, publicity men, cameramen, the press, film editors, directors and producers. Whether they worked in and around New York, worked out of Chicago like Essanay, or Philadelphia, like Lubin, they had a convivial home where they could meet informally, do business and let off a little steam. It was a very powerful idea. Their avowed purpose as expressed in their statement of organization was "to unite, advance and preserve the motion picture art." And further, "to raise the industry to the highest status of respectability and dignity and eliminate existing evils."[4]

From that time onward, King was almost always described not just as a popular actor and leading man, but as the founder of the Screen Club. Eventually, as the film industry's focus and activities began to shift westward, the Club's influence and fortunes would decline. Yet, in its time, it was the most important social organization in the film world, with a membership of more than 500.[5] It should be noted that the membership figure represented only the men in the industry. Women were welcome at some, but not all of the club's functions, but were excluded from being members.

It has sometimes been said that Irish men marry late in life compared to other nationalities. In Ireland, back in the nineteenth and into the early twentieth century, that was often true. Because of the country's chronically poor economy, most young men took a long time to have enough income to support a wife. Immigrants to the United States continued the practice, and did it for just about the same reason. King's father William married when he was 32. King took even a little longer, but now he felt secure enough in his future that matrimony was no longer out of the question. He had left the knockabout world of the theater with its openings, closings and long inevitable stretches of being on the road. In fact, he had come to equate his participation in films as "coming home." He once said:

> I am not sorry that I made the decision to go into pictures. In fact, I am rather proud that I am a figure in motion picture life.... The movies have brought the actor to the dignity of a citizen. Very few of us [in the theater] had homes that could be called homes in the common acceptance of the term. Many of us had homes somewhere, where we went during the off season, but none of us had permanent homes for fifty-two weeks in the year, as we now have. This gives us an opportunity to engage in civic life and to become more substantial. We are many times removed from the gypsy element of theatrical life. Some of us have automobiles and farms and various business interests ... [We] look upon the idea of traveling and doing one-night stands as a laughing matter, as some kind of dream we hope will never come true again...[6]

Now the film business was booming and he was a star with IMP. He was writing and directing many of his own films and had even managed to contribute to the social fabric of the industry. It was time to get married.

Surprisingly, in spite of all the beautiful women he had known from both the stage and screen, he chose to wed a non-professional young lady named Ruth Constantine. Unfortunately, very little is known about her. She was born in Boston in 1889. Her father's name was Fenwick and her mother was Ann or Annie Robinson — both were from Nova Scotia. She had a brother named Charles, born in 1887. At the time of her birth, her father's occupation was listed in the city directory as "tinsmith."[7] She may have known King for at least two years before their marriage. The *New York Telegraph* had the best and most lengthy description of their nuptials. The article stated that they had been engaged "for more than two years." It also mentioned that she was the daughter of "a well known Boston family," and that she and her mother "had made New York their home for the past several years."[8] If this was true, she may have met King sometime after his personal appearance in St. Louis in 1910 and before IMP's excursion to Cuba in 1911.

The wedding took place on Tuesday, December 3, 1912 at Cella's Park Hotel in Fort Lee, New Jersey. Cella's was well known to the industry. From before the turn of the century, the Fort Lee-Edgewater-Leonia areas were used for outdoor location shooting, and these areas were fairly accessible to New York filmmakers. They could take the subway to ferries at 42nd Street or 125th Street to cross the Hudson River. Once landed at Edgewater, they

Cella's Park Hotel, circa 1910. A popular meeting place for film companies working in the Fork Lee, New Jersey, area. King and Ruth Baggot were married here in 1912. Photograph courtesy of the Fort Lee, New Jersey Film Commission.

could take a trolley or hire a livery to many different northern New Jersey locations. Cella's, in Fort Lee, was only a quarter of a mile from Main Street.[9]

The wedding was not a splashy affair. Indeed, it almost had the air of being done in some haste. Tuesday was not a traditional day for a wedding. Then too, there was no prior announcement in the press. The New York Telegraph picked up the event days later on December 8, and the trade papers did not publish the news until December 14. Even the make-up of the wedding party was rather unusual. King's good friend William R. Daly was his best man, but if Ruth had a maid of honor, that information did not appear in any of the sources. Nor did they mention Ruth's mother being present. The service was performed by Judge George Kinsler in a civil ceremony. For all King's openness about his Catholic faith, it seemed they were not married in the Church, so it may be presumed that Ruth was not a Catholic. The wedding took place in one of the hotel's private parlors at 5:45 P.M. Mr. and Mrs. Peter Cella acted as host and hostess for a dinner held immediately afterward.

They returned to New York that evening with Robert Daly and stopped briefly at the Screen Club, where King presented his new bride. Then they were "whisked away" in their motor car to Pennsylvania Station, where they took a train to Philadelphia and Atlantic City. They returned to New York on Friday and on December 7 they sailed for a honeymoon in Bermuda.[10] There is a strong possibility that neither King's nor Ruth's family approved of the match. King's family may have been against the marriage because Ruth was most probably not a Catholic. Ruth's mother may have had her own concerns about her daughter marrying an actor. Although Philadelphia and Atlantic City were on the newlyweds' itinerary, no mention was made of a visit to St. Louis.

From late fall, after the release of *Human Hearts* until the end of the year, King did not make any important pictures. The Screen Club may have taken up a great deal of his time just then. What he did produce were mostly one-reel comedies and dramas, and it is likely that he directed these himself, since no other director's name appears in the credits. The only exception was *John Sterling, Alderman*, which was a two-reeler directed by James Kirkwood, who had been an actor with Biograph, and was just coming into his own as a director. King was credited as the scenarist. It was released during the last week of October, and was praised as a film dealing honestly with political graft and bribery. Just the same, his films at this time were simply not "blockbusters."

12

Higher and Higher

On the evening of February 11, 1913, a remarkable event took place at the Astor Hotel. It was the Screen Club's first public occasion and the Screeners were there to honor King and Ruth, first on their recent marriage, and also to publicly thank King for being the driving force behind the founding of the Club. Harry Raver, general manager of the Film Supply Company, observed a unique feature of the evening when he was interviewed by the *New York Clipper*. He said: "[F]or the first time in the history of the dramatic profession a considerable number of its members sat down together at dinner, while at the same time millions of people all over the country were applauding their acting."[1] By all accounts it was a glittering affair, with a rooftop dinner in the Belvedere Room for over 200 people representing every facet of the industry. Columns of type were devoted to mentioning all the well-known people who gathered there. The menu was presented on a three-foot strip of raw film stock, printed in gold and bound together with ribbons of various colors.

John Bunny was the toastmaster, and as each course of the meal was served, speeches were delivered with wit and affection by King's colleagues. Special tributes were presented by Frances X. Bushman, Florence Turner, Carl Laemmle, Arthur Johnson, Herbert Brenon, Calder Johnstone, George Blaisdell, William R. Daly, Arthur Blinkhorn, Billy Quirk, Joseph W. Farnham and Matt Snyder.[2]

When the speeches were finished, there was a short cabaret entertainment, followed by a special presentation to King and Ruth made by Arthur Johnson, Tefft Johnson and Calder Johnstone. It was a gift of a magnificent mahogany chest containing seven dozen pieces of sterling silver. When King's turn to speak came, the press reported:

Mr. Baggot, as the silver was placed in front of him, hesitated. "It is beautiful," he said. "Let me go for a little while," he added when he found his voice. "Just let me look at this. Let my wife look too, look at it, so we may realize and know what friendship is." ... He confided to his hearers that when he came in he had all prepared a speech in which he had been rehearsed by his wife all week, "but this bomb of friendship landed and took it away from me." He thanked his friends for their gift and predicted for the Screen Club a success that will make it the greatest theatrical club in the world."

Carl Laemmle, too, had warm words for his star and his words were an indication that the rumor about King's intention to leave IMP had some merit. He said, perhaps in a veiled reference to that rumor, "as between the guest and myself the relationship of employed and employer does not exit ... he is my friend. I think the world of him whether he is with me or not." As the evening was winding down, one more star appeared to wish King and his new bride well. Mary Pickford, "garbed in a simple costume," dropped by with Owen Moore after the close of the evening's stage performance of *The Good Little Devil*.[3]

During the early months of 1913, IMP was preparing a version of *Dr. Jekyll and Mr. Hyde*, starring King, and directed by Herbert Brenon. Written by Robert Louis Stevenson in 1886, it had thrilled theater audiences ever since it became a stage vehicle for Richard Mansfield in 1887. Other adaptations followed. It has sometimes been called the screen's earliest horror film, but IMP was not the first company to undertake it. The Selig Polyscope Company filmed it in Chicago in 1908. There were two other versions released in 1910 by foreign producers: a British release with the title *The Duality of Man*, and one by Denmark's Nordisk Company. Just the year before, Thanhouser did another version starring James Cruze as Dr. Jekyll and Henry Benham as Hyde.[4] IMP's version was the longest so far — two reels. It was released March 6, and the reviews for King were raves. The transformation of the good Dr. Jekyll to the evil Mr. Hyde was done with dissolve effects that had the reviewers reaching for new adjectives to describe its impact on them. The review in *Moving Picture World* was especially laudatory. George Blaisdell said:

> It is seldom that one man or one woman dominates a play or a picture. In these two reels King Baggot holds the center of attention all the way.... The leading man of the Imp Company outdoes himself. It is a forceful characterization, and shows much care and study. In the periods when Mr. Baggot portrays Mr. Hyde the horror of it holds you. It may be said in cold blood that Mr. Baggot has done nothing for the screen that will rank higher as an artistic piece of work than will his exposition of Mr. Hyde — the transformation of the charitable physician into a fiend.[5]

This film is available on video today. Baggot plays Dr. Jekyll as a calm, kindly man until Hyde emerges. As the fiend, he is an eye-popping monster whose actions hearken back to early film acting. There was no "repose" in this character. He jumps about and gestures like the wild man he is playing. One can imagine that he and Brenon had a certain amount of enjoyment making this film.

King was working hard during this time. Ads for him began appearing in the trade press that year and continued into 1914, calling him "A face as well known as that of the man in the moon." He made a series of one-reel comedies and dramas interspersed with more two-reel features. For the World's Best Film Company, he wrote the scenario for *The Wizard of the Jungle*, which starred the famous lion tamer, Capt. Jack Bonavita. It was directed by Harold Shaw, who would soon be going to England, and it was shot near Tampa, Florida.

At this time, Ruth Baggot had what was probably her only first-hand participation in the film business — she wrote the scenario for the two-reel film *The Leader of His Flock* — in which good triumphs over evil. King most likely directed it. He played the part of the minister, while Jane Gail was the young woman who was "falsely accused." Another important two-reel film from this time was *The Rise of Officer 174*, written by Walter MacNamara, a crime story where graft and corruption are

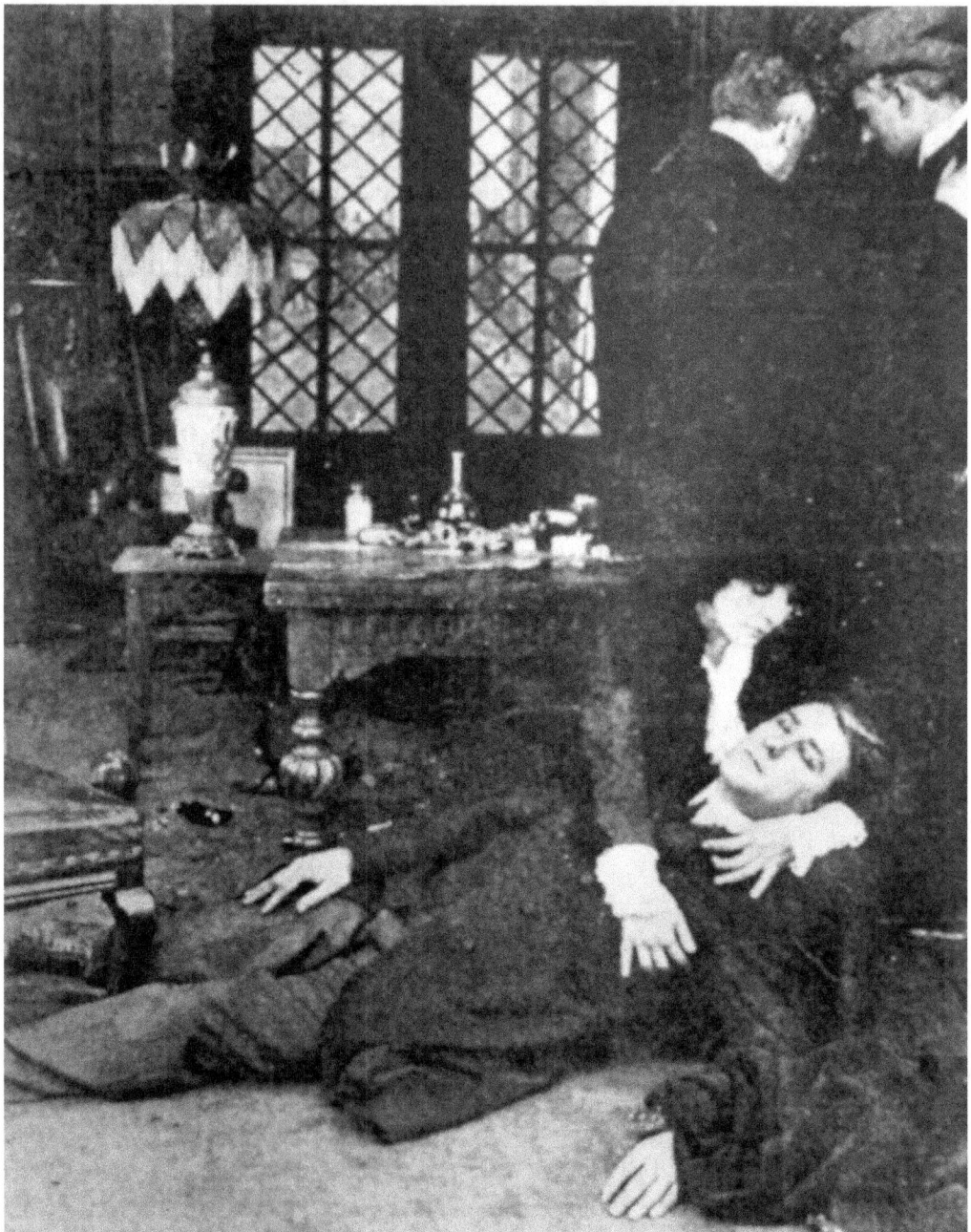

Jane Gail and King Baggot in IMP's 1913 production of *Dr. Jekyll and Mr. Hyde,* directed by Herbert Brenon. Photograph courtesy of Wisconsin Center for Film and Theatre Research.

thwarted by Officer 174 and his sweetheart, again played by Jane Gail, by listening in on the plot using the office dictaphone. Another two-reel film of note was *The Comedian's Mask*, directed by Herbert Brenon.

It is unfortunate that although this film is owned by the Museum of Modern Art, and at least can be seen, it is missing the beginning titles, the reels are out of sequence, and the print is not a very good one. King plays a kind of "Pagliacci" character — once a world famous comedian, but now a has-been whose wife is about to go away with the handsome tenor in the company. On stage he gives the finest comedic performance of his life, then tries to commit suicide by taking poison. Still, for all its mechanical flaws, one can see the dramatic power that he now brought to his work. Brenon's growing skill as a director was clearly visible as well.

It was announced in May that members of the IMP Company were going to Europe to do some filming. This was not a first. The Kalem Company had gone to Ireland in 1911 and shot quite a number of films there with Irish themes.[6] Yet what IMP was about to do was in some ways more ambitious. They planned to go first to England, then to France, and finally to Germany. They would be gone for at least three months. This time it was not necessary to put all of their eggs in one basket.

Herbert Brenon would direct, and King would be the star. They also hired Leah Baird, formerly with Vitagraph, as King's leading lady, but would team up with European crews and actors to fill out the company. Brenon was sent over first to make preliminary arrangements. He left May 3 with his wife, Helen, aboard the *Olympic*. King, Ruth and Harold Shaw, who was leaving to direct for the London Film Company, all sailed May 21 on the *Kaiser Wilhelm der Gross*. Universal executives and members of the Screen Club met in Hoboken at the North German Lloyd docks to wish them bon voyage. The *Dramatic Mirror* published a long list of those who were present. Ruth's mother, Mrs. Constantine, was among them.[7] If there had been any rift between her and the newlyweds, it was now mended. Leah Baird, who had just joined IMP the week of May 26, left June 2.

13

Assault on England

Brenon's first task was to set up an IMP office in London at 100 Charing Cross Road. He worked closely with the Ideal Studios and Frank Brockliss, a distributing agent for Universal. Then began the daunting task of hiring actors and crew, scouting locations, giving interviews to the press and settling on which films they would produce and where. It is telling that although the Company had an overall "game plan," at that juncture they may not have had a full complement of specific stories to shoot. Brenon actually placed an ad in the British trade press soliciting suitable scenarios for five pounds each.[1] When King arrived, he too was kept busy meeting with buyers, viewers and exhibitors as well as being interviewed by the press.[2] Somehow, though, they were ready to begin filming by June 4.

Their first film was *Across the Atlantic*, and Brenon timed the shooting of the first segment to coincide with the running of Derby Day at Epsom Downs. The footage was incorporated into the plot for this three-reel drama about famous aviators, international intrigue, plans for a secret new airplane, a murder the hero (Baggot) never committed, and a thrilling chase after a Japanese spy (played by Brenon) over the rooftops of London. An important historical event happened that Derby Day, but when Brenon set up his cameras, he missed placing one at Tattenham Corner. That day, as a protest, a suffragette, Emily Davidson, threw herself under the hoofs of King George V's horse and was killed. The Gaumont Company of London was also covering the race. According to an account in *Moving Picture World*, they had 15 cameras and at least one was strategically placed at "The Corners."

> The first batch of horses goes thundering by; suddenly a woman in dark clothes springs from the rail and as the last three horses appear, quickly grabs the bridle of the King's entry, throwing the horse into a complete somersault. precipitating the jockey headlong through the air, falling herself under the hoofs of the horses which follow...[3]

The article went on to say that every London illustrated paper used clips from the Gaumont film. It was shown in New York as a documentary about the Derby race and might also have figured in a Gaumont drama released in December *The Suffragette's Revenge*.

Brenon was given a fairly substantial budget for these European films and he was able to hire and use some well-known people. Leah Baird was not in this first film — perhaps she did not arrive in time. The leading lady was an English actress, Evelyn Hope. He also obtained the services of two famous aviators, Gustave Hammell and Claude Graham White, who in addition to flying their own planes, acted in the film as well. Soon after the filming was completed, Hammell was killed preparing for a transatlantic flight. Brenon worked hard to incorporate as many views of London as he could, including Hendon Aerodrome, Buckingham Palace, Westminster Abbey, the Strand, St. Paul's Cathedral and Fleet Street. One review called it "a dramatic travelogue with contemporary news interest." However, this first film would be just a warm-up for what was to come.

Their next vehicle was a more ambitious one. It was no less than Sir Walter Scott's classic *Ivanhoe*. During the course of the shooting and long afterward, the film captured the respect and affection of the English people for the intrepid IMP Company. Until that time, nothing quite like it had been done on English soil. All the major British papers covered it in great detail. Some sent special correspondents on location and a few members of the press were actually hired to play small parts. The correspondent for the *Cinematograph Exhibitors Mail* gave Helen Brenon credit for suggesting a production of *Ivanhoe*. He related that the Brenons were attending a stage performance of *Ivanhoe* at the Lyceum Theatre in London and she thought it would make a very fine film.[4] She was right.

A cast and crew was assembled with great speed. They left from Paddington Station and arrived at the little town of Chepstow in Monmouthshire on Sunday, June 22. This out-of-the-way place was chosen because it was the site of a half-ruined castle called "Chepstow." Brenon had the cooperation of a town booster, Mr. Clifford Thomas, who lived there, and who helped them lease the castle for a month from its owner, the Duke of Beauford. It proved to be a perfect location, situated on the banks of the River Wye and surrounded by beautiful trees and grassy parklands. It was an ancient site, first constructed by William FitzOsbern about 1067 and was in almost constant use from the time of the Norman Conquest until after the Reformation. It belonged to Oliver Cromwell after the Civil Wars and he kept it repaired and garrisoned until the Restoration in 1660.[5]

When they arrived, this small town of about 3,000 gave the company their unstinting support. During the two weeks that filming took place, almost everyone in the town was involved in some way with the production. The arrivals from London were put up at the Bell Hotel owned by Mr. and Mrs. J.H. Thomas. Local people assisted with the costumes and the "Church Boy's House," a large social hall, was turned into a costume, props and make up facility. As time went on, the townspeople would do even more.

Filming was scheduled to begin on Monday, but being England, it rained buckets that day. Tuesday was merely overcast, so some of the principal shooting began. King played Ivanhoe and Leah Baird was Rebecca, the Jewess, who falls in love with Ivanhoe, but who loses him to Lady Rowena (Evelyn Hope). Brenon gave himself the meaty part of Isaac of York, Rebecca's father, who in one chilling and all too realistic scene is tortured by the Normans with red-hot branding irons. The rest of the cast was made up of seasoned English actors: Wallace Bosco as Ivanhoe's father Cedric, Arthur Scott Craven as Richard the Lion-Hearted and Walter Thomas as Robin Hood. Helen Brenon used her old stage name "Helen Downing" and had the small role of Elgitha.

It was an amazing film for its time and

parts of it still hold up today, even if viewed with Dutch intertitles from a copy made by the Museum of Modern Art from one owned by the Nederlands Filmmuseum. Herbert Brenon's battle scenes carry the picture. He employed more than 300 supers recruited from the local iron foundry and the townspeople. They were paid five shillings a day for two very hard days' work. About half were designated as either the Knight's Templars or Robin Hood's Foresters and the other half were the Normans. Every horse in the town had been conscripted. All of Chepstow took a holiday to come and watch. The foundry and the school were closed because so many of the Chepstonians were involved in the shooting.

Rehearsals began on a bright and sunny Friday morning, June 27. Brenon drilled his troops until he was satisfied that they could handle the broad swords, bows and arrows, battle-axes and horses proficiently — as well as perform the sweeping charges and clashes of hand-to-hand combat that would make those scenes so thrilling. Often standing on the camera platform in his shirtsleeves, he used a whistle, a pistol and a megaphone to signal his intentions. They performed beyond all expectations; the only exception occurred when some of them were required to fall in battle when the whistle blew. It was hard for them to remember to lie still. Brenon had to repeatedly say, "Remember to lie still when you are dead!" For those who happened to fall on stony ground or into a patch of nettles, that was not an easy thing to do.[6] The battle began on the grounds in front of the castle. Brenon exhorted his men, "Fight like blazes, boys, and there's sandwiches and beer when you get inside."[7]

Those Welshmen fought with so much enthusiasm that a few became totally carried away. That was when Baggot was injured. In rehearsals, he was to defeat a number of soldiers single-handedly in a carefully orchestrated broadsword combat. He was facing the camera and had his back turned to the masses of men fighting near him. Suddenly one of the supers came charging toward him swinging his weapon. Perhaps he thought Baggot was another super. Baggot turned and the sword caught him flat on the chin, just missing his mouth. He staggered, but resisted the impulse to faint until he saw the camera operator's hand stop turning — then he collapsed.[8] That bit of action was kept in the film. Watching closely, he can be seen to stagger as he was hit.

King Richard's fighting men breached the oaken castle doors, sweeping the Norman defenders aside, while Robin Hood's men scaled the castle walls. They knew how to do this because Brenon showed them in rehearsal. More than once it was said that the townspeople admired the company, and especially Brenon, tremendously because he never asked them to do anything that he could not do himself and because the professional actors were supportive and helpful in so many small but meaningful ways. In some of these scenes, a camera was stationed on top of the battlements and achieved stunning views as waves of men surged forward through the castle gates while other men, being struck by swords and arrows, fell backward. The two cameramen employed on this film, Ernest Palmer and Stewart Kinder, were English. They stood out there on those camera platforms hour after hour and day after day, sometimes in very hot sun. Their work was quite remarkable and Brenon and IMP were fortunate to have them. (Some years later, Palmer would come to the United States and become a well known cameraman.) It is sad to reflect that these strong young Chepstow lads playing at war on sunny days in Monmouthshire would soon be fighting with real weapons in a real war when Great Britain declared war on

Germany in August 1914. All of Europe would be in flames.

Filming the battle scenes took two days and it required another week to finish the picture, but on Saturday evening it was time to say goodbye. The leading citizens of Chepstow gave a party that night at the Bell Hotel for the cast. Many of the actors had to return to London to be able to rehearse for new roles on Monday. There were songs, and recitations, some magic tricks were performed—and many affectionate toasts were given on both sides. Brenon said that he had never worked with a better group of people and they said they had never before had the experience of working with such a talented and professional film company. It had been a mutual love feast and a special time for all of them. Strangely, Ruth Baggot did not seem to have been in Chepstow. There were two newspaper accounts of the party and everyone who attended appeared to have been named, but she was not mentioned. Nor did her name appear in any of the almost daily accounts given by all those members of the press who were there. Perhaps she stayed in London; if so, she missed a very memorable time.

Correspondents for the English press who were on location lavishly praised Brenon and Baggot even before the film was released. Of Baggot, it was said by the unnamed correspondent for the *Cinematograph Exhibitors Mail*:

> What a wonderfully perfect actor is Mr. King Baggot, and what an enormous amount of energy he puts into his work. He seems to inspire the rest of the company whenever he is in the picture, with the result that they put much more force into their work than they would otherwise deem necessary. He takes his work completely to heart, and this past week I am sure he has forgotten that he is King Baggot, the best film actor in the world—and has been eating, drinking, sleeping, and working as if he were the very Ivanhoe of centuries ago come to life again to pay homage to his king and to fight and win the hand of fair Lady Rowena.[9]

A fellow actor, Arthur Scott Craven, whose background was largely theatrical, also paid tribute to him, saying:

> As an actor of some standing and long experience on the London stage, I had been wont to take to the work of the "picture actor" all too lightly ... and had regarded it as an art easily acquired. I was quickly undeceived. I found it to be the most difficult and subtle accomplishment. The way that Mr. King Baggot succeeds in getting his extremely magnetic personality into every picture is a little short of marvelous, and actors of the largest standing on the London stage might study many of his methods with advantage. He can convey more in a single expression or gesture than many actors of high repute on the ordinary stage could convey in a page of close type, and this is no mean histrionic art, no matter from what exalted level we may criticize contemporary dramatic productions.[10]

Ivanhoe was released in England on September 11, 1913, but did not make its American debut until September 22. It was billed as a "Universal De Luxe." The advertising copy boasted that in Europe it smashed all selling records and that it was the most expensive picture Universal ever made. They also declared that over a thousand extras were used, which can typically be expected from advertisers' hyperbole. While IMP was making their version, another British producer, Zenith, was at work on their own, using the company of the Lyceum Theatre—the very company that inspired the Brenons to undertake it as a film. Who can now know which company had the original idea? Zenith's *Ivanhoe* was nearly twice the finished length of IMP's at over 6,000 feet. However, there was a severe limitation placed on Zenith: They were able to use the Tower of London for

The making of *Ivanhoe*, IMP, 1913. Herbert Brenon in white trousers directing while the townspeople of Chepstow, Monmouthshire, take a holiday to watch the filming. Photograph courtesy of Tom and Mary Baggot.

the battle scenes, but were only allowed to shoot between 5:30 and 9:30 A.M. It was released in the U.S. as *Rebecca the Jewess*, but for production values it did not hold a candle to the IMP version.[11] Judging the original length of IMP's *Ivanhoe* is a bit tricky. Early information called it a three-reel film, but it was more than 3,000 feet. IMP ads, at the time of its release, described it as 3,700, which was closer to four reels. Wear and tear on the copies which still exist makes each of them a slightly different length. An English source revealed that Brenon shot about 20,000 feet of film, then reduced it to about 3,000. This source also said that £3,500 were spent making it.[12]

14

On to Paris

Brenon did not have a moment to lose in order to produce as many films as possible during their European junket. Immediately after the filming of *Ivanhoe* was completed, the company embarked for Paris and began shooting their next film while still en route — probably during the first week of July. It was *Mr. and Mrs. Innocence Abroad*. Part comedy and part travelogue in one reel, it told the story of a young couple, King and Leah (Baggot and Baird), going to Europe for the first time. While on the ship to Calais, they filmed the cliffs of Dover, then their arrival at Calais and finally their entry into the great city itself, Paris. This film may no longer exist, but photos that accompanied the reviews show them enjoying the sights. They climbed the many levels of the Eiffel Tower and in one shot they are leaning over a handsome wrought iron railing, pointing and exclaiming at the view below.[1]

Their next undertaking was *The Anarchist*. Another one-reel feature using an all–French cast except for Leah and King. King is the anarchist and Leah is his sweetheart. It is a dramatic story wherein the anarchist and his sweetheart have an argument over a rival who wishes to win Leah away from King. One day as King is walking in the streets of Paris, he meets a little girl. As it happens, she lives in the same building on the floor above him. He buys her a toy horn to cement their friendship. Soon after, his rival tells the police where he lives and that King and his fellow anarchists are making bombs. Leah manages to warn him that the police are on the way and in a melodramatic moment the anarchists decide to blow themselves and the building to smithereens. But just then he hears the little girl upstairs playing the horn he had given her and realizes that she too would be killed. Flashes show the child sitting on the floor above playing with two kittens and the horn he had given her. The hand of the anarchist drops; the police storm in and take him prisoner. The reviews praised both Baggot and Baird for fine acting. They also had kind words for the French actors, especially the little girl and the rival. It was noted that real gendarmes were used and that the "chief of police" did a very realistic job. One review mentioned that the copy of the film shown was without intertitles but that none were needed.[2]

Brenon was now on a roll. With each film he gained strength and confidence in his own abilities. He was ready to tackle a project somewhat more narrow in scope than *Ivanhoe*, but dealing in four reels with a subject that would be sensational enough to be a true box office smash. He chose the theme of absinthe, the internationally notorious drink of France that turned habitual users into addicts, ruining their lives in a downward spiral that led to madness and, finally, death. Most other countries had already outlawed its sale and use and so would France, but not until the Great War was underway in 1915. In fact, war was already underway in Europe when the IMP Company arrived in France, but at that point in time it was far removed to the east and over the Danube in the Balkan States where fierce fighting was taking place between Bulgaria, Turkey, Serbia, Rumania, Greece and Montenegro. The French government was already preparing and had instituted the three-year conscription of its citizens that February. But the bombings, killings and atrocities had not yet touched France and would not do so until August of 1914 when Germany declared war against the French people. The little group of Americans making their European IMP films was still safe and relatively unconcerned.

Preparations for *Absinthe* took a week or more. In addition to writing the scenario with the help of the talented George Edwardes Hall, whom Brenon had brought over to assist him, he and the cast did some intense background research. Baggot spent what was said to be a week living in the tenderloin of Paris observing absinthe drinkers, the colorful apaches and other denizens of the Latin Quarter; their dress and manners and the way in which they carefully prepared the absinthe before imbibing it. When King was shown preparing it in the film, he did not just pour it into a glass. As the French custom dictated, the green liquid was dribbled slowly and tediously, drop by drop, into water.[3]

Absinthe could be called a "one man" picture. Baggot's role as Jean Dumas, a Parisian artist who falls under the influence of the insidious drink, is a morality tale depicting what can happen to a previously normal individual. He comes from a middle-class family. His mother and father love him very much. He is their only son. Trouble begins when he falls in love with an opportunistic little laundress, played by Baird. She is an absinthe user and introduces him to it. She marries him, but wants more in the way of material things and convinces him to rob his parents' house. They catch him and are devastated by his actions, but he is unconcerned, slipping further and further under the spell of the drink. When his money is gone, she leaves him for a rich man. The bottle becomes his constant friend and he joins an apache gang that make their living robbing people. One night, he and his gang notice a wealthy looking couple. The woman, loaded with jewelry, is put into a cab by her escort. Jean takes the place of the driver and drives off with her. Suddenly he realizes that she is his former wife. He is inflamed with unreasoning anger. A terrible ride follows. While still driving the cab, he proceeds to beat and choke her, finally driving down the Bois de Boulogne and into the woods where he drags her from the cab, robs her and leaves her for dead. Arriving home, he begins to drink to the point of delirium. His degradation is complete. The next morning he awakens a wreck and staggers back to his parents. They do not know what to do to rehabilitate their son. Outside they hear soldiers marching by — volunteers going to war. His father puts his old gun in his son's hands and sends him out to join them. He is last seen a ruined man, dragging his gun along behind him, following the soldiers and being jeered by a band of city street urchins.

That scene in the cab provoked a rift between director and star that would take a long time to heal. Reports in the trades

Herbert Brenon, 1880–1958. Sparks flew when IMP's youngest director was working with Baggot in France during the making of *Absinthe* in 1914. Photograph courtesy of the Francis Howard Goldwyn Hollywood Regional Library, Special Collections.

suddenly announced that Baggot would be returning to the United States and that William E. Shay had left for Europe to join the IMP troup for their last leg of filming in Germany. No explanation was given for the switch and perhaps the cause would forever have remained a mystery except that some of Brenon's papers were given to the Frances Howard Goldwyn Hollywood Regional Library in 1987. In the early 1950s, Brenon sought the help of William Laidlaw, George Geltzer and William Everson to write and publish his memoirs. As far as is known, the project was never completed, but there are copies of some of Brenon's responses to questions asked by these men in his correspondence. Writing to William Laidlaw, Brenon explained:

> The impass between Baggot and me came as a result of rank insubordination. We had a mighty row over the taking of a scene, going through the streets of Paris in *Absinthe*. The photographer and I were in one car, Baggot and Baird followed closely in another car. It was an important scene — ending in his manhandling her. We had rehearsed it carefully. There were hardly any retakes in those days. Left the hotel, and when I gave the signal for action from the car ahead — he DID JUST WHAT I TOLD HIM NOT TO DO. A difficult scene in Paris traffic, and I hit the ceiling. He was insulting as to my directorial abilities. We had an abusive row, and, then well — it was he or I.[4]

Brenon's anger and bitterness toward King some 40 years later were shown in another passage that he wrote to Laidlaw when he was describing the making of *Ivanhoe*. He reflected:

> Baggot was not so bad at first, but he had that "directing" bee in his bonnet. [And no doubt he did — he had been directing his own films for a year or more while Brenon was still a scenario editor at IMP.] It was when we went to France that he "acted up" and on one occasion declined to take direction. It must be done his way.

> We were going on to Berlin to make another series there, and I cabled Laemmle, that rather than go there with Baggot, I preferred to resign. That's why Stern [Julius Stern, IMP's general manager] was sent over — to patch things up — no soap. So I asked for my favorite leading man, William Shay to [take] his place. Bear in mind that Baggot was, then, the biggest drawing card for Universal. He was a six-footer — handsome fellow — but unmanageable....[5]

As acrimonious as their quarrel might have been, there were still films to be made. So, presumably while they were waiting for Stern's arrival, the company made one last film in the City of Lights. It was *The Child Stealers of Paris*, based on real-life incidents in Europe where roving gangs of criminals were stealing young children and virtually selling them into slavery, often renting them out to professional beggars to appeal to the sympathies of those who might give them money. Again, Brenon used local color to tell the story. The settings were the streets of Paris, the Champs Elysees, the Arc de Triomphe, the Bourse and the Louvre — and the beggars were real beggars. In the film, King and Leah were a couple who separated soon after their marriage. A few years later, Leah visits Paris with their little girl whom King, now a wealthy financier, has never seen. The little one is lost and falls into the hands of a child stealer who rents her out to a beggar. King sees her on the streets and, realizing her plight, buys her from the beggar and takes her home. Meanwhile, Leah is frantically looking for her missing daughter. Then, one day, she finds her child looking out through the iron fence of the mansion where she now lives with her benefactor. The three are brought back together in a joyful reunion.

Brenon certainly had a right to be angry about King's refusal to take direction, and making that final film must have been an uncomfortable experience for all of them. Brenon was developing into an exceptionally fine director, but art is art and talent is talent. Many months later, in November, when he had returned from Europe, he was sitting in a screening room with George Blaisdell, then a reviewer for *Moving Picture World*. The film was ready for release and Blaisdell was getting the benefit of the director's experience making it. Apparently it was a moving and well-made film. Even Brenon could not help being proud of the poignant scene where King has just found the little girl and they are sitting in a park near the Champs Elysées. Almost in wonder at King's ability as an actor and his own as a director, he said, "Can you conceive that situation as it was? ...King is talking English and the child is speaking French, yet between them there seems to be a perfect understanding." Blaisdell liked the film very much and said many laudatory things about the backgrounds, the acting and the plot, but he also made a case for the ability of a one-reel film to tell a wonderfully moving story. He said, "There are those who insist that a story cannot be told within the limits of a thousand feet of film. Such pictures as this will always serve as a standing refutation of such an assertion."[6]

When *Absinthe* was finally released in January 1914, it indeed caused the kind of sensation and box office appeal that Universal and all concerned had hoped for. It was billed as a "Universal Special," and exhibitors had to pay more for it than Universal's regular fare. Accompanying the film was wonderfully lurid advertising art which, no doubt, helped draw the large crowds. Yet, Universal did not show the film exclusively in selected large theaters first, as had been done for *Traffic in Souls* the year before.[7] Possibly the thinking was that *Traffic In Souls* was six reels, while *Absinthe* was only four. It was released nationwide and exhibitors merely upped the admission price from their usual five cents to ten. It played to packed houses and turn-away crowds. It was revealed that during the shooting of the wild carriage ride scene, Baggot and Baird fought so realistically that King suffered a split lip and a broken tooth and Leah fainted. This could be a case of post-production hype, but given the intensity of the scene as it was described at the time, it may have been true.[8] Interestingly, there was another production of *Absinthe* that pre-dated Universal's version. It was released back in January 1913 by a small concern, Gem Motion Picture Company. By the following, year Gem would become one more company under the Universal umbrella. That film still exists and is held by Nederlands Filmmuseum, but a frame enlargement taken from the actual film, which was about one reel, shows it was a cheap and crude bit of filmmaking. Regrettably, a print of Universal's *Absinthe* has yet to be found.

15

Triumphant Return

King came back to New York in triumph. When the S.S. *St. Paul* docked in the New York harbor on September 13, 1913, a hero's welcome was waiting for him. Hundreds of people lined the pier to cheer for him, including his friends and associates from the Screen Club and the executives of Universal. The banner on the welcoming tugboat read "Welcome King Baggot. King of the Movies." And at that moment he was. No mention was made of his quarrel with Brenon. In fact, the official story would later be that he was being rewarded as the foremost movie star in the world by being given his own company at IMP. He would have the artistic freedom to write, act in, cast and direct his own films.[1]

Less than two weeks later, on September 23, *Universal Weekly* announced that King and Ruth had left New York for a short visit with King's mother in St. Louis, and that then the IMP company would be off to Kentucky with a unit that included Ethel Grandin, character actor Frank Smith and Thomas McAvoy to film another "big picture" in conjunction with a week-long celebration in Louisville commemorating Kentucky's participation in the War of 1812. The focus would be upon the "Battle of the Thames." Not the English Thames River, but the one in Ontario, Canada, where a brave Kentucky regiment, led by Col. Richard M. Johnson's cavalry, defeated both British and Indian forces led by Thomas Proctor and swept them back into Canada. King was to play a young trapper who joins Col. Johnson's forces and becomes a captain. Planning had apparently gone on for some time. Permission had been obtained to shoot various battle scenes and incorporate them into the film. They would have a large pool of participants from which to choose in the filming, including 1,500 members of the Improved Order of Red Men, the First Unit of the Kentucky National Guard, the Turner's Society and "a host of Indians."[2] However, something went wrong and this film was never made. Instead, King began making a series of interesting but unremarkable one- and two-reel offerings to fill out the year.

This did not matter so much in terms of his fame at that moment, for all those exciting European films in which he starred were being released throughout this time: *Ivanhoe*, on September 22; *The Anarchist*, October 23; *The Child Stealers of Paris*, November 20; and *Mr. and Mrs. Innocence Abroad*, December 8. Then, moving into

1914, *Absinthe* was released on January 22. Universal's strategy seems to have been to give the public one every month. Still, King and his unit had to produce something, but these films were far from exceptional. When the big Kentucky battle picture failed to be realized, he, Ethel Grandin and Charles Eldridge, formerly with Vitagraph, made a two-reel comedy, *Love vs. Law*, in which Charles Eldridge, as Ethel's father, plays a war veteran constantly bragging about what he would do if accosted by a bandit. When a real bandit comes along, he flees. King expands on this gag by dressing like a bandit to scare Ethel's father, and gets arrested. Ethel finds the real bandit and pleads with him to go to court to prove King was not really a bandit. The bandit holds up the court with a gun and then confesses to the crime, which frees King—and then he escapes. King and Ethel are married on the spot. This is hardly the stuff of *Absinthe*, or *Dr. Jekyll and Mr. Hyde*. He seemed to be reaching backward to the simplistic plots of films he made in 1910 and 1911.

Publicity still of Baggot at the height of his fame circa 1914. Photograph courtesy of Wisconsin Center for Film and Theatre Research.

His next films were no better. He reprised Tony, his simple little Italian character, from *Tony and the Stork*, which he made in 1911. *The Return of Tony* was so bad that the reviewers could not grasp the plot—and this was a one-reel film! *Moving Picture World* kindly blamed "the scenario writer," but it most probably was King's work. The reviewer even gently hinted that King was not strictly convincing in the part.[3] As the year was winding down, it was time for a "Christmas" picture. IMP's yuletide offering was another one-reel "quickie," *The Actor's Christmas*. In it, King as a down-and-out actor is hired to play Santa in a rich man's home, where he is tempted to steal toys for his child. He is caught, but the spirit of Christmas and his reasons for the theft lead to a happy

King checking his extensive wardrobe at the IMP Studios in New York, 1913. Photograph courtesy of the Quigley Photographic Archives, Georgetown University Library, Special Collections Div., Wash., D.C.

ending. If the plot sounds familiar, it should. That pathetic theme of a crime committed with good intentions ran through a very large number of plots, not just in IMP films, but in so many other companies as well that by now it was a war-horse. Jane Gail played opposite King. She was fresh from her triumph in *Traffic in Souls*, which took the film world by storm and made a great deal of money for Universal. Before this film was released she would be on her way to England to star in George Loane Tucker's films for the London Film Company.[4]

For his last effort of the year, King turned to a kind of film that had fascinated him for some time and which would continue to do so on and off for the rest of his career as an actor—it was the detective genre. Crime detection, and especially the use of scientific principles to catch criminals, whether in literary form or in film, delighted the American public from before the turn of the century and, indeed, continues to the present time. Back in 1911, shortly after the Pickford contingent left IMP, he made *King, the Detective*. There are no known credits but it is possible that he may have written and directed this one-reel film himself. Now that he was more or less free to produce what he wanted, he began to develop this idea into a series, beginning with *King, the Detective in the Jarvis Case*. However, it was apparent that he still had a great deal to learn about the nuts and bolts of filmmaking. The *New York Dramatic Mirror* was not as kind to him as *Moving Picture World* had been:

> ...a two reel detective drama.... Mr. Baggot takes the lead with distinction in the early part of the offering ... with a considerable amount of mystery attached to it. Some of the mystification, however, comes from the fact that there is not sufficient explanation to make it understandable.... Mr. Baggot has allowed his sense of the ridiculous to get the best of him and the film turns abruptly into a farce.[5]

To add injury to insult, while *Jarvis Case* was being produced back in November, the company was working outdoors at Leonia Heights, New Jersey. As they were digging a tunnel in an embankment, the hillside collapsed due to previous heavy rain and partially buried King and his friend and associate, Frank Smith. Smith's back was sprained and King had a bruised and lacerated hip.[6] That review must have stung as much as the cave-in injuries.

Yet, King's focus on being an accomplished actor led him then, as it would continue to do for most of the rest of his life, to support his profession in every way he could. Late in 1913, he joined Actors Equity Association. He certainly did not need to join, for Equity had nothing to do with screen actors. However, as a group they were struggling to expand their ranks. At that time they had only 631 members, of which a mere 67 were women. Frank Smith, who had once been a promising theatrical actor himself, joined with him.[7]

16

The Good Life

Baggot's work during this period shows that as a screen actor he was thought by many to be one of the best and most popular in the world. However, artistically, he was still struggling to find his place as an accomplished scenario writer and director. Just the same, his rise in the industry was considered a major accomplishment. In his 1914 book *The Theatre of Science* Robert Grau had this to say:

> Mr. Baggot has been with "Imp" four years, increasingly in influence and popularity steadily, until at this writing he is one of the six most idolized favorites of the screen. Mr. Baggot is quite as celebrated as a director as he is as a photoplayer and he writes many scenarios of the productions in which he appears and others in which he does not personally act. On the theatrical Rialto the career of King Baggot is discussed as being of the Arabian Nights order. As usual, there is little cognizance taken of the fact that this man is what he is today because of the seriousness with which he invests his work, because he is a prodigious worker, and finally because he has remained steadfast to the organization which he joined as an experiment, and as he contributed materially to the growth of the organization, his constancy and capacity have been rewarded so rapidly that his annual earnings now are said to be 2000 per cent greater that four years ago.[1]

The salary figure may have been a bit exaggerated, but King himself was pleased with his accomplishments and all seemed right with the world. In an interview that year, a reporter asked him, "Do you think life is worth living?" He replied, "It has been very good to me so far."[2]

It was during this time that the popularity of the stars began to be measured by polling movie fans. One of the earliest was undertaken by *Photoplay* in August 1913. During the contest, film fans could buy an individual copy or multiple copies of each issue. Each contained a coupon worth 50 votes, which were mailed to the magazine. Fans could also buy a year's subscription at $1.50 — worth 600 votes, or a special two-year subscription at $2 worth 1,500 votes. Additionally, fans had the option of buying ten postcards of their favorite star for ten cents (coins or stamps) and vote by purchasing the cards. By November 1913, seven million votes had been cast and the standings were: J. Warren Kerrigan of Victor, 129,100, Mabel Normand (Keystone), 125,450, and Baggot, 118,600.[3] When the contest ended on April 20, 1914,

Margarita Fischer of the American Film Manufacturing Company was the winning leading lady with 318,100, Kathlyn Williams of Selig was second with 274,350 and Mabel Normand placed third at 272,450. Mary Pickford, then with Famous Players, was fourth with 260,150 votes. Of the leading men, J. Warren Kerrigan won with 362,050. Since he could not be called "King," he was proclaimed "Jack of Hearts." Arthur Johnson of Lubin was second with 276,750 and Baggot third with 262,701. Francis X. Bushman of Essanay finished fourth with 235,700 votes.[4]

While the *Photoplay* contest was underway, *Ladies World Magazine*, published by the McClure Company, devised their own, more elaborate popularity poll. It began in January 1914 with the publication of a story by Louis Tracy titled *One Wonderful Night*, which featured a "typical screen hero." Their readers were to vote for their favorite star who would actually play the role on screen, but their choices were limited to only seven pre-selected leading men: Maurice Costello (Vitagraph); Kerrigan and Baggot representing Universal; Crane Wilbur (Pathé); Arthur Johnson (Lubin); Carlyle Blackwell (Kalem); and Bushman (Essanay).[5] Coupons from the magazine entitled each reader to 50 votes. But unlike the *Photoplay* contest, where the publishers were merely trying to achieve a larger circulation and perhaps sell some postcards, the studios were more involved this time. They took out full-page ads in *Ladies World* and the trade papers, printed advertising cards for streetcars, and produced slides for the exhibitors in order to promote their stars. When the contest concluded in May, *Moving Picture World* reported that Essanay had out-spent their rivals and Bushman won the contest with 1,806,630 votes. Kerrigan was second with 1,262,740 and Maurice Costello came in third with 1,088,400. Those under one million were Crane Wilbur with 575,650, Arthur Johnson at 284,050, Baggot with 261,650, and Carlyle Blackwell at 161,640. The total number of votes cast was 5,440,760.[6] At the time of the contest, *Ladies World* had a circulation of about 1,500,000. The old saying "vote early and vote often" can be seen to apply here. Essanay filmed the story using New York City as a locale and *One Wonderful Night* was released in four reels July 18, 1914.

King seemed literally to dance through the early months of 1914. Filmdom's most glittering social occasions were its balls and in 1914 they may have reached their zenith. The first was the most modest, but it was really only intended as a family affair. The Board of Directors of Universal gave a reception and ball for their employees and business associates on January 3 at the Leslie Rooms on 83rd Street and Broadway — their first annual. Over 200 people attended. The highlight was a presentation to Carl Laemmle of a huge silver loving cup, but it was done in an unusual way. First, J.C. Graham, Universal's general manager, urged Laemmle to the podium under the pretext of having him give a short speech. However, as he began, a large box draped in an American flag was carried to the platform. Out of the box popped a little curly haired two-year-old boy, Master Philip Weiner of London, who presented Laemmle with the cup. Mr. and Mrs. Laemmle then led the grand march.[7] The dancing went on until four in the morning. One other event occurred that evening that grabbed some headlines:

> King Baggot got into an argument with J.C. Graham on the floor and it looked for a moment as though all the men on the floor would soon be mixed in a free-for-all fight. Four policemen were called in, but they could do little with the surging mob of men. Women were frightened and taking to shelter, and cries of "shame" came from the balcony guests. Mr. Powers and Mr. Swanson pushed their way

into the thick of the melee and did their best to stop it. The orchestra struck up a tune to divert attention. Nobody seemed to know what the argument was about, but truth to say, it was about nothing. When it seemed about time to send in a riot call the guests were greatly surprised to see King Baggot start turkey-trotting with one of the cops and some of the boys who were in on the joke danced it with the three other policemen. The fact is, they were four husky gents that Baggot had previously rigged up in studio uniforms. They do say that Pat Powers and Bill Swanson swallowed it hook, line and sinker. They were not alone in their innocence; everyone who was not in on it fell for it, only Pat and Bill fell hardest.[8]

The Cinema Club of the Bronx Ball was next, held on Wednesday evening, January 14, at Hunters Point Palace. This one was given by the motion picture exhibitors of the northern part of New York City. It was their first annual event of this kind and was well attended by close to 800 people, including representatives from all the major producing companies in the New York area. King and Gene Gauntier, who was at that time producing her own films with Warner's Features, were the special attraction and led the grand march. Both Universal, who also provided variously shaped and colored hats to the crowds, and Warner's Features Film Company screened some of their multi-reeled films. Again, they danced until four in the morning.[9] But the largest and best was yet to come.

The Screen Club held its second annual reception and ball on Saturday night, January 31 at the Grand Central Palace. The *New York Dramatic Mirror* called it "probably the highest class ball ever given in New York...,"[10] while *Motion Picture News* declared it "a brilliant affair."[11] Over 4,000 people flocked to the Grand Central Palace in a rainstorm just to be there. The event was heavily advertised in the trades and the popular press. This was no intimate gathering for insiders—the public was invited to see "the flower of filmdom" for a "star gemmed night." Tickets were $2 a couple, but boxes seating ten were available at $50. The decorations were described as "lavish." Women guests received hatpins with the Screen Club insignia as favors. The crowd was so large that the Longacre Hotel nearby had to be engaged to serve dinner. King, billed as "The King of Hearts," and Mary Fuller, then with Edison, led the grand march. Colored spotlights played on the crowd as they performed "intricate figures" around the floor to the delight of the on lookers:

> Practically all the representative people of the industry were there, millionaire manufacturers, high salaried actors, scenario editors, State rights men, and with them a host of the public who had come to see their favorite players as they were in real life. The boxes blazed with diamonds worn by beautifully gowned women, champagne corks popped merrily, everyone danced with everyone else and the night was given over to frivolity and joy.[12]

A dramatic highlight occurred when King climbed onto a table to auction off a special souvenir program signed by many celebrities in the film world. Charles O. Baumann and Adam Kessel of the New York Motion Picture Company started the bidding at $1000, but out of rivalry and pride Screen Club members led by C.A. "Doc" Willat formed a pool and upped the stakes to $1500. Adolph Zukor assisted the pool by bidding another $500. In the end, the program was sold to the Screen Club for $3,500—the largest sum ever obtained for a program to that time. No one wanted the evening to end and for some it didn't. Members of the Club and their guests returned to the clubhouse and continued the party there, where a few managed to last until eight o'clock Sunday morning—wending their way home just in time to meet the righteous on their way to church.

The sounds of music continued into the month of February. King was featured on the cover of a piece of sheet music titled *In the Evening by the Moonlight in Dear Old Tennessee,* composed by Keithley and Thompson, and published by Frank K. Root & Company. Shortly after that, a ragtime piece was dedicated to him called *The King Baggot Rag,* composed by G.W. Lowe of Columbia, Kentucky, and registered under copyright at the Library of Congress on February 20, 1914.

It was in April of this year that King returned to the theater. To be sure, it was not a long stint, but he had not set foot on the boards since 1909 when he appeared with Marguerite Clark in the touring company of *The Wishing Ring.* Universal did a replay of their notion that the public loved to see film stars "up close and personal" as a promotional tool. They engaged the Republic Theatre in Times Square and members of the IMP Company became stage actors twice a day at four and nine P.M. for a week. The purpose was to let the public see how movies were made in a way that combined actual film with a conventional script and stage acting to illustrate the process. But first, the audience had to see the six-reeler *Samson* which starred the up-and-coming leading man J. Warren Kerrigan. Harold Lloyd, who would become so famous a few years hence, appeared as an extra in this film.

At nine o'clock, the theater curtains parted on a movie set complete with Cooper-Hewitt lamps, burning their fierce blue green glow. It had cut-away sets, actors, props, a director, cameramen and all the trappings of a film studio. A telephone on a desk rings and it is answered by Frank Smith, in real life one of IMP's best character actors (and Baggot's assistant director). He relates to the players and the audience that King Baggot, although needed for the next scene, has been delayed at the Screen Club, and will be a little late. They decide to go to the "projection room" to view the first part of the picture. The curtains close and the projection screen is lowered to show the first 800 feet of a film called *The Baited Trap.*

The story's central theme is "white slavery"— once again trading on the immense popularity of *Traffic in Souls* from the previous year. King is seen on the screen as an Irish immigrant boy, Dennis, "come to America" with the hope of saving enough money to bring his winsome sister Norah (Arline Pretty) over to join him. Unwittingly, he takes a job cleaning out a saloon owned by a gang involved in the white slave trade. They are aptly named Black Louie, Craven and Blondie. The crooks see Norah's picture and decide to capture her for the trade. They plant a wallet full of money — the bait — on Dennis while he sleeps, and with their assurance that it is all right to keep it, he joyfully sends for Norah. On his way to the docks to meet her, he is waylaid by the gang, who accuses him of theft. He is arrested, but once he convinces the police of his innocence, the chase is on to save Norah, who by now has been "nabbed."

The film stops there and the curtain opens again on the movie set. King arrives in grand fashion and proceeds to make up as Dennis — with a red wig. But now everything goes wrong. King is hoisted up on a trapeze over the stage in preparation for jumping down into the scene from the "skylight," but the grips get it too high or too low. A locked door isn't locked at the right moment, guns fire or don't at the wrong time, the vase does not shatter on cue, the camera runs out of film. All these "mistakes" elicit groans of despair and frustration from the cast and crew, but after many retakes they get it all right. Norah is saved and the film is completed.

Audiences loved it. Despite some grumbling on the part of the industry about giving away secrets and destroying illusion, *The Baited Trap* was widely covered and praised.¹³ The public had a chance to hear King Baggot and other screen actors "speak" and see them in person. They were able to view an approximation of a movie set and see the details that went into actual filmmaking. Every night during its run, the Republic played to turn-away crowds and standing room only conditions, but all too soon it was over. *The Baited Trap* was completed as a two-reel film and IMP's moviemaking went back inside the studios.

One could search in vain for any mention of Ruth Baggot during this time. The last mention of her in the press occurred shortly after she and King returned from Europe in September 1913. Because of King's public persona as a matinee idol and as the "King of Hearts" to millions of women, there is no doubt that she kept a low profile for the sake of her husband's career. If she was not present at those large glittering social functions, it might have been to keep the spotlight away from herself and on King. But there was another reason: She had become pregnant in December of the past year. The *New York Dramatic Mirror* was first to announce the news:

> AN HEIR TO THE THRONE. There is now an heir to the throne; a son arriving in the family of King Baggot at 12:30 on Tuesday, July 7. The young Crown Prince is evidently to play leads, for he already balances the scales at ten pounds. Mrs. Baggot and the youngster are now reported to be doing nicely. Screen Club members showed their joy over the arrival of the president's son in evident fashion. All present in the club when the news arrived sent telegrams of congratulations, and as the news spread throughout the day the stream of messages increased in strength. The total last reported was well over the hundred mark.¹⁴

He was named Robert King Baggot — the "Robert" in honor of King's good friend and best man at his wedding, William Robert Daly, and he would be King Sr.'s only child. However, he was never called "Robert" but always "King," and a family tradition was begun. Robert King's oldest son was named "King" and his son's oldest son the same. At this time, there are four generations of King Baggots.

Now that King was a father, he seemed to be reaching even higher into his creativity and his art. Dual roles had become one of his trademarks—*The Double*, as early as 1910, *After Many Years, The Breakdown, His Other Self,* all in 1912, and, of course, *Dr. Jekyll and Mr. Hyde* in 1913. What a *tour de force* it would be to portray even more characters all in one film! He did. By this time he had become an extremely versatile actor with a keen interest in playing many kinds of roles. He enjoyed the challenge, the disguises and the chance to act in parts where his persona was not typically that of "the hero." In an interview with *Blue Book Magazine* at the time he was appearing on stage in *The Baited Trap*, he gave a thoughtful assessment of his own outlook and his perception of the evolution of film acting to date:

> When the motion picture industry was gaining a foothold with the public ... all that was required of the hero was that he be good looking, preferably with curly hair. It was the popular supposition among those who engaged him that as no one could hear what he had to say for himself, no one had a chance to "give himself away," and the public would remain in blissful ignorance as to whether he had a brain worthy of respect, or whether he was merely a cheerful tailor's dummy togged up in the proper clothes and possessed of a little more than the usual amount of self confidence. Nowadays, the public expects much more of the picture-play hero. The dashing and reckless sort of fellow who held the villain off with one hand while he snatched the heroine from certain death with the other, has passed. The public wants the

hero of mentality, in preference to the physical type.

I have been called "the studio actor" because I always rely on my mind to get my personality across. There is a greater opportunity for the mental effect in the silent drama than there is in the spoken drama, though most folks won't believe it. The camera almost photographs thought. In pictures, the actor can pause, let a thought "register," change to another scene and bring it home all the more vividly, while in the legitimate he is confined to three or four acts, and attention is riveted to his every word. On the stage, the lines of the mummer create the thought in the hearer's mind. In motion pictures, the actor must think and act the part in order to get the effect.[15]

At this stage of his career, he had enough artistic control to "think big." The vehicle he chose was called *Shadows*, a name suggested by the many exteriors shown in the film in which the rays of a low sun played a "picturesque" part. He called on the talented scenario writer George Edwardes Hall to write it. It was a two-reel detective drama in which he played ten different parts, including two women. By this time the techniques of filmmaking could comfortably handle double and triple exposures and they were used to great effect in the making of this film.

Essentially, the plot tells a well-rounded story of banker William Clark and his wife who lead a lonely life in the country. Their sole companion is their Chinese servant. Years before, their only son, a wayward, fun-loving boy, had left them. As the story opens, the boy returns, but his father decides to give him enough money to start a new life and sends him away. A thief breaks into their house and, encountering the Chinese servant, robs him of his life's savings. Among the coins obtained are a few Chinese coppers. The father hears the scuffle and is intercepted by the crook and murdered. The servant did not get a good look at the thief and the son is arrested and charged with the crime. The police are called, and King Baggot the famous detective is put on the case. Searching for clues, King visits a tavern where the crook and his sweetheart are having an argument. The sweetheart throws the money he has given her in the crook's face, but one of the coins rolls to where King is seated. As he picks it up, he realizes that it is a Chinese coin. He trails the thief to his lodging house and is convinced of his guilt. From a nearby phone, he calls to request a plain clothes policeman to assist in the arrest. With this backup, they break down the crook's door and a terrific fight ensues. King chases the thief up to the roof where a gun battle takes place. King wings him and he falls to the ground several stories below, but he lives long enough to clear the son. In a closing feature of the film, there are a series of short scenes showing King in the make up of each character, then removing the make up as each scene fades into another.

This film was not easy to produce, in fact, much more difficult than King had originally thought:

> When I started making the picture ... I had no idea of the amount of work it would involve. I believed that I could do it at odd moments, but it took me the better part of five weeks, as I had regular work to keep up with. I have received most efficient assistance from Mr. Schellinger, the cameraman; he has taken a deep interest in making the double and triple exposures synchronize. Some scenes we had to take three or four times to get the results we wanted. I found one of my greatest difficulties in the dovetailing the gestures of the triple exposure.[16]

When *Shadows* was released in October, it was greeted with acclaim both here and abroad. There are numerous examples of dual role films from 1912 onward. Just the year before King made *Shadows*, Grace

Cunard played three parts in *The Twin's Double*, released by Universal–Gold Seal in November 1913, and as late as 1929, Paul Muni played seven roles in *Seven Faces*. Just the same, for its time, it was hailed as a remarkable acting achievement.

Universal needed many more "big pictures" for its programs and embarked on a new campaign to produce "the best pictures in all the world." As creative as Baggot's efforts had been, he was only one man attached to one of Universal's companies. So, at this time, King was given a new director—whether he wanted one or not.[17] His name was George A. Lessey. A graduate of Amherst and a long-time stage actor, he had spent the past two years at Edison, where he had become somewhat well known for his "Cleek" detective stories, which would coincide nicely with Baggot's penchant for that genre. It was said of Lessey that he was a "furious worker," but one who balanced that with care and attention to detail. In his first year with Edison he was credited with having produced "fifty thousand feet of negative, every foot of which was released and proved successful."[18]

Before the year was over, Carl Laemmle felt the need to expand the Universal empire. He purchased a tract of land of about 230 acres east of Pass Road in North Hollywood and began to build a city—Universal City—that would be the largest self-contained motion picture production facility in the world. But that was only half of the plan. At about that same time, he acquired land and had blueprints drawn up to build a very large plant at Fort Lee, New Jersey. Although not envisioned as so grand as Universal City, it was to have two lakes, a bridge, a waterfall and the largest glass-enclosed buildings in the United States. The projected cost would be a quarter of a million dollars. Laemmle envisioned a consolidation of all of Universal's East Coast facilities, personnel and studios at Fort Lee. At the time, Universal's holdings in the East were scattered. There were plants at 110th Street, where they recently had a fire, another plant at 43rd Street and 11th Avenue, as well as two other New Jersey operations at Coytesville and at Bayonne.[19]

This had been a very full and fulfilling year for King. He had become one of the foremost film actors in the world. He had enjoyed two years as president of the Screen Club and had built it into one of the most popular and important organizations of its kind. He had a son and enough money to live his life just about any way he wished. And what he probably wished for was to continue in the career that he loved and that life could go on that way, forever.

17

Fame and Change

George A. Lessey continued to direct King in most of his films from late 1914 until almost the end of 1915 — about 28 in all. They were good solid works, mostly in two reels, but occasionally in three and four. Some were comedies, but most were dramas with emphasis on social themes, which had become quite popular with film going audiences. King was able to play a wide range of characters now, and not just "heroes." From the scope and length of some of these, it is obvious that Lessey was able to command more money and time for his productions with IMP/Universal than King could do alone. In *The Man Who Was Misunderstood*, with a cleverly twisting plot by George Edwardes Hall, he plays an old, itinerant violin player who, with his faithful little dog, ekes out a precarious living going from door to door to entertain. He is invited into the home of a little girl and her mother and encouraged to tell his life's story. Here the plot dissolves back into the past when his character, Ned Jackson, is a young man betrayed by a rival. He loses a horse race, his fortune and the hand of the woman he loves. As the film ends, the broken old man and his dog are walking sadly into the distance. The last intertitle reads, "And so we drift away, waiting for the sunshine of a happier day." Although somewhat damaged this film had been preserved by the Library of Congress. In it, King's versatile talent as a mature actor in a moving and sympathetic role is plainly evident.

The plot of in *The Mill Stream*, a murder mystery, was suggested by a real murder known as "The Carmen Case," which took place on Long Island. In *An Oriental Romance*, King plays a young Chinese man in love with the sister of his Caucasian college roommate and she returns his affections. Unfortunately, the family objects and love does not conquer all, at least not in 1915. "Hop Kung" breaks off the romance by pretending to be attracted to another girl. Still, the reviewers of that day were impressed with the sensitive handling of the race question.

King played more multiple roles during this time, although none could match *Shadows*. In *The Story the Silk Hats Told*, he plays an old second-hand clothing dealer who falls asleep in his shop near a section of shelving containing a row of silk hats. In his dream, each former owner of a hat comes forward and tells his story. The characters are a politician, a lover, a doctor, a businessman, a German burlesque comedian and a bank clerk. In this film, no elaborate use was made of double and triple exposures; rather, it was another opportunity for King to show his ability as a character actor as he played each role.

A more ambitious film was *The Corsican Brothers*, from the novel by Alexander Dumas, père. At the time, it was still a very familiar story to audiences, both as a novel and a play. Edison had done a 1912 film version which featured George Lessey, who, then an actor, played the lead and performed the dual role. However, this time it was in three reels with a modern setting. As the film begins, King is standing in front of the camera dressed as himself with a copy of the novel in his hands. He bows to the right and Fabien appears— then to the left where Louis makes his formal entrance. Double and triple exposures were used to obtain the effects. Briefly told, two brothers, Louis and Fabien Dei Franchi, are Siamese twins joined at birth but separated by a doctor hours later. Although their lives take them in opposite directions, they remain united mentally. When Louis is killed in a duel, Fabien, still at home in Corsica, feels a pain in his side. Touching the place with his hand, he finds it covered with blood. He rushes to Paris and avenges his brother's death, then returns to Corsica with his body. It was a demanding role for King, but it was considered an artistic success by the reviewers.

Later that year, the entire cast had a chance to play dual roles in a four-reel film version of Charles Selby's 1864 play *The Marble Heart*. It featured a prologue in which King's character, Raphael, an artist of the modern day, dreams he is a sculptor, Phidias, in ancient Greece. Phidias is commissioned by a wealthy man to carve statues of three beautiful women, but when they are completed he cannot bear to part with them, especially with Asphasia, with whom he has fallen deeply in love. Diogenese (Frank Smith) encourages him to ask the statues if they wish to stay or go with the wealthy Georgias. They come to life and all elect to go with Georgias, which breaks Phidias's heart. In real life, Raphael is faced with a very similar situation with almost the same results. The characters in the dream became modern versions of their counterparts and "dissolves" were used to tell both stories. Elaborate sets for the Greek street scenes were built on Staten Island and it also included a wild chariot race in which one of the participants suffered a very real broken leg during the filming. A well-known Russian dancer of her day, Yona Landowska, appeared in two dance sequences. Although this could not be called an "epic" film, it did well with audiences and was considered another significant film for King and for George Lessey.

That year, 1915, Baggot and Lessey made one more important four-reel drama—*The Suburban*, which was based on still another popular and well-known play by Charles Turner Dazey. Interestingly, this was another vehicle with which Lessey had personally been involved before when he was an actor in one of its many stage productions. Lessey made prodigious use of multiple locations to tell the story. The main elements of the plot included blackmail, a disinherited son (King), class distinction, justifiable homicide, theft and suicide. But the core of the action was, a horse race called "The Suburban." No production information exists to tell us how long it took to make, but it was advertised as having over 200 scenes in 50 locations. It was a "big picture," but curiously, it was not marketed as such. In the advertising copy for the film in *Moving Picture Weekly* (which was actually owned by Universal), it was described as an "IMP four-reel drama, with Frank Smith and Ned Reardon supporting Universal star [King Baggot] ... a Broadway Feature in all but name."[1] This meant that although it was in four reels, and that a large amount of money was

Baggot in *The Corsican Brothers,* IMP, 1915. He played both brothers and appeared as himself in the film's introduction. Baggot had blue eyes, which often registered as almost blank on the orthochromatic film of those early days. Photograph courtesy of the Wisconsin Center for Film and Theatre Research.

spent on its production, including purchasing the film rights to the story, Universal did not attempt to give it exclusive screenings in large theaters at higher prices before its general release. This was Carl Laemmle's doing. At the time, he still resisted the move toward special features in large downtown theaters, calling them "wasteful." He favored what he called a "balanced" program of one-, two- and three- reel pictures.[2] If he had chosen to market King's films in a more visible way and on a larger scale, it might have prolonged his stardom, but he did not. Four-reel films were just not considered worth the expense. Yet, audiences had a lot of picture for their money. They filmed north woods scenes in Upper Canada. Dramatic action took place aboard three kinds of ships, a steam yacht, a three-masted schooner, and a steam launch — all filmed on Long Island Sound. Naturally, it also included the inevitable "big race," filmed live during the running of the Belmont Handicap with thousands of actual spectators as background.

Still, King was receiving a great deal of publicity during this time. His old friend and fellow club member Hugh Hoffman, who had been working for *Moving Picture World* for the past five years, left to become a motion picture press agent. King became one of his clients.[3] Suddenly King's name became more prominent than ever before. Flurries of interviews were published in all the major motion picture fan magazines, including *Photoplay*, *Picture-Play Weekly*, and *Motion Picture Supplement*. In *Photoplay* for March 1915, he was featured in their "Tantalizing Eyes Contest," where only the eyes of 16 such stars as Maurice Costello, Mary Fuller,

Margarita Fischer, Ford Sterling and other top performers of the day were shown. The fans had to guess which eyes belonged to which star. Hoffman was also personally credited for one stunt announced in the *New York Clipper*: "King Baggot is to be highly honored. They're going to name a ten-cent cigar after him. Hugh Hoffman engineered the deal with the American Tobacco Co."[4]

By now the salary he was making, while if not "kingly," was at least "princely." Back in 1909 and 1910, he first made $100 per week; then, when Mary Pickford joined the company, he was raised to $125 and later to $150. Real salary figures had always been hard to obtain in the film industry. However, in 1915, *Photoplay* tried to find out what inquiring fans wanted to know. The piece was titled *What They Really Get*. Writer Karl K. Kitchen, pointed out that the women stars almost always received more than the men did. He reported that Clara Kimball Young, Florence Lawrence, Blanche Sweet, Norma Phillips and Anita Stewart were paid in the neighborhood of $200 to $500 per week and that only Mary Pickford and perhaps Marguerite Clark got more than that. As for Baggot, Francis X. Bushman, Maurice Costello and Carlyle Blackwell—they were in the $100 to $400 range. He quotes J. Warren Kerrigan's salary specifically as $400, with only Charlie Chaplin in the really big league at $1,200. It can be assumed that King would be making that top step of at least $400 a week if credence can be given to Kitchen's research.[5]

By this time, personal appearances by film stars had become almost mandatory. Every week the trades brought fresh news of who had just appeared where, and King was no exception. In order to publicize *The Corsican Brothers*, in March he was sent by Universal to address some 800 members of the Century Theatre Club at the Hotel Astor. The afternoon's program was devoted to Universal's progress making "photodramas" an important aspect of the "dramatic arts" in general. They showed *The Corsican Brothers*, and Baggot explained the wonders of double exposure while the film ran. Mary Fuller, who, at that time was with Victor, appeared with him, courtesy of Universal. They showed the first reel of her latest release, *Mary's Duke*, a three-reel comedy written by Elaine Sterne. Only the year before, Sterne began her career by winning the $1,000 prize for the best scenario in the *New York Sun* contest. She gave a short talk on "The Photoplay from the Viewpoint of the Scenario Department," and was introduced as "one of the most promising of the present day scenario writers ... who has written dozens of successful photoplays which have been produced by nearly every film concern in America." Miss Fuller was also asked to give a little talk. In it, she told the audience that this was really her first public speech and it was reported that "she did tremble, but [she] was given a large ovation at its conclusion."[6] It may be difficult to realize now, but at the time these were experiments and pioneering efforts by film companies trying to reach the public in any way possible.

They were not even adverse to exploiting a "captive audience." Universal sent King to Sing Sing Prison to show two of his films and chat with "the boys." They screened *The Streets of Make Believe*, a one-reel light comedy where a clerk in a dry goods store and a laundress try to impress each other by pretending to be other than whom they really are. After they sort out their misunderstandings, they find true love. The second film was *An All Around Mistake*, where King plays the henpecked husband of a very jealous wife. He and his friends manage to get out for a while and behave very badly in a tavern after getting extremely drunk. The next day he wakes up with a terrible hangover. He has a few more drinks and looks at the morning paper. There he sees a story about an axe murderer who has just killed his mother-in-law and convinces himself that he has committed the crime. When he goes to the police station to turn himself in, he finds himself in very deep trouble until the police discover that the newspaper is a year old. The themes of a submissive husband, a controlling wife, drunkenness and thoughts of killing one's mother-in-law were indeed a cause for hilarity in 1915. King wound up his visit by inviting questions from the audience; and the press noted:

> One young man wanted to know how they make things disappear.... Baggot answered, "Why, the cameraman stops turning his crank when he hears the director yell to the players to hold their positions. The object they want to disappear from the scene is removed and they continue the action with the camera. Now, isn't that as simple as pie?" Another young man wanted to know how they make people jump or fly up a hill. "Why, there's nothing to that either," replied King. "The person jumps down the hill and the cameraman, instead of turning the crank the ordinary way, simply turns the crank backwards, and when the film is projected on the screen the person is jumping up the hill instead of down." This almost created a riot among the audience.[7]

In the fall of 1915, it was time for the Screen Club to hold its annual elections. The Club had come a long way under Baggot's two-year presidency in 1912 and 1913. After serving for two terms, he had gracefully bowed out. James Kirkwood, handsome leading man to Florence Lawrence and Mary Pickford, and now a director, had become president in 1914. The clubhouse was moved to more spacious quarters a few blocks away at 165 West 47th Street. Club membership was at an all-time high and it was considered prestigious by all branches of the film industry to belong. Their social occasions had become legendary and everything they did was noted both in the trade press and newspapers. King was proud of all that he had personally helped them to accomplish, and he had every right to be. But this election would prove to be his Achilles' heel and cause his otherwise well-deserved good reputation to become tarnished for the first time.

Initially no one, not even the press, wanted to talk about conflict or scandal in the Screen Club ranks and no wonder — so many of them were members themselves. With veiled irony *Moving Picture World* reported:

> BILLY QUIRK SCREENERS NEW HEAD Nearly two hundred members turn out for the election on Saturday, October 2.... It was natural that in the assembling of such a large number of Screeners there should be a get-together, and this is what happened. There was the best of feeling over the result of the counting of the votes which began at 9 o'clock. On the whole, the election was a quiet one and was conducted with a minimum display of partisanship.[8]

Variety, however, was a little more forthcoming:

> SCREEN CLUB SQUABBLE. As an aftermath to the annual election of officers at the Screen Club last week, Dallas Fitzgerald (then an actor) has been notified by registered mail to appear before the Board of Governors on October 26 at 8 P.M. to answer to the charge of having hurled a vile epithet at King Baggot. Fitzgerald threatens countercharges against his accuser, alleging Baggot had declared the successful candidates were "a pack of bar flies." Guy Hedlund [another actor], a friend of Fitzgerald's, has joined with the latter and announced his intention of associating himself with the countercharges.[9]

The installation of officers was held on a Saturday, October 30. Reporting on the event, *Moving Picture World* was still reluctant to engage in telling the real story. The paper gingerly characterized the meeting as:

> ...one of the most interesting occasions in the history of the organization. Outgoing president, James Kirkwood, in the absence of Vice-President Ben Wilson, asked Sam Spedon to install Billy Quirk as president, which he did in a few extemporaneous remarks that were heartily applauded. It was the second time during the evening that Mr. Spedon in his inimitable philosophical style had entertained the members.[10]

The article went on to say that Baggot had been appointed chairman of the committee for the coming ball and that he gave a report on what had been done to date to insure its success. The affair might now be a mystery if *Variety* had not published a report on those troublesome doings. Heading the section of motion picture news, a bold headline proclaimed, "King Baggot Under Charges By Four Screen Club Members: Petition Signed Asking That Former President be Placed on Trial on Charges Contained in Quartet of Affidavits— Alleged He Conducted Himself in Ungentlemanly Manner on Night of Annual Elections."

It appeared that King's concern for the future of the organization, which he had so often been credited with founding, led him to continue to want to control its course by seeing to it that the future presidents were men who had the same vision as himself— and perhaps would be more likely to take his advice. That was a very human response, but it was only natural that his fellow club men at some point would want to take charge and assume the power to direct the club's destiny without their famous past-president's interference. Apparently, King's choice for president that year was Paul Scardon, a popular actor with Broadway Star/Vitagraph, who had just that year become a Vitagraph director. In the previous year, 1914, it was brought out in the testimony, he may have influenced the Board of Governors in the election of James Kirkwood. The "King of Hearts" and "Prince of Men" was behaving in a very emotional and unsportsman-like way.

Variety obtained copies of the affidavits that were submitted in support of the charges against him — and they were not pretty:

> Guy Hedlund: On the night of Oct. 2, I was in the Screen Club and King Baggot abused me for my part in the election. Among other things he said was: "You have elected your man, but let me tell you something; I still control the Board of Governors." He called those who voted for Mr. Quirk "bar flies." Mr. Fitzgerald and Mr. Sadler were present. I took issue with Mr. Baggot on most of his remarks, particularly the one in which he said: Kirkwood was a rotten president.
>
> William J. Sadler: Mr. Baggot, in speaking of those members who voted for Billy Quirk, used the expression "bar flies" and did not conduct himself worthy of a former president. He abused Mr. Hedlund and Mr. Fitzgerald.
>
> Arthur Leslie [writer and publicity agent]: On the night of Oct. 2, Mr. Baggot said: "Well you won and your damn campaign literature elected Billy Quirk." I replied, "You didn't damn it last year when I wrote what you told me to write about Billy Quirk and Joe Farnham and you helped pay for the printing and postage stamps for Kirkwood's election." He said, "Don't fool yourself that you've beaten me. I still control the Board of Governors; every servant in this club tips me off on everything, and I'll frame you up yet, see if I don't." I said, "That sounds more like a King Braggart than King Baggot." He said, "Think you're smart, don't you? Let me tell you something. I'll rule or ruin this club. Inside of a month I'll have Billy Quirk eating out of my hand and I'll have you up on charges. I'll also get those louse pals of yours."

Dallas M. Fitzgerald: "Mr. Baggot said that those who voted against Paul Scardon were a bunch of 'bar flies.' He repeated this several times."

The *Variety* article went on to say:

A copy of these charges was, as is customary, served on each member of the club, a large number of whom strongly believe in availing themselves of the widest possible publicity as a means toward quickly eradicating any existing deficiencies in management. They maintain that inasmuch as the regular channels provided for the proper government of the club are obstructed this course is now necessary.

However, there is a small but active minority who feel that no matter how serious such evils might be they should be hushed up and there should be no departure from the usual conservative procedure and that the course adopted by the others is inadvisable. The trial of Mr. Baggot will probably be ordered about the middle of next month.[11]

In part, the conservative members were correct in so far as it hurt the Club's reputation — not to mention Baggot's. But as far as it is known, no formal charges were ever brought against him. The sorry affair just subsided. The Screen Club would continue to be very popular for at least one more year, and Baggot would carry on, working with some of those very men with whom he had just had such a contentious dispute. In fact, Baggot, Fitzgerald and Scardon would all be fellow directors at Universal in the 1920s. But from that time forward, the Club would never have exactly the same cachet or glitter it once had. It was not just the open airing of the scandal that caused the Club's decline at that point — the call to the West had been heard by the industry. One by one, then in droves, the producers, actors and everyone connected with the motion picture industry began leaving for California. As early as 1913, the *Dramatic Mirror* noted that in one year, the number of film companies in California had gone from six to 39.[12] By 1919, the Screen Club in New York would lose their clubhouse and soon after, all but disappear.[13]

Why did Baggot behave so badly, one wonders? Perhaps his stardom and his sense of power had gone to his head. Perhaps his feelings of possessiveness overcame his good sense. It is also possible that alcohol played a part in the behavior of the whole group. Intemperate words often go with intemperate drinking, and social drinking was the very cornerstone of the Club. Double-page cartoons in the trade press often portrayed most of the members with glasses in their hands. One even had coy little arrows drawn toward their glasses that said "milk"—and this was quite a long time before Prohibition in 1920. Large numbers of people in America, and certainly within the industry, saw nothing wrong with drinking—not even getting drunk on occasion. Films often portrayed drunks as comic figures. King himself had played those roles in many of his films. That there was no disgrace about the topic can be seen when *Moving Picture News*, in 1913, could laughingly tell a story about Arthur Johnson—then a very big star with Lubin—when he came over to New York from Philadelphia for a visit. It was reported:

His confreres at the Screen Club learned of his coming, and laid in an extra supply of "firewater," in anticipation of the "Indian's" arrival. Arthur's extreme fondness for animals is proverbial, so an apropos story is not ill-timed. After an elaborate feast of pure food products both "liquid" and "solid," Arthur was seen to garner what sugar remained from the coffee service, and when later he, in the company with several of his intimates, emerged from the club "Lil' Arthur" became sequestered in a maze of pedestrians from the various theaters.

Rigid search finally revealed him

Candid shot of Baggot on the fire escape circa 1915. Caption: "King Baggot observing the fire laws — taking a smoke outside his dressing room at Universal Studios." Photograph courtesy of the Wisconsin Center for Film and Theatre Research.

standing at the hood of Owen Moore's car, with several lumps of sugar in his outstretched hand.

"For the love of Mike! what are you doing?" asked Bob Daly.

"Feeding the poor horse some (hic) sugar!" answered Arthur, a trifle unsteadily. "Poor old fellow, he's (hic) l-o-n-e-s-o-m-e."[14]

This handsome and talented actor died of alcoholism just three years later.

18

The Parade Moves On

It was not long after the release of The *Suburban* that King's director, George Lessey, departed for what he hoped were greener pastures at the Eastern Film Corporation in Providence, Rhode Island. He directed the only three films that the company ever produced: *Cap'n Eri* and *Partners of the Tide,* from novels by Joseph Lincoln, and *The Minister,* based on Oliver Goldsmith's *The Vicar of Wakefield.* Then the company sank like a stone. He was fortunate enough to be rehired by Universal and finished out the year making *Graft,* a 20-part serial. Upon his departure, however, King was given another new director in the person of Henry (Harry) McRae Webster. Apparently Universal did not think too highly of Lessey toward the end of his association with King, for in their own *Moving Picture Weekly,* it was stated that, "King Baggot has at last found a good director. He is Harry McRae Webster, late of Essanay and points West."[1] Unfortunately, Webster's credentials as a director were less impressive than Lessey's had been and it showed in the work that they briefly did together.

No Baggot films were released in October 1915, but he and Webster were most likely working on two three-reel films that would be released in November — *The Reward* and *Man Or Money? The Reward* was a social drama with some fairly seedy overtones. King played another "hero" role as a bartender in a roadhouse. Themes included illegal gambling, prostitution, a wealthy man with a sinister double life and, of course, a love interest. This is a "lost film," so its merits cannot be judged today, but no rave reviews from its time have been found. *Man Or Money?* was no better. Much of the action takes place in the "Northwest." The central theme is a love triangle between King, his former sweetheart (Edna Hunter), who has married a scheming crook, and the man himself (Ned Reardon), who at the end tries to do the "right thing" by his wife, and almost dies trying. As the story ends, King places their two hands together, wishes them happiness and bids them a last farewell. The symbolic "placing of the hands" had become a well-worn cliché and the storyline was just as ancient. King and Webster were not breaking any new ground here.

A long and loving interview with King appeared in the November *Moving Picture Weekly.* It was titled "Dean of the Screen" and, in a way, it was a tribute to King's longevity with IMP/Universal. Writer Peter

Pepper pointed out that "[he] has remained longer on the payroll than any other person, with the exception of Carl Laemmle, who hired him."[2] King was now 36 years old, which was not exactly elderly by contemporary standards, but he began to realize that his days as a matinee idol would, at some point, be over. In the interview he said:

> One reason I like to play characters ... is to let people see that I am not afraid of grease paint and wigs. They might get the idea that I am afraid to soil my hands and face by playing a ragged hero. I want everybody to feel that I am willing to play every part that is assigned to me if it is a part worth playing. The mere fact that it requires me to cover up my countenance with paint and whiskers doesn't bother me at all. Furthermore, I like to do these things to make it clear that I know my profession in an all around way. There may come a time someday when they ring the bell on me as a leading man and then I will have to play characters. The little fun I get out of playing them now will also provide a good experience for me if ever I get to playing character old men after I am sixty years of age.[3]

Unfortunately, King was not given any further opportunities to play character parts just then. From mid–1915 to the end of his career with IMP Universal, he played "hero" type leads in mainly one- and two-reel comedies and dramas. For a time there was some hope in the person of Henry Otto for, in April 1916, King was given still another "new director." The two had actually known each other as early as 1902. Otto, like King, was a native of St. Louis and the two worked together as amateur actors at the Players Club of St. Louis. King was then their leading man; by August of that year, Otto became president.[4] Their paths were not known to cross again until Otto was hired by Universal, first to direct some of Hobart Henley's films on the West Coast, then to come to New York to direct Baggot. At the time, Otto had acquired a reputation for being "the artistic producer" and for directing "pictures which count," such as *Undine*, a five-reel film from the novel by Pierre de la Motte Foquet.[5]

Their first two films together were made under the IMP brand. The two-reeler *The Haunted Bell*, released in April, was a science-crime drama based on a story by Jacques Futrelle. This was followed by *Won By a Make-Up,* a one-reel film about an actor and the deacon's daughter. They fall in love and deceive the girl's parents when the actor assumes a "make-up" that allows them time to escape the parents and elope. It then seemed that Otto and Baggot would get down to business. Their next work together was *Half a Rogue*. For the first time in his career, King would be making a five-reel feature. It is difficult to know exactly why it took so long for this to happen. One tiny clue is found in an article that appeared in *Motion Picture News* early in 1916. It announced that Joe Brandt, then general manager for Universal, had changed the brand name of their longer features from "Broadway Universal Features" to "Red Feather Productions." He was quoted as saying:

> Exchange managers had been reporting for some time that theater proprietors had been complaining that their patrons were confusing the big Universal features with the regular Universal program, not differentiating between the two. Many people would see a release on the regular program, and when they saw a feature advertised, would connect it with the one and two-reel releases, thereby creating a false impression and hurting the big feature."

The article went on to mention King:

> For the first time King Baggot will make a picture for release in the feature program. He has preferred to do the one and two-reelers which have made him famous, rather than going into the making

of the longer pictures. The constant demand for his appearance on the feature program has prompted him to make the change. Beginning with the advent of the Red Feather Productions King Baggot will appear regularly on that program.[6]

When Baggot became a film star in 1909, the usual length of a film was one reel. Many in the industry kept insisting that one, or at most, two reels were all that an audience would sit still for. Theater owners initially agreed, for they could turn an audience over and sell more tickets with short programs. Yet slowly, inexorably, the length kept expanding. In 1912, an article appeared in *Moving Picture World* by Ingvald C. Oes, American general manager of Great Northern Film Company representing Nordisk Films of Denmark. He observed that in the past two years, more two- and three- reel films were being produced and the demand for them had already proved they were viable. He did caution that quality had to be maintained for demand to continue. He said, "In my judgment, within the next six months the majority of films projected will be two and three thousand foot films."[7] In 1915, Thomas Ince, now an esteemed producer with the New York Motion Picture Corporation, prepared a paper to deliver at the annual conference of the Motion Picture Exhibitors League of America. In it he said, "To say that the feature has come to stay would be putting it mildly." But he hedged his bets a bit by adding, "In my opinion ... the single and two-reel film will never pass..."[8] By 1916 there were so many multi-reel films being produced that a plaintive article by W. Stephen Bush in *Moving Picture World* was titled, "Are Short Subjects Coming Back?"[9]

Just the same, Carl Laemmle seemed to have had no long-term faith in the coming predominance of the feature film. In December 1915, he was quoted thusly:

Carl Laemmle, president of the Universal Film Manufacturing Company, believes that the moving picture regular program is coming back into its own. "The tired business man doesn't want to see a big feature play ... with a deep and complicated plot after a hard day's work. He doesn't mind a one reel, or two reel, or even three reel, possible four, but when it comes to five, six and seven, he cannot be enticed into the theater. The feature has convinced the exhibitor that the moving picture is filling the need required of it, and for which it was actually created; to furnish an interesting, educational and instructive program of amusement to those who could not afford to attend the legitimate theater and pay the high price for comfortable seats. But the people do not care to see a long production, for such performances can be seen at the legitimate theaters. The patrons of a picture show enjoy seeing a little bit of everything."[10]

This was the man responsible for some important early features — *From the Bottom of the Sea*, in two reels (1911), the extremely successful and much imitated *Traffic in Souls* in six reels (1913), Herbert Brenon's famous *Neptune's Daughter* in seven reels (1914) — and while Baggot was playing in his little two-reel film *The Baited Trap* in 1914, Laemmle starred the up-and-coming J. Warren Kerrigan in *Samson* — another six-reel film. In his *History of the American Cinema, Vol. 3, An Evening's Entertainment*, Richard Koszarski shed some light on his attitude. Koszarski pointed out that Laemmle, in spite of launching the "Broadway Features" (five-reelers with big name stars) in 1915, he never really liked them, and that he resisted the move away from short subjects much longer that most of his competitors. He asserted that: "While Aitken (Reliance-Majestic), Zukor (Famous Players) and others moving heavily into the production of features continued to promote the star, Laemmle resisted long enough to leave his studio almost bereft of big-name talent by the postwar period."[11] If King's mentor and staunch supporter had those feelings, perhaps he shared them, but now he was slated for immersion in the five-reel world.

Some pains were taken to make *Half a Rogue* an important film for Baggot, Otto and for Universal. Produced under the Red Feather brand, this would be the first time King had ever made a film that was not an IMP, with the exception of the small cameo role he played in *The Great Universal Mystery,* produced by Universal Nestor in 1914. The advertising copy ran: "The star of a thousand characterizations— King Baggot in a sparkling photo drama, *Half a Rogue.*" *Half a Rogue* was based on a best-selling novel by Harold McGrath, originally published in 1906. (McGrath was paid $250 for the rights to the story). Henry Otto wrote the adaptation and also played the part of "Ex-Senator Henderson." There was money in the budget for location shooting in Savannah, Georgia, and some night shooting was done on "The Great White Way." Special artwork enhanced the promotion. Exhibitors could obtain two six-sheets with four-sheet streamers to be used for combination 16-sheets, or separately, in addition to the regular two three-sheets, two one-sheets and the window cards.[12]

No major stars supported him, but the cast was made up of some experienced and well known actors, including character actress Mathilda Brundage and Howard Crampton—one of IMP's stalwart supporting men of many seasons. It was a political tale of scandal and false accusations, but, of course, it all comes out right in the end.

When location shooting was done in Savannah, one scene called for King to address a very large crowd. In order to get that large free crowd, Baggot was advertised in the local newspapers as wanting to thank the citizens of Savannah for their courtesy to the Universal Company during their visit. As a result, a multitude packed the center of the city to meet him. While he was addressing them, the cameras were busy filming the scene.[13] This crowd-getting trick worked as well as it had back in 1910 at the St. Louis railroad station, but at least those citizens were able to obtain a photograph of Florence Lawrence for their trouble. Apparently, this time, a chance to see and hear King Baggot in their own city was reward enough. The reviews were kind, but there were no raves for it. Otto and Baggot's next film together was quite a bit better.

The Man from Nowhere was released in mid–June 1916. Although it had no "big locations," it did have a good story written by William H. Clifford, once an actor, now an accomplished scenario writer. It was a melodrama produced as a Red Feather photoplay in five reels. The reviews were more enthusiastic than any King had had in some time. Peter Milne in *Motion Picture News* said:

> Without stretching the point at all this melodrama is by far the best picture shown under the Red Feather brand in the past two months.... It has a story furnished by William H. Clifford, of pronouncedly strong and gripping qualities, handled in such a manner as to quite eclipse a number of impossibilities, apparent when the picture is stripped to the bone. Thankfully too, the story can do full justice to five reels of film.
>
> ...King Baggot, who has for a long time been denied the opportunity to render a performance befitting an actor of his ability, is afforded a real part in this picture. In the role of Jim, Mr. Baggot acts with sincere and effective feeling. He plays to the sympathies of his audience and he reaches them by methods worthy of praise....
>
> The work of Henry Otto is always artistic. Never, when an opportunity has been afforded him to strengthen a scene by the use of light effects has he refused the chance and the results certainly show for themselves. The subtitles of the

pictures are perhaps a little too dreamily poetic, but this is a minor matter. More pictures like *The Man From Nowhere* and the Red Feather brand will be meritoriously established.[14]

Even *Wid's*, whose reviewers were often more critical in their assessment of the films than some of the other trade publications, had more praise than damns for it:

> This is a straight melodrama with a little bit of love interest, produced along routine lines as to the development of the situations and the convenient placing of coincidences, but the whole has been well done as to settings, lighting, playing and atmosphere, so that it ranks as a little better than acceptable.... King Baggot is always an impressive figure and he has a part which is decidedly well suited for his work, with the result that we get some good scenes from him.[15]

With the release of *The Man from Nowhere*, King's fortunes should have taken a new turn. He now had an effective director and the chance to act in those longer features that would give him more exposure and critical acclaim. The studio, the press and his audiences were solidly behind him when some dreadful news broke. It was first announced in *Universal Weekly*, June 3:

> Officials of the Universal have issued the following statement concerning the studio at Fort Lee, N.J.... Beginning immediately ... will transfer its eastern production companies to Universal City, Calif.... To eliminate all waste, thirty-five companies will eventually be operated in one place with one overhead charge. Universal's new glass studios in New Jersey will be held for emergency purposes....[16]

Throughout the following week, there was much confusion in the industry press about the move. At first, with all the rumors swirling about, it was thought that Universal would still allow a small amount of production to continue on the East Coast. *Moving Picture News* reported that Baggot, Mary Fuller, Violet Mersereau, Jane Gail and William Garwood would continue to work on the East Coast, and even announced the title of King's next film — *The Chance Market* — which he had written, and in which he would star, direct and play a dual role. At this critical juncture, Henry Otto departed and went to work for Metro Pictures. But the rumors were wrong. The whole true story was carefully spelled out in the June 10 issue of *Motion Picture News*:

> Removal of "U" Studios To West Definitely Decided
>
> It has been definitely decided to transfer all the eastern producing companies of Universal to the west and hereafter all pictures ... will be made at Universal City, Cal.... The transfer has been the result of much consideration on the part of the officers of Universal and it is believed that the eastern officials were largely influenced by H.O. Davis, general manager of Universal City.... It is computed that $8,000 a week will be saved by the shift. Heretofore the expenses of the Fort Lee, N.J. plant have totaled $12,000 a week....
>
> Some of the eastern producing companies are already on their way to the coast. Director Matt Moore's company, headed by Jane Gail and himself, left on Monday, May 29th....
>
> The list of prominent directors and stars who will hereafter work at the California film city includes Violet Mersereau, Mary Fuller, Jane Gail, Edna Hunter, Edith Roberts, Irene Hunt, Dorothy Phillips, King Baggot, Hobart Henley, William Garwood, Harry Benham, Paul Panzer, Matt Moore, Francis J. Grandon, William Bailey, Robert Hill and cameraman, Tony Gaudio.... The closing down of the Fort Lee studios will throw about 500 other employees out of work.
>
> Mr. Davis will leave for Universal City with the last of the migrating

easterners, it is believed. During his stay in New York, he has procured at least $12,000 worth of stories for production.... It is Mr. Davis' intention to devote more time to the making of pictures dealing with outdoor life, believing that here the camera finds its natural scope. Mr. Davis wants to get away from the morbid society melodrama as much as possible and consequently his purchase of stories laid in the open.[17]

But King did not wish to go to the coast. It was a decision that would change the entire course of his personal and professional life.

19
Cast Adrift

This must have been a very trying time in King's life. He had hitched his wagon to Universal's "star," and, in fact he was IMP's biggest male star — their nova — for almost seven years. His faith in the future of the motion picture business was rock solid and his loyalty to Laemmle had always been unwavering. Yet, that business in which he had begun was growing and changing, and he, at that point in time, was extremely reluctant to change with it. He undoubtedly loved New York. It was the place of his greatest success. He had been a big frog in a big pond. His wife and son were there. So many of his friends were there. Everyone knew him. Why would he want to go to California, where he would be in competition with over 30 other companies? He had not been to California since he toured there with *Mrs. Wiggs* in 1907. He probably did not like what he heard from those who had been there in recent years. He had acquired the skills of a renowned film actor, and a writer and director as well. When H.O. Davis, the new general manager, declared that "social melodramas" would be out of favor, what sort of roles could he possibly have? And how was he to vie for continued recognition with a whole new generation of younger leading men? No, it would be best to stay in New York.

One more film was released under the Universal IMP brand, directed by Henry Otto: *The Man Across the Street,* which was completed before the news of the move broke. He had a contract still in force, but from July through September his films were issued under the Universal/Big U name. These were one- and two-reel films with the exception of *The Chance Market,* which had already been announced. This was in three reels and released as a Universal/Gold Seal production. In fact, from September 1916 well into 1917, the films of King Baggot continued to be released by Universal, but careful scrutiny shows that a number of them were films either still in "the pipeline" in 1916, films made earlier but for one reason or another never previously released, or worse — films made long ago — but re-released under a totally different title. It was not uncommon to find that character names had been changed and sometimes even the names of the actors had been altered. Laemmle had done the same thing in the case of Mary Pickford after she left IMP in 1912. She was able to air her displeasure in the press and eventually persuade him to, if not apologize, at least admit he was responsible for the deceptions.[1] Deciphering these "credits" requires a certain amount of detective work. The words "special release" attached to the announcement can act as a red flag to sort out this practice, as well as a careful look at the plots to see if they duplicate earlier films.

At least six such examples can be found from this time period and some are masterpieces of deception. One of the most outstanding was *The Bigamist*, released in September 1916. It was actually Baggot's famous *Lady Audley's Secret* from 1912. In order to try to disguise its real identity, actress Jane Fearnley's name was changed to Jane Vernon, Thomas Welsh became William J. Welsh, and Herbert Brenon's name was substituted for that of Otis Turner, who originally directed it. Carl Laemmle and Universal were not the only producers to employ this trick and, to be fair, they *did* actually own the rights to these films. But to use a star's name in such contexts is a misrepresentation to the filmgoing public and exhibitors, and it is enough to give a filmographer nightmares almost a century later. Baggot's *The Flaming Diagram* from 1914 had become *The Blazing Secret* in 1917. *The Rise of Officer 174*, made in 1913, was now called *The Heel of the Law* in 1916, giving director credit to George Loane Tucker, who was busily engaged by the London Film Company at the time. In this one case, Tucker may actually have directed it in 1913, but no specific credit has been found. Other examples from 1913 include: *The Child Stealers of Paris*, which became *Lost in the Streets of Paris* in 1917 under the Rex brand, *King, the Detective in the Jarvis Case*, as *The Secret Cellar* in 1916, *The Wanderer*, as *Undoing Evil* in 1916, *The Anarchist*, filmed in Paris, as *The Voice Upstairs*, and *Mr. and Mrs. Innocence Abroad*, also shot in Paris with King and Leah Baird, as *So This Is Paris*, also in 1916. Knowing what he did about the film business, King probably agreed that Universal had the rights to his work, but it must have been galling to see the company continue to profit from that work when he himself was now unemployed.

There was a sense of finality in the item published in *Variety* on August 18:

> FULLER AND BAGGOT LEAVE U.
> Mary Fuller and King Baggot have severed their connections with the Universal Film Co. during the past week. Baggot, who was one of the original members of the old IMP Co. when Thomas Ince, Mary Pickford, Owen Moore and Lottie Pickford were members, was the eldest star in service that Universal had had in its employ.
> At the time it was announced the Fort Lee studios were to be abandoned and all Universal pictures would in the future be made in Universal City, Baggot immediately declared he would not go to the western plant and work. Efforts were made by the officials of the concern to get him to go, but he was obdurate and insisted that his contact called for him to work in the east and that he would live up to this agreement. As a result, when his contract expired recently no overtures were made to him for a renewal by the concern. It is understood that at present he is negotiating with several of the large producing concerns in New York, and probably may close shortly with Vitagraph.

The news for Mary Fuller was even more unsettling:

> Miss Fuller, who was secured from the Edison Co. two years ago, has been considered one of the best drawing cards of the Universal for a long time. But it is understood that her last few pictures were both financial and productional disappointments to the concern and at the expiration of her contract she was allowed to depart.... Miss Fuller has offered her services to several concerns along Broadway, but it is understood that they were turned down with the remark, "You are no longer [a] film type."[2]

These transitions were difficult for the pioneers. Mary Fuller actually entered film a year before King, in 1908 with Vitagraph. Her work with Edison in early serials such as *What Happened To Mary?* and *Who Will Marry Mary?* made her a star before she joined Universal. However, now that she had been categorized as being "no longer a film type," her days were predictably numbered. She made only a few more films in 1917, notably *The Long Trail* with Lou Tellegen for Paramount; then her career was over.

A bit more hope was held out for King. The story about his break with Universal that appeared in *Motion Picture News* suggested:

> As an actor Mr. Baggot has established for himself a reputation for unusual versatility. He also directed several of his own pictures [a gross understatement] and has many original scenarios to his credit.... He is a master of the art of make-up, an accomplishment which [has] served him well...[3]

But it was *Photoplay,* with cold, clear eyes on the current scene, that dared to announce that a new era had already begun and that a whole galaxy of the biggest stars was about to come crashing down from the sky:

> The most cruel thing to wish upon a player is a great success. The star who once touched a mile-a-minute gait must keep pace or be spoken of as a has-been.... Henry Walthall, a year ago [was] acclaimed the screen's very finest intellectual-poetic male product.... Somehow, his [latest] ventures have been flashpan misfires.... There are other fellows, other complaints. Carlyle Blackwell, essentially one of the cleverest of leading men, is altogether too prone to carelessness. Crane Wilbur is just solemnly absurd. Robert Warwick carries on as no human being ever carried on over land and sea. So does Francis Ford. Robert Mantell upon the screen is a sort of scene-eating monstrosity. King Baggot belongs to the old school of gesticulative grandeur. Courtenay Foote gets nowhere. Billie Reeves ought to get somewhere — just where we won't say.[4]

Despite the rumors of King's impending move to Vitagraph, or to any other company, he did not sign with another eastern studio. In the fall of 1916, he became a film producer in his own right. Negotiating with Universal directly, he was able to purchase the negative and the territorial rights to one of his most famous (and, for Universal, one of the most lucrative) of his films: *Absinthe*. Not only was it considered one of his triumphs as an actor, but it also had a war theme. It was shot in 1914, before the general conflagration in Europe, called "The Great War," had become a reality. As the original film ended, the father gives his old gun to his wayward son and sends him off to march with soldiers going to battle. By now, 1916, practically all of Europe was at war, and although the United States did not enter the fray until April 1917, in the public consciousness, U.S. participation was inevitable. The situation had already caused a great financial upheaval in the film industry; its profitable foreign markets almost dried up entirely as the fighting reached Western Europe.

The first announcement appeared in *Moving Picture World* in early December when *Absinthe* was close to release. Audiences would have a chance to see Paris in all its glory as it was before the war; King personally re-edited the film, changing some intertitles and adding a new reel with "actual scenes from the present war. The French trenches, artillery in action, and the armies on the march will be shown."[5] Just as no trace of the original *Absinthe* can be found today, this remake is also, sad to say, among the long list of "lost films." In order to drum up as much business as possible, King elected to "troupe it," once again going on the road just as he had done so often during his theatrical career. He had a manager, one Charles H. Greene, who was described as a "veteran manager and screen director," but of whom nothing can be found.[6] Greene booked King's many personal appearances into large, medium and small theaters in towns all over the Midwest for the states rights buyers.

By March 1917, his tour was in full swing. It must have reminded him of the old days, traveling from one town to another and braving the Midwest cold. However, this time his accommodations were more elegant, or at least as comfortable as the towns could provide, befitting his status as a film star and not a supporting player. The *New York Dramatic Mirror* described his grueling schedule in Michigan, mainly for the Butterfield theater circuit:

> The popularity of this well-known screen actor, King Baggot, if it were ever in doubt, has certainly been proved with a vengeance during his present itinerary, in which he has appeared in person at numerous theaters throughout the state of Michigan. He has been greeted with veritable ovations at each appearance, dined by the mayors of all cities, welcomed by committees at the trains and generally received with acclaim…
>
> He has played Ann Arbor, Bay City, Battle Creek, Saginaw, Flint, Jackson, Ypsilanti, Kalamazoo, Pontiac, Lansing and Grand Rapids….

When he arrived in Detroit, he had kind words to say for the city, which must have been much changed since the days when he played there almost ten years previously:

> "Detroit…is the busiest city I have ever seen. The streets are crowed day and night. There is an abundance of money; hotels overcrowded." He will go to Ohio next to continue his successful tour.[7]

The tour closed in Indiana on April 22. It was originally announced that King would return to New York to organize his own company with the help of Greene, but those plans never materialized. *Absinthe* continued to be shown around the country with Argosy Films as the distributor at least through June 1917, but King's career as a star, at that point, was seemingly at an end.

20
New Hope

The first announcement appeared in the *Dramatic Mirror* on November 24. "King Baggot's coming back!" And so he did. No more city-to-city junkets for months on end; he could come in out of the cold. By a wonderful stroke of luck, all those detective parts he had played for so many years would pay off, for he was hired by the Whartons to play the lead in a 20-episode serial featuring the exploits of an amateur detective. It was titled *The Eagle's Eye*. The story was suggested and written by William J. Flynn, recently retired chief of the United States Secret Service, on a most timely topic: Imperial Germany's attempts at espionage in the United States. War had been declared against Germany on April 6, and although many people did not want the United States to participate, including President Woodrow Wilson, by July a million American troops were fighting in Europe. Propaganda films became the order of the day for film producers and this one was especially effective in its depiction of insidious plots by Germany to disrupt the government and the peace of U.S. citizens on their own shores.

The Wharton brothers, Leopold and Theodore, had been independent producers even before they started their own production company in Ithaca, New York, in 1912. They had both known King since at least 1913, for at that time Theodore was a member of the Screen Club. By now they had become specialists in serials, which they often produced and directed themselves. Two well-known examples were *The Perils of Pauline* and *The Exploits of Elaine* with Pearl White. When King was first interviewed on the new serial, the press noted:

> "What else could I do?" he asked laughingly as he signed the contract which is to make him the hero of twenty episodes of the Super-Serial. "I've been a personal friend of Chief Flynn's for years. My greatest admiration has always been for the Secret Service — some way the name always has held a magic something for me. In the days when I was writing my own stories, and then playing them, I always was happiest when I could get the idea for a good secret service picture. Then, too, the fact that this serial is about the biggest thing I've ever struck has its influence also. The result was that I gave up all thought of a speaking stage contract which I was about to sign and took the part which the Whartons offered me in the new serial."[1]

Marguerite Snow was signed to play

opposite King. She came from a theatrical background, playing in stock companies in Denver and on the New York stage before joining Thanhouser in 1911. She worked her way up to starring roles including *The Million Dollar Mystery*, a very successful 23–episode serial in 1914, and also worked briefly for Metro before coming to the Whartons for this film. King's old director George Lessey was assigned to the preliminary directing chores while the well-known fiction writer Courtenay Ryley Cooper was hired to transform William Flynn's account of German espionage activities into 20 two-reel scripts.

Filming began near the end of November and by late December the first episodes were completed. They were filmed at the Wharton studios in Ithaca, in New York City and in Washington D.C. The first story told of the intrigue that led to the sinking of the passenger ship RMS *Lusitania* in 1915. Although she was a British ship of the Cunard Line, she was said to be unarmed and flying the American flag when she was torpedoed by a German submarine. Over 1100 people were killed, of whom 123 were Americans— men, women and children.[2] The second episode, titled *The Naval Ball Conspiracy*, told of a thwarted plot by the Kaiser's agents, also in 1915, to blow up the Ansonia Hotel in New York while high-ranking officers of the Navy's Atlantic fleet were in attendance. Parts of this particular episode were actually filmed at the hotel between midnight and four in the morning, with over 400 people in the cast and crew.

In the overall plan for the serial, King played Harrison Grant, president of the Criminology Club, an organization made up of prominent men in all parts of the world who have made a specific study of crime. The club volunteers to assist the U.S. Secret Service defeat spy plots and Grant becomes an operative under the direction of the Chief. Dixie Mason (Marguerite Snow) is a beautiful and successful actress with more than average intelligence, who had quietly become a commissioned captain of women operatives in the Secret Service.

When casting the roles of the German officers and agents, a certain amount of trouble was taken to select actors who bore a close resemblance to them. With the government's help, photographs were provided to assure authenticity; Captains Karl Boy-Ed and Franz von Papen were played by John Wade and Paul Everton, Count von Bernsdorff by Bertram Marberg, and Dr. Heinrich Albert by Frederick Jones.[3]

The country, by now, took the war effort very seriously indeed. Anything that would help in that effort was of great importance, including the making of *The Eagle's Eye*. While the company was filming in Ithaca the week of January 14, the city experienced an explosion in their power plant, the Ithaca Light and Power Company. It was reported in the *Theatrical News* of Buffalo, New York that:

> ...Ithaca has again shown its civic pride in having a big motion picture-making plant in its midst—the studios of the Whartons who are producing the serial photodrama *The Eagle's Eye*.... That not a day might be lost, the street car system of Ithaca last week was made subservient to the demands of the Whartons and electric power that usually goes to run the trolleys was diverted to the lamps and arcs used to light the sets of the picture.
>
> There was not power enough to run the street cars, light office buildings and run the lighting system at the Wharton studios. So arrangements were made for the Whartons to work at night. The street cars and other users of power shut down at a certain hour, so that it could be diverted to the studios.[4]

Cynics might say that the Whartons and their distributor, Four Square, would engage in any sort of publicity to exploit this film, but a case can be made for their utter sincerity as they and other companies making such films felt they were helping win the war by using the powerful tool of the motion picture to engage the hearts and minds of the public. There was a blizzard of free special showings all over the country, especially of the first episodes. In early February, the first three were shown in Washington D.C. for the Committee on Public Information and the National Press Club. Some of the actors who played the German operatives made a personal appearance.[5] In New York it was screened for representatives of patriotic societies at the Hotel Biltmore on Washington's Birthday.[6] In that same article, the remarks of William J. Flynn were quoted that touched on a very controversial issue that surfaced even before the film was released. He remarked:

> I have arranged this private showing because I desire the opinion of Americans as to the value of this production as a means of creating a greater patriotism and inspiring a more intense loyalty. A prominent motion picture exhibitor controlling a great number of theatres, has criticized *The Eagle's Eye*. He claims its revelations of Imperial German intrigue, espionage and propaganda in America would be too great a contrast to the thoughts and opinions of his German patrons.[7]

The "prominent motion picture exhibitor" was Marcus Loew, and apparently he was backed by his partner, Joseph Schenck. He later denied making those remarks and actually claimed to have been misquoted — that the reason it had not been booked was because "he had heard that the picture was pro–German."[8] Of course, the fact that he could think that a film written by the former head of the Secret Service would be "pro–German" inspired widespread incredulity both in the regular press and the trades. The controversy soon blew over; yet, the sensitivity of the film industry toward public opinion about the war had become quite pervasive. Margarita Fischer, one of King's early leading ladies, dropped the "c" from her name and began spelling it "Fisher" in order to sound less German.

The first episode was released on February 27. Four Square exchange men mounted a nationwide publicity campaign. The *Dramatic Mirror* called it "the greatest ever used to exploit a motion picture."[9] They tried an experiment to see if newspaper advertising alone would draw more audience than a combination of magazine advertising and newspapers together. *Moving Picture World* declared, "[N]ever has a National campaign of this magnitude been made for a single picture."[10] It is not known what, if anything, was concluded by this experiment, save that a prodigious amount of publicity was generated for this film. Full-page ads appeared in the newspapers of every city where Four Square had an exchange and it was also covered extensively in the trade press. But before filming was completed, the Whartons dropped everything for a week in order to make a gift for "war charity." It was called *The Mission of the War Chest*.

Many motion picture producers during the war used their facilities, their personnel and their time to create short films that were shown not just in theaters, but in hotels, halls and club rooms as well, and they did this at their own expense. Their purpose was, quite simply, to raise money for the war effort. *The Mission of the War Chest* was targeted specifically for the Red Cross, the YMCA, the Salvation Army and other civic organizations. The story was written by the Wharton brothers and concerns a man who would not contribute, until his son enlists and begins writing letters home describing the work these organizations were doing on the battlefront. Finally the father realizes that his own son is willing to give more than money — he would give his very life for his country so

Baggot as secret agent Harrison Grant making sure the German spy will not get away in *The Eagle's Eye*, Wharton/Foursquare, 1918. Photograph courtesy of Wisconsin Center for Film and Theatre Research.

that "Dad" can stay in the safe haven that is America. He finally sees the light and becomes a subscriber. King and Marguerite Snow starred and footage of actual battle scenes, including Vimy Ridge, were incorporated into the action. It was officially presented to the Chamber of Commerce in Rochester, New York near the end of June, but there were plans made to distribute it on a national basis.[11]

The twentieth episode of *The Eagle's Eye* left the Whartons' cutting room the week of June 17 and was shown in U.S. theaters into July and August. But it was destined for a longer afterlife. While signaling the conclusion of the series, *Moving Picture World* remarked:

> *The Eagle's Eye* has fulfilled more purposes than that of an ordinary serial, as it has been used to combat the intrigues and the propaganda of Germany and has been used by Liberty Loan committees to further the buying of bonds. It is also said to have been used in Mexico to forestall German propaganda, and it soon is to have widespread circulation abroad that foreign countries may see the difficulties with which America was beset before it entered the war.[12]

No doubt *The Eagle's Eye* had stiff competition from other companies also engaged in filming pictures for the "war effort," but those particular months when it was being shown were extremely critical ones for the U.S. forces fighting in France. While the battle of Château-Thierry was being waged from May until September, Gen. Pershing led his troops into Verdun and the Argonne Forest and sustained terrible casualties between August and October. It was not until the capture of Sedan, south of the Meuse River on the western German border, that Germany at last admitted defeat and signed the general Armistice on November 11, 1918. In the course of some 17 months, the number of U.S. soldiers killed in battle topped 53,000 and over 200,000 were wounded, but for the time being, the world was now safe for democracy.

Although the war officially ended in November, the country would continue to be haunted by the havoc it caused. War and its aftermath did not immediately leave the American consciousness. Books, plays and films kept arriving — almost as if the telling and retelling would bring some relief and eventually closure to those still recent, traumatic events. Metro Pictures was a company that continued to make this kind of film for quite some time after the war was over. It was not surprising, then, that King would move almost seamlessly over to them to make another fund-raising film while the war was still raging. It was called *Building for Democracy* and was scheduled for production in late August. It was made in cooperation with the U.S. Treasury Department as part of the fourth Liberty Loan Drive.[13] Two others in the Metro series were *Edith's Victory* with Edith Storey and *Liberty Loan Jimmy* with Harold Lockwood. Emily Stevens was King's co-star, but for the first time in his long career and not since his brief work with Mary Pickford in 1910, in all the production stories and other publicity, he was referred to as *her* co-star.

Miss Stevens did not have as long and as illustrious career in motion pictures as King did, but she was the niece of the very famous stage actress Minnie Maddern Fiske. She may have gotten her start for this reason. In December 1914, a small but up and coming producer, Benjamin Albert Rolfe, launched B.A. Rolfe Photoplays. He tried to engage Mrs. Fiske to work with him, but she broke off negotiations in January 1915.[14] Emily Stevens' career began that same year. She starred in five films for Rolfe released through Metro between 1915 and 1916. Then in 1917, the Metro/Rolfe association ceased when Rolfe was absorbed by Metro and she starred for Metro in nine others through 1918. *Building for Democracy* was her last film released by Metro.

21

A Slippery Slope

King originally went to Metro not to be Emily Stevens' co-star, but to star in his own right in another espionage film. Still fresh from his role in *The Eagle's Eye,* he was recruited by a fellow St. Louisian, director Harry L. Franklin. According to the *Dramatic Mirror,* Metro bought the rights to a successful patriotic war drama, *The Man Who Stayed at Home,* in late July or early August 1918.[1] However, something happened to delay its production. Instead, Franklin began making what would be a fairly awful film, *Kildare of Storm.* It was based on a 1916 novel by Eleanor Mercein Kelly—her first venture into novel writing. She was better known for her short stories. From the beginning, King was billed as playing "in support" of Miss Stevens, but he did have a meaty part as a cruel and brutal alcoholic with an illegitimate son.

It was probably filmed at Metro's leased Fort Lee studios—at least for the plantation scenes—with perhaps some filming at their New York studios on West 43rd Street. The review that appeared in *Variety* on September 27, with characteristic unkindness, noted:

> Miss Stevens appears to have grown heavier before the screen and in this picture younger as the film progresses, although there are a couple of long lapses. The book may have enjoyed popularity—the picture won't. It's too commonplace.[2]

King managed to survive this film without much loss of dignity, but poor Emily Stevens had to be hospitalized two years later for a nervous breakdown due to dieting.[3]

Then, while the country was still holding its collective breath and hoping for an end to the Great War, another calamity struck: the infamous influenza epidemic of 1918, the most severe of its kind that the world had ever seen. Indeed, it was rightly termed a "pandemic" since it involved almost the entire world. Sometimes called the "Spanish influenza" because at the time it was thought to have begun there, it spread to almost all the corners of the globe. It is now known that the disease is a virus traveling from person to person by means of airborne droplets. The conditions of war greatly exacerbated its duration and its reach as the unusual concentration and movement of troops carried the infection with them.

By mid-summer 1918, the United States began to feel its severity and by the fall, not only were military personnel abroad dying, but also large numbers of regular citizens. Drastic measures were called for, and those measures greatly affected the entire motion picture industry. Leading man Harold Lockwood was a casualty, as was Mary Moore, sister of Joe, Owen, Matt and Tom Moore; she died while working for the Red Cross in France. Others who died were actors Julian L'Estrange, Walter Long, James Fitzgerald, Philip Lang and Anna Harron, Bobby Harron's sister. Public health officials finally began to understand that the disease spread more rapidly where large crowds of people congregated. All over the country, shops, factories, churches and schools were closed by municipal orders. Theaters and motion picture houses were shut down as well. A three-page report appeared in *Moving Picture World* on October 26, declaring that "because of the deplorable epidemic of influenza [that] has gripped the entire country ... the clock of the motion picture industry has been stopped as of October 14."[4] The National Association of the Motion Picture Industry decided to halt not only the distribution of films, for most theaters could not show them, but to stop, their production as well. The article went on to enumerate, on a state-by-state basis, the activities that were being postponed. There were a few rural pockets in small towns that remained unaffected, but film-related work in all the big cities and in some cases whole states came to a grinding halt. New York, Chicago, Atlanta, Cincinnati, California—the list rolled on. It was only when winter arrived that the virus finally subsided. By early November, the *World* was able to report some hope for the stricken industry and work resumed.[5]

Naturally, the epidemic affected Metro along with all the other producers. A good two months elapsed between the release of *Kildare of Storm* and the start of production on *The Man Who Stayed at Home*. Actually, a bit of shooting had been done some time in June, for the title was announced in an article about King which appeared in the July issue of *Photoplay*, "Sleuthing as a Fine Art."[6] The interview was conducted on the Metro set and described a scene being directed by Herbert Blaché. The interview pointed up his work in *The Eagle's Eye* and tied it to this new film. This time there was no doubt about who was the star. He was quoted and praised with the same reverence his fans had come to expect. In late October, Metro made a more formal announcement that named many of the members of the cast and noted "the engagement of King Baggot to visualize the character of Christopher Brent ... is expected to give a masterly representation of this important part."[7] It is not clear why *Kildare* was released first or why his status had slipped to that of co-star, but shooting definitely resumed in October, and by the end of November press releases were reporting on the progress of its production.

The Man Who Stayed at Home was originally a stage play produced in London in 1914 for their own "war effort." It was written by Lechmore Worrall and J.E. Harold Terry and played briefly in New York under the title *The White Feather*, but did not do well until the United States entered the war. It reopened in Boston under its original title with much greater success and eventually made it back to New York. Louis B. Mayer may have had something to do with its purchase for, as one of Metro's founders, he was a great believer in acquiring the rights to plays for adaptation to the screen. It became Metro's eighth patriotic production, preceded by *To Hell with the Kaiser*, *Lest We Forget*, *My Own United States*, *The Slacker*, *Draft 258*, *The Legion of Death* and *Her Boy*.[8] King had a different leading lady this time in the person of Claire Whitney, who had a solid background in film beginning with Solax playing leads at least as early as 1913. She may have been chosen for this role by Herbert Blaché, for whom she had worked in 1914. Although this film is one of so many among the missing, some lobby cards still exist and she appears to be a lovely and graceful-looking woman.

From mid–1918 to the end of the year, Metro Pictures was undergoing a period of growth and change. They had been able to acquire the services of a number of important stage actresses, including Ethel Barrymore, Alla Nazimova and Viola Dana, and a production entity known as Screen Classics was developed to market them. In June, they rented the top floor of the Biograph studio specifically for Screen Classics, but more importantly, they began expansion on the West Coast as well. Buzz about a major move started as early as May. The *Dramatic Mirror* broke the news:

> Inspired by a spirit of war economy Metro Film Company plans to move its New York Film Company to California beginning July 1.... The New York company of players will be transferred to California and the entire organization, so far as the actual filming of pictures is concerned, will work at one studio. The executive offices will remain for the present in New York.... It is considered doubtful whether Metro will be successful in inducing all of its stars who are engaged at the New York Studio to take up residence in California. Several of them including Ethel Barrymore, Emily Stevens, Mabel Taliaferro, Emmy Wehlen and the Dolly Sisters, appear regularly on the stage and it is thought that they will prefer to remain in New York.[9]

Their first move was to a barn-like structure in Hollywood at Lillian Way and Eleanor Street, but almost immediately they began work on a much larger facility at Cahuenga Boulevard and Romaine Street, which Richard Rowland, then president of Metro, purchased directly from one of Hollywood's founders, Cornelius Cole, for $30,000. The plan, although not as grand as to envision an entire city, was Universal redux, with ultra modern facilities, large stages, state-of-the-art lighting, carpentry shop and mill, at least 50 dressing rooms with special rooms for the stars, spacious grounds and accommodations for up to ten companies. In short, a major move west was imminent.[10] Louis B. Mayer left the company that year and signed on with First National. Fate would have bigger plans for him, but those would come later.

King's pond was becoming smaller and smaller all the time. So many of his old friends and colleagues had gone west by this time that his New York must have seemed a lonely and different place than just a few years before. All of the old IMP Company actors and personnel had scattered to the four winds. Many of them went to California at the time of Universal's great migration. Others had long ago been hired away by other companies, some of them to sink into total obscurity and some to achieve great fame. His best friend William R. Daly, as well as Thomas Ince, J. Farrell MacDonald, Ethel Grandin, Leah Baird, George Loane Tucker, Jane Gail, Francis X. Bushman and Arline Pretty — all had gone west, and a few were now dead. Even his beloved Screen Club was a mere shadow of its former self. Although he stayed in touch, his relationship was never the same after the contentious dispute over the elections in 1915. By 1917, he would give both the Lambs Club and the Screen Club as places to contact him. He was too busy on the road to participate the way he once did; more to the point, the purpose of the Club was now moot as the center for film production moved away from New York.

The Screen Club fell on very hard times after 1917, and it was foundering even before that. All three previous presidents had been actors and directors — Baggot for two terms, James Kirkwood, one, and Billy

Quirk, two. None of them proved to be good managers, but in good times that did not seem to matter. The frequent changes to new quarters, the elaborate furnishings, the glittering balls, the lavish entertainments all took their financial toll. By the end of 1917, they were in rented quarters at the old Friars Club at 117 West 45th Street, and the wolf was definitely at the door. The membership — what was left of it — elected Joseph Farnham to be their next president. He had always been a stalwart supporter, a frequent officer, and was a charter member. His background was quite different from the previous presidents. He had been a newspaperman, press and publicity director and the general manager of the All-Star Feature Corporation. At the time he was elected, he was in charge of production and sales for the Frohman Amusement Corporation.[11] In other words, he was a businessman. A long and thoughtful commentary on the Club appeared in February 1918 in the *Dramatic Mirror*'s "Without Fear or Favor — By an Old Exhibitor" department:

> Joe Farnham should be assisted to pull it through by true friends of the industry, especially on the producing side where seventy-five per cent of the membership has come. It is lucky, at this rate, that Farnham is an executive in this critical hour of the Club's life; for Joe has never submitted to a licking in his entire business experience. He will not fail the Screen now. The Screen's troubles, as this may lead you to believe, have not been due to its executive officers, but to the advertising spirit on the part of the whole membership that forced the membership to bite off more than it could chew. It is a spirit that you can find the length and breadth of the motion picture business — the call of the "big front!" — and the Screen membership is not to be blamed if they inherit it! Perhaps with the new war taxes and the closing of the Screen Club threatening, we will be content to let the other fellows make the noise. Perhaps a club as young as the Screen, and representing so young an industry, will be content with quarters like the modest and "*safe*" ones kept on Forty-fifth Street when the Screen started. We had to rival the Lambs and Friars, nothing else would do! Vast, sumptuous, *idle* rooms were preferable to small, *crowded* and profitable ones. Well, Farnham is going to pull the Screen through its tense period. And when that is accomplished, let him house the Club somewhere on its sound starting basis and permit it to grow gradually. It will find its true level in time — that of the Lambs and Friars — but continue to "force" its growth and ten Farnhams will be of no avail.[12]

Unfortunately, Farnham could not "pull them through." By the end of the year, they were forced to vacate their 45th Street quarters. And there was a further indignity — their former landlords William H. Cowen and Robert H. Davis sued them in Superior Court for unpaid rent amounting to $2,500 and contended that they, the landlords, were now unable to rent to anyone else. The Club defended on the grounds that the disposses proceedings had terminated the lease and that the club therefore owed no rent for the period that followed while the premises were vacant. The court sustained this contention and directed judgment for the defendants.[13] So it was that what many once hailed as the foremost social club of the film industry died a slow and quiet death. There were few left in New York to really care, and although there were various attempts to start a new "screen clubs" in other industry centers like Los Angeles, they could not recapture the short-lived glamour of the original.

All the work that went into the making of *The Man Who Stayed at Home* did not immediately see the light of day. It was not released until July 1919, more than six months after it was completed. This may have had something to do with Louis B. Mayer's departure, for in January 1919 his former partners, Rowland and Ruben, sold their interest to Marcus Loew — the same Marcus Loew who a year earlier was so solicitous of the feelings of his German patrons. Many changes occurred after Loew acquired Metro. It is not clear whether King was asked, once again, to move to California. There were many personnel changes in the company and he may not have even been given the opportunity, but with characteristic Irish stubbornness, he continued to cling to New York as his home. He had often said in interviews that when his career in films was over, he would return to the stage, and in the year 1919 he did. At first he toyed with the idea of going into vaudeville. It was announced that he had been placed under contract to Joseph Hart for a tour with the idea of securing an act that would have a costarring role for a "woman picture favorite."[14] But nothing came of that. Then, in March, *Moving Picture World* announced his return to the stage in a play by H.S. Sheldon called *The Violation*.[15]

22

Troubled Times

To say that *The Violation* was an ill-conceived venture would be putting it mildly. Things went badly from the very beginning. When the play opened in Columbus, Ohio, on March 6 at the Hartman Theatre, the critics were bemused by this melodrama and noted that it needed work; however, they were kind to King. They wrote hopefully that the play would improve. The *Ohio State Journal* of Columbus noted:

> Nearly a capacity house witnessed the launching of *The Violation* and all seemed pleased down to H.S. Sheldon, the author and Harry Hunter, the producer. The actors worked under a strain. They had just completed a tiresome journey from New York and were forced to put on their final rehearsal in the ballroom of the Deshler Hotel during the afternoon.... The first act was a bit rough, enunciation, stage presence and things; the second act was better and the third better yet.... "All it needs is more rehursals," Mr. Hunter said. "By Saturday night we expect to have things going smoothly."
>
> Mr. Baggot walks through his part, and it is an unusually long one, with suavity. His voice and enunciation are good. His big scene comes in the second act. Last night's audience liked it so well it couldn't let him go without a curtain speech. "After eight years before the cold, calculating eye of the camera, this is wonderful to me," he said.[1]

However, when it opened in Cincinnati at the Grand Theatre, the critics, especially J. Herman Thurman of *The Enquirer*, were most unkind. He did not like the way King spoke his lines. He called Baggot's delivery "of the elocution school variety." He said the play was "a horror" and compared it to *Passing of Hans Dippel* and other atrocities."[2]

Reviews said the play was "naughty." In a way they were right, but it was not unlike so much of the entertainment of its day and of years past—full of innuendo, but with a nice moral conclusion. King plays the governor who is married to a harridan of a wife who just happens to have a gentleman friend with whom she is planning to run away. A former sweetheart of the governor approaches him and asks him to pardon her brother, falsely convicted of murder. For reasons that are hard to understand from the reviews, he agrees, but stipulates that she must spend a week at his hunting lodge in exchange for the favor. Her virtue is on the line, but the wife and her paramour are conveniently drowned at sea while they are on a trip to

Europe, thus paving the way for a happy ending.

When the play reached Detroit on March 13, critics could see how ragged it still was and although they were less vociferous than J. Herman Thurman had been, they called it "a melodrama in the making" and a production "still in the loom." It reached Peoria, Illinois, the week of April 6, and on April 10 King collapsed. A clipping datelined April 12 reported:

> King Baggot, playing here in *The Violation*, was taken ill Thursday night during the first act of the play and had to be taken to his hotel. It is said that shock caused by news of the death of his friend, Sidney Drew, was the cause of the actor's illness. Physicians say Mr. Baggot will recover after a complete rest.[3]

What transpired on the tour or what might have caused King to collapse might have remained a mystery if not for film historian Kevin Brownlow, who had the good fortune to interview one of the participants, Frank Blount, in 1967. Although Blount had been a cameraman since film's very early days, he toured with the production of *The Violation*. His recollections came almost 50 years after the event, but he told Brownlow:

> "Doc" Willat [C.A. Willat] and a man named Roy Hunter [his first name was more probably Harry Hunter] financed a play and King Baggot was to star in the play. Doc knew King and I were pals. "Frank," he said, "I want you and King to room together. Stay together all the time and when you're through with the play go to California to Irvin's [C.A. Willat's brother]. What ruined King Baggot was drink. "Keep him sober," see? We closed the show in St. Louis in April and Doc sent the company back to New York and I took the train to California.[4]

King's association with the Willat brothers can be traced all the way back to the IMP Company's sojourn to Cuba in 1911 when "Doc" and Irvin were in charge of transporting the raw stock there. King and "Doc" Willat remained good friends. Willat was a founding member of the Screen Club and a real film pioneer. After the play closed, Frank Blount did indeed "go to California to Irvin." In September 1919 he was a cameraman for Irvin at Paramount when he directed *The Grim Game*. He stayed at Paramount to film *Behind the Door* and *Below the Surface* in 1920, then went with Irvin Willat as a cameraman when he and W.W. Hodkinson produced *Down Home* for their own briefly formed company in November of that year.

Did King have a collapse that night in Peoria, overcome with grief at the death of Sidney Drew, or could drinking have played a part? No evidence can be found that King and Drew were especially close friends. Drew was the son of Sidney Rankin and uncle to Ethel, Lionel and John Barrymore. All had long and illustrious careers in the theater, but in the "teens," Drew and his second wife Lucille McVey became very popular film performers. He did die on April 9 in New York of what was said to be exhaustion and uremia.[5] Drew did not belong to the Screen Club, but he no doubt belonged to the Lambs. They were all working together at Metro in 1918 where they could well have formed a closer friendship. Yet, because of King's ten years in the theater, where the dictum was "the show must go on," that should have precluded his giving in to his emotions to the extent that he could not do the play that night. Did he have other emotional baggage just then? Yes. King was no longer a young man; he was nearly 40. The company had a grueling schedule — five cities in four weeks. From the reviews, it was obvious that the company was in disarray. The play kept changing. The critics had personally savaged him in Cincinnati. His hopes that he could simply go back to the theater and magically become a star all over again were dashed. If "Doc" Willat, who had known him for so many years, was concerned with "keeping him sober," then alcohol may well have played a part. That in itself was surely painful to him and all who knew him.

Drink, to the Irish, was what thrift was to the Scots. Although it would be unfair to characterize an entire nation in that way, there is a certain amount of truth in that observation. Today it is known that alcoholism is a disease, often with heredity roots. Some people can drink and some simply cannot because they are biologically and chemically incapable of doing so. It was becoming apparent and more public that King did have that disease. Drinking to excess went back to his earliest days in film. Herbert Brenon, who would later have his own problems with drinking, observed this back in 1911 and 1912. He was describing to one of his potential biographers what it was like trying to make a film in those early days:

> On the Tuesday, we would get down to the real business. Usually, Billy Shay [William E. Shay], of whom I was so fond, and Vivian Prescott were in my one-reelers. Baggot would never condescend, nor did Daly [William R. Daly]. But I broke the "clique." I do not know why I was not popular, unless it was that in those days, I drank very little alcohol and they, between scenes, with Pop Turner [director Otis Turner] not on the "qui vive," would consume a bottle of scotch between them. I was far from a prude, but they just didn't mix, as I found out for myself later on.[6]

The Screen Club was another source of temptation, if it was even considered a temptation at all. Drinking was an important adjunct to their social occasions as well as a daily and nightly occurrence for so many of the members. Drunkenness in private or in public was more of a joke than a source of social stigma. What this did to King's home life can only be imagined, but it must have been a source of serious friction in the family. Almost no mention of Ruth Baggot is made in print after that bright and beautiful celebration of their marriage back in 1912, except for their trip to Europe together in 1913 and the notice of the birth of their son King Robert, in 1914. If she went with him for location shooting, or trips to St. Louis to visit the family, or to accompany him to the glamorous balls and parties, not a line was written. Now, in 1919, it seemed certain that Ruth's husband had just drank himself out of the theater and possibly out of the film business as well. But the luck of the Irish would hold for yet a little while.

23

California, Here I Am

Louis B. Burston, although not one of Hollywood's best known producers, was a moderately successful one for a time. He was an associate of Charles Bauman, Adam Kessel and Fred Balshofer back in 1909, and acted as their attorney when they formed Bison Films, then began his career as a producer with Equitable Films about 1915. By 1917, he was president and general manager of the King-Bee Comedy Company. Their studios were in Jacksonville, Florida, and their home office in the Longacre Building at Broadway and 42nd Street in New York. He produced the Billy West comedies and sold them on a states rights basis; however, the company only lasted about a year. In 1918, he came to California and formed a company called Silent Mystery Corporation. Together with Hiller and Wilk, they produced a 15-reel serial, *The Silent Mystery*, starring Francis Ford, Mae Gaston and Rosemary Theby. It did well enough that he was able to form his own company, Burston Films. Another serial followed, *The Mystery of 13*, again released as states rights. Francis Ford not only starred, he also directed this one. While it was still in production, he and his brother George began writing a new serial based on a story by Nan Blair, *The Hawk's Trail*.

It was sometime in May 1919 when King, now "at liberty," was approached by Burston and hired for the lead. For at least five years, companies had been begging him to come to California and each time he had said no. But by now, even this stubborn Irishman realized that he did not have much choice if he wanted to continue working. Not only that, but this vehicle was tailor-made for him.

The Hawk's Trail was in 15 parts—each in two reels. Our hero, Sheldon Steele, is a scientific criminologist and man of wealth who solves crimes as a hobby. Of course, in order to solve them, he must assume various disguises and visit many interesting parts of the underworld. The chapters had wonderfully creepy titles like "Yellow Shadows," "Stained Hands," "The House of Fear" and "Tides That Tell." Fortunately, the serial still exists and is owned by the Library of Congress. The episodes are delightful to view, even today. The villains are unspeakably evil, the two sisters he saves (Grace Darmond and Rhea Mitchell) are lovely and grateful, and the location shooting is fascinating. Many of the plots required location shooting around downtown Los Angeles. They used the real Chinatown of 1919 as well as scruffy old warehouses and office buildings, and filmed scenes depicting contemporary street life. King's star quality had not left him. Seeing him today, one can realize that even at 40 he was still a graceful, dynamic actor. When he appears on screen, viewers cannot take their eyes from him.

This film was notable for another reason. Burston hired Woody Van Dyke to direct it (it was Van Dyke's first film for Burston). According to his biographer, Robert Connom, Van Dyke was going through some hard times just then. He and his wife Zina were separated. He was living in a small house behind the Charlie Chaplin Studios with Edgar Kennedy and Bert Henderson and, although this was not a dream job, he made the most of it. He would arrive an hour before the cast and round up anyone he could find, walking them through scenes he had planned — entrances, exits, bits of business — so that the shooting would go off without a hitch. Burston discovered that Van Dyke worked faster than anyone he had ever had on his lot, and in addition to being fast, he was also very good. It was in films like these that his reputation as "one take Van Dyke" was born.[1]

When King first came to Hollywood, he stayed at the Hollywood Hotel, at that time the best in town. Originally built in 1903 on the northwest corner of Hollywood Boulevard and Highland, it is no more. It was razed in 1956. King must have known that his break with New York was final for he brought his family with him. His son King Robert, who was about five years old then, told his family that when they first came to California, he remembered playing on the hotel's wide and spacious porch.

Production of *The Hawk's Trail* "wrapped" in December and *Moving Picture World* commented:

> Louis Burston, president of Burston Films, Inc., announces the completion of his latest fifteen episode serial. King Baggot, with Rhea Mitchell, Grace Darmond and a big cast of principals, directed by Woodrow Van Dyke. Producer Burston's statement that he has succeeded in producing an original type of serial is said to be borne out by the few episodes that have already been shown.
>
> King Baggot assumes a different character in each installment. The suspense at the end of each chapter is achieved through tense situations, which developed for two reels, reach their climax as episode endings. This does away with the necessity for interpolated stunt endings. In this respect the serial may be likened to a novel which is published serially in a weekly magazine.[2]

The Hawk's Trail ran in theaters from December 1919 into April 1920. Then, there were no other films for King to make for Burston. In fact, no record of any Burston films can be found for 1920. Burston did produce another serial, *The Great Reward*, in 1921, then died in an automobile accident near Hollywood on March 25, 1923, ending what might have been a more distinguished career.[3] Fortunately, King was not out of work for long. In April 1920, he was engaged by the American Film Company to star in *The Thirtieth Piece of Silver*.

The American Film Manufacturing Company had a long history in the industry. They were based in Chicago from about 1910, less than a year after King began his career. As part of "the great exodus" from the East to the West, they established a Santa Barbara plant in 1912 and another at Niles, California, in 1913. Their logo was a winged A and they were sometimes referred to as "Flying A." Over time, they were associated with or controlled some nine separate production companies including Beauty, which starred Margarita Fischer (with her husband Harry Pollard as her director). This was the same Margarita Fischer who, had worked for IMP and was

Baggot being "held up" in episode 13, "Face to Face," *The Hawk's Trail,* Burston Films, 1919/1920, dircted by Woody Van Dyke. Photograph courtesy of the Academy of Motion Picture Arts and Sciences.

King's leading lady in a few early IMP one-reel films: *The Girl and the Half-Back* and *A Lesson to Husbands* in late 1911, and *The Trinity* in January 1912 — just before IMP started their first Western IMP company. She and Pollard were on that first train West. By 1920, Beauty had been dissolved and Margarita Fischer was working directly for American. In that time period, her films were being distributed by Pathé.

The Thirtieth Piece of Silver was an entertaining film with no pretensions to greatness. It was based on a story of the same name by Albert Payson Terhune, who was on the staff of the *New York Evening World* at the time and is remembered to this day for his dog stories such as *Lad: A Dog* and *Buff: A Collie,* enjoyed by both children and adults. King played the part of an amateur coin collector who loses the valuable "thirtieth piece of silver," but in the end, by a stroke of luck, he regains it. A publicity blurb on King appeared in *Moving Picture World*, the kind that by now must have become annoying to him, characterizing him as an "old timer." It also makes it clear that he is playing in support of Miss Fischer:

> King Baggot, "the star of a thousand romances," who is Margarita Fisher's leading man in *The Thirtieth Piece of Silver*, has a past in motion picture experience which tells something of the business itself. For instance, after nine years on the speaking stage King Baggot transferred his big following of admirers to the pictures, and there can be no doubt that such men as he, through their own personal

popularity added much to the prosperity of the growing industry.

In those days, when the name of the player was not announced on the screen, King Baggot was known as "the Man with the White Streak," a conspicuous streak of gray over the temples [actually, the streak was in the front of his hair] always marking him through any disguise. Realizing the actors' need of getting together for mutual interests he founded the Screen Club and was its first president.

King Baggot has appeared in over 300 pictures, and during his career he has written, directed and starred in his own pictures. He has played everything from comedy to tragedy, from western to society parts, with such well known actors as Thomas H. Ince, George Loane Tucker and Mary and Jack Pickford.[4]

It did not take long to shoot this picture — it was released in mid–May. King was then hired back by Metro, but this time on the West Coast. His old director Henry Otto may have had something to do with this, for he was the director of this film, *The Cheater*, which was produced as a "Screen Classic." The star was the winsome May Allison, who had worked for Metro from about 1916. Her co-star and popular leading man for many years had been Harold Lockwood, one of the unfortunate stars who died during the influenza epidemic of 1918.[5] Lois Zellner wrote the screenplay based on the play *Judah* by Henry Arthur Jones, which was first produced in London in 1890. In the original production, Edward Smith Willard starred as Judah Llewellyn, but in the film, the female role was emphasized. It was well received by the reviewers. As an interesting sidelight, Rudolph Valentino had a small unbilled role as one of the gang members. More than one pointed out its similarity to *The Miracle Man,* released the year before by Mayflower for Paramount. That production was written and directed by George Loane Tucker and starred Thomas Meighan, Betty Compson and Lon Chaney

It is unfortunate that *The Cheater* cannot be viewed today because there are hints in the reviews about what may have been happening to King's acting style with regard to popular taste. One review mentioned that the supporting cast was very much subordinated to allow the star every opportunity. Of Baggot, *Moving Picture World* said, "King Baggot in the male lead gives a satisfactory and dignified portrayal. The picture registers a slight note of burlesque and graduates into a highly dramatic situation."[6] Another merely notes that "King Baggot is a gentleman to perfection." And in still another, "May Allison is fairly convincing as the heroine, but King Baggot gives his usual restrained performance." One senses quite a bit of sarcasm in those words. It is possible that at this time, critics and the public were growing weary of the old dramatic or melodramatic style and were looking for something less broad and a little lighter.

Almost immediately, King went to work on his next film, but this time his role was so small that no reviewer even mentioned him. The film was *Life's Twist*, produced by B.B. Features and released as a Robertson-Cole special feature in August 1920. The director was William Christie Cabanne with Bessie Barriscale in the leading role. King had never worked with them before, but there were several old friends working on this picture who may have seen to it that he had that small part. The scenario was written by Harvey Gates, based on a magazine story by Thomas Edgelow. Gates and King went back together as friends and associates to 1914 when Gates was a publicist for Universal. Gates was also a staunch member of the Screen Club. The cameraman was Eugene Gaudio, Tony Gaudio's brother. Tony Gaudio, as may be remembered, was IMP's long-time cameraman and had participated in IMP's Cuba trek in 1911.

King Baggot with May Allison in ***The Cheater***, Metro Pictures, 1920, directed by Henry Otto. Collection of the author.

Bessie Barriscale was both a stage actress and a very experienced film performer. She was with the old Domino and Broncho companies back in 1913. In 1914, she worked for Thomas Ince and starred for Jesse L. Lasky in *Rose of the Rancho*, which Cecil B. DeMille directed. Eugene Gaudio was complimented for his fine camerawork; reviews also noted that not much was done with the double exposures that were used for the two roles played by Bessie Barriscale, but that by now they were "no longer a novelty." The film was released in early August 1920, but by then King was already at work on his next film.

At least in this film he had a leading role even if his leading lady, Claire Adams, was billed first. Considering that it was titled *The Dwelling Place of Light*, it had some rather grim themes including insanity, a big strike, sexual harassment, prostitution and a gun battle between strikers and the police. Benjamin B. Hampton's company produced it. The director, Jack Conway, was well regarded and had a long career as an actor, as least as far back as 1909 and 1910 with Kalem and Nestor before joining the directorial ranks. Although he was slated to direct a number of pictures for Metro's Screen Classics in 1919, it appears that he completed only one, and so it was that in 1920 he was working for Hampton.[7] It took seven reels to tell the story, but it had such a dark and melodramatic plot it is no wonder that a reviewer for *Harrison's Reports* sniffed:

> …the story is too worn out to appeal to the better class of picture-goes. Besides, it is too suggestive, the heroine's sister being depicted as having become a prostitute,

though in the end she is brought home by the hero. It may prove acceptable for second rate theatres and down the line.[8]

King was working steadily now. The quality of his next film was a bit better, thanks to Allan Dwan's good direction. This one was called *The Forbidden Thing*. Dwan produced it for Associated Producers. Dwan had been directing for many years, beginning with American Film Manufacturing Company at least as early as 1911. He worked for Triangle in 1916, for Selznick with Norma Talmadge in 1917 and 1918, and that same year he directed Douglas Fairbanks for Artcraft. He had been a good friend of Mary Pickford and Owen Moore when in 1915, he and his then-wife, Pauline Bush, renewed their marriage vows together with Pickford and Moore at Mission San Juan Capistrano.[9]

The leading man in this film was James Kirkwood. Here was another old friend of King's who, it may be remembered, became president of the Screen Club in 1914— immediately after King's two terms. They knew each other even before that. Kirkwood began his film career as an actor with Biograph in 1909, the same year King began working for IMP; Kirkwood directed him in *The Parson and the Moonshiner* for IMP in 1912. By this time he had worked for an astonishing number of companies, transitioning back and forth between being an actor and director, sometimes as both in the same film. It should also be noted that he was born in 1883; he was four years younger than King. Admittedly, he was the star of this picture. His leading lady, Helen Jerome Eddy, while a well-known name by now, had played far more supporting roles than leads until this film.

The title, *The Forbidden Thing*, referred to suicide. It came from a short story by Mary Mears, which appeared in *Metropolitan Magazine* earlier that year. King played a minor role—that of a fisherman who conveniently drowns in order to bring the two stars back together in the end. The reviewers loved it. They praised the locales, which used the spectacular rugged coastline near Oxnard and Port Hueneme, California. They thought Kirkwood was excellent—that the photography by Tony Gaudio was spectacular—and that Dwan's directorial ability made the film superb. *Motion Picture News* was especially enthusiastic:

> One feels inclined to place a gold seal opposite Allan Dwan's name in his first production for Associated Producers.... He has constructed the feature in narrative form and has placed remarkable emphasis upon its rugged simplicity. The tale is peopled with figures who are actually lifelike—whose joys and sorrows are touched upon with genuine feeling. It is dramatic to the core—but not the drama of the theatre, but of life ... [Kirkwood] has needed no recourse to melodramatic incident ... its human flavor stamps him as one of the most vital figures on the screen.[10]

Those words, "life-like," "genuine feeling" and "no recourse to melodramatic incident," all suggest that a new kind of realism was beginning to filter into film acting style, with the approval of filmgoers and reviewers. King was a practitioner of a more "natural" style early in his career. He had made fun of the gesturing and jumping up and down that he had seen when he first visited IMP in 1909. But it would seem that his acting was still tinged with the accepted melodramatic tendencies of former times, and that not only was his age catching up with him, but it appears film acting was gradually pulling away from the kind of heightened dramatic intensity that audiences had formerly loved. By now he may have been incapable of further artistic growth as an actor even if he perceived there was a need to do so. The 1920s spelled many changes in the country's moral habits and social

Helen Jerome Eddy receives some bad news but soon marries Baggot, the simple fisherman, in Allan Dwan's first film for Associated Producers, *The Forbidden Thing*, 1920. Collection of the author.

attitudes, which would continue throughout the decade. Change was inevitable.

He had one more acting job that year. In December 1920, Carter De Haven cast him to play his wife's father in a light comedy called *The Girl in the Taxi*. King had just turned 41. It was produced by De Haven for First National and starred Mr. and Mrs. De Haven. The De Havens had been working for Universal, and then First National for some time. De Haven had done a bit of scenario writing for them in 1919 and now he and his wife, Flora Parker De Haven, signed on to produce a series of "high class comedies."[11] It is not certain why the De Havens hired King, but there may have been an Irish connection. Carter De Haven was born Francis O'Callaghan. Ten years earlier *The Girl in the Taxi* was a play written by Stanislaus Strange and produced on Broadway as a farce. Filming took place at Charlie Chaplin's studio— rented by the De Havens for this production. The reviews were tepid and barely mentioned King's role.

24

Crossroads

King had now, for all intents and purposes, reached another dead end. With each film in the past year, the downward spiral continued. Even his work as an actor was now under criticism. He was not the industry's darling any more. A whole new crop of younger leading men had taken his place as the heroes and idols of the screen. It must have been a very discouraging time for him to be so far from his real home—New York—and to be in the midst of people who considered him an "old timer," or even a has-been. If there was even any doubt about his present status, it was keenly brought home to him in an article that appeared in *Picture-Play Magazine* in January 1921, written by Herbert Howe and titled "Who Will Be Who in 1921?"[1]

Howe forecasted what the coming year would bring in a long and serious discussion of the past year in the industry and where it might be going. In a box editorial on the first page, it was claimed that Howe's piece was: "brilliantly written, and backed by a thorough knowledge of the film industry, it is recognized as an annual guide-post, not only by PICTURE-PLAY'S large following among the fans, but also by the men and women of the industry, who regard Mr. Howe as an authority on matters pertaining to the screen."[2]

It was a cogent article in which he pointed out many of the film industry's foibles and propensities that could stand some correction, and he predicted some new trends. The article made much of the "ten bests" for the coming year, just as is still done today. His top ten in the leading men's line-up included Charlie Chaplin at number one, and in descending order; Richard Barthelmess, Charles Ray, Wallace Reid, Harold Lloyd, Douglas Fairbanks, Antonio Moreno, John Barrymore, Thomas Meighan and Will Rogers. His discussion of "stardom" brought up an interesting point about salaries in the early 1920s:

> It is a demonstrable fact that many a player makes more as a leading man than he does as a star.... A player is recognized by the public for his merits. The word "star" means nothing. Yet actors and constables do cherish it. Richard Barthelmess, unstarred, was esteemed quite as highly as any of the bestarred gentlemen. The only reason he is being featured now is that he exerts such a potent attraction that the exhibitor would be a numskull not to realize on his name.
>
> Those actors who have passed already from stellar eminence into starless

roles with higher salaries are Marc MacDermott, King Baggot, Maurice Costello, Montagu Love, Edward Earle, Carlyle Blackwell, Roy Stewart and Irving Cummings. I dare say all of these gentlemen are earning much more now than they ever did before.[3]

One wonders if this statement was really true. However, if King was making more money now but enjoying it less, it would not be about money, but about creative freedom. At this point in his career, he had none. After burning his bridges with Universal, he tried to stay in control of his own work. He had purchased *Absinthe*, created an up-to-date ending and toured with it, but that was only one film. He probably did not have the capital to set up as a producer on his own. His venture back into the theater was close to a disaster, and after only a few more films in New York he was forced to come to California because the entire base of film production had shifted there.

He soldiered on, now working in what would be almost his last film as a major actor. It was in January that he was hired "to head an all-star cast" in a picture originally titled *The Soul of the Butterfly*, but retitled *The Butterfly Girl* before its release in June. The director and writer, John Gorman, produced it for Playgoers Pictures. Hollywood in the early 1920s became fascinated by the symbolism of butterflies. They flitted through the titles of quite a number of films of that period and were associated with the images of the young women who were the "flappers" of the Roaring Twenties. Marjorie Daw was the "butterfly" in this film — a flirty young thing whose highest ambition was to have a score of admirers at her feet. King plays the part of a banker — an older married man who becomes captivated by her youth and beauty — which almost destroys his marriage. *Variety*'s review by Leed was rather pointed in its criticism:

> The acting is fair enough. Miss Daw is pretty, extravagantly well dressed and Fritzi Brunette comes through with her usual solid performance. The two juveniles, du Briac and Raymond, [Daw's two boyfriends, Jean du Briac and Ned Whitney Raymond] unfortunately have something about them continually suggestive of the Gold Dust twins. King Baggot, now a stout middle aged man, was fair enough as the banker, while Lisle Darnell gave a dignified, reassuring interpretation of the banker's wife.... There is too much kissing, however, in this picture. Edith is forever kissing her boyfriends, too general a habit since the war...[4]

This kind of picture could have been the beginning of the end of King, struggling from film to film and company to company — still a recognizable name — but in smaller and smaller parts until he faded from view altogether. That was the fate of many of his contemporaries. In his heart he already knew that could happen to him. In an interview back in 1914 he had said:

> One of the greatest fears that a person in my profession has, it that of old age. The motion picture camera is heartless. It allows no deception. If a man is fifty, he looks fifty — perhaps a little older, for the highlights and shadows accentuate the wrinkles in his face. The observant eye of the lens is harder on the leading man than on the comedian, for the comedian always looks happy and happiness gives the appearance of youth. The hero must portray seriousness or pathos, and naturally, is made to look older. To the hero of the movies, there is an element of tragedy in the public's insistant demand for a youthful idol. Age dims the glamour, which has been built up around him. When the lines begin to appear in his face and when his breath comes a little harder, he is cast aside. A new hero, a younger man, supplants him on the pedestal.[5]

Surely he did not want to end his career in this way and luckily, he did not have to. He had one more option open to him and he took it. He became a director.

The modest initial announcement appeared in *Variety* on February 11. "The Universal has engaged King Baggot as a director. Mr. Baggot's first will be the handling of Edith Roberts."[6] Early in March, several equally brief statements elaborated on the news that he signed with Universal to direct three special features, that he would direct Carmel Myers in *Thou Art with Me* and that, as of June, Universal had under contract King Baggot, Fred LeRoy Granville, Jack Conway, Reaves Eason, Jack (John) Ford, William Worthington and Robert Thornby to direct special features.

Just exactly how King was able to come back to Universal in this new capacity is not certain. "Boy Wonder" Irving Thalberg was then in charge of production, but could scarcely have known King except by his reputation. Thalberg became Carl Laemmle's personal secretary in 1918, two years after King left Universal. As a studio head in 1919, he still would not have any personal in-depth knowledge of his potential. It is possible that Carl Laemmle himself chose King. He, better than anyone, would have known his abilities, and Laemmle had a long-standing reputation for taking care of not only his relatives, but others who had worked for him in the past whom he considered deserving. He was known for paying their old debts and finding employment for many who needed a job. Laemmle was a kind and charitable man and he was not likely to forget King's unswerving loyalty to him from his earliest days. However, the record is silent in this regard.

There is no doubt that King had credentials as a director. Although many titles were never credited, he was directing himself in films as early as the end of 1911 when he produced the first of his *King, the Detective* series. His peers in the industry also acknowledged him for his directorial skills.

In 1914, he was asked by the *New York Dramatic Mirror* to write a first person article about his duties as a film director. Titled "The Director's Work," it described him as "King Baggot, IMP author, director and leading man, founder of the Screen Club." Above and below the piece were photographs of other well known directors of their day. In addition to King, there were photos of Lloyd Carlton of Lubin, James Kirkwood of Famous Players and C. Jay Williams of Edison; surprisingly, lumped in with the others was D.W. Griffith, then with the Mutual Company. Of course, today, only Griffith's name is well-known.[7] However, no matter how many films King directed, these were only one- and two-reel efforts. As his credits show, he directed just two three-reelers: *Jim Webb, Senator* (1914) and *The Chance Market* (1916). He had no credits directing feature-length films. But now he would have a chance to show what he could do and he did quite well.

Universal's 1921 output of feature films was considerable. During that year they produced approximately 55 features. Other directors with whom he would be working that year were Stuart Paton, Rollin Sturgeon, Norman Dawn, and Tod Browning.[8] Two other names from out of King's past flag the attention — Paul Scardon and Dallas Fitzgerald — both with a Screen Club connection. Scardon was King's choice to succeed him as president in the 1915 election, and Fitzgerald was one of the men who testified against him that year for the "bar fly" epithet. It was hoped that six years later, all that would be water under the bridge. For now, with his acting roles in *The Girl in the Taxi* and *The Butterfly Girl* behind him, he was ready to direct his first feature film.

His initial assignment was *Cheated Love*, a remake of *The Heart of a Jewess*. (It was first produced by Universal's Victor Company in 1913; Lois Weber and Phillips Smalley co-directed and starred in it.) The new version was written by noted author and scenario writer, Lucien Hubbard and Doris Schroeder, another very experienced and talented scenarist. Carmel Myers, the daughter of a rabbi in real life, and by now an established star for Universal, played the Jewess.

An exploitation catch line read, "One man wanted her but loved his career. The other man loved her and wanted nothing else. Which did she choose?" Set in New York's Jewish ghetto, it featured Myers playing a young and beautiful immigrant. David, a settlement worker, loves her, but her heart is set on Mischa, a medical student whom she knew from Odessa. She gives him her meager savings to help establish his career, but he spurns her for a wealthy woman. She is working in the local Yiddish theater, but is refused an important role in a special performance because another woman is jealous of her beauty. While she is in her dressing room in tears, a boiler in the theater bursts and starts a fire. The audience is in a panic, but she goes on stage and quiets them. She becomes an heroic figure in the community and learns to love David.

This film no longer exists, which is the case with most of the films King Baggot made for Universal during this period. That is unfortunate because his work can scarcely be properly judged, except through the reviews—and they were excellent for this film. One exclaimed:

> Everything belongs to the credit side of this lifelike picture which gives Carmel Myers a chance to display her refreshing personality and talent to their best. In fact it is the best offering in which she has ever appeared and in all likelihood will meet with a very enthusiastic reception everywhere. King Baggot has turned director here and shows he knows how to construct a picture and make it palpitate with life. He has been at the game long enough to know what he is about and his experience has given him a ripe knowledge in knowing how to build moving scenes and balance them with genuine humanities...
> Not a touch is out of place, the director catching every incident and visualizing every characteristic of the race.... The punch scene is a panic in the theatre when the boiler explodes with the heroine calming the audience by giving an impromptu performance.... The picture is easy to anticipate, but is charged with such realistic touches and intimate detail and is so exceptionally played that its entertainment value is immense.[9]

Fritz Tidden of the *Moving Picture World* was no less enthusiastic:

> There are two distinct things, besides the customary appeal and talent of the star, Carmel Myers, that make *Cheated Love* the entertaining picture that it is. The first is the general excellent direction, and the other is the careful selection of the types to interpret the story.... The director who performed such an excellent task is none other than the well-known player, King Baggot, who supervises the making of a feature for Universal for the first time. All through the picture are instances of expert work, and his direction of the panic scenes in the East Side theatre is especially proficient. Both he and the scenarists build up in the drama the mildly melodramatic but always appealing and interesting story contents.[10]

With his next assignment, he was not so lucky. The vehicle was *Luring Lips*, based on a John Moroso story called "The Gossamer Web." The leading lady was Edith Roberts, who, by all accounts was a perfectly capable actress, having recently been signed as a star for Universal. But the problem was the plot. It was not a very strong one, and the two supporting leads—Darrel Foss and Ramsey Wallace—were not able to do much with their roles. "Sime"'s *Variety* review summed it up dismissively:

> About the one novelty bit in the film is the reproduction of a picture show in

prison [it was a newsreel], wherein the husband sees his wife meet the banker at Trinity churchyard, New York. That entails mental stress through jealousy and is the only imaginative point of the picture. In its scope, the entire direction may be mildly commended. Otherwise, excepting for a little twist to the story here and there, the thing has been done threadbare in pictures. There is nothing attractive about it or the playing.[11]

His next picture had a bit more going for it. Irving Thalberg decided to make the former Mack Sennett bathing beauty Marie Prevost into a star. After hiring her away from Sennett, he saw to it that she got a great deal of publicity from the very start. He began by taking her to the company's summer meeting in Chicago to introduce her. There, he announced that he had already personally selected two vehicles in which she would play as leading lady: *The Butterfly*, later retitled *Moonlight Follies*, based on a story by Percival Wilde, and *Kissed*, a novel by Arthur Somers Roche. Thalberg then sent her to New York's Coney Island where she publicly burned her bathing suit before enthusiastic crowds.[12] King was assigned to direct her first feature.

Filming for *Moonlight Follies* began in mid to late June. With no aspirations to being a "great film," the plot traded heavily on the public's newfound appreciation for those vivacious young things who had become icons of the Roaring Twenties.

In order to garner more publicity for Marie, it was solemnly reported that while shooting on location at a pool on the Cofin estate in Pasadena in mid–July, she saved Baggot and assistant director Nat Ross from drowning:

> Working under terrific sun, Ross, although a splendid swimmer was overheated when he dove into the cool pool. The shock doubled him up and he went down. King Baggot, also a powerful swimmer, jumped in after him. He slipped on the wet concrete, struck his head and went out. [Miss Prevost] dragged Ross out and King Baggot revived himself and got out.[13]

As can be seen from this report, that although Marie had burned her bathing suit at Coney Island, the public could be assured that she would be wearing one in this film.

Two more publicity events occurred in September when the film was released. The first was a segment of King directing a bathing girl scene with Marie for Screen Snapshots—a newsreel-like series which featured the doings of celebrities. They were shown in theaters as a sort of "filler." These "Snapshots" were produced by Pathé and released through the Federated Exchanges. The second was the now-familiar personal appearance event at theaters. *Moonlight Follies* had its West Coast opening at Tally's Theatre in downtown Los Angeles. The event lasted for the entire week of its run at Tally's, both at the 7:30 and 9:30 showings. It took the form of a prologue in which some of the scenes from the film were re-enacted. On stage, King directed Miss Prevost and another actor from the picture, George Fisher, who played one of her suitors, Rene Smythe. Michael Boylan, who also wrote the subtitles for the film, wrote the dialogue.[14]

After opening night, Grace Kingsley, writing for the *Los Angeles Times*, penned a clever piece, lightly tinged with sarcasm, but with some apparent praise as well titled "Marie in Clothes," it read in part...

> I think Marie Prevost ... is going to be a great screen favorite—even clothed and away from her professional bathing suit. She appears in the flesh and blood, too, every evening at 7:30 assisted by King Baggot and George Fisher.
>
> Entirely disguised by clothes, except when she takes a bath in a regular

Mary Prevost in her first starring role for Universal with her new director, King Baggot, in *Moonlight Follies*, 1921. Collection of the author.

bathtub and later when she appears at a swimming pool party. Miss Prevost proves herself possessed of an expressive face and a vivid and arresting screen personality. In addition to which, she shows evidence of developing into a brilliant screen comedienne.... [She] adopts the most obvious methods of bringing her lover to her feet including the wearing of a wicked bathing suit, announcing "A dimple in the knee is worth two in the chin."[15]

The unsigned *New York Times* review was a lot less kind to her. It questioned Universal's ability to make an actress out of a former bathing beauty, but admitted it was not the first time this had been attempted. Calling the film a "trifle," it questioned the need for it being made in five reels when two would have done as well. With regard to King, it was humorously noted that "King Baggot directed the production and deserves credit for his success in filling up all of the film allotted to him. He left no blank spaces. Every scene is at least a picture of something."[16]

Apparently neither Thalberg nor the studio was daunted by such lofty criticism. Prevost's first feature was a popular success and they immediately gave King her next feature to direct. This one was *Nobody's Fool*, from a story by Roy Clements with a scenario by Doris Schroeder. Harry Myers, an actor-comedian whose career stretched back to the early teens, was her leading man. As stories go, it was admittedly a bit of "fluff." *Motion Picture News* called it a light but satisfying comedy-romance, commenting that there was no substance to the story; however, "*Nobody's Fool* serves its purpose — which is to present Miss Prevost in the best possible light. She knows her own limitations as an actress. And it is to the credit of Universal that this company is not putting her in stories which might tax her ability."[17]

So it was that King came back to Universal and that some of his career pressure had been alleviated, at least for the time being.

25

Settling Down in Hollywood

When King first moved his family to California, they lived in hotels—the Hollywood Hotel, then the Christie Hotel, which was just down the street on Hollywood Boulevard at McCadden Place. Hotels had been a way of life for him from his earliest days in New York, but he had an idiosyncrasy that is hard to explain—he moved like a vagabond almost every single year. In New York, between 1911 and 1918, he can be traced from hotel to apartment to hotel with bewildering regularity. His first known address was 16 West 104th Street in 1911. He was living at 155 West 47th Street in the King Edward Hotel when he was courting Ruth. The couple moved briefly to an apartment at 113th Street, then to The Shelbourne in Brighton Beach, New York. Next, it was back to an apartment on 112th Street, followed by a move to the Hendrick Hudson Apartments on Cathedral Parkway and Riverside Drive, and finally to the Bretton Hall Hotel located between 85th and 86th Streets on Broadway. That constitutes eight known moves in less than ten years. This continual moving about would be part of an interesting but inexplicable pattern for most of the rest of his life.[1]

Now, in 1922, he abandoned the hotel life and moved into a residence at 6905 Franklin, just north of Hollywood Boulevard. It was a house then, but today it is part of the parking lot for a magician's club called the Magic Castle. The few houses that still remain in the neighborhood are not mansions, but they are stately, and exude a feeling of quiet gentility left over from a by-gone era. No real estate records can be found that show he purchased it, so it must be assumed that the Baggots were renters. Universal Studios were not far away—just a few miles up the Cahuenga Pass. It was an easy commute.

In less than a year, he had become securely established as a Universal director. *Universal Weekly* throughout this time published numerous mentions of how his work was progressing and gave little snippets about his former life and career. Late in 1921, a long and very flattering article about him appeared in *Motion Picture Supplement*, written by Hazel Simpson Naylor. She interviewed him at Universal, and from the tenor of what she wrote, one could tell than she was totally charmed by him It also shed some light on his physical appearance and his mental outlook at this time—even if the piece was studio-inspired.

Naylor constructed her article around the idea that King was a jovial Irishman. She titled it "Cabbages and Kings," no doubt from a phrase in Louis Carroll's poem "The Walrus and the Carpenter" in *Alice Through the Looking Glass*—"cabbages" for that Irish dietary staple and "kings" for Baggot himself. She begins with the start of a lyric from an old Irish song:

> My mother and father were Irish, and I am Irish too—Somehow the old couplet kept running thru my mind as I heard King Baggot's voice echo and re-echo thru the corridors of the Universal studio.

Then she brought him on stage:

> "Sure an' if-you're a going to cast that man as the hero—I'll don the greasepaint and play it myself. Man alive, he's older than I am!" The door was flung open and in burst King Baggot, his brilliant blue eyes blazing, his tan silk shirt-sleeves rolled up in a business-like manner, exposing two brawny arms, which seemed to me ample reason for his winning any argument. He was followed by the casting director of the studio who was laughing heartily, and said: "Satisfies me, King—go ahead and play the lead and direct. You might as well be drawing down two salaries, as some other people I know." "No, no, go 'way with you, but if I'm going to direct this picture I want a *young* hero."
>
> We all laughed—then the nice publicity manager at Universal introduced me, and all tip-toed from the office, leaving Mr. Baggot and me alone. He drew himself up to a seat at the table, folded his arms and looked at me very much as I imagine the victims of the Inquisition would have looked.
>
> I giggled.
>
> The stalwart cinemite stared, then he too, smiled and said: "I'll bet you're Irish." Much as I wished I could lay claim to that kinship with him, truth compelled me to shake my head "no." "Well, at any rate, you have the true Irish sense of humor,'" he said.

This was followed by a mildly exaggerated but brief description of how he became an actor and the role that he, Universal and Carl Laemmle played in the early days of motion pictures. She then explored, in a kindly way, how he had transitioned from actor to director:

> Mr. Baggot is now exactly thirty-nine years [of age]. [Actually, he was a month short of his 42nd birthday]. He has turned to directing pictures instead of acting in them—not because he has grown a bit portly, but because he has been cast in so many poor parts. Whenever a director had a weak part in his scenario, it seemed as if he called on Baggot, and said, "Here, King, this role is the one weak part in the story, you'll have to take it and make something of it. You're the only person who can." And even tho he did his best, no man can make tremendous successes of weak parts. So he turned to directing, but every now and then he chomps at the bit and aches to get back into the greasepaint—so there is hope that he will not always be behind the camera.

The interview also touched briefly on his wife and son:

> He is married to a Boston girl, and they have a son nine years old. [King Robert was really eight at this time.] It surprises him to find that the boy, unlike most children, has no desire to act in films. "He often watches me act or direct," confided the father, "but he has never even asked me to turn the camera on him." "Will you wish him to become an actor when he grows up?" I asked. "Whatever he wants to be will suit me. I can still remember being forced into the [real estate] broker's office. My son shall choose his own career. He probably won't go into pictures—not if his mother can help it. She thinks one actor in the family is enough."

She concluded the article by saying:

> He is very much a man's man, this matinee-idol who has turned director—too big a man to be concerned with feminine

foibles, but possessed of a deep respect and wholesome courtesy for those of the weaker sex. King Baggot is still handsome, if in a somewhat more heavy and mature way, but as he said; "It doesn't matter how we look but how we feel — does it?" And he stretched himself to his full height. "And I — why, I feel like a million dollars!"[2]

In the early 1920s Universal had slipped quite a bit in terms of box office numbers, big stars and general creativity in its films. Consider that Paramount had both Rudolph Valentino and Gloria Swanson, and produced films like *The Sheik* and *The Affairs of Anatol* in 1921. In 1922 there were big features such as *A Doll's House* with Alla Nazimova for United Artists, and producer Robert J. Flaherty's *Nanook of the North* from Pathé, with its fresh documentary style. On the Universal lot, the stars shined a little less brightly. Gladys Walton, Carmel Myers, Edith Roberts, Frank Mayo, Herbert Rawlinson and Harry Carey were, in their day, all well-known names, but hardly the stuff of legend. Even the name Hoot Gibson, still recognized today for his work in Westerns, was in no way a superstar, except to Western fans. No doubt they were trying, but their lineup of romantic comedies, Westerns and melodramas did not inspire the kind of audience appreciation that they enjoyed just a few years before. There was one exception — Erich von Stroheim. His first film for Universal in 1919 was *Blind Husbands*, followed in 1920 by *The Devil's Pass Key*, which was marketed as a "Universal Jewel" for its lavish scope and financial cost to the studio. These were box office successes, and at that time Universal was willing to put up with his Prussian excesses. Whatever his faults — and they were large and plentiful — he knew how to tell a dramatic story in purely visual terms. He was also a legendary perfectionist, whose proclivities in that direction would eventually get him into trouble.[3]

Early in 1922, King started work on *Human Hearts*. It was definitely time for King to do a more serious kind of film after directing all those butterflies, follies and the kissing. Most likely he proposed this project himself, and it was a credit to Universal's good sense that they backed him. This was the third time King made *Human Hearts* for Universal. In the 1912 and 1914 productions he played the hero, Tom Logan. This time he would direct it. It would be what the trade called "a big picture," and it was produced as a Universal Jewel — the first time he had been given that kind of latitude in terms of budget and time. At almost seven reels, it was also the longest he had ever directed to date. Lucien Hubbard and Marc Robbins wrote the screenplay. Ruggedly handsome House Peters, whose star was rising, was signed to play Tom Logan. Another good choice in the cast was Gertrude Claire as the blind but indomitable Ma Logan. George Hackathorne was the pitiful half-witted brother Jimmy, who got that way when a grandstand collapsed on him. Edith Hallor, formerly known as Edith Halleran before 1914, played the thankless role of the wicked city girl. Mary Philbin was the faithful sweetheart Ruth, while Snitz Edwards played hayseed Ran Schreiber for comic relief.

It takes some understanding for the modern viewer of this film to appreciate its values. It can be seen today on video, but it is easy to miss what an important film it was for its time, even in the 1920s. Unabashedly a melodrama, it depicts the harsh realities of rural life to which many filmgoers could still relate. Hal Reid first produced *Human Hearts* as a stage play in the early years of the twentieth century. It was not just a run-of-the-mill melodrama, but a classic, and it endured as both a play and a film from as early as Selig's production in 1910. This was material King knew very well and by all accounts he did an excellent job with it. "Sime's" *Variety* review was especially complimentary:

> A sob bucolic, with a rugged father, a blind mother, an idiotic son, an unfortunate marriage, a couple of murders and a jail. And yet withal a laugh here and there, a tear more often and a tenseness all of the while. If those ingredients make a picture, then *Human Hearts* is. On the screen it spreads out, not so much in territory as in scope. This U runs about 80 minutes. It starts out wobbly, but races along pretty soon, and towards the finish it's traveling right to the heart strings.
>
> It isn't the story so much. Parts and all of it have been told in as many different ways on the screen. It's rather the blending or adaptation or scenarizing and direction that could cram the comedy with the pathos and hold an audience for 80 minutes straight-away, which audiences filled the Central to capacity downstairs Tuesday evening.
>
> That speaks rather well for Broadway and Forty-seventh Street, a section blasé and tough on pictures, and in Times Square, where sentiment centers on bankroll more than on unfortunates, for the section has enough unfortunates of its own, of every kind. *Human Hearts* will catch the human hearts, and for the inhuman at least it will show that there is still peace to be had in the country if you can keep your family away from the breaks.
>
> As a feature it is a good U production, well if fervently played at times, and it is absorbing, for all of us, no matter how tough we think we are, still have a heart while we can stand up. But *Human Hearts*, away from Times Square will still be a bigger picture, an educational in its way, telling country yokels to stick to their own.... But play *Human Hearts* because it takes in so much; it is clean and it is quite apt to do business in all communities, for there is a mother, and who can resist a mother, and who is so tough that a blind mother won't make him wilt.[4]

This was a visually interesting film apart from its dramatic impact. Location shooting was done around rural areas of California's Owens Valley, and some good use of soft focus shots gave the look of the film an extra dimension. Although completed about March 25, 1922, it was not released until August in order for the studio to mount a suitably large publicity campaign. Upon its release, *Universal Weekly* quoted Carl Laemmle as saying that "after this picture is shown, King Baggot will be known as one of the truly great directors."[5]

While waiting for the release of *Human Hearts*, King was given another Marie Prevost vehicle to direct. It was titled *Kissed*— one of the films Thalberg had announced for her the previous year. Needless to say, it was a lightweight romantic comedy featuring those "flappers." Once again, Doris Schroeder wrote the screenplay, based on a 1918 story from *Ainslee's Magazine* by Arthur Somers Roche. Lloyd Whitlock and J. Frank Glendon — her inevitable suitors — supported Prevost, and Lillian Langdon, who had played a meddlesome fortuneteller in *The Thirtieth Piece of Silver*, played her mother.

It was an entertaining little story, but some reviewers observed that King had to stretch to put it into the usual five-reel format. Only the last reel remains of this film. It is owned by the Museum of Modern Art in New York from a copy provided by the Nederlands Filmmuseum in Amsterdam. A clever touch employs a bit of film animation: In the last reel, when Marie is kissed, an animated thermometer registers its warmth. It is apparent from this that filmmakers were still ignoring those critical quibbles that there was presently too much kissing in films.

Now that the studio was solidly behind him, he was in a much better position to call his own shots. The studio briefly discussed doing a remake of *Ivanhoe* around the middle of June. This would have been another chance to cash in on box office draw from a film that he made for Universal in

Poignant scene from *Human Hearts* directed by Baggot for Universal, 1922. L-r, unknown black actors, Mary Philbin, Russell Simpson, unknown actor, Gertrude Claire, and George Hackathorne. Photograph courtesy of the Frances Howard Goldwyn Hollywood Regional Library, Special Collections.

1913, and which had contributed to his great fame as an actor. The studio went so far as to plan the construction of sets along Lankershim Boulevard, but that project was scrapped in favor of a more modern, but probably no less costly production of a different kind of action film — *The Kentucky Derby*.[6]

From all accounts, a lot of planning and hard work went into it, but *The Kentucky Derby* must have been an enjoyable picture to produce. King probably had a hand in selecting it for, at this time, it seemed to be a pattern for him to repeat some of his earlier films. This was a remake of *The Suburban* in which he starred in 1915. The new production was in six reels, allowing more time to develop the plot. And this time, instead of being shot at the Belmont Track in New York, it was filmed at the Churchill Downs track in Kentucky during the running of the country's most famous race. Reginald Denny, whose career with Universal was in high gear just then, played the hero, Donald Gordon.

The cast and crew spent three weeks in the Louisville-Lexington, Kentucky, area in May. They received the usual lionizing treatment from the Bluegrass sporting gentlemen of those cities and from the press. The company had a special train car to travel in, and Carl Laemmle was there to watch the proceedings. King and some of the players, including Denny, made personal appearances at Lexington's Strand Theatre, where Universal's boxing series *The Leather-Pushers*, which starred Denny, was playing. During their visit, the Mayor of Louisville met King and some of the cast for a photo session. Naturally, King filmed the actual race, which ran on May 13 that year. It was attended by 40,000 fans who watched "Morvich, the Wonder Colt" win.[7] The press rumored that King and Reginald Denny wagered and "cleaned up" on Morvich.[8] When the company returned in June, more hard work ensued—for in addition to the trip to Kentucky, filming was done in 22 separate locations in California before the film was completed.[9] While the reviews were most favorable when it was released in October, the consensus was that it was a well-done film which would do good business at the popular priced houses as a special feature, but should not be considered as one of the best pictures of the year.

King was developing a reputation for making Universal's young female stars "look good." He had performed this service for Carmel Myers, although she was not considered a "starlet," but a very good actress. He had done the same for Marie Prevost three times now, and so it was that he was assigned to direct Gladys Walton in both *The Lavender Bath Lady* and *A Dangerous Game*. *The Lavender Bath Lady* was certainly no "Jewel," but a lightweight romantic comedy. At this time, Walton was working very hard for the studio. She made eight films in 1921—but with titles like *All Dolled Up, High Heels* and *Short Skirts*, there was some indication that she was more object than actress. In 1922, she made another eight, but it was apparent that the studio considered her window dressing—and her role in *The Lavender Bath Lady* was, indeed, that of a window dresser. It was not a very good story and the reviewers said so. None of them could understand the significance of the title, except that she referred to lavender bath salts several times in the film.

A Dangerous Game was no better, although King had a chance to team up with his former publicist Hugh Hoffman, who was now working as a scenario writer for Universal. The title was taken from a story by Louise Dodge—"Gret'n Ann"—published in *Ladies' Home Journal*. King found a good part in it for his old friend William R. Daly and cast the lovable comedienne Kate Price to liven things up. However, there was not much to be done with either Walton or the picture. *Variety*'s reviewer "Rush" was brutally frank:

> Designed as a simple pastoral romance of a childhood, the picture develops into a bare-faced theft of footage. There isn't enough material in the five reels to make a reasonable two-reeler. In fact, there isn't material enough in the story to make a picture of any kind.... In a frenzied effort to stretch it out into the regulation length they project close-up after close-up of the star in which she does nothing but register concentrated thought and does it for minutes at a time...[10]

Work began in December on another Gladys Walton feature—Hoffman again wrote the scenario. Titled *The Love Letter*, it was not ready for release until early February 1923. But as 1922 came to an end, King could count a few blessings. After all, he had the opportunity to direct two Universal Jewels and had done so admirably. He had been assigned to help shape the careers of a number of young actresses—with mixed results—although his experiences did not differ greatly from those of his fellow directors on the lot just then. The sad fact was, at that moment in time, Universal, with the exception of *Foolish Wives*, produced by von Stroheim that year, was not a first-rate studio in terms of resources or creative imagination.

26

Ups and Downs

Perhaps it was studio politics, or maybe the wishes of the star, but for whatever reason, King was directing Gladys Walton over and over again. Having finished *The Love Letter*, he was given *Gossip* as soon as the year began. *The Lavender Bath Lady*, *The Dangerous Game* and now *Gossip* were inexpensive little pictures to produce, based mainly on magazine stories and, with a few exceptions, non-stellar supporting players. As the reviewers all said, they were "old hoke" with no "punch," fit only for exhibitors who needed to have something to fill in on a double-feature day. One would think that all involved would finally give up and try for better projects, but they did not. Irving Thalberg left the studio in February to become Vice President of Production for Louis B. Mayer, and the one bright note remaining for Universal was *The Hunchback of Notre Dame*, which Thalberg had in the works before he left.[1] It would be many months before King would have the chance to direct another "big picture."

No sooner was *Gossip* completed than the team of Baggot, Hoffman and Walton began *The Town Scandal*. This one had a slightly better plot, although a highlight in the story has Walton, as New York chorus girl, doing a "cute little shimmy." Reviews were generally favorable, terming it "a corking little comedy drama" and "a worth while little program feature," but that pretty much pegged it for what it was.

Several small bursts of artistic fulfillment came to King after the completion of *The Town Scandal*. Working with Hugh Hoffman, he was able to write the story for Walton's next feature *Crossed Wires*, with some additional support from Raymond Schrock, who had worked off and on as a scenario writer for Universal since 1915. Schrock had been a member of the old Screen Club and knew King very well. *Crossed Wires* was a fairly lightweight comedy, but at least he had more of a hand in shaping it. He was also able to cast some other old friends whom he considered to be dependable actors Lillian Langdon (with whom he had worked successfully before), Kate Price and, once more, William R. Daly. Unfortunately, there was not much to it. The *New York Times* reviewer called it "a program picture with flashes above the average," and praised King for the staging of a dance contest and a free-for-all action scene in a hotel suite.

The second break from strictly directorial duties was a brief escape back into the theater. The run was for just a week, but the vehicle, The *Hold Up*, had interesting antecedents. The play was only in one act, but it packed some punch. William S. Hart had made a success of it in 1910. In his autobiography *My Life East and West*, Hart recalled his own 1910 experience with it:

> When we returned to New York [after completing a successful tour with *The Barrier*], Taylor Granville, an actor with whom I had worked some years before, came to me with a vaudeville act that he had tried out, *The Hold-Up*. It had been a failure. They would not book it. He had a carload of scenery and two excellent railroad effects. I rewrote the act and we tried it out in Brooklyn, with myself as the star. It was a hit. We went into the American Theatre for a run and it drew the first critics of the city to review it. We then went to Chicago for three weeks. The act was a big hit and very valuable. Granville quarreled with me. I parted with an interest in a fine piece of property for seventy-five dollars.[2]

Now, 13 years later, King played in it at Grauman's Million Dollar Theatre in downtown Los Angeles the week of April 9. By an interesting coincidence, Taylor Granville was, at this time, Grauman's production manager. Kingsley Benedict, a former actor and scenario writer, and William Dyer, another longtime Universal actor, appeared in the sketch with him. Sid Grauman himself did the staging. The play was a Western melodrama with a moving train and elaborate lighting effects—a tribute to Grauman's showmanship. Not surprisingly, there was a Universal connection. Also playing the same week in conjunction with *The Hold Up* was a Universal feature film, *The Midnight Guest* with Grace Darmond, Mahlon Hamilton, and Clyde Fillmore.[3]

Crossed Wires was released on May 14; by then, King was already at work on another film. It went through several working titles; first, *Wanted, a Home*, then *Whose Baby Are You?* and finally *The Darling of New York*. The star was Baby Peggy Montgomery—not yet five years old. The daughter of screen extra–stuntman Jack Montgomery, she started in films in 1920 at 20 months of age, co-starring with Brownie, the Wonder Dog in a series of two-reel slapstick comedies at Century Studios. When Brownie died a few months later, the studio starred her in close to a hundred of her own "Baby Peggy Comedies." Because Century was owned by the brothers Abe and Julius Stern, and because Julius was Carl Laemmle's brother-in-law, all of her comedies were released through Universal. In 1923, Universal recognized her star qualities and, to compete with the popularity of child star Jackie Coogan, Laemmle personally brought her over to Universal to star in feature films, beginning with this one. Baby Peggy has often been called "the Shirley Temple of her day," but that is a most unfair comparison. *The Darling of New York* no longer exists, but there are other vehicles that do, and to see her films like *Captain January* or *The Family Secret*, it is evident that she was more than an adorable moppet—she was an accomplished actress whose presence on the screen could be positively mesmerizing. During those years, Jackie Coogan was considered her only rival.

Universal gave King and the little star good opportunity to make a quality film. *The Darling of New York* had the Jewel status with a budget and time to match. However, the studio's largest financial outlay at this time was being poured into *The Hunchback of Notre Dame* with its huge cast and the construction of Notre Dame Cathedral on Universal's back lot. King and Raymond Schrock wrote the original story of a little orphan girl from Italy who becomes separated from her nurse en route to New York where she is to live with her wealthy grandfather. On board the ship a member of a gang of jewel thieves (Sheldon Lewis) takes charge of her, and hides his stolen diamonds in her rag doll. The gang takes her to their hiding place in a New York tenement, where one of the gang, unaware of the jewels' new hiding place, unceremoniously dumps her and the doll into a trash can when she becomes a nuisance. They mount a frantic search for her, but she is discovered by some newsboys. For a time she is taken in by a Jewish family, but one of the gang members, Kitty (Gladys Brockwell), reclaims her and hides her in her room. Almost immediately, the police raid the place and a fire starts during the scuffle. Kitty dashes back into the flaming structure, grabs the little girl and makes a flying leap into a net three stories below. After all these adventures, the little girl is almost miraculously reunited with her grandfather and the diamonds are returned to customs' authorities.

King had quite a bit of latitude when it came to telling the story. A steamship that sailed between Los Angeles and San Francisco was chartered to shoot the shipboard scenes. The company then traveled to New York for more location shooting. They filmed the Statue of Liberty and Ellis Island to capture little Peggy's arrival in New York, and some fairly elaborate sets were constructed for scenes around the New York ghetto, and for the tenement where a fire was to occur. There were some tense moments during the filming of the latter. While Baby Peggy today exists only on film, the real woman, Diana Serra Cary, now a successful writer, allowed us some insights, young as she was, into the making of that scene:

> I remember it was quite cold and we had to work with water being sprayed over us, supposedly from the fire hoses, which made this night work even colder. In a long shot, Gladys Brockwell had a male double jump in her place from the tenement window with a rag doll "child" in her arms (supposed to be me), into a "net" held by the firemen on the street below. Later Miss Brockwell and I did a close-up together, which entailed a shorter jump directly into the net. Even so it was scary for both of us, and very tricky to make sure we landed just right.

> But the real excitement happened during the interior fire scene, filmed on the set of Miss Brockwell's tenement apartment. I was alone in this shot in which I was shown to be trapped by the fire. Mr. Baggot and my father walked me through the set before the take, showing me the three windows through which I would be unable to escape, and the door which would *not* be on fire, and was going to be my only safe escape route. While they explained the action they wanted from me, prop men were busy smearing sawdust soaked with kerosene along the inside of all three windowsills. This flammable mixture would then be torched just before the take.

> "But the prop men are *not* going to set fire to the door," Mr. Baggot said, "so after you run from one window to the next and realize you can't get out through them, you go to the door, open it and go right through it." Then he added a word of caution. "But this set can only burn once, Peggy, so you have to make absolutely sure you do the scene exactly right on the first take. Do you understand?"

> Having been working steadily, eight hours a day, six days a week for the past two years, I understood very well the importance of getting a scene right the very first time. I nodded and Mr. Baggot and my father went back to the camera which was set up to shoot directly through the window located above the kitchen sink in the set. Seconds before Mr. Baggot called, "Action!," prop men swarmed over the set's interior, setting all three windows on fire. When the flames were at their height the director started the scene. As was the custom in silent films, he then "talked me though the action":

> "Now you go to the first window and you see it's on fire, and you are frightened. That's right. Good! So now you run

over to the second window..." and so on.

When I got to the door and took hold of the door knob it was hot, and when I opened the door a crack I realized the prop men had made a terrible mistake. They had misunderstood Mr. Baggot's explicit orders and set fire to the door as well! But from where Mr. Baggot and my father were, seated by the camera, they couldn't see that the door was actually in flames, because I slammed it shut almost as soon as I opened it.

"Now, go through the door Peggy!" the director cried, and when I hesitated for a moment trying to figure out what to do, my father repeated his orders. "Go through the door! It's safe!" I turned around instead, remembering that the window beyond which the camera was set up was *not* burning as fiercely as the other two (probably because it would have interfered with the photography), I headed for it as fast as I could go. I clambered onto the sink and went directly on hands and knees toward the safety of the camera. While both the director and my father kept telling me to go back to the door, I knew I couldn't make it out alive that way, so I just kept coming at them. They got a great close-up with a lot of genuine terror registered on my face! I made it though so fast I didn't get a single burn on my hands or legs.

After the scene was over I led Mr. Baggot and my father over to the door to show them why I deliberately disobeyed their orders. By then the door was completely black and burned through and the prop men were all over the set with buckets of water, putting out the flames. Both men were shaken by my close call and greatly surprised that I had made such a split-second decision on my own against their repeated orders. My father took great pride in my "instant obedience." But he never understood that I had early on developed an instinctive secret monitor that I relied upon for my survival in dangerous scenes. I had learned early on that my father and the director did not always know the danger I alone could see when I got right on top of the situation, because they were usually too far away to realize what was really happening. Obedience was one thing; survival was another![4]

Some notable actors (in addition to Gladys Brockwell and Sheldon Lewis) were in the supporting cast. Max Davidson and Minnie Steele portrayed the kindly Jewish couple with a dash of comedic flair, and Frank "Junior" Coghlan played "Ross Kid," the leader of the newsboys. Carl Stockdale, Pat Hartigan, William J. Quinn and Frederick Esmelton all had good roles. The original may have been as long as eight reels, but it was reduced to a bit more than five by the time it reached the theaters. Filming was completed by the first week in August, but it was not released until December 3.

King took a well-earned break when it was finished. It was announced that he repaired to Catalina Island for some deep sea fishing with Hal Roach, Dustin Farnum and Zane Grey.[5] When he returned to the studio, he had another opportunity to do some acting. Raymond Schrock and Edward Sedgwick had been working on a story tailored for Western star Hoot Gibson. It was a fast-paced burlesque (with an astonishing number of plot switches) called *The Thrill Chaser*. Part of the plot involved Hoot working on a studio lot as a screen actor's double. Sedgwick directed and took the opportunity to grab and use a few Universal employees who were temporarily between pictures. He rounded up Mary Philbin, Norman Kerry, Reginald Denny, Hobart Henley, King and Laura La Plante. He even gave himself a small role. Contemporary reviews did not quite spell out what these "high priced extras" did exactly, and no print is known to exist to help out with an analysis, but Gibson was given good marks for this entertaining bit of film.

By the first of October, King began pre-production work on his next feature, adapted by Raymond Schrock from a play by Rita Weiman. It was first called *Blackmail*, but later changed to *The Whispered Name* when it was released in January 1924. While he was working on it, he had a visitor — someone out of his distant past from St. Louis. It was Thomas W. Cahill, the man who made him a soccer star so long ago in his old hometown. Cahill had come to Los Angeles from New York on business for the U.S. Soccer Football Association, of which he was the founder and now secretary. *Universal Weekly* devoted several paragraphs to King's former exploits that give us a better understanding of King from those far-off days:

> King Baggot, old-time Universal star and now director of Baby Peggy hasn't kicked a football for 20 years and says he couldn't run more than 100 yards now without two prescriptions, but there was a time when the veteran motion picture director could zigzag down a soccer field through the opposing team and could do a "century" in ten seconds flat.
>
> Memories of the days when he was one of the outstanding stars of soccer football in America were recalled the other day in Baggot's office at Universal City by much conversation between Baggot and his coach and friend of earlier days.... It was just about 27 years ago that Cahill first saw King in a soccer game. Cahill said, "He was just a kid — about 14 or 15 and he was playing center-forward on the Christian Brothers College team in St. Louis. He was a big rangy chap and could run rings around anybody else on the team. The next year I signed him to play on my Shamrock team — the first professional team in that part of the country and one of the first in America."[6]

The Whispered Name was a mystery drama. It had some potential from the plot, but the acting was not the best. King seemed not to be able to raise it above the level of yet another program picture. The leads were played by Ruth Clifford and Niles Welch, with Charles Clary and William E. Lawrence in support. Ruth Clifford had been starring for Universal's Bluebird brand, and then directly for Universal, from the teens — with several brief forays to other studios at various times. She was a hard-working actress, to be sure, and she continued to work (in bit parts) almost up to the time of her 1998 death, just as King would do; however, she never became a large bankable star in the way that Laura La Plante or Mary Philbin did. Niles Welch was a durable supporting leading man, but he had neither the looks nor the star quality to put him into the first ranks. The film was made fairly quickly. Shooting began the first of November and the cutting was completed near the end of the same month. When it was released in January 1924, *Variety*'s review was a bit cruel, but probably honest enough:

> The characters move through the scenes in jerky, clumsy sequences and poses, and when the big climactic moment arrived the director lost a splendid opportunity for the dramatic smash that should have crowned the situation. However, the director was handicapped by a cast of players at best so-so and at worst poor enough. Ruth Clifford and Niles Welch are the leads. Miss Clifford is pleasantly capable-looking as the young woman reporter, but too much rouge on her lips hurts her full-face shots. Welch is the leading man who, when he played opposite Elaine Hammerstein and Norma Talmadge some years ago, was heralded as having a great future...[7]

Another year with Universal was almost over. Not much about King and his family is known from this period. They had moved from the Franklin Avenue address to a very modest bungalow at 6371 Fountain Avenue, but in close proximity to Hollywood Boulevard. That property is still standing today, although the neighborhood must have been more inviting then than now. One can look in vain for glimpses into his social life. No mention of him can be found in the society pages or the trades that described the doings of the old Hollywood guard — their grand parties, excursions or other social functions. Maybe he disdained them or perhaps they disdained him. However, some time during that year he joined the Motion Picture Directors Association, a precursor to the modern Directors Guild of America. After his heady involvement with the Screen Club, the toast of the industry and of New York, it is apparent that these two clubs were not in the same league, but he needed a social connection to his peers and the Association could provide it. But as luck would have it, he and his fellow directors were soon involved in short-lived but heated controversy.

The group planned a ball at the Biltmore Hotel, which had just opened in October. But in Los Angeles, by the 1920s, a police permit was required to hold large public gatherings. In earlier years, the police were more flexible when it came to what would be considered a socially acceptable group. Unfortunately for the directors, the city had recently hired a new police commissioner whose mission was to "clean up" Los Angeles. There was a statute on the books that prohibited public dancing after midnight. In the past, that law had only been selectively enforced — but for some reason a point was made of fulfilling it to the letter this time. Four policemen were sent out to close their ball down at midnight, causing great distress among the attendees. The situation became more galling when they learned that the Shriners had a ball at the Ambassador Hotel the same night, but were not required to stop dancing at midnight. Fred Niblo, then president of the association, leveled charges that the police had discriminated against the film community, which led to a great deal of finger pointing and civic grumbling.[8]

The incident caused a very large amount of flap in the film community and in the public press for days after the event. It had far-reaching social consequences, pitting those who favored the enforcement of "blue laws" against those who did not. As a result, the Wampas Association, which had been denied an extension of the midnight curfew, decided to hold their annual ball in San Francisco rather than Los Angeles, and Louis B. Mayer was said to be entertaining the idea of removing his studios to the City by the Bay, as well.[9] But, no studios left Los Angeles, and after a time flaring tempers cooled.

Yet some sort of public revenge seemed in order. It got at least to the planning stages, and King was a member of the planning committee when the Motion Picture Directors Association announced that a revue would be staged at the Philharmonic Auditorium in downtown Los Angeles in January 1924. Other committee members were Eddie Cline, Philip Rosen, Fred Niblo, George Marshall, Harold Shaw, William Beaudine, Reaves Eason, Erle Kenton, Wally Van, Al Santell and Charles Parrott (Charley Chase). In a nose-thumbing gesture born out of frustration and resentment, it was titled *After the Ball* and was to be a satire on those local "blue laws." The Motion Picture Directors Association would be assisted by other industry groups including the Screen Writers Guild, the American Society of Cinematographers, the Assistant Directors Society, the Writers Club, the Society of Motion Picture Engineers, the Catholic Actors Guild and the Motion Picture Producers of America.[10] No evidence has been found that it was actually produced, but by then Mayor Cryer, the Crime Commission, the general public and even some church groups who were originally proponents of the curfew withdrew their support from enforcing it.

27

Winds of Change

King's next assignment was *The Gaiety Girl*, which was not an original work done by seasoned scenario writers, or even an attempt to pictorialize a best-selling novel. Instead, it was an adaptation of an Ida Alexa Ross Wylie story called "The Inheritors" published in *Good Housekeeping*. For reasons known only to themselves, the Universal front office gave it the "Jewel" designation. Actually, at this juncture Universal's new general sales manager, Al Lichtman, announced during their fall sales meeting that at least 36 "Jewels" were going to be scattered throughout their programming during the coming year, and that more money would be expended on "big pictures" to improve Universal's overall drawing power.[1] In terms of stars, Mary Philbin was the only important name. She had already come to some prominence for her work as the little Austrian girl in von Stroheim's production of *The Merry-Go-Round* and as the little Bowery girl in *Fool's Highway*. This was yet another film that cannot be viewed today, but from what was said about it — both by the lack of any great hoopla in pre-production reports from *Universal Weekly*, and from the reviews — no great care or expense seems to have been given to its production values. It contained neither casts of thousands, nor elaborate sets to distinguish it from other features.

Briefly told, the plot concerns Irene Tudor (Philbin), this time as a little British blueblood, whose sick grandfather has been forced out of his ancestral castle. The two are now living in poverty in London. Their former home is purchased by millionaire John Kershaw for his lout of a son, Christopher (Freeman Wood). Irene has been waiting for the return of her sweetheart Owen Tudor St. John (William Haines) from Africa, hoping he can buy the castle back from the Kershaws so that her grandfather can die in peace. When Owen does not return, she finds a job with the Gaiety Theatre Company. She mistakenly hears of Owen's death and accepts the attentions of Christopher Kershaw. In an attempt to have her grandfather spend his final days back at the castle, she promises to marry Christopher if he will grant her that wish. Her wedding night begins as a nightmare when the groom becomes intoxicated and tries to force himself on her. But just in the nick of time, Owen returns. A chandelier conveniently falls on Christopher — killing him. As the *Variety* review said, "That leaves the bride free to grab her true love and the audience its hats."[2] The review went on to point out that although Baggot directed with a great deal of skill and that Philbin, as an actress, got as much out of the part as she could with "poignant wistfulness," the story was trite and did not live up to its billing as a Jewel special. Mary Philbin had a much better opportunity the following year when she was cast in *The Phantom of the Opera.*

Not every production is a hit, even if the director does the best he can. Months before its July release, King probably knew what kind of reception this film would be getting, and his discouragement may well have been mounting at this time. He might even have entertained thoughts of taking his talents elsewhere when at last he got a good break and the opportunity to show the stuff he was really capable of doing. Filming of *The Gaiety Girl* was practically completed in May, and soon after he was given a truly ambitious film.

The Tornado really was, in every sense of the word, a "Jewel." It was billed as a "King Baggot Production" and based on a Broadway play by Lincoln J. Carter (originally sub-titled "A Spectacular Comedy Drama In Five Acts"), first produced in 1891. There were some lighthearted moments, but for the most part it was a melodrama in the better sense of that term. It embodied a man's struggle with a raw and unforgiving environment, and at the same time, showed his attempts to tame his own raging human emotions. The hero is House Peters, now the boss of a lumber camp in the far north — gruff and brooding from some dark secret. For that, he is known only as "Tornado." By one of life's twists, some visitors come to the camp: Ross and Ruth Travers, played by Richard Tucker and Ruth Clifford. As the plot unfolds, Ross was once "Tornado's" best friend, and the lumberman's bitterness comes from losing his sweetheart Ruth to this man. However, what he did not know was that Ruth was persuaded to marry Ross because he tricked her — telling her that "Tornado" was killed in the war. He then moved her away before her true love returned. All these years she really loved him, and now her husband, in addition to having a sullen nature, is being physically abusive to her. There is a showdown in which Ross forbids Ruth to talk to "Tornado." But she manages to slip away for a poignant meeting where she tells him the truth. Ross finds out and starts to beat her, but "Tornado" comes to her rescue. A fight begins between the men, but "Tornado" stops himself before he can do great bodily harm to Ross. After warning him never to touch her again, he tells the couple to leave in the morning on the next logging train. Just as they are departing, a tornado strikes. It tears through the town, destroying everything in its path — then the winds whip up the waters in the nearby river, creating a logjam which threatens to inundate what is left of the town. The two are trapped inside the train as it is about to be washed over the bridge. "Tornado" and his men are furiously breaking up the logjam when they see the train going into the water. "Tornado" is able to save Ruth from the swirling waters, but Ross is washed away. The town is saved and Ruth and her true love are reunited. Comic relief is provided by a gangly and painfully bashful Snitz Edwards (Peewee) courting an exceedingly plump and amorous Kate Price (Molly). There is also an adorable little boy named Hurricane, played by Jackie Morgan, but the real star of the film is the violent wind and lashing waves that come close to destroying the town and everyone in it.

In order to do justice to this tale of the north woods, King found a location worthy of that name. It may have been one of the most difficult shoots of his career. The first week in June, together with his production manager W. (Bill) J. Rau, art director Elmer Sheeley, and cameraman

Friend Baker, King traveled to the town of St. Maries in northern Idaho, a region known for its lumber camps and logging activities. Bordered on the north by British Columbia, on the east by the Bitter Root Mountains and on the west by Idaho's Coeur d'Alene region, it was an area of spectacularly breathtaking beauty and scenic opportunity. The scouting party toured the area, stopping to photograph several buildings in the little town of St. Joe, which would later be replicated as sets back at Universal City. They plotted the logistics of filming Idaho's true "back country," visiting Marble and Boulder Creeks and the St. Joe River. Some of these places were accessible only by primitive roads or by logging trains. Local officials were ecstatic, for no film company had ever journeyed to that particular part of Idaho before. The filmmakers returned to Los Angeles on June 6 to make the necessary preparations for a fairly long shoot.[3]

They were back in St. Maries on Tuesday morning, June 17, with wind machines, rain-making equipment and a full company of 27 people all ready to take on the challenge of the task ahead. A lengthy newspaper article in the *St. Maries Gazette-Record* named everyone in the cast and quite a few of the crew as well. For instance, King's assistants were Joseph Barry and Gilbert Kurland. The chief cameraman was the able and gifted John Stumar and the still cameraman was Henry Freulich, the son of Jack Freulich, who was himself a fine still photographer with Universal. The article also proudly named all the lumberjacks who had been selected to do the difficult and dangerous stunt work. For posterity, they were Elmer McIntyre, Archie McGowan, E. Dennis, Tom McDermott, Ernie Broman, Jack Hays, E. LeDue, Pete Clair, James Manning, Bob Boble, Bob Wilson and Harry Figuhr. According to the article, they were paid "top-notch wages" (ten dollars a day for a week to ten days work). Wherever the film crew went, people from the town and from all over the region followed them by horse, by boat or on foot, to watch the fascinating sight of an actual film being made.[4]

Of course there were rain delays, and when it was not raining and they needed it, the rainmaking equipment sometimes failed to function. Their work day often began at four o'clock in the morning when they left their various hotels in St. Maries to board special logging trains in order to reach far-off shooting locations. Not infrequently, they returned long after sunset. Considering the rough terrain and the dangerous working conditions they faced every day, they got off easy with only one accident: Snitz Edwards sustained a badly bruised foot when a horse stepped on it, and he had to go about on crutches for several days. The work was completed on July 3, and the hardy band returned to Los Angeles to finish the picture.[5]

On July 5, House Peters' photo appeared on the cover of *Universal Weekly* and the film was formally announced. Silly publicity gambits were nothing new to Universal or to dozens of other studios either. (Recall that pioneering publicity stunt achieved by IMP in 1910 when they planted the story that Florence Lawrence was killed in an accident, then proclaimed that she was alive and about to make a personal appearance in St. Louis.) This time the "bunk," not surprisingly, involved a tornado. It was near the end of August when *Moving Picture World* published a breathless little piece announcing that King Baggot was about to engage in the most fanciful adventure of a lifetime — he was setting a trap for a tornado! Despite the fact that by the time this item appeared, the company had been back from Idaho for over a month, it was reported with a perfectly straight face that:

> [Baggot] has established headquarters at Coeur d'Alene, Idaho, from which base

he will dispatch expert cameramen to various parts of the region usually visited at the season by tornadoes. The cameramen will have their instruments enclosed in strong iron cages, firmly anchored to the ground, with windshields to protect the operator from the terrific force of the blast.

At the first sign of a tornado, the operator in its path will enclose himself in a miniature fort and focus his camera on the approaching storm.

"The only danger we can see," says Baggot, "is from flying wreckage getting through the bars of the cage, which will be set as close as possible, allowing for the camera lens to protrude. There will be shields behind the camera, which can be adjusted as the force of the storm breaks. I will be in the cage with Friend Baker, Universal's chief technical cameraman, who will be in charge of the lens men."[6]

Much the same report appeared a week later in *Universal Weekly*, with a few further embellishments. Quoting King again, it stated, "We realize there is some danger, but have absolute faith in the cages, designed by Arthur Shadur, city engineer at Universal City. He calculated their strength to withstand almost anything."[7] It was not often that King, aided by the publicity department, revealed a "P.T. Barnum" side of his character, but it could be seen here. And yet, the actual special effects he was able to achieve were almost as stunning as any that could be accomplished by the real thing — and for once this is no longer a lost film.

It was in 1990 that the dogged persistence of Tom Trusky, head of the Idaho Film Collection at the Hemingway Western Studies Center, Boise State University, paid off. While looking for films shot in Idaho, he traced *The Tornado* to the Nederlands Filmmuseum in Holland. The Museum of Modern Art in New York and Boise State now have copies. The intertitles are still in Dutch, but Trusky had them translated. The film was presented there in October 1994, using actors to speak the parts in English. The film was the centerpiece of a grand celebration of historic films shot in Idaho. In 1998, *The Tornado* had a new West Coast premiere after 74 years. It was presented at Cinecon 34, the annual festival of the Society for Cinephiles, at the restored Alex Theatre in Glendale, California. The Boise State translation was used in the form of voiceovers by King Baggot's grandson Bruce Baggot and this author.

To see *The Tornado* is to recognize the work as an astonishing piece of filmmaking. It starts out slowly to establish the character of the broodingly handsome House Peters in his moody forest setting — then the two people out of his past are introduced. It gradually gains speed as the tension develops between Peters, Ruth Clifford and Richard Tucker. Wonderful attention is paid to detail, such as in the scene where Peters has his first glimpse of Ruth through his cabin window. The camera moves to his hand holding the curtain as he draws it closed, and the way the hand is poised manages to convey all of his sorrow and regret in that one gesture. The action builds as the couple quarrels, and ratchets up again during the confrontation and near-fight between Tucker and Peters. When the tornado hits with all its fury, the town seems literally to explode as bushes, trees, furniture and people are swept before the storm. Out on the water, the power of nature lashes at the men frantically trying to loosen the logjam. So seamless is the action, viewers then and now are often hard-pressed to decide, even with a practiced eye, exactly when they are seeing live action and when they are seeing the staged shots. Since almost no film historians have had a chance to view it, it may still be some time before a proper judgment will confirm what a great Universal film it was, as well as to credit Baggot as a skillful director of the action drama genre.

The Tornado was scheduled for its New York premiere on January 4, 1925, at

The only known family photograph of Ruth Baggot, seen here with son King Robert at about age ten and brother-in-law Marmaduke, circa 1924. Photograph courtesy of Mimi Baggot Landberg.

the new Picadilly Theatre; however, it was being shown around the country as early as November 1924. Although it could not be considered a "blockbuster film," it did quite well. In Syracuse, during the week of November 29, it broke all house records. In Norwich, Connecticut, it topped the box office returns garnered by Harold Lloyd, who had just been voted the most popular star in America.[8] The townspeople of St. Maries had a chance to see themselves and their neighbors on the screen at the Dream Theatre on January 18, 19 and 20. King could feel better about himself and his work, and no doubt he did.

Work began on *Raffles, the Amateur Cracksman* in October, although it would not be released until the following April. The story of Raffles, the debonair, cricket-loving and witty gentleman safecracker, had long been familiar to audiences on both sides of the Atlantic. Raffles appeared in a series of novels by E.W. Horning between 1866 and 1921, and was the subject of a 1903 Broadway play of the same name by Eugene Wiley Presbrey. On the screen, John Barrymore portrayed him in 1917 for Hyclass Producing/Weber Photo Dramas. Now he was reprised by Baggot with the help of House Peters and an interesting cast. It was designated as a "Jewel," but it was a "Jewel" in name only — unfortunately for King. And there was a significant change in the billing of the picture: The credits did not read "A King Baggot Production." The main title credit read, "Carl Laemmle Presents House Peters *In Raffles*, Universal Jewel." King's name did not appear on that first credit.

This may have been an indication that his work had slipped in the estimation of the studio or it may have been only an insider's trade joke, for in "Sisk"'s review in *Variety*, he commented:

> There may be a laugh at the beginning of the picture for the trade. Instead of the

name of the film at screening, a full picture of Carl Laemmle, president of Universal, is shown and that fades into "Carl Laemmle." Then comes the explanation to the world that Carl Laemmle is president of Universal and then that Universal presents the picture. There are some more credits and once more "A Universal-Jewel Production made by Universal Pictures. Carl Laemmle, president." After that it sounds set that Laemmle had something to do with it.[9]

Yet none of the regular studio-generated publicity found thus far — neither the print material nor the stills — gave King directorial credit in the main title.

The plot, while a bit superficial, still tells an entertaining story of the dashing thief and his ability to steal at will for his own amusement, and then return the goods to their owners. Also in the cast were Miss Du Pont (also known as Marguerite Armstrong and Patricia Blanche Heiser), Hedda Hopper and a few of King's tried and true supporting players: Frederick Esmelton, Freeman Wood and Lillian Langdon. Kate Lester was supposed to play the part of Lady Amersteth, but on October 11, 1924, a gas heater exploded in her dressing room and she died of her injuries the following day. According to *Picture-Play*, she was replaced by Mathilde Brundage, "made up as nearly as possible to represent Kate Lester." But the credits, well into 1925, continue to use Lester's name.[10]

"Sisk"'s review acknowledged that sufficient money had gone into creating the sets, but a small alarm bell goes off when he mentioned two of the film's faults. He was bothered by bad editing which left "a host of subtitles and close-ups in the picture." He also did not care for Miss Du Pont, calling her "saccharine and minus a front moniker" and, later, "colorless and blonde." He observed that House Peters and the rest of the cast held things together, and that Baggot's direction "was always sure." But one is left to wonder if King had any responsibility for editing this film or for choosing Miss Du Pont.

28

Tumbling Around

King's first film in 1925 was *The Home Maker*. It was in pre-production as early as March of that year and was a rather unusual film for its day. The story came from a recent novel by Dorothy Canfield — a domestic drama with a twist. Today, role reversal in family life is taken for granted, but at the time, a man staying at home while his wife went out to work was not the normal order of things. In the story, Lester Knapp (Clive Brook) is a businessman in middle management. He is a failure who hates his job. His wife Eva (Alice Joyce) is a stay-at-home mother with three children. She hates her job, too, and knows there must be something more to life. Lester is fired and out of despair for himself, and hope that at least his insurance will sustain his family, he tries to commit suicide, but only succeeds in becoming a cripple. Eva must go to work as a saleswoman in a department store and discovers that it is work she was born to do. Meanwhile, Lester, at home in his wheelchair, finds he has a special way with the children that his wife did not have and he takes great satisfaction in finding creative ways to do household chores. The children are now happy and so are Lester and Eva, until Lester finds his paralysis is going away. He knows that if he recovers, they will all revert to their former state of unhappiness. He and the family doctor conspire to keep things the way they are.

At the time of its release, most of the reviewers were not sympathetic to the notion of domestic role reversal. The *New York Times* critic, Mordaunt Hall, had no tolerance for Lester's supposed weakness and the *Variety* critic mentioned "too much delving into child psychology ... [where] the picture definitely gets on the wrong track..."[1] Nevertheless, it was a fine piece of filmmaking. Today its stock has soared. A restored 35mm print was made from a 16mm diacetate print by the Stanford Theatre Foundation Film Preservation Center, which is held by the UCLA Film and Television Archive. A special showing held during UCLA's 2000 Festival of Preservation reveals Baggot's directing in a much more positive light. Today, when viewed with more acceptance of the theme that two women (Dorothy Canfield and scenario writer Mary O'Hara) tried to give it in the 1920s, it has become a film noted for being ahead of its time. It is by no means a "flashy" picture. Rather, it has a quiet but forceful power to portray a human family and their difficulties in a touching and very believable way. It is completely real. We are living their everyday life as if we were their neighbors instead of seeing them as mere actors on the screen. In one delightful scene the children, with their father's encouragement, use kitchen implements as musical instruments to show they are learning in a joyous and spontaneous way. In another understated but highly dramatic scene, Brook finds he is regaining the use of his legs. The audience feels all the emotions he goes through during that pivotal discovery. Now, as the reestimation of his work continues, it may be considered as one of Baggot's finest films.

The Home Maker was not released until August 1925. Back in Universal's April production schedule, Baggot was next slated to do *Peacock Feathers*, starring Virginia Valli, but he did not. Perhaps he had enough of those "fluffy" kinds of pictures. His next film would be more artistic and challenging than any he had directed since *The Tornado*.

It was at this time that King became involved in the newly formed Masquers club, a fraternal organization made up of both well known and lesser-known actors, although producers, directors and those from other facets of show business were also welcome. This club was more in the spirit of the old Screen Club than the Motion Picture Directors Association. These fellows wanted to have a good time. In fact, the club's motto was, and still is: "We Laugh To Win." It was officially founded June 1, 1925, when they rented a two-story white club house at the end of McCadden Place, at 6735 Yucca Street. Their first president, or "Harlequin," was both a Broadway star and long-time film actor, Robert Edeson. Just five months after forming, a group picture was taken on the sprawling front porch of about 48 of their members, or "Jesters." King can be seen standing in the back row, looking a bit shy or pensive. Others in the shot included Roy Atwell, Bert Lytell, Charley Chase, Lincoln Plummer, Montague Love, Frederick Esmelton and Paul Scardon. As a social club, the members had an opportunity to get together away from their studios, to network with one another, to dine and most likely to do some social drinking. Prohibition was still the law of the land at the time and private social clubs were one way to avoid the worst of the raids by police on more public establishments where drinking took place in spite of the law.

There is not a big stretch from making an epic north woods logging picture, to making an ambitious Western, yet the circumstances under which King came to his next film were rather unusual. "Bill Hart 'Set' to Start for United Artists Corporation," the headline read in *Moving Picture World* on August 15. William S. Hart had signed a contract with United Artists to produce two films; the first would be *Tumbleweeds*, and King Baggot was to direct. Furthermore, Hart's company had obtained space at Universal City for offices, dressing rooms and sets.[2] For one thing, King had not made a film for a company other than Universal since 1921. Unfortunately, no contracts or production records can be found for this time period so it is difficult to know whether King's agreement with Hart was separate from his usual studio or as a "loan-out" on a one-time basis. Yet, there was no precedent for it. Hart did not undertake to direct this film himself either; rather, he chose King. The fact that they knew each other is indisputable; Hart most probably played some part in King's doing his play *The Hold Up* in 1921. It can only be guessed how they came to work together, for no definitive account of their past friendship can be found.

Hart had name recognition larger than life by now. Like King, he started in the theater at an early age and originally was first known for his Shakespearean roles but later for the dramatization of Westerns, notably *The Squaw Man* and *The Virginian*. Both men had both done extensive work in stock companies. Hart entered films in 1914, five years later than King, and he was quite a few years older when he met Thomas Ince and went to work for him at the New York Motion Picture Company. He immediately achieved starring roles and went on to act, direct and even write many of his films—just as King had done. Yet, by the mid 1920s, his career was in trouble. He insisted on sticking to his tried-and-true formula for making films, emphasizing plot and characterization over action for its own sake, but the public, then as now, wanted more and more action.[3] When he signed the contract with United Artists for two pictures he was elated. As he wrote in his biography *My Life East and West*, "I had almost 'failed.' The United Artists contract had come just in time. It had let down the bars. The big iron gate had swung open."[4]

Tumbleweeds would be Hart's last film, but he did not know it at the time. He merely thought that he had been given another chance to make good Western films and it was his intention to make this a very good one. He chose the story by Hal G. Evarts and engaged C. Gardner Sullivan, with whom he had collaborated back in 1914 on *The Bargain*, to write the screen adaptation. Almost prophetically for Hart, the core of the story revolves round the historic settlement of the old Western frontier by homesteaders and the ending of the "Wild West" as the cattlemen and cowboys had once known it. The title, *Tumbleweeds*, refers to that ubiquitous Western native plant which blows in the wind and which is analogous to the role of the cowboys who once prided themselves on their rootless and roving nature. In the first part of the film, the government has just ordered the removal of the cattle from a region called the Cherokee Strip in preparation for its settlement. Vast herds are seen being driven across the landscape. Hart, in his role as Don Carver, one of the last of his kind, removes his hat and remarks, "Boys, it's the last of the West."

The character of the true cowboy is established as embodied by Carver—the rugged individualist who does not kill a rattlesnake because he knows it has just as much a right to be there as he does. He is boss of the Box K Ranch, but with the cattle gone, the scene soon switches to the growing town of Caldwell, Kansas, where more settlers are arriving every day. Here he meets Molly Lassiter, (Barbara Bedford) and of course, falls awkwardly but completely in love with her. He plans to join the race for land and stake out the old Box K Ranch for himself and Molly. However, the two villains of the piece, Molly's half-brother Noll Lassiter (Gordon Russell) and his pal Bill Freel (Richard R. Neill), who is also in love with Molly, plot to have Carver arrested under false pretenses and thrown into the government stockade in order to keep him from joining the land rush. (Historically, this was a very real land rush. In 1889, the U.S. government opened some 1200 square miles of wild prairie to settlement).

When the big day comes, thousands of people are there waiting for the signal. At high noon, a cannon booms and the rush is on. Masses of people stream onto the Cherokee Strip in every conceivable kind of conveyance: wagons, carts, horses and their riders, even a bicycle. Carver uses his knife to cut his way out the stockade, leaps onto his faithful waiting horse and gallops across the prairie in an amazing demonstration of speed and action footage, headed for the ranch. Although he is way ahead of the pack, he finds Noll and Freel already there. Checking their horses, he discovers they are rested—the two have obviously cheated the deadline. He drives them off and stakes his own claim but, arriving back in town he finds that Molly

King Baggot directing William S. Hart in *Tumbleweeds,* 1925. Photograph courtesy of the Los Angeles County Museum of Natural History, Seaver Center.

believes he is a "sooner" who also jumped the deadline. She rejects him. He is despondent and vows to leave for South America. But before that can happen, he finds the villains terrorizing two old settlers in an attempt to take their newly claimed land. He captures the pair and turns them over to the law. He and Molly are reunited.

Visually, this is an enthralling film, and it has become a Western classic. The camerawork by Joseph August is magnificent, and as an action picture it has few rivals. Film historian Kevin Brownlow went so far as to call it "among the finest sequences of pure action in film history."[5] As productions go, it was meant to be an epic. Nearly a thousand extras were used in the land rush scenes, as well as 300 wagons, a thousand head of horses and mules, goats, dogs, and other livestock. The action scenes were shot at the La Aguerro Rancho near Newhall, California. As many as 19 cameras were there filming.[6] Over the years, reams of commentary have been written about the kinds of cameras employed, the use of "pit shots" where horses and riders and wagons travel directly over cameras dug into earthen berms, and the shots of Hart and his horse, literally airborne in the dash for the ranch. It was stunning filmmaking.

Yet, as the years have gone by, an error has crept into the writings about this film. The error concerns King Baggot's participation. At the time of *Tumbleweeds'* release (December 1925), no reviewer suggested that William S. Hart directed it, or that Baggot merely "assisted." It was only later, after King's name and the films that he made became lost and all but forgotten, that film historians began to suggest such a notion. Consider the case beginning with Hart's own words. At no time in his autobiography did Hart take credit for the film's direction. In fact, he specifically credits Baggot, saying:

> What a joy it was to go to work! King Baggot, my director, told me half-apologetically, that the first scenes would be taken at 5:30 A.M. I was there, made-up, mounted, and ready to go at five. While we waited for the rising sun, the morning was like a long, cool drink—the elixir of happiness. I love acting. I love the art of making motion pictures. It is the breath of life to me!
>
> *Tumbleweeds* was a big story and an expensive picture to make. [Hart said that it cost him $312,000 dollars.] The many hundreds of vehicles and thousands of people used in the scenes showing the opening of the Cherokee Strip ran into mighty big money. We wanted a big picture and we got one. King Baggot did some splendid directing, and all of the principals made individual hits.[7]

It should also be remembered that Hart was a big star with an ego to match. If he did the lion's share of the directing, this is a man who would have said so. And what of King's reputation at the time? He was fresh from directing action films like *The Kentucky Derby* and *The Tornado*—most probably that was the reason why Hart chose him in the first place. He was hardly a charity case. Did King direct the film with no help from Hart? That is scarcely likely either, given Hart's past experience as a director of some of his own films, but King was clearly the more experienced of the two. It is unfortunate that King's excellent work should today have become so misunderstood and misrepresented, but the process of film evaluation continues to evolve. The more film historians get to see of the films and dig ever deeper into the records of the past, the more accurate their assessments will become.

Poor William S. Hart. All his new hopes for a career renewal were dashed when the film was released in December. Originally slated for release December 27, it was pre-released by United Artists December 20, the week before Christmas, which Hart claimed was the worst week of the year. Still, as Hart said, "its success was instantaneous. The night of its first showing, dozens and dozens of wires kept coming all night long. It is hard to describe the joy they gave me."[8] But that joy was short-lived. As he watched the weekly box office figures, he found that it was out-grossing such big films as *Stella Dallas*, *The Phantom of the Opera* and *The Big Parade*... but only in the smaller and independent houses. United Artists did not book it into the large theaters in the big cities where an expensive film must be shown to get adequate returns. They had, in effect, purposely created a box office failure. He later took them to court and won a judgment of $278,000, but he had no more big money to spend on another big film. His career was over and he retired to his ranch in Newhall to write his memoirs.

The film was granted a new life in 1939 when it was reissued by Astor Pictures (probably, as film historian William K. Everson suggested, "to cash in on the great new Western cycle launched by *Stagecoach*"[9]). It was re-edited and re-titled, and the sound effects were synchronized with a musical score by James Bradford and Arthur Gutman. Hart appeared in a seven-minute prologue where he gave a dramatic and emotionally moving speech about the death of the Old West. Reviewers and audiences of that time were amazed to hear this former silent film great speak, for apparently they did not remember that he came from the theater. The sound of his deep and mellifluous voice thrilled them and sealed Hart's reputation for all time as an icon of the Western film genre.[10] By 1939, Baggot's career was over and forgotten; *Tumbleweeds* had become Hart's film alone.

29

Trouble Ahead

Having nearly finished *Tumbleweeds*, King appeared to be returning to the Universal fold, possibly at the behest of his friend Raymond L. Schrock, who had been recently appointed the new head of production. *Universal Weekly* announced in late September:

> King Baggot has just signed a new long-term contract with Universal Pictures Corporation, according to an announcement from Raymond L. Schrock, studio general manager. Baggot has been associated with Universal for almost 10 years, first as a star and later as a director. He left the company for a short while, and signed to direct William S. Hart in his present production for Joseph Schenck.
>
> He will return as soon as the Hart picture is finished, for a period of several years, and will direct as his first production under the new contract *Perch of the Devil*, Gertrude Atherton's popular novel of this season."[1]

King and the family had moved again. They were now living at 1771 Vista Del Mar, a charming little street just two blocks north of Hollywood Boulevard. The original house may have burned down or drastically altered, for it has obviously been replaced by a rather ugly but typical one-story stucco dwelling more in keeping with houses of the late 1930s or early '40s. Others on the same block which still remain from that earlier time, although not impressively "grand," have a more dignified and refined character. Today the Hollywood Freeway cuts across Vista Del Mar so that the street dead-ends just there; the roar of freeway traffic reminds us of the price of progress.

In 1926, Universal continued to dither and shuffle films and personnel around. Less than a year after his appointment as production manager, Raymond Schrock was replaced by a former director, Henry MacRae. Looking at King's directorial credits for 1926, based solely on release dates, it would appear that in 1926 he made only one film, *Lovey Mary*— and that one was made for MGM, not Universal. Did he break with Universal and go to work for Irving Thalberg that year? It would be a natural assumption, but it would be inaccurate, to say the least. King's name and reputation were clearly in evidence throughout that year at Universal as a diligent search of *Universal Weekly* shows. Production began on his next film, *Perch of the Devil* in January, and the cast was selected by February 6. It was completed near the end of April and slated for release on October 24.[2]

The selection of *Down the Stretch* was first announced in late February. The March end issue has an all-color brochure with King on the roster for their 1926-27 season. On May 1, his portrait appeared in a full-page ad on the back cover. In the May 14 issue, photos of King and director Lois Weber were at the top of the new directors' list, while on June 12, a short article explained that he just signed a new contract. Nothing was said about what happened to that "many year contract" from the year before. The trouble was that those films he began in January and February were not finished until much later that year and not released until the following year.

It was on April 10 that Universal held a testimonial banquet for Carl Laemmle at the Ambassador Hotel to celebrate his twentieth year in the motion picture business. This important annual occasion was originally scheduled for February 28, closer to the real anniversary, but Laemmle was ill and it had to be postponed. Henry Mac-Rae was the toastmaster and King was at the speaker's table, as well he should have been as one of the company's most enduring employees. There were many tributes to Laemmle in *Universal Weekly* at that time and King's personal one was among them. He wrote:

> My dear Mr. Laemmle: With this your 20th anniversary of activity in motion pictures, I am becoming more and more impressed with the fact that the industry is growing up.
>
> Besides you, I am still a comparative newcomer in pictures, having been connected with the screen only slightly more than a decade. In that time I have been associated with you and your company almost continuously, as an actor, and director, and in that time, I have always been conscious of the genius and acumen which has made you the acknowledged leader of all picture activities.
>
> My sincere congratulations go to you, Mr. Laemmle. You have played a major part in building the greatest industry of our times and posterity will not forget it.[3]

It would seem that King had either lost track of time, or was merely referring here to his career as a director with Universal, for in spite of the fact that he was away between 1917 and 1921, his work for the studio totaled closer to 15 years. Then, too, the tone of his remarks seem curiously submissive — almost fawning, as a dutiful son to a father. It is possible that the basis of their long relationship was characterized by these roles that the two played out.

King's work for MGM was on a loan-out basis. Some pre-production work began in early February and by the end of March the entire cast was on board.[4] The first announcement for *Lovey Mary* appeared in the March 20 issue of *Moving Picture World*. King would direct Bessie Love after a long search to find the actress most suitable to portray the sympathetic heroine of this story.[5] *Lovey Mary* was a sequel to the venerable play and novel *Mrs. Wiggs of the Cabbage Patch* by Helen Hegan Rice. It may be recalled that King himself was in a 1906 New York production of *Mrs. Wiggs* playing Mr. Bob, the big city reporter from "up north," and that the cast went on to tour with it all over the western states in 1907. King was on familiar ground again directing a story of rural life that contained drama, tenderness and humor — just as he had done with the same kinds of themes in *Human Hearts* (1922) and many other films from the teens.

Lovey Mary was a "King Baggot Production," and he was given all the latitude he needed to do a good job with the story. Lovey Mary (Love) is a mischievous but kind young girl living in an orphanage. She has become devoted to little Tommy (Jackie Combs) and is taking good care of him when his wayward mother, actually her

Reunion of Vivia Ogden and King Baggot during the making of *Lovey Mary* at MGM, 1926. Collection of the author.

sister Kate, (Eileen Percy) returns from prison to claim him. He does not want to go with her, so Lovey and Tommy flee the orphanage and end up in "The Cabbage Patch" where they are taken in by Miss Hazy, (Vivia Ogden). Vivia Ogden played Miss Hazy on the stage in that 1906 production with King. Now here she was, 20 years later, working with him again.

Miss Hazy is awaiting the arrival of her new suitor whom she has met only by mail. She is to be a mail order bride. He is Stubbins (Russell Simpson), a bum, a drunk and an opportunistic villain of the worst sort. By another stroke of bad luck, when he arrives to claim his bride, Stubbins recognizes Mary. He had been a casual workman at the orphanage when she and Tommy ran away. Being as rotten as he is, he threatens to tell the authorities. To stop him, Mary waits until he passes out from too much drink, then locks him in a box car on the neighborhood's near by railroad siding and watches elatedly as the train moves away. However, her joy is short-lived for when she returns to her "Cabbage Patch family," she finds that Stubbins has already told the authorities and they are taking Tommy away. Meanwhile, Kate, in a fit of despair, has taken poison and is dying. Mary is asked to bring Tommy to see her in the hospital and in a tender scene she coaches him to call Kate "Mamma"—the last word she hears before she dies.

William Haines does not enter the picture until the second half as Mrs. Wiggs' son Billy, Mary's love interest. Mrs. Wiggs was played "splendidly," as the review said, by Mary Alden. For once, the New York reviewers were in accord in praising *Lovey Mary*. Even Mordaunt Hall, writing for *The New York Times* (whose reviews were often so critical as to be downright churlish), could find little fault with it. He was especially impressed with Bessie Love's performance.[6]

There are great disadvantages in trying to write about films and events of 75 to 100 years ago. As time goes by, there are fewer and fewer eyewitnesses to describe and explain what actually transpired at any given point in time. In the case of *Lovey Mary*, there was one such witness—Willard Sheldon, who. was interviewed by this author in 1997. Later in his career, he became an assistant director, second unit director, director and unit production manager (and received the Frank Capra Achievement Award from the Directors Guild of America in 1993)—but he began his career with MGM in 1925, when he was only about 20 years old and was assigned to be a script clerk on *Lovey Mary*.[7] One of the things he remembered most vividly about King was his engaging personality and his generosity to a young man like himself. He recalled that they were in pre-production for about three to four weeks. The directors had offices on the lot that were like "cubby holes," with an inner office for the director and an outer office for assistants. He said King treated him like a valued member of the production staff. He made sure that the young man sat in on every story conference, including discussions about things like the proper psychological interpretation of Bessie Love's character. Sheldon said, "King never made you feel that you were not wanted. He was always comfortable to be with." When asked if he knew whether the rumors about his drinking problem were true, he replied that he never saw King drinking on the set or any indication whatever that alcohol might have been a problem in his life. He also remembered that King did not drive. If he had a driver, Sheldon was unaware of it. He thought King used taxis and he sometimes drove King home himself to "a large home off Hollywood Boulevard." He did not remember many details about the actual filming, but he remarked, "You never knew what was going on at MGM" and that often no call sheets were used.[8] (Sheldon died in 1998.)

King was back on the Universal lot in May, and on May 8 he was again reported as the director for *Down the Stretch*. A short time later, a curious set of events took place. In the May issue of *The Motion Picture Director*, in the section called "What the Directors Are Doing," it stated that King was preparing for Jackie Coogan's next MGM picture, *Johnny Get Your Hair Cut*. The same information appears again in June.[9] He may have been on another loan-out to them for this picture, but with two others in the works, that would have been a bit of a stretch. However far the negotiations had progressed, they were all scrapped when *Moving Picture World* reported in July that:

> Millard Webb, the youngest director in Hollywood, is now directing the youngest star in the movies. Webb, whose rise to fame was heralded by his expert direction of John Barrymore, in the *Sea Beast*, was called to direct Jackie Coogan when King Baggot, originally slated for the directorial post, was released by the elder Coogan to return to Universal City to complete a series of pictures.[10]

As it turned out, King was well out of the making of this film. By late August, Jack Coogan, Sr., had gone through a total

King Baggot with Jackie Coogan when it was announced that they would make *Johnny Get Your Hair Cut* for MGM, 1927. Mercifully, King was replaced. It was not a successful film. Collection of the author.

of four directors. *Variety* reported "2 Directors Now on Coogan Picture" (Millard Webb had been relieved of his duties after only a few days shooting). Coogan was quoted as saying that although Baggot was originally signed to it, "[Coogan] was unable to locate him when he was ready to start shooting." This is a puzzling statement in light of the fact that Universal had recalled him to complete those two previously assigned pictures.[11] But now, in August, Coogan was working with Archie Mayo to direct the story and Reaves Eason to direct the racetrack sequences in San Francisco. When it was released, both directors received screen credit, but it was thoroughly trashed by critics who pointed out the obvious: that it was simply an exploitation of the young star.

Perch of the Devil, although completed in March and originally scheduled for an October release, did not actually appear on the screen until March of 1927. Just the same, it was designated as a Jewel, and could be characterized as a "society melodrama"—one of Universal's stocks-in-trade. Mae Busch, sometimes remembered as a comedienne, was at the time considered a very competent straight actress in films like *Foolish Wives*, *The Christian* and *The Unholy Three*. This film presented still another example of King's directorial ability with action drama that today cannot be seen or evaluated. There was an exciting death struggle in a mine shaft between Busch and Jane Winton that the reviewer Paul Thompson (in *Motion Picture News*) called "one of the most effective and melodramatic climaxes to a picture that one can well conceive and is mighty well done."[12]

Down the Stretch would be King's last film for Universal. It is not certain why it was originally announced in January, then dropped and reassigned in May — but that was the case. At the time of its first announcement, it was said to be based on John Tainter Foote's racing story "Blister Jones." The May announcements in *Universal Weekly* say much the same thing. However, on July 24, Gerald Beaumont's name was attached to it (from his *Redbook Magazine* story "The Money Rider") and it was reported that it was his last story, Beaumont having died "two weeks ago." Pre-production continued into August when Robert Agnew was selected to play the jockey, and in September King was in Chicago and on his way to Aurora, Illinois, to scout and do location shooting at the new million dollar racetrack with a crew of five cameramen headed by John Stumar. More location shooting took place in October; he then returned to Universal, where the picture was completed. When it was finished, a longish piece in *Universal Weekly* described the film and noted that "King Baggot directs it ... and [it] has many startling photographic innovations." Stills accompanied another notice of the film in November.[13] Yet, it was not released until the following May.

Down the Stretch can be seen at the Library of Congress and it is evident that this was not the stuff of a Jewel film in any sense of the word, although the racing scenes are marvelous; King had not lost his touch. Horses and their jockeys gallop straight into the camera. The scope of the spectacle is well portrayed with panning shots of the crowd in the stands and the track itself. The viewer is right in the middle of the action. But, as the *Variety* review put it, "Continuous, undiluted suffering (on the part of Robert Agnew as the jockey who tries to starve himself down to weight) grows obnoxious."[14] Agnew had neither the looks nor the acting ability to make the story very believable, no matter how strong the direction was.

30

Beginning of the End

After October 23, 1926, there were no more items about King Baggot in *Universal Weekly*. The man who had been their first male star, and a solid, sometimes brilliant director for them for the past seven years, was suddenly "out of the picture." There is no explanation. Did he quit in disgust because of the lack of quality films he was given to make for Universal? Was he fired for some cause? The record is as silent as the films he had been directing. Only a tiny item in a November *Moving Picture World* told what happened next:

> Baggot to Direct
> King Baggot will direct Sam E. Rork's next production about December 1 on a script adapted from Patrick Hastings play, *The River*.[1]

Something went very wrong between King and Universal in those last few months; Carl Laemmle's long absence during that time may have exacerbated the situation. In July, while on his annual trip to Europe, he suffered an attack of appendicitis. His situation was so serious that he had to have surgery and blood transfusions. In a bizarre quirk of fate, his daughter Rosabelle, who accompanied him to Europe, also had an attack less than two months later. As a result, Laemmle did not return to the United States until October. He was away for almost four months.[2] While he was gone, if King and the studio were having differences, he would not have been there to mediate or intervene. By November, it might have been too late. But that is only speculation.

Another event occurred around this time that adversely affected King's life. He and Ruth were separated. A combination of his drinking and his long absences from home led to the break. Ruth could take no more. Their son King Robert was 12, a sensitive time for the young boy. From that time forward, for the next ten years, she and King would live apart. Yet, although they both continued to move frequently, they never lived more than a mile or two from each other.

At that point, King went to work for Sam E. Rork. He was only an independent producer for a few years, but during that time he hired some "big names" and had ambitious plans. Rork's first known production was *Curtain* (1921), followed by *The Rosary* (1922), in partnership with William N. Selig. As time went on, he began releasing through First National and hired quite a few seasoned personnel with long track records, including George F. Marion, Donald Crisp, Svend Gade, Maurice Tourneur, Jane Murfin, Gilbert Roland and Tony Gaudio.

King's production for Rork was taken from Sir Patrick Hastings' novel *The River*, retitled *The Notorious Lady*, with the screenplay by Jane Murfin. It was a lively adventure story of the English in South Africa. The plot featured diamonds, murder and lots of menacing "natives." It was shot in Hollywood but the reviews raved over the picturesque settings made possible by of Tony Gaudio's fine photography. King had not had an opportunity to work with Gaudio since the making of *The Forbidden Thing* in 1920. Filming seems to have gone forward with no major incidents. The reviewers criticized Barbara Bedford for being "too perfect sartorially" and for wearing too much jewelry out in the bush, but Lewis Stone got good marks for an understated performance. Ann Rork, Sam Rork's daughter, played the native girl and was singled out as being "well on her way to emotional heights."[3] King's work was cited as being satisfactory, but there were no raves. It was simply another program picture. The film is available on video; viewed today, one can see how a lack of a decent budget affected it, especially in the river and jungle scenes. But, the recurrent use of a comedic "deck walker" in the shipboard scenes and the feats of spear-throwing natives are nice touches.

Perch of the Devil was released March 3 and *Down the Stretch* on May 29, with *The Notorious Lady* in between them on March 27. After that, the pace of King's output definitely slowed. No items about him can be found in the trade press or the newspapers around this time. However, he was still active in the Masquers. Their records show he proposed three men for membership in the group: Jimmy Starr, Addison Burkhart and Jacques Pierre.[4]

King now found himself in a very precarious position. Not since his break with Universal the first time, back in 1917, had his professional future been so uncertain. He was 47 years old and his looks were gone. His face showed the traces of a life almost too well lived, and his always stocky but powerful physique had become quite portly. He was separated from his wife and son and after the making of *The Notorious Lady* he had no current employment. And then there was that specter of his possibly serious drinking problem hovering over him He did, however, still have earning potential. Even though he was no longer a salaried director with Universal, many ex–Universal directors before him had gone on to carve out impressive careers after leaving. He had done well with *Tumbleweeds* and *Lovey Mary* on his own, and he could still command good money for his services in order to support himself and his family. All he needed was a new studio and some good stories.

Finding solid salary figures within the motion picture industry has always been a tricky proposition. Publicists and agents inflate those figures for the benefit of their clients and the press, while the studios downplay (or are loathe to disclose) them, for obvious reasons. Box office figures, too, are equally hard to substantiate, even to this day. Exactly how much money had King been making in the second half of the 1920s? A perfectly accurate figure cannot be placed on his income, but perhaps a ballpark one can be determined from an insider's source.

Richard Koszarski, in his book *An Evening's Entertainment*, managed to unearth an internal memorandum from Universal that has bearing on this issue. In November 1926, when Carl Laemmle had just returned from his long trip abroad, he asked Paul Kohner (later a well-known publicist and agent, then a producer with Universal) to canvass the industry and discover what salaries were being paid to directors. Kohner found information on over 60 of them and assured Laemmle that in most all cases they were fairly correct. Whether they were completely correct or not, the list makes fascinating reading. The majority of these directors were working on an annual contract basis and were paid weekly. However, there were a few major-league directors who received their pay "per picture." The list can be divided into four categories: common or normal, high, extra high and astronomical.

The report found that well-known directors working for established studios with fairly good track records were making $1,000 to $1,500 per week. In 1926, that list included Clarence Badger, George Archainbaud, Frank Borzage, Tod Browning, Irving Cummings, Victor Fleming, Edmund Goulding, Raoul Walsh and Irvin Willat. The next tier, although still making a weekly salary, were commanding from $1,600 to $2,500: John Ford, William Beaudine, Herbert Brenon, Sidney Franklin and Hobart Henley were in this category. Those receiving $20,000 to $50,000 per picture were Henry King, James Cruze, Allan Dwan, Charles Brabin, King Vidor, George Fitzmaurice, and Marshall Neilan. Erich von Stroheim, at $100,000 per picture, and Ernst Lubitsch, at $175,000, were at the top of the list. However, there were a few for which Kohner could find no exact figure: Donald Crisp, Rupert Julian, Maurice Tourneur, and Sam Wood. King's name was not mentioned here, but he was still technically on Universal's own payroll, so they already knew it. His salary may have been a little less than for the above mentioned gentlemen, for Universal was well known not to pay well — one of the reasons so many of their good people moved on. But he could have been making somewhere in the neighborhood of that first group, or even into the second when the film was a "King Baggot Production."

If only another break could materialize — a new studio and brighter prospects. But that did not happen. He had always landed on his feet before, but this time the luck of the Irish deserted him. In October, he was signed by Tiffany Productions.[5]

He was given *The House of Scandal* to direct, from a story by E. Morton Hough about Irish-Americans. Pat O'Malley was chosen to play the lead, Pat Regan. King and Pat knew each other from Universal where they worked together as recently as *Perch of the Devil*, but they undoubtedly went back much further than that. O'Malley's film career began even earlier than King's. As a young man of about 17, he began with Edison in 1907. He was a remarkably durable actor, having worked for Essanay, Kalem and other pioneer studios. He was acting almost up until the time of his death — his last film was *Apache Rifles* in 1964, just two years before he died — but at this time, he was still playing romantic leads. His leading lady was Dorothy Sebastian who entered films in 1924, but whose career had not yet made her a star. The story did not give any of them much to work with and the *Variety* review commented that it "just missed," and that "either the time limit or something mixed in, with the story fading away faster than it started ... a fine chance muffed."[6] That would be King's last work for Tiffany and a far cry from his films of less than two years earlier at Universal and MGM.

Now he took one more step downward. In about May or June, he found one last job as a director with a less than distinguished company called A. Carlos. *The Romance of a Rogue* starred two previously well-known actors who A. Carlos might have hoped still had some good box office appeal left in them. The leading lady was Anita Stewart, once the darling of Vitagraph as far back as 1911, and well-known in the industry for having lost a well publicized contract battle with them in the courts in 1918.[7] Her career was still bright into the mid–1920s. In 1921, she was listed as one of the industry's 15 top female stars. H.B. Warner was hired to play the male lead. Like his father before him, he had a fine reputation as a stage actor and was recruited into films in 1914 by Famous Players. Just the previous year, he had won acclaim for his role as Christ in De Mille's *King of Kings* and would remain a solid film performer for many years. Later he received an Academy Award nomination for his portrayal of Chang in the 1937 production *Lost Horizon*. Adrian Johnson, a longtime and well-regarded writer, did the scenario. It was based on a novel by Ruby M. Ayres. Yet, their efforts fell short of the mark. It played for over a week at Keith's Broadway in New York, but the critics found a great deal wrong with it. According to the *Variety* review, it consumed "60 slow-moving minutes" and was handicapped by the "leaden, unexpressive characterizations of H.B. Warner and Anita Stewart." The plot involved a man who was sent to prison on the eve of his wedding and seeks vengance on the man whose lies sent him there. However, the villain is "paralyzed and confined to a wheelchair," which must have limited the potential for action. There may not have been a great deal there with which to work, but whether that was an accurate estimation or not, King was blamed for its major faults. "Direction is responsible for the numerous draggy sequences where all that is shown are a couple of people talking, without titles to tell what they are saying."[8]

And then his career as a director was over.

31

The End of an Era

A new era dawned on the film industry in 1928. It began with a whisper but quickly grew to a roar. Sound had come to films. As Kevin Brownlow pointed out in *The Parade's Gone By*, experiments may have began as early as 1889 or 1901, but nothing much came of them then in a commercial way.[1] It was Sam Warner, in 1925, who began working with Western Electric Company to explore the possibilities of making sound films and who, in 1926, signed a formal agreement with that company to use the Vitagraph Sound System, that signaled a cataclysm of the first magnitude. About this time, other experiments in electronics led to more possibilities and a whole host of sound technologies were soon being tried by various film companies. But it was *The Jazz Singer*, released in October 1927, that changed the dynamics of the industry for the simple reason that although the technology still had a long way to go, it made a spectacular amount of money for Warner Bros. As Alexander Walker put it in *The Shattered Silents*, "its box-office grosses were the galvanic coil that passed a kind of visionary thrill through the whole industry."[2]

Not since the rise of the feature film between 1912 and 1915 had the industry been confronted with such a do-or-die situation. As was the case in the teens, many studios hoped that "talking films" were just a fad and would soon fade from public favor. When that did not happen, they had no choice. This time it was not a matter of inclination or creative sensibility, but of extremely large expenditures of cash. The transition took an incredibly short amount of time, so that by 1930, for all intents and purposes, in the United States, at least, the silent era was over. During this period, the upheaval caused by such a monumental change touched the lives, in one way or another, of all of the thousands of those people who were working in films, be they studio heads, stars, directors, cameramen, musicians, theater owners—everyone. Some survived this sudden great change and some did not.

King Baggot was unfortunately in the later category. He had already been cut loose from his old studio and his career was definitely on a downward slide; in 1929, for the first time in his entire life in films he made not a single film. He may have tried to find other work as a director, but if he did he was turned aside. As *Photoplay* put it in 1928, "To expect a good director of motion pictures to make fine sound pictures today is like asking the first violinist of an orchestra to play his own instrument with one hand and the drums and traps with the other."[3] There was such panic going on within the industry at the time that "old-timers" from silent film, no matter how distinguished their careers may have been, were, for the most part, considered no longer useful. Sadly, so many became anachronisms to the industry that had originally spawned them. A few of his colleagues were able to hang on and prosper — Raoul Walsh, John Ford, Irving Cummings, Clarence Brown and King Vidor — but all of them were younger than King.

Almost nothing is known about how he spent that year; adding to his woes the country was hit by the Great Depression in 1929. By 1932, over 12 million Americans were out of work. Back in 1915, when King was at the height of his fame as a matinee idol, he anticipated how he would end his career. He spoke then of his delight in playing character parts to show his versatility as an actor. He had said:

> There may come a time some day when they will ring the bell on me as a leading man and then I will have to play characters. The little fun I get out of playing them now will also provide a good experience for me if ever I get to playing character old men after I am sixty years of age.[4]

Those were prophetic words. He did not know when he said them that he would get a good long ride out of being a director before it came to this, but the time had finally arrived. However, in his fanciful calculations, he was off by a decade — he was only 51.

After King was out of work for over a year, his old studio, Universal, was the first to hire him back — but as a character actor. The vehicle was *The Czar of Broadway*, based on the life of political boss and underworld czar Arnold Rothstein. It was made using the Movietone sound system and starred John Wray and Betty Compson, an actress who was able to make a smooth transition from silent films to sound. A plus for King undoubtedly was his speaking voice — stage-trained and resonant, the very kind that the studios struggling with the new medium were happy to get.

The year 1930 was to be one of the worst in King's entire life. It was learned later that back in 1925 he bought a house for Ruth located at 7249 Franklin Avenue. She and King Robert lived there from the time of her separation from King in 1926. There may have been some attempts at reconciliation, for King actually listed this as his address in the 1929 city directory. While not palatial, it was grander than any of the others, with a spacious porch and graceful columns in front. However, if any reconciliation had been attempted, that was now out of the question. Just a few days before the release of *The Czar of Broadway*, King was arrested and fined for being drunk in an automobile. If he had ever been arrested before, it would probably have been hushed up, but not this time. The *Los Angeles Times* reported that he had been arrested and fined $50 for the offense. A William Collins, described as a mechanic, was taken into custody with him. The car was parked at Franklin and Wilcox in the early hours of that morning — a location not far from where Ruth and King Robert were now living.[5]

That was the last straw for Ruth. The following month, she sued him for divorce. This was not just local news. The *New York World* got the story from the A.P. wire and reported it to the East Coast. It was headed "Movie Director Divorced on Coast, Wife Says King Baggot Was Habitually Drunk" and went on to relate...

> King Baggot, motion picture director, has been divorced by Mrs. Ruth Constantine Baggot. The decree was granted after Mrs. Baggot testified her husband had indulged in habitual intemperance. She said she

left him four years ago, taking their son, Robert, who was then thirteen years old, after Baggot ignored her ultimatum that if he persisted in drinking she would leave him. The decree was granted on the grounds of desertion. They were married at Fort Lee, N.J., December 3, 1912.

A property settlement under which Baggot agreed to pay his wife $325 a week from the time of their separation and one-half of all he earned over $850 a week was approved by the court. Baggot agreed to pay $100 a month for the support of his son.[6]

Ruth's original decree was filed on June 24, but according to court records, King did not respond when he was served with the papers. It was not until September 17 that he answered the complaint and made the concessions that appeared in the newspaper article. He agreed to pay the balance due on the $17,500 house on Franklin Avenue, which would become Ruth's property when it was paid off. He was also allowed to see his son "at reasonable times under proper conditions and circumstances."[7]

As scandals go, Hollywood's movie people had endured far greater ones that this. The public was by now quite used to scandals, but within the family it was devastating enough. King's personal situation was now quite clear—he could not control his drinking enough to work steadily. At this point, he was admittedly an alcoholic. It should be noted that alcoholism was his only known vice. At no time had he ever been accused of connections with women other than his wife, nor would he be for the rest of his life. His mistress was the bottle.

Somehow life went on. His next known address was a little bungalow court at 1624 North Vista, not far south of Hollywood Boulevard, and by the summer he was working again. King, Francis X. Bushman and George Fawcett all played supporting roles in *Once a Gentleman*, a society comedy which starred Edward Everett Horton as a butler and was produced and directed by James Cruze. It is a great pity that this is a "lost film," for the critics were unanimous in praising Baggot and Bushman for fine performances. There is a touching irony—almost a mocking ring—to the fact that these two men who once vied with each other to be the most popular leading man in America now played side by side. Once they were the foremost "gentlemen" in the country, if not the world.

There were a few other changes in King's life worth noting. He had been listing himself in *The Standard Casting Directory*, a precursor to *The Academy Players Directory*, from the late 1920s as a director. Now, from September to December 1930, he had a second listing as a character actor and he had obtained an agent: Loretta Fitzpatrick, whose agency was at 5617 Hollywood Boulevard, not far from the Central Casting Office at Hollywood Boulevard and Western Avenue. His selection of Fitzpatrick to represent him might have been pure happenstance, but her Irish surname may have inspired more confidence. Month after month in these listings, another change had occurred. He was spelling his name as "Baggott." All his life on stage and in films, that spelling had popped up from time to time, but those instances can be written off as typographical errors. It was a common mistake throughout the industry in earlier days to misspell names, but now it seemed to have been a conscious choice on his part. On legal documents the spelling was still "Baggot." The new spelling appeared only professionally. There is an old saying about changing your name and changing your luck. He may have been desperate enough by then to believe it.

The year 1931 was another dismal one in terms of his work. He made only two known films: *Sweepstakes* for RKO/Pathé and *Scareheads* for Richard Talmadge Productions. At least these were speaking parts. In the first he played "Weber's trainer," in the second he was a policeman. He was able to get a little more money by writing the scenario for the film *Sporting Chance* for small-time producer, Albert Herman; it was released through Peerless Productions and starred Buster Collier, Jr. One of the reviews noted that the racing footage was composed mainly of "stock shots." Mahlon Hamilton was also in the cast. He was never as big a star as King, but he was a popular silent leading man, and the two would work together many times in later years—their roles often unbilled.

King was arrested again in July 1932 in front of 6724 Hollywood Boulevard. This time he seems to have been driving. With him was Edward Moffat, identified as a writer. They both pleaded guilty to the charges in Judge Woodward's municipal court and each paid a $50 fine. It was reported that King was behind the wheel, but that Moffat was arguing with him and interfering with his driving.[8] The business of his driving is a minor mystery throughout his life. Did he drive or not? Once, when he was interviewed in 1912, he was said to have taken a taxi from the interview location to the IMP studios. In 1915, when he was interviewed by Hugh Hoffman, he had a driver. However, again in 1915, he joined in a much-publicized daylong outing at Brighton Beach sponsored by the New York Motion Pictures Exhibitors League. He participated in an automobile race where the stars drove "flivvers."[9] Then, too, in several of those early one-reel films, driving an automobile was part of the plot, and he undoubtedly did his own stunts. His daughter-in-law, Mimi Baggot Landberg, recalled that he never drove and did not own a car. Willard Sheldon, when working with him on *Lovey Mary* in 1926, stated that he often gave King rides home.

After the divorce was final, Ruth and King Robert moved from the Franklin Avenue house to an apartment at 1344½ North Formosa Avenue. It may be surmised that she needed the income that the rental of the house might bring, and that despite King's legal obligation to provide for her and their son, he no longer had the means to do so. The $325 a week he had promised could hardly come from a man now playing small character roles whenever he could find them. The two moved again in 1932 to another apartment complex at 1916 North Las Palmas, not far from Hollywood High School. That year, King Robert graduated from the school. Another great mystery in the life of King Baggot remains as to what became of all the money he made during his palmy days. He did not live in expensive homes. It is believed that King Robert was sent to a local military school for several years about the time he was 12, but even that could not be considered a large expense. If he made some bad investments or loaned money to unworthy individuals, there is no record of them. The divorce proceedings show no great personal assets to divide. There is some hearsay evidence that he gambled. Perhaps he lost money in the stock market crash. This is simply an unanswered question.

A bit more acting work came his way in 1932, all speaking parts. The best of them was Monogram's *Police Court,* a veritable old home week for some former silent stars. Henry B. Walthall played the lead. The cast also included Al St. John, Lionel Belmore and Edmund Breese. The theme involved the downward spiral of a once-famous screen actor due to alcoholism. A 16mm print owned by a private collector still exists and it is a fascinating story. Walthall's performance is riveting as his career declines. Thanks to his director Harry Field (King), near the end he is given "one more chance." He gives the performance of his life in the last scene, which literally kills him: he dies while the cameras roll. What must it have been like for

King to have participated in this film? Did he see Henry Walthall or himself there, or was it just another chance for him to continue acting?

There were only five other films for him that year and the parts were very small. *Girl of the Rio* was released by RKO in January; he played an unbilled part as the maitre d'hôtel at the Purple Pigeon café. In June, *What Price Hollywood* was released by RKO-Pathé with George Cukor directing. King played a studio department head. The following month, Columbia released a Buck Jones feature titled *Hello Trouble*, written and directed by Lambert Hillyer. According to a brief blurb in the *Los Angeles Record*, King and Bert Roach were slated to be in it, but neither appeared in the print viewed by the American Film Institute Catalog team. He had the part of a newspaper managing editor, Mr. Hinkle, in an Educational Film Exchange short, *The Big Flash*, and near the end of the year, a walk-on as a police officer in Universal's *Afraid to Talk*.

His mother Hattie died of a stroke in St. Louis in March 1933. She was 73. Her death certificate noted that she evidenced senility. Mercifully, she may not have known what had become of her once-so-famous son. He had almost no work that year — just three films and one of those, *Secrets*, could be considered a "charity case." It was to be Mary Pickford's last film. King, his former leading lady Florence Lawrence, Paul Panzer and another former great star of the silent era, Francis Ford, were given tiny roles. The four former stars were probably grateful to have work at all and were no doubt being as "professional" as they could be about their situation. However, their gratitude must have been tinged by the bitter realization that Pickford had once envied Florence Lawrence and followed her twice — once to Biograph, then to IMP on her upward journey to stardom, and that King had been Mary's leading man in all those one-reel films for IMP so long ago. Now Mary, still as rich and as famous as ever, was able to cast a few scraps in their direction so that they could at least act in one more film.

That year, too, marked another irony. Prohibition, that "noble experiment," was finally repealed. So many lives had been lost or ruined. So many millions or billions of dollars had been siphoned away into the pockets of criminals. It was too late for

Baggot became a character actor in the 1930s. Publicity still from *Beloved*, Universal, 1934. He played the inglorious role of "the second doctor." Photograph courtesy of the State University of New York, Purchase College.

King. That is not to say he would not have been undone by drink if Prohibition had never been enforced, but making it a criminal offense had definitely heightened the thrill of doing what was once legal, and then was not. The very challenge of it destroyed the lives of countless citizens. It had seemed so right at the time. Who could have known that such good intentions would wreck the havoc that that law managed to achieve?

King's situation did not change much in 1934. He managed to be cast in seven films, the best of which was probably *Beloved* for Universal, which was actually in production from the previous year. It was a big musical film staring John Boles and Gloria Stuart, produced by Carl Laemmle, Jr. The cast was a large one and included many old silent players. King had the inglorious role of "the second doctor," but some of his former colleagues had parts with real character names attached to them: Edmund Breese, Mae Busch (whom he had directed in *Perch of the Devil*), Bessie Barriscale, another of his early leading ladies, and Fred Kelsey.

The nomadic Baggot moved again in 1934. King was now living back at the Christie Hotel, as he had in 1921. It may have been a logical move being closer to Hollywood Boulevard and the streetcar lines and, too, the Depression may have forced their rental prices down to a more affordable level.

32

The Last Days

Work picked up significantly for King in 1935. Universal used him in no fewer than ten films, including three serials. He played two policemen, a druggist, a businessman and an airplane inspector; in five others, he was simply a "bit player." The films were *Tailspin Tommy, Call of the Savage, Night Life of the Gods, A Notorious Gentleman, It Happened in New York, Chinatown Squad, She Gets Her Man, Diamond Jim, Three Kids and a Queen* and *The Adventures of Frank Merriwell.* Although not released until 1936, there was a small part for him as a "character man" in the melodrama *Next Time We Love* with Margaret Sullavan and James Stewart. He managed to squeeze in one film at Paramount as well, playing a gambler in *Mississippi* with Bing Crosby, W.C. Fields and Joan Bennett. At MGM he was a dignitary on the platform in the Marx Brothers' *A Night at the Opera.* The stars of these films were a whole new breed. Sound was improving and filming techniques had now changed radically from just a few years before. Many of his old friends dropped out and retired (J. Warren Kerrigan, Francis X. Bushman, Maurice Costello). From his earliest days in the theater he simply picked himself up and went on trying and he was doing this now no matter how humiliating or difficult it might be. Baggot was first and foremost an actor — that was his life.

Carl Laemmle celebrated his Thirtieth anniversary in the moving picture business in February 1936. Since King was still with Universal in the early months of that year, he was invited to the celebration. The luncheon, given for Laemmle by his West Coast staff, was held at Universal City on the set for *The Phantom of the Opera.* Guests entered the studio through a reproduction of the lobby of the White Front Theatre, his first in Chicago in 1906. About 250 people attended, including ex-vaudevillian song and dance man, now Senator Francis (Frank) T. Murphy, who was said to be the first actor Laemmle ever hired. However, for King, the seating arrangements were a bit different than for all those previous celebrations for Carl Laemmle. This time he did not sit on the dais with the dignitaries and give a laudatory speech. Instead, he was assigned to a regular table with a newcomer to the screen, Shaindel Kalisch; an actress of long standing, May Robson; and a pioneer trade publisher, Bill Johnston. There was a photograph of the foursome in *Universal Weekly* and also a photograph of King and Laemmle taken later that day.

His loss of "A Table" status was just one more reminder of who he once was and who he had now become.¹

Production for a new song-filled melodrama at MGM began in early 1936. It was *San Francisco*, which would be MGM's top-grossing film for that year and which is still loved and admired today. No expense was spared. Woody Van Dyke, the director, was at the top of his form. Clark Gable and Jeanette MacDonald had the leads. The musical numbers were lavish and the 1906 earthquake, which destroyed the city, was reproduced in painstaking detail. It is not certain whether Louis B. Mayer came up with the idea of using many silent veterans or if it was Van Dyke's, most probably the latter, for to produce this film, he literally needed a cast of thousands. However it came about, Mayer got the credit for the announcement in the press:

FAVORITE STARS OF SILENT DAYS
MAKE COMEBACK
Pioneers of Screen Given Preference in
casting *San Francisco*
   ...Before the advent of sound ... many were the famous names that basked in the limelight that now shines on the Gables, the Crawfords, the Garbos. Some have entered other walks of business, some have chosen to remain in pictures.
   Realizing the pioneer work performed by the earlier stars in the film industry, instructions were recently passed on to directors, producers and casting officials by Louis B. Mayer of Metro-Goldwyn-Mayer that the screens pioneers were to be given preference in casting roles in MGM productions.
   In keeping with the new production order, one picture alone is bringing to the screen more famous screen personages of the past than have ever been presented before in one picture...
   Among the familiar Stars of Yesterday who play important parts are: King Baggot, who starred in 300 pictures prior to 1920 and Rhea Mitchell — together they were the stars of the first million dollar serial, *The Hawk's Lair*, directed by Van Dyke in 1918. [Actually the title was *The Hawk's Trail* and the date was 1919].²

The press release went on to mention Flora Finch, the "queen of film comedy" who had starred with John Bunny; Naomi Childers, "top-most star of the old Vitagraph"; Mahlon Hamilton, "a leading star of fifteen years ago"; Fritzi Brunette, "whose screen experience began with the early Yankee films"; Helen Chadwick, "former star of Astra-Pathé"; Frank Mayo, "star of Lois Weber productions"; and Donald Hall, "baritone lead in the first *Floradora* show and who appeared with Anna Held and Fritzi Scheff."

Other names mentioned were Al Shean, Harry Myers, Rosemary Theby, Jean Acker (first wife of Rudolph Valentino), Jane Talent, Lillian Rich, Kathleen Key, Russell Simpson, Eddie Hearn, Willard Mack, Mary MacLaren, Myrtle Stedman, Bob Ingersoll and Arthur Belasco. A number of publicity stills were taken on the MGM lot at this time. In one, the former stars were dressed in various period costumes and were shown signing contracts. King appeared in this shot wearing a top hat and tails. Florence Lawrence was in the photo, but curiously her name does not appear with the others in the printed article about MGM's new hiring directive. In the second photo, King was dressed as a minister. Despite this nice bit of publicity, almost none of these actors received any screen credit for whatever parts they may have played. We must take it on faith that he was there for, when seeing the film today, because of its huge cast, it is impossible to spot him. He may have been in three other MGM films that year: *The Devil Doll*, *We Went to College* and *Mad Holiday*; in each case, small press blurbs announced him in them, yet he received no credits in the final releases — nor could

Carl Laemmle's 30th anniversary in show business celebration, 1936. This time Baggot did not sit on the dais. L-r, Fred S. Meyer, trade publisher, Carl Laemmle, and King Baggot. Collection of the author.

he be seen in the prints viewed by the American Film Institute Catalog staff.

Family members have related that about this time King Robert, who had now graduated from Hollywood High School, got a job at MGM, too—in the film laboratory. Later he worked as a film loader. No evidence can be found that father and son ever worked together on the same film, but it is interesting to know they were on

Publicity photo from MGM, 1935, announcing that the studio had hired many "noted stars of yesterday." Shown signing their contracts are: l-r, Florence Lawrence, King Baggot, Flora Finch, Jack Gray, Helene Chadwick, Robert Wayne, Naomi Childers, Jules Cowles, and Mahlon Hamilton. Photograph courtesy of the Wisconsin Center for Film and Theatre Research.

the same lot at the same time. Ruth and King Robert moved again; they were now living at 7149 Hawthorn Avenue, a few blocks south of Sunset Boulevard, in another four-unit apartment building. On about December 8, Ruth had an abscessed tooth and went to the dentist. By December 12, she had an infection that invaded her bloodstream and she became quite ill. King Robert had been working the night shift and on the morning of December 22 he returned home to find a hearse in front of their apartment. Ruth had died of septicemia. She was only 47.[3] There were no antibiotic drugs in those days. Today Ruth's death from this cause would be quite preventable. She was cremated and her ashes consigned to a wooden box in a niche at Hollywood Cemetery — now known as Hollywood Forever Cemetery.

Ruth left a will which she had prepared at the time of her divorce from King in 1930. King Robert was then only 16 years old. She was advised, probably by her attorney, to appoint the Bank of America as trustee of her estate. She directed the bank to satisfy all her creditors and to pay her funeral expenses. King Robert and her mother Ann were each to receive $75 per month from the rest of her estate. While this made a certain amount of sense in 1930, by 1936 King Robert was 22 years old and probably would have been quite competent to be the executor, but no change had been made in the original will. Unfortunately for the family, the bank decided that her only real property — the house on Franklin Avenue — had to be sold. It went for a paltry $8,000. When King bought it for her in 1929, he paid $17,500 for it; the

Depression may have been partially responsible for this much lower figure. And the bank, of course, charged monthly fees for maintaining the trust. The house was purchased by a "John Mosso [sic]," one of the proprietors of the famous Musso & Frank's Hollywood restaurant. The house was still owned by his family members in the 1990s. By September 1939, the money that Ruth had left to her son and her mother was completely gone.[4]

Although King had a long-term contract with MGM, it is difficult to tell what work he did for them in 1937. He may have participated in any number of films as an unbilled bit player, but only three have been documented: One was a two-reel short titled *Torture Money,* an entry in MGM's *Crime Does Not Pay series*, in which he played a witness to an accident. He played a customs official in *The Emperor's Candlesticks*, directed by George Fitzmaurice with a distinguished cast that included William Powell, Luise Rainer and Robert Young, and had a small bit in the Marx Brothers' *A Day At the Races* as an official at the track. Still, he continued to take an active part in his profession. Records from Screen Actors Guild show that he joined the organization in May. His membership number was 9,900. SAG was founded in 1933, but in the early years the Guild had no power to make actors join. It was not until 1937 that SAG reached an agreement with the Directors Guild of America. He may have waited because he needed the support of those studios that might employ him; it may have been a case of not wanting to bite the hand that fed him. However, by this later date it was more a mark of respectability than an act of rebellion.

For a time after Ruth died, King had no contact with his son, but that year King Robert met a beautiful young woman at a party named Miriam (Mimi) Cornely from Burlingame, California. She was a part-time model and active with the Hackett Players of San Francisco, and was also going to school at San Mateo Junior College. Her father would not have approved of her marrying at such an early age — she was only 19 — so the young couple eloped to Nevada on July 5.[5] By this time, King Robert had moved to an apartment at 232 North Clark Drive in the West Los Angeles area with his grandmother, Ann Constantine (the family called her "Nana"). He supported and cared for her for the rest of her life; at the time of her death in 1941, she was living with the family.

King moved once again. In 1937 he had been living at an apartment hotel on the corner of Wilcox and Sunset Boulevard, but the following year he moved to the Culver City area. Since he seemed to be working exclusively for MGM, it made sense for him to live closer to his place of work. A diligent search has turned up no telephone directories for this location and period, so it is not known exactly where he lived, and no credits for 1938, 1939 or 1940 can be found. His parts (if any) must have been unbilled. A touching article appeared in a January 1939 *Los Angeles Examiner*. His former leading lady, fellow supporting player and friend, Florence Lawrence, had died on December 28, 1938. Her death sent shock waves through the industry, both because of the terrible way she died and because she represented so many of those "former stars." Ill, broke and in despair, she swallowed a mixture of cough syrup and ant poison. She died in agony.[6] Two photos accompanied the piece about King. One was a publicity still by the photographer Witzel, from around the time he directed his 1922 production of *Human Hearts*. He stands tall and confident, mature, yet still a handsome man. The other was a photo by the *Los Angeles Examiner* taken for this interview. Seventeen years had exacted their toll. A hat covers most of his gray hair. He does not look directly at the camera, but rather to some middle distance beyond it, as early film actors had been taught to do. Those tired eyes have seen quite a bit of life and pain. His jowls are sagging and his tie is askew. He is 59 in this picture, but could be taken for a decade older. The article recapped his career, but his quotes about his present situation reveal his mental toughness and eternal optimism:

> KEEP PITCHING, BAGGOT'S ADVICE
>
> He was the screen's great star before many of the present-day "greats" were born. A noted director before many of them were out of swaddling clothes.... So yesterday King Baggot looked back along the years that he had seen names come and go and gave this New Year's advice:
>
> "No matter what happens — just stay in there and pitch. Because if you're in there pitching all the time, any day may start that New Year you've been waiting for."
>
> And King knew whereof he spoke — he's still in there pitching, playing character parts and playing them regularly, after not one, but two notable careers.
>
> But there was one note of sadness in his advice. One of his oldest friends wasn't in there pitching any more. Last week Florence Lawrence chose suicide to escape ill health...
>
> [When] times changed, King Baggot didn't care particularly if he worked or not — he didn't have to. But came the depression — Florence Lawrence and King Baggot were two of the first of a dozen "old timers" signed by M-G-M. "So," said Baggot as he hurried through the studio gate, "don't forget, the thing to do is stay in there and pitch."[7]

A short time after King Robert married Mimi, she brought a reconciliation between her husband and her father-in-law. He came to visit them on a number of occasions and he clearly enjoyed having a young and vivacious daughter-in-law. However, from the *Los Angeles Examiner* photo one can see that he was not well. In September he tried to get some help. He checked into the Kimball Sanitarium in La Crescenta and elected to undergo electroshock treatment for his alcoholism.[8] Although it did not provide a cure, at least it did not seem to create memory loss or other side effects associated with its use.

As the years passed, it becomes just as difficult to unearth his screen credits as it was in the early days at IMP when actor's credits were so unevenly reported. He may have been too ill to work toward the end of 1939 and into 1940. The next credit found was not until 1941: *Come Live with Me* directed by Clarence Brown with James Stewart and Hedy Lamarr. He had the role of a doorman. Since the film was released in January of that year, it would have been in production at the end of 1940. The only other clue that he was still employed by MGM can be found in a 1941 *New York Times* article. It was a fascinating report on stars of the silent screen who were still working, albeit in far smaller roles. Some names mentioned were Lillian Gish, Gloria Swanson, William Farnum and Leah Baird. The writer cited the use of stock contracts by some of the studios to keep these old former stars employed. He quoted a casting director as saying that they were the most competent and conscientious bit players available. Warner Bros., according to the article, was paying their older players about $60 per week. At MGM he named six old stars under stock contract there: King, May McAvoy, Barbara Bedford, Naomi Childers, William Farnum and Mahlon Hamilton. The article also noted that Childers, Baggott (with two T's), Farnum, and Hamilton were currently working on the film, *A Woman's Face*.[9]

The year 1943 slipped by with no credits found. In 1944 he may have had an unbilled role in *Barbary Coast Gent*, which starred Wallace Beery and Binnie Barnes. At least, his name appeared in the production charts. In 1945, he could be seen in

Abbott and Costello in Hollywood, released in June of that year. He is not easy to find, but with repeated viewing he can be spotted as a patron in the barber shop scene. As he hurries by, he reveals only his right profile and shoulder. His old friend and colleague from his IMP days was in this film as well: Robert Z. Leonard played the part of a "film director," which indeed he was for so many years.

That might have been just about the end of King's known credits if it had not been for actor Roddy McDowall. From an early age, McDowall had been an enthusiastic admirer of King Baggot and others of the silent screen. He said that, growing up, he loved silent films and that many of these pioneer actors were his heroes. Not long before he died in 1998, he related that King had been in his film *Holiday in Mexico* in 1946. He said that King was a dress extra and that when he recognized him he walked up to him, offered some words of praise for his work and asked for his autograph, which King gave him. McDowall was 18 at the time. Roddy graciously viewed a video of the film himself, hoping to recognize him; he was unable to do so. But small wonder — in some of those scenes, especially in the nightclub, there were what seemed to be hundreds of extras.[10]

In the summer of 1948, King was living at the Aberdeen Hotel in Venice, California, less than a block from the ocean and just steps from the trolley cars that took him to his assignments at MGM. He may have been ill for some time, but suddenly his condition became critical. On July 9, King Robert took him to a sanitarium in order to get better care. But he did not improve. He may have had a series of small strokes before a final cerebral hemorrhage caused his death three days later, on July 11. His death certificate also mentioned that he was suffering from malnutrition.

There was no grand funeral service with hundreds of mourners, no banner headlines, no tributes to him by the famous. He died with no assets and left no will to dispense them even if he had. His clothes were so unacceptable that his son gave up his best blue suit in which to bury him. He was interred at Calvary Cemetery in East Los Angeles with a flat granite marker giving the year of his birth incorrectly as 1880 and the year of his death, 1948. The stone read, simply, "King Baggot." A few days later, in the major papers, there were some stock obituaries covering his career, but only one tried to capture his life in a meaningful way. It was the *Los Angeles Examiner*, which just eight years before had published his admonition to his fellow actors to "just keep pitching."

> King Baggot Gets Last Cue
> "No matter what happens — just stay in there and pitch." King Baggot, one of the screen's early-day stars and a top director, often gave that advice to younger actors. But yesterday the 68 year-old thespian let his cue slip by. He died at a sanitarium at 2020 South Western Avenue, victim of a stroke. He had been ill for three days. His death brought an end to a notable career...
>
> But bitterness also came with the sweetness. His wife of 18 years, Ruth Baggot, divorced him in 1930. He didn't care whether he worked or not after that.
>
> With the depression, Baggot sought work again and along with 11 other "old timers" was signed to an acting contract at Metro-Goldwyn-Mayer. He played many character roles in his later years and he played them with all the gusto of a big-time star.
>
> Baggot lived alone the past five years at the Aberdeen Hotel, Venice. It was here that he first took ill. Efforts were being made yesterday to reach his son, Robert King Baggot of West Los Angeles. Until then, funeral arrangements are pending.[11]

Fame is usually finite and so he left the world as anonymously as he had entered it. He was born into one world and died in quite another. Filmdom's first publicized leading man had a career that burst into existence like a skyrocket. His fame was once so great that he was world-renowned. When that rocket was spent and fell back to earth, up he went again, though not quite so high. He was a part of the infant days of the motion pictures, one of its true pioneers, and he wholeheartedly participated in its evolution, welcoming each new step as it happened until events outpaced him. When that occurred, he never succumbed to self-pity. His fierce love of his profession propelled him on for as long as he could go. The stubborn Irish boy from St. Louis had quite a ride.

Coda

One might wonder why so little is known today about this once famous man. Where are the family photographs, the memorabilia, the family history? The answer is simply that like so many of his films, they are all gone. During the last years of his life, King created a great deal of resentment on the part of his wife Ruth and son for his uncontrollable behavior. It is believed that in anger, Ruth destroyed every family photo that might remind her of him. The family's constant moving from one place to another also took its toll. King Robert was so ashamed, hurt and disgusted with his father that he barely spoke of him to his own family. Life went on.

At the time of the writing of this book, over 100 years have passed since Baggot's birth. There is almost no one left to ask. King Robert died tragically in May 1965. He had become a cameraman after his service in the Navy during World War II. While filming offshore background footage for *Lt. Robin Crusoe, U.S.N.* for Walt Disney Pictures, near Knudson's Beach, Poipo, Kauai, his boat was struck by a heavy wave. He was thrown from the boat and died of his injuries.

King Baggot's daughter-in-law Mimi was a young woman when she knew her father-in-law. She has little to remember. Several times they lunched together at the Cotton Club in Culver City and they sometimes exchanged presents, but the family was not close. She had little opportunity to completely understand what an important man he had once been — and besides that, she had two boys to raise.

Her sons, King Stephen and Bruce, were young children when their grandfather died. King, born in 1943, was only five and Bruce, who was born in 1947, was a bit more than a year old. Not surprisingly, both have worked in the motion picture industry, King Stephen as a cinematographer and Bruce as a film editor. But aside from knowing the basic facts about his life, they could know little about the man himself.

King's many siblings all died long ago. His youngest sister, Harriet died at age 31 in Missouri. His sister Marion was the anchor of the family back in St. Louis. Her unmarried brother Amos lived with her in the family home on Union Street until his death in 1954. Marion came to California to visit King Robert and the family, but that was not until the 1950s, a number of years after King's death. She died in the 1960s in Clayton, Missouri. Their brother

Thomas Gantt married Hortense McChesney and in 1929 or 1930 moved to California, where he was an insurance executive for many years. Their son Tom Baggot, who became an attorney, remembers King visiting their home a number of times, but he was a little boy at the time. John Marmaduke also moved to California some time in the 1940s and died in 1975. Arthur Lee was a family mystery. Legend has it that he was working in the film industry, perhaps as a distributor, when some time after 1933 he went to Arizona and suddenly disappeared. If he was killed, his body was never found.

What do those still living family members recall about him, personally? They remember his piercing eyes, that he gestured forcefully with his hands, that he was a man of few words but gave the appearance of strength, and that when he walked into a room, he would take everything in with his eyes before proceeding. They used words like "kind," "loving," "dignified."

Although those wisps of memory are not enough to paint a picture of the whole man, they give us a glimpse of him.

Film archives, both here and abroad, are not much help either. Most of his films have not survived. Film history as a discipline is still evolving. Until about 15 years ago, there were few research tools, and study of the early film pioneers was almost non-existent. Today the situation is somewhat better, but there is still much work to do on the industry of King's day and the people who created it. So much can never be retrieved now, and what remains urgently needs attention.

King Baggot's career, especially in those very early days of film, was an odyssey of unprecedented proportions. Perhaps if he had died rich and free of any scandal, or even had he led a far more notorious life, he might have been better remembered. Yet all that he did for his profession deserves to be recalled and celebrated. He was, indeed, "The King of the Movies."

Filmography

Introduction

King Baggot's film career began in late 1909, and he worked until 1947, a year before his death. In a 1920 interview, he commented that he had already made over 300 films. Documenting the work of any of those true film pioneers is no easy task. In the very early years, between 1909 and 1912, it was not a common practice for producers to give the names of their film performers. Then too, when the usual length of a film was about 1,000 feet, they were making many films in a given year. In Baggot's case, it is equally difficult to find all the films he made between 1930 and 1947 because near the end of his career, he appeared in many films as a bit player, mostly in uncredited roles. For those reasons, the exact number of his films will never truly be known.

Many sources have been consulted to arrive at this compilation. The following have been found to be the most useful:

Books

The American Film Institute Catalog of Motion Pictures Produced in the United States. New York: R.R. Bowker, Vols. 1895–1910, 1911–1920, 1921–1930, 1931–1940, 1941–1950.

Richard E. Braff. *The Universal Silents.* Jefferson, North Carolina: McFarland, 2000.

Annette M. D'Agostino. *An Index to the Short and Feature Film Reviews in Moving Picture World: The Early Years, 1907–1915.* Westport, CT: Greenwood Press, 1995.

Einar Lauretzen and Gunar Lundquist. *American Film-Index, 1908–1915 and 1916–1920.* Two volumes. Stockholm, Sweden: Film-Index, 1976 and 1984.

The Library of Congress Catalog of Copyright Entries. Motion Pictures, 1894–1911, 1912–1939, 1940–1949. Washington, D.C.: U.S. Copyright Office, Library of Congress.

Paul C. Spehr with Gunar Lundquist. *American Film Personnel and Company Credits, 1908–1920.* Jefferson, North Carolina: McFarland, 1996.

Periodicals

The Implet, March 16–June 1, 1912.
Moving Picture World, 1907–1927.
Motion Picture News, 1908–1913.
Universal Weekly, 1911–1928.

For the years from 1909 to 1919, considerable effort has been made to include all the information about each film that could be found. The basic arrangement is chronological. The actual words of the reviews or synopses have been paraphrased in order to capture the flavor of that time.

By providing detailed descriptions, it is possible to see what kinds of films were being produced and viewed by the public. It sheds interesting light on what the people of that time were thinking about — the social and moral sensibilities of the age — as well as how these elements were depicted on screen. It is also hoped that plots and other production information might be of help to film preservationists in documenting films when only fragments still exist.

The components of the 1909 to 1919 group include:

Title

Production entity The studio and releasing company.

Release Date Since films were not shown in theaters in all parts of the country at the same time, it seemed best to use the date when film producers generally made their films available to exhibitors, usually by means of their ads and release charts in trade publications.

Length In feet, minutes or reels.

Library of Congress registration number Included when found. Production companies did not always register their films in the early years.

Dir Indicates the name of the director.

Scen The scenarist or screenwriter.

Cast The spelling of actors' names could vary widely, including Baggot's. Paul Spehr's *American Film Personnel* is the largest and most comprehensive source to date attempting to arrive at standard spelling for their names and has been used here as a name authority. When known, character names have also been included.

Notes These give any production information, shooting locations, discrepancies or interesting sidelights found during the course of the research.

Loc Location of existing prints of the films.

BFI	British Film Institute, London
BSU	Boise State University, Boise, Idaho
GEH	George Eastman House, Rochester, New York
LC	Library of Congress, Washington, DC
MOMA	Museum of Modern Art, New York
NF	Nederlands Filmmuseum, Amsterdam
UCLA	University of California. Film & TV Archive, Los Angeles
VID	Indicates a commercially produced video, or in a few cases, a video owned by a private collector.

At times, not all of the components could be found. If any are missing, it means no sources searched provided that information.

From 1920 to 1947, tools to document films became more readily accessible. Advertising, reviews and film documentation in general become more available to the researcher. At this point, extended casts, character names, and synopses, in some cases, after 1930, writers' credits have been omitted.

King Baggot was a remarkable man. He was a masterful actor of great versatility and accomplishment, a screenwriter of some note, and a talented director. To see and acknowledge the breadth and depth of his work is to realize what an important figure he was, and still is, and what an integral part he played in shaping the early history of film.

1909

The Awakening of Bess
IMP, 12/27/1909. 950 ft.

Dir: William V. Ranous.
Cast: Florence Lawrence, King Baggot, George Loane Tucker.

Synopsis: A love story, not mushy, but powerful and convincing.

Notes: George Loane Tucker's participation was given by Baggot in an interview in the *Los Angeles Express* 10/1/1921, where he said Tucker "played the heavy."

1910

Never Again
IMP, 1/24/1910. 615 ft.

Cast: Florence Lawrence, King Baggot.

Synopsis: When "Mrs. Henpecker," temperance crusader, somehow gets throttled by the demon she is trying to pursue, a series of complications result. The unfortunate worker is given whisky so frequently and so liberally that she becomes a shining example of how not to do it.

Notes: Split reel with *Rose of the Philippines*, 730 ft.

Jane and the Stranger
IMP, 2/21/1910. 900 ft.

Dir: Harry Solter.
Cast: Florence Lawrence, King Baggot.

Synopsis: An unfaithful father deserts the girl he has wronged and migrates to the west, where he is discovered by the girl's brother. The wrong is revenged in a highly dramatic manner which introduces Jane, the pet of the ranchmen. She innocently causes the arrest of the brother, who took the law into his own hands, but saves his life when she learns through a letter that his crime was justifiable. She lets the ranchmen in on the secret and they plan a pleasant surprise for the man who expected to get it in the neck. The plot contains a strong love story. The picture ends with the lovers surrounded by their friends, who offer hearty and vigorous congratulations.

The Time-Lock Safe
IMP, 3/17/1910. 960 ft.

Cast: Florence Lawrence, King Baggot, Owen Moore.

Synopsis: A mother arranges to go to a matinee with a friend and plans to leave her little daughter with her husband at the office, but he is not in. She entrusts the girl to the care of the office boy until the father returns. A laundry man with a large basket appears to change the towels at the employee's washstand. Suddenly the office boy is called away on an errand. The mother and her friend return from the theater and cannot find the child. The father returns from his business errand and they realize the child is missing. They think she may be in the time-lock safe, which cannot be opened until the next day. The police are called and a professional safe-cracker is employed for a large sum of money to open the safe. He goes into a private office where the safe is located and discovers the child asleep in the laundry basket. He summons the anxious parents and makes a hasty exit before it is discovered that his services were not required after all.

Notes: Although no credits exist for this film, the viewed incomplete and titleless print clearly reveals the actors listed above played the main characters. The plot suggests that *Time-Lock Safe* is the correct title. The only character named in the intertitles is the safe cracker; "Spike Murphy" played by an unidentified actor.

Loc: UCLA.

Transfusion

IMP, 3/28/1910. 960 ft.

Dir: Harry Solter.
Cast: Florence Lawrence, King Baggot.

Synopsis: A young girl takes her horse to the local blacksmith's shop to be shoed. The blacksmith falls in love with her, but she already has a suitor and does not realize his situation. Her horse runs away with her, causing a serious accident. Doctors are called and it is determined that she needs a blood transfusion. The suitor is too cowardly to give the needed blood and arranges for the blacksmith to provide it. While the girl is unconscious, incisions are made in both their arms and a tube provides the blacksmith's blood to the stricken girl. When she recovers, she thanks her sweetheart for providing his blood. Conscious-stricken, he admits that it was the blacksmith who saved her. The blacksmith and the girl are united.

The Miser's Daughter

IMP, 4/4/1910. 980 ft.

Dir: Harry Solter.
Cast: Florence Lawrence, King Baggot.

Synopsis: A miserly father in need of money promises his daughter to a wealthy old bachelor. The girl already has a sweetheart, but her father insists. When the bachelor comes to the house to be introduced, the girl has their unlovely domestic give him a lively reception, but he persists in his attention to the girl. She decides to have some fun with the situation and agrees to wed right then and there. Upstairs she goes to get dressed and down comes the eager bride-to-be with a modest veil over her face. They walk toward town, where they just happen to run into a minister — actually, it's the sweetheart in disguise, who agrees to marry them on the spot. Dad collects his bag of cash and the knot is tied. The eager newlywed lifts the bride's veil and to his consternation finds the homely servant girl beaming at him. He realizes he has been tricked and attempts a getaway, but the ardent damsel considers her luck too good to lose and with arms flailing she seals his fate for him in no uncertain way.

His Second Wife

IMP, 4/7/1910. 970 ft.

Dir: Harry Solter.
Cast: Florence Lawrence, King Baggot.

Synopsis: A dashing young man meets two beautiful girls at a ball and chooses one of them to marry. They have a little girl, but after a few years the wife falls ill with the white plague (tuberculosis). As she is dying, and with her old friend in attendance, she places her husband's hand in that of her former rival and admonishes her to take care of her child. She dies and the two are wed. However, the little girl keeps asking for her mother, which so distracts the new wife that she tries to strangle the little girl. The little girl writes a note and prepares to run away, but she becomes suddenly ill and falls unconscious. It is smallpox. The note comes to light and the stepmother's maternal instincts return. Defying the chance of contagion, she nurses the little girl back to health and is rewarded. The house is once again bathed in sunshine and happiness.

The Eternal Triangle

IMP, 5/23/1910. 950 ft.

Dir: Harry Solter.
Cast: Florence Lawrence, King Baggot, Harry Solter.

Synopsis: An old man has a young wife. A young man comes on the scene and makes violent love to her. It results in the death of the old man at the hands of the younger one. When the wife realizes what has occurred and her part in it, she deliberately walks off a cliff to her death, joining her husband in his last sleep in the chasm below.

A Game for Two
IMP, 6/30/1910. 970 ft.

Dir: Harry Solter.
Cast: Florence Lawrence (Mrs. Henderson), Owen Moore (Mr. Henderson), King Baggot (Clark).

Synopsis: A wife becomes jealous of her husband's male friend. She bestows unwelcome attentions upon the friend in order to drive him away. Unfortunately, the husband misunderstands the reason for his wife's attentions and begins some uncomfortable shooting about the place. But, happily, the tangles are all unraveled and peace once more folds her wings and rests within the household.

Bear Ye One Another's Burdens
IMP, 7/29/1910. 975 ft.

Dir: Harry Solter.
Cast: Florence Lawrence, (Mrs. Rand), King Baggot, (George Rand).

Synopsis: George Rand, a businessman, is overcome by a series of strokes. His crooked broker tells Rand's wife that the bonds she tries to cash are worthless. She returns home to her invalid husband and is determined that he never know of their reduced circumstances. She establishes a little workroom adjacent to his room but keeps it screened. When near him, she wears her fine clothes and maintains his room with all the trimmings of their former days. One night their child accidentally tips over a lamp, and soon the room is ablaze. Rand realizes that his family is in danger and that knowledge acts as an electric shock to his palsied limbs. With a surge of strength he springs up and carries the child to safety. As he puts out the fire, he looks around and realizes for the first time all of the sacrifices his wife has been making. The last chapter is a reunion and a reincarnation.
   Loc: LC.

The Irony of Fate
IMP, 8/1/1910. 995 ft.

Dir: Harry Solter.
Cast: Florence Lawrence, King Baggot, Owen Moore.

Synopsis: An author with a lovely young wife is so preoccupied with his books that he ignores her. A friend comes to visit and he insists that the friend keep his wife company. They begin to fall in love and the friend tries to leave, but is asked to stay while the husband takes care of some business in the city. While there, he has an attack of sunstroke. At home, under a doctor's care, he is told to avoid excitement, which could kill him. In the library, the friend confesses his love for the wife and tells her he must leave. The husband sees the two together. He flies into a jealous rage and faints. The doctor is called and gives the husband an injection of morphine to calm him; however, the husband and wife have another quarrel and he dies of the excitement. The friend sees the morphine and syringe and thinks the wife has killed his friend, but he hides the evidence to protect her. The doctor exonerates her, explaining that the death was due to sunstroke. However, the friend feels that the death was partially his fault and decides to go west and be heard of no more.

Pressed Roses
IMP, 9/26/1910. 987 ft.

Cast: Florence Lawrence, King Baggot.

Synopsis: A young man has pawned his last loose property in order to take a girl to the theater. There is a mix-up in which roses are sent to the tailor to be pressed while his trousers go to the girl, with instructions to "wear them tonight." Ultimately the snag is straightened, everyone is happy and the girl presses the trousers.

The Count of Montebello
IMP, 10/24/1910. 994 ft.

Dir: Harry Solter.
Cast: Florence Lawrence (The Heiress), King Baggot (Percy), Owen Moore (Gerald).

Synopsis: Percy and Gerald are friends. Percy inherits a tidy fortune. They move to luxurious quarters and proceed to enjoy them together. While at the tennis court surrounded by eligible "summer girls," they meet "the heiress" and both fall madly in love with her, but she rejects their proposals. They plot revenge on the haughty one and discover an organ grinder who will help them with their plan. They dress him in finery, take him to a reception at the home of "the heiress" and introduce him as the Count of Montebello. The plan is to have the heiress fall in love with and marry the Count. But he falls in love with a pretty little French maid instead. Their plot is discovered by the heiress, who devises a plan of her own. She announces her intention to marry the Count, much to the joy of the pair. The wedding day arrives and the ceremony is performed. The two plotters denounce the Count as an organ grinder and began to laugh, but as the bride's veil is lifted, the face of the pretty maid is revealed and a seemingly old maid aunt removes her disguise and stands before them as the heiress.

As they return sorrowfully to their bachelor quarters, they are relieved of the last of their money by the bridegroom, who collects his fee. The landlord throws them out for nonpayment of rent and back to their hall room they go, devouring baloney sausage and dry bread donated by a sympathetic little slave.

Notes: This was part of a series featuring two office clerks, a.k.a. *The Hall Room Boys,* Gerald and Percy. Other titles in the series were *Fruit(s) and Flowers,* released 5/19/1910, *The Widow,* released 8/29/1910, *The Count of Montebello* and *The Aspirations of Gerald and Percy,* released 12/5/1910. Baggot's participation has only been verified in the latter two.

The Double
IMP, 11/14/1910. 996 ft.

Scen: Katharine Boland Clemens.
Cast: King Baggot (Col. Robert King and Joseph Dansby).

Synopsis: Charming Maude Wentworth is in love with Robert King, a dashing soldier who must go off to war in Cuba. This soldier has an exact double, whom the girl meets and mistakes for King. At first Joseph Dansby tries to explain the situation, but she will not listen. However, he soon falls in love with her and decides to assume the role of King. Things drift along in this manner until King, fighting in Cuba, is killed. When Maude reads the news, she falls into a faint. Dansby summons her maid to her assistance, then leaves. At home, he writes her a note telling her the truth and states that he will go away forever. When she reads the note she realizes that she loves Dansby as much as she ever loved Robert. She goes to him and begs him to remain, which he does.

Notes: Mrs. Clemens, the wife of a St. Louis doctor, won $100 in a scenario writing contest sponsored by the *St. Louis Times.* This was one of Baggot's first dual roles.

The Aspirations of Gerald and Percy
IMP, 12/5/1910. 994 ft.

Cast: King Baggot, Owen Moore.

Synopsis: After losing their positions in a shop, the Hall-Room boys appear in a new role, as would-be performers in a theater—with disastrous results. The variety and number of things hurled at them are surprising. They then enlist in the Army, which results in desertion; their old friend Tony suffers until officials are convinced of his innocence. But Tony succeeds in obtaining redress from the gay youths and leaves them attired in a barrel.

Unreasonable Jealousy
IMP, 12/29/1910. 990 ft.

Cast: King Baggot, Isabel Rea.

Synopsis: A wife is jealous of her husband's medical practice and the patients who take him away from her. She meets an actor and they go to supper together. The doctor is informed and goes to the cafe, where he sees them together. The wife returns home and the couple quarrel. She goes up to her room, pleased to have aroused his jealousy. Later, the doctor is called to attend the actor whose skull is fractured. At first he refuses, but then relents and performs the operation, which saves the man's life. When the wife hears of it, she understands her husband's nobility of soul and asks forgiveness for her foolish escapade.

1911

Phone 1707 Chester
IMP, 1/26/1911. 997 ft.

Dir: Joseph Smiley.
Cast: King Baggot (Ralph Vincent), Eleanor Kershaw (Effie Vincent).

Synopsis: A story of how a young married man is cured of a sporting life. Ralph makes a bet, which he wins. He goes to the city to collect it and runs into a fast crowd. He begins drinking and gambling and forgets about his wife and child. Effie goes to the city and finds him in a cafe drinking out of a woman's slipper. As she turns away in tears, he sees her and realizes that he has just lost his whole future. Some hours later, he comes to his senses in a Turkish bath. He is broke, but surrounded by his friends of the evening. One of his new friends, Fred Strong, finds Ralph's phone number and calls Effie at Hiram Hayes' grocery store (the Vincents rent rooms above the store). Effie and the baby are brought down to the phone and negotiations for Ralph's return are begun. Fred and the rest of Ralph's friends are at one end of the wire in their bathing costumes and Effie and the baby are at the other end in their nightclothes. Effie asks Ralph to return. As he dresses to leave the Turkish bath, his friends take up a generous collection for his baby. Ralph swears off the sporting life and the next time he receives a tip by wire, he tears up the telegram and throws it away.

An Imaginary Elopement
IMP, 2/2/1911. 500 ft.

Cast: King Baggot (Guy Judson), Maude Burns (Dora Judson).

Synopsis: Dora is asked by her father to go out for a little excursion. She leaves a playful note for Guy saying she has "gone away with a handsomer man." Guy assumes the worst and hires out-of-work detective Abel Sharpe to find her. The bumbling Sharpe takes a box of beards, wigs, and other disguises and begins dragging every woman he can find to Guy's home, hoping it is Dora. He grabs one about to catch a train and another in the street. He finally arrests Guy's colored cook as she leaves the front gate for an airing. Guy becomes so enraged, he kicks Abel out. Then all of Abel's victims arrive on the scene accompanied by a policeman and he is taken off to the police station. When Dora arrives back with her father, Guy discovers who the "handsomer man" really is.
Notes: Split reel with *The Mix-Up*.

At the Duke's Command
Imp, 2/6/1911. 1000 ft.

Dir: Thomas Ince.
Cast: King Baggot (Edward, the Duke's nephew), David Miles (Duke of Chatmoss), Anita Herndon.

Synopsis: In sixteenth century England, a beautiful young court maiden, Irma, is introduced to the Duke and his nephew. Edward falls in love with her and it is reciprocated. However, the old Duke becomes infatuated with her and sends his hunchbacked serf to her apartment to summon her to his presence. He tries to overwhelm her, but she repulses him. She runs to Edward and tells him. Edward confronts the Duke, and after a bitter exchange of words, Edward draws a sword. The Duke has Edward thrown into the dungeon. He also has Irma seized and taken to the cell where Edward is confined. A mock trial is held and Edward is ordered to the torture chamber. The Duke informs Irma that the price of her lover's life is herself. When she is taken to view Edward being seared and tortured on the rack, she consents to sacrifice herself and the torture ceases. The hunchback is commanded to bring the girl to the Duke's chamber, but before she goes, she sears her face with a red-hot poker, horribly disfiguring herself. She is led into the chamber wearing a veil. The Duke lifts the veil and renounces all pursuit of her. He then calls Edward and tells him he must now marry Irma, thinking he will no longer want her. Edward lifts the veil, and although shocked at the result of her sacrifice, he draws her tenderly toward him in an embrace and leads her away, loving her in spite of her disfigurement.

Notes: In the viewed print, Mary Pickford appeared in a small part as one of the court ladies. Although Anita Herndon was credited in this film, from the viewed print it was not possible to tell what role she played, or if she was indeed in it.

Loc: LC, MOMA.

Pictureland

IMP, 2/20/1911. 1000 ft.

Cast: Mary Pickford (Rosita), King Baggot (Pablo).

Synopsis: Pablo, of humble origins, loves Rosita, a beautiful maiden. Wallace Crawford, an American tourist now appears on the scene. He rides up to Rosita's house and asks for a drink, and Rosita looks after the tourist with altogether too much concern. Pablo calls with his guitar and plays to her as he usually does, but the girl seated beside him allows her thoughts to drift into sleep where she dreams. In her dream, Crawford offers her jewels and wins her with his lovemaking. Pablo discovers them and brings Rosita's parents to the scene. Rosita innocently believes Crawford means honorably by her and leads him to a church, but this is more than he had in mind. He declines. He is attacked by Pablo, and only the intervention of the Holy Father saves the life of the faithless American. During the struggle, Rosita awakens to find it is all a dream. The drama closes with the venerable Father uniting Pablo and a now-contrite Rosita in marriage.

Notes: Semi-documentary. This is the first IMP release filmed in Cuba. Part one showed the cast and crew setting up to shoot the picture, part two told the story they shot, and part three showed the IMP company packing up and driving off after the film was completed.

Tracked

IMP, 3/6/1911. 1000 ft.

Dir: Joseph Smiley.
Cast: King Baggot (Roger Densmore).

Synopsis: Dan Barret, a forger, is sought by Balfour, a detective. He goes to Cuba to escape arrest. There, he comes to the tobacco plantation of Roger Densmore. He is taken ill and is cared for by Densmore and his wife. He becomes infatuated with the wife and invites her to accompany him on a horseback ride. Before they leave, he forges a letter to Roger saying that his wife no longer loves him and has gone away with another man. The unsuspecting wife is led away to an isolated spot where Barret seizes her and, throwing her across his horse, gallops away. The note is found and a furious Densmore sets out with a servant to find them. When he does, the wife tries to explain, but he will not listen. He gives the cur a chance for his life by removing all the cartridges from his gun but one. Then spinning the cylinder around, he commands the destroyer of his happiness to shoot, but Barret proves a coward and pleads for his life. Barret is about to be run through by the servant with a machete when the detective, Balfour, appears and saves his life. Balfour explains that Barret is a forger and is shown the note. Then Densmore begins to understand. Barret is led away and Densmore takes his faithful wife in his arms, begging her forgiveness.

Notes: Filmed in Cuba.

The Secret of the Palm
IMP, 3/13/1911. 1000 ft.

Dir: Joseph Smiley.
Cam: Antonio Gaudio.
Cast: King Baggot (Cecil Abbott), Anita Herndon (Mother of Don Alvarez).

Synopsis: Cecil Abbott is foreman of the Canby fruit ranch in Cuba and a favorite suitor for the hand of Edna, daughter of the ranchman. The mother of Don Alvarez, an old friend of Canby, sends her son to visit the ranch, where he falls in love with Edna. But she prefers Cecil. Cecil is entrusted with the company mailbag and rides off to the post office. On the way back, he meets Edna and stops for a little talk. Don Alvarez observes them and, while they are distracted with each other, he steals the mailbag. Returning home, Cecil is accused of having robbed the ranchman. Alvarez hides the bag at the top of a palm tree. Later, his mother sends him a note saying she has sent him money via the former mail. He climbs the tree to retrieve the bag. Looking down, he sees Cecil and Edna. He falls, still clutching the bag, and is found bruised and dying at the foot of the tree. Cecil carries his former rival to the ranch with Edna following, mystified. When Alvarez sees the bag, it rouses him and with his dying breath he confesses his crime, absolving Cecil of all blame. Cecil takes Edna in his arms and the inference is that Cecil is promoted from ranch manager to son-in-law.

Notes: Filmed in Cuba. An uncredited Anita Herndon was spotted in the viewed print.
Loc: LC, UCLA.

The Penniless Prince
IMP, 3/23/1911. 1000 ft.

Dir: Thomas Ince.
Cast: King Baggot (Prince Gustave), Isabel Rea (Dolores), Anita Herndon (Inez).

Synopsis: Prince Gustave, a young bankrupt German nobleman, alights from a vessel at Havana, Cuba, to earn a livelihood. He applies for a job at the office of a tobacco planter where he meets the planter's daughter Inez, who immediately falls in love with him. Gustave is given a position in the office as a bookkeeper but soon is attracted to Dolores, who is employed on the plantation. Inez is jealous and induces her father to remove him from the office and put him to menial work on the plantation. She then mails him a letter informing him that his presence is required at the office of the German consul. Gustave is hopeful that there will be good news from his family home, but he cannot go in the shabby clothes he now wears. Dolores rescues him by going to a dealer in hair and sacrificing her beautiful tresses. Gustave is surprised, hurt and grateful. He tries to thrust the money back in her lap, but she bids him keep it. He visits the consul only to learn there is nothing to be done for him and he returns humiliated. Inez rejoices in his disappointment, but Dolores comforts him. He returns to the fields, but one day he receives a visit from a German official who tells him that his brother has died and he is now heir to his father's estate. He takes Dolores in his arms. The consul congratulates the prince and the girl he has chosen and they walk away leaving Inez, the intriguer, disappointed and desperate.

Notes: Filmed in Cuba. Although uncredited, Anita Herndon was seen in the viewed print.
Loc: LC.

Sweet Memories

IMP, 3/27/1911. 1000 ft.

Dir: Thomas Ince.
Cast: Mary Pickford (Polly Biblett), King Baggot (Edward Jackson), Owen Moore (Ashton Orcutt), Charlotte Smith (Lettie Terrell Jackson), Jack Pickford (Young Earl Jackson), Lottie Pickford (Young Lettie Terrell).

Synopsis: Edward Jackson brings his betrothed, Polly Biblett, to his mother for her blessing. As the lovers walk away to plan their future, Mrs. Jackson falls into a reverie and dreams about her own youth. First she sees herself as an infant seated beside Earl Jackson, who is destined to become her husband. The children are eating sweets and cooing; childish innocence personified. At 14, Lettie is a beautiful young girl. Earl paints her portrait and kisses her. They walk away oblivious to all else except their own happiness. Earl has a rival, Ashton Orcutt, who attempts to woo Lettie by force. Earl arrives on the scene and they duel using rapiers. Ashton is slightly wounded and Earl's honor is satisfied. Lettie and Earl are married and their union brings them a son, Edward. But later in her life, when Edward is 14, Earl dies and Edward is all she has to lean upon. The scene reverts to the grove. Lettie awakes in sadness. Her face is tear-stained and her body convulsed with sobs. Edward and Polly approach. She takes the young girl in her arms, admonishing Edward to cherish and protect her. The young people receive her blessing.

Notes: Although Charlotte Smith (Charlotte Pickford) was uncredited, she can be seen in the viewed print. Filmed in Cuba. Reissued by IMP as *Sweetheart Days*, 9/14/1914.

Loc: LC, VID.

The Lover's Signal

IMP, 4/3/1911. 980 ft.

Dir: Thomas Ince, Joseph Smiley.
Cast: King Baggot (Raymond Williams).

Synopsis: Allan Roberts is in financial straits and takes his problem to his wealthy friend Maurice Anderson. Anderson offers to marry Robert's lovely daughter Grace to ease his burden. Anderson agrees. Next door live John Williams and his son Raymond, but they are not known to Roberts. Raymond strolls onto the grounds of the Robertses' property and meets Grace. They fall in love, but Raymond is ordered off by Roberts and Anderson. The lovers meet in a secret place and resolve to continue meeting by means of a signal, a shrill whistling note. One day in their trysting place, Raymond tells Grace he must take a train and deliver some important papers for his father. He dallies too long and misses the train, but Grace does not know this. She sees a newspaper which reports that the train was wrecked, killing all on board. She loses her reason. Raymond comes to the house and finds her in this state. He suggests an experiment and by means of the whistle he restores her. All objections to their marriage are removed and Grace and Raymond are happy in their unrestricted love.

Notes: Filmed in Cuba.

The Scarlet Letter

IMP, 4/27/1911. 1000 ft.

Dir: George Loane Tucker, Joseph Smiley.
Scen: Herbert Brenon.
Cast: King Baggot (Reverend Dimmesdale), Lucille Younge (Hester Prynne), William R. Daly (Roger), Anita Herndon, Robert Z. Leonard, J. Farrell MacDonald.

Synopsis: Hester Prynne has left Holland in advance of her husband Roger, an older man whom she does not love, to join the colonists in Salem, Massachusetts. Roger follows, but is captured by Indians, and Hester waits for him in vain. Reverend Dimmesdale, the handsome minister of Salem is beloved by his parishioners. He meets Hester clandestinely and an unlawful love is the result. Hester is discovered with a baby and is arrested and made to stand in the pillory. For the remainder of her life she must wear the letter "A" on her breast. The governor of the colony commands her to name the father of the child, but she refuses. Roger is released by the redmen and comes to Salem the day Hester is pilloried. By mutual agreement, they maintain silence and Roger takes the name Chillingsworth. Being a physician, he is called to prescribe for the minister, who has fallen ill. He knows that Dimmesdale is the father of Hester's child. As time passes, the minister grows weaker in bodily strength. His guilty secret gives him no peace. Meeting Hester and little Pearl by accident, he tells Hester of his terrible mental punishment and they decide to go away to another country. Hester's tears the letter from her breast, but Pearl finds the letter and returns it to her. The pair realize they cannot escape the consequences of their sin. On a holiday, Dimmesdale preaches a strong sermon on sins of the flesh. Afterward, in the marketplace, members of his congregation cheer him, but he is overcome by emotion at his own hypocrisy. He slowly and deliberately mounts the pillory and acknowledges Pearl as his child. Hester smiles through her tears. She will no longer have to bear the shame alone. However, the strain of the guilt he suffered so long proves too great a tax on his strength and he falls dead at the foot of the pillory. Hester supports his head. Tears course down her cheeks. Vindication has come, but with it has gone the man she has loved so long in secret.

Notes: Billed as an "IMP de Luxe." Filmed on Eastman stock. From the novel by Nathaniel Hawthorne.

Second Sight

IMP, 5/1/1911. 1000 ft.

Dir: Thomas Ince, Joseph Smiley
Cast: Mary Pickford (Gertrude Edgar), King Baggot (Tom Moorland), Owen Moore (Owen Jackson), George Loane Tucker.

Synopsis: Gertrude flirts with Owen, but really loves Tom. Tom is invited to go on an expedition to discover the headwaters of the Amazon River. Uncivilized savages capture the party and he is the sole survivor; however, a newspaper report suggests that all have been killed. Gertrude's grief is pitiful. She wanders down to an old gate where she used to meet Tom and, fixing her eyes into space, sees Tom alive in the wilds. She goes to Owen and tells him she knows Tom is still alive. She begs him to go and find Tom and promises that if Owen will save him, she will marry him. Owen organizes a search party, finds him and brings him back to Gertrude. At their return, Gertrude is at first overjoyed, but remembering her promise, tells Tom she must marry Owen. Then Owen shows his true character. He places the hand of Gertrude in that of Tom and walks away.

Notes: Possibly filmed in Cuba.

The Temptress

IMP, 5/4/1911. 1000 ft.

Cast: King Baggot (Gilbert Irving).

Synopsis: Gilbert Irving and Bertie Erroll are boyhood friends. At a house party, Mrs. Allen announces the engagement of her daughter, Lucille, to Gilbert, but while there he meets and falls madly in love with Madam Eloise. This evil woman decides to cause trouble between the friends. She makes Gilbert jealous and also writes a letter to Bertie saying she is in love with him. Bertie denounces her and tries to get her to leave, but she tells Gilbert that Bertie has written her an insulting letter. Gilbert challenges Bertie to a duel. Then Lucille falls ill and dies. Bertie arrives first and in his grief he throws himself in anguish over the form of the girl. Gilbert, entering, sees this and becomes angry. The two men meet on the field of honor. Bertie fires his pistol in the air, but Gilbert shoots Bertie. As he is dying, Bertie tells Gilbert the truth about the perfidious woman. Convinced of Bertie's innocence, Gilbert is stricken with remorse. He confronts the woman, who denies everything. He orders her from his house and collapses in grief and sorrow.

Notes: No printed credits for this film have been found; however, on page 928 of Moving Picture World, 9/29/1911, there is a quarter-page ad that clearly depicts Baggot in this production. Possibly filmed in Cuba.

The Fair Dentist
IMP, 5/8/1911. 700 ft.

Dir: Thomas Ince.
Cast: Mary Pickford, (Edith Morton), King Baggot, Owen Moore, George Loane Tucker, Isabel Rea (The Maid).

Synopsis: Three young clubmen, Claude Marlow, Eugene Wilson and Fred Strong, consider themselves irresistible to women. Claude is the first to spot the beautiful new dentist in town, Edith Morton. He goes back to the club where he raves of her charms to Wilson and Strong. Each independently decides to pay a visit to the young dentist, pretending to have a toothache in order to woo her. Marlow arrives first, but the dentist is all business. First she takes his cash, then relieves him of a tooth. In turn Wilson and Strong appear in the waiting room, each confident that they will charm her, but all leave the chair minus cash and some teeth. As they compare notes in the waiting room after their ordeal, the fair dentist has another surprise for them. She ushers in a man whom she introduces as her husband. Their racy little dreams of flirtation shattered, they file out sadder but wiser men.

Notes: Split-reel with The Four Lives, 300 ft. Reissued by IMP as Mary's Patients, 10/26/1914. Possibly filmed in Cuba.

The Master and the Man
IMP, 5/15/1911. 1000 ft.

Dir: Thomas Ince.
Cast: Mary Pickford (Elsie Graham), King Baggot (Basil King).

Synopsis: Henry Jenkins is released from state prison with an admonition from the warden to lead a straight life. He looks up his old friend and partner in crime, Basil King, who is now masquerading as an affluent society man. Basil is not overjoyed to see Jenkins, but employs him as a butler. Basil has a reception and a quartet of gentlemen leave the crowded parlor for a quiet game of poker. Jenkins arranges the table and manages to steal a bill of a large denomination, which Basil bids him return. Basil loves Elsie Graham, but she is in love with Ralph Webster. At the party, Ralph asks Elsie to marry him and she accepts. He has forgotten the ring and leaves to get it. One of the guests is wearing an expensive necklace and Basil cannot resist the temptation to steal it. The loss is discovered and, the next day, the woman who lost the necklace invites all who were present to join her in trying to discover the thief by employing a medium. Basil arrives late and takes a position behind a screen. The medium falls into a trance and declares that the thief is a clean-shaven man. Both Ralph and Basil are beardless. Basil makes off unobserved and suspicion falls on Ralph, who is driven from the house. In his grief, Ralph calls on Basil. Basil is penitent at Ralph's plight. He telephones Elsie to join them and assures them he will clear up the mystery. He produces the necklace and the pair leave elated. King summons Jenkins and gives him the necklace and a letter to take to the woman whose jewels he has stolen. In the letter, he confesses to the crime. Jenkins stops in a park, reads the letter and tears it in half. He writes that he, Jenkins, is the thief and can be found at Basil's home. After delivering the letter, he returns to find Basil dead in a chair. Out of friendship and compassion, he calmly awaits his fate. He returns to prison to serve time for a crime he did not commit.

Notes: Possibly filmed in Cuba.

Back to the Soil
IMP, 6/8/1911. 1000 ft.

Dir: Thomas Ince.
Cast: Mary Pickford (Sadie Allen), King Baggot or Owen Moore (George Dupont).

Isabel Rea, Mary Pickford and King Baggot in *The Fair Dentist*, IMP, 1911. Baggot's ardor just caused him to lose a tooth. Photograph courtesy of the Academy of Motion Picture Arts and Sciences.

Synopsis: George Dupont, a young farmer with artistic talent, lives with his parents, while Sadie Allen, his sweetheart, lives on an adjoining farm. He decides to go to the city believing that his talent as a painter will bring him a better life. His mother gives him all of her savings and he departs. He enters an art school where an unscrupulous teacher encourages him, knowing he has money. But after a year, when the money runs out, he tells George that he has no talent and dismisses him. George stops writing to his family and Sadie decides to go to him in the city. By chance she finds lodgings in the same house in the next room to his. He tries to pay his rent with a painting, but his landlady refuses. Sadie buys the painting without his knowledge. George decides to return home, still not knowing that Sadie has been so near. Arriving home, George finds Sadie there and they concoct a little joke. Finding some boots in the barn, he dons them and goes to work in the field with the other hands. The father rings the dinner bell and all come in. Without being noticed, George seats himself at the table, then breaks down in grief. They pile his plate high with food and the wanderer is welcomed home with warmth by all.

Notes: *The Dramatic Mirror* review, 6/14/1911, lists Baggot as the son, while *Moving Picture World*, 6/24/1911, notes Owen Moore in the role. Possibly filmed in Cuba.

A Piece of String
IMP, 6/15/1911. 1000 ft.

Dir: George Loane Tucker, Joseph Smiley.
Scen: Herbert Brenon.
Cast: King Baggot (Anton Paxton), Lucille Younge (Greta Anderson), Robert Z. Leonard, J. Farrell MacDonald, Lassie, the dog.

Synopsis: Anton, a young man of saving habits, walks to the village. He stops at the house of his sweetheart Greta and finds her talking to the blacksmith, who is his rival. But the girl shows her preference for Anton and the blacksmith goes away in a rage. At his forge, the blacksmith tightens the shoe of a horse owned by a hunter. In dismounting, the hunter drops his purse and his dog picks it up and runs into the forest, where she drops it among the rocks. Anton leaves his sweetheart to go into the village and, near the blacksmith's shop, he picks up a piece of string, which he pockets. When the hunter realizes his loss, he posts a note on the wall of the inn. The blacksmith tells the hunter that he saw Anton pick up the purse and he is publicly accused of the crime. Both his sweetheart and his mother believe the accusation. He is searched and no purse is found. He produces the piece of string, but is not believed. Roaming through the woods, the dog finds the purse again and takes it to his master, who goes to the inn and announces it has been found. Anton becomes hysterical with joy, believing he has been vindicated, but the evil blacksmith accuses Anton of hiding the purse in the forest. All present agree with the smithy and Anton is driven to raving madness. He drops dead, to the consternation of the villagers, who believe him innocent after he expires.

Notes: From a story by Guy de Maupassant.

In the Sultan's Garden
IMP, 7/3/1911. 1000 ft.

Dir: W.H. Clifford.
Cast: Mary Pickford (Haidee), King Baggot, Owen Moore, Isabel Rea, George Loane Tucker, Mr. Rae.

Synopsis: Lt. Robins is smitten with the favorite inmate of the Sultan's harem. She becomes interested in the handsome American and manages to get a note to him as his warship is in the harbor. She begs him to effect her rescue. When he comes ashore and climbs the wall of the palace, the Sultan's guards capture him. He is confined to a dungeon and sentenced to execution at daybreak. Haidee is condemned to be sewn into a sack and cast into the Bosphorus to drown. However, a servant has given her a knife. She cuts her way out of the sack and swims to the ship. Once aboard, she tells the Captain the fate of his officer. A battle ensues and the lieutenant is freed. Back aboard the ship, he is reunited with his Oriental sweetheart.

Notes: Reissued by IMP, 7/20/1914, as *The Sultan's Garden*. Filmed in and around the Hudson River in New York. Viewed print out of sequence. Reviews did not give the full cast. The print was of poor quality and it was not possible to tell whether Baggot played the lieutenant or the captain. In the reissue, Pickford's character was called "Haydee."

Loc: LC, VID.

For the Queen's Honor
IMP, 7/6/1911. 1000 ft.

Dir: Thomas Ince.
Cast: Mary Pickford (The Queen's Sister), Owen Moore (The King), King Baggot (The Villain/Hero), George Loane Tucker, Isabel Rea.

Synopsis: The setting is an Italian court of the sixteenth century. The king is good-natured and unsuspecting, though the queen is beginning to think too much of one of the courtiers. The queen's sister is aware of this and saves the queen by taking her place. This deceives the king, but he requires that the villain and the queen's sister be married. She loves another courtier and a terrible situation develops. The villain turns out to be heroic and sacrifices himself.

A Gasoline Engagement
IMP, 7/10/.1911. 1000 ft.

Cast: Mary Pickford (Flora Powell), Owen Moore (Arthur Lennox), King Baggot (Rev. John Maxwell).

Synopsis: Flora Powell and Arthur Lennox are lovers, but her father prefers the minister Rev. Maxwell. Arthur calls on Flora and produces a marriage license, but the father orders him out of the house. Arthur receives a note from Flora telling him her father is taking her on an automobile tour with Rev. Maxwell. Arthur manages to arrange with the local garage to become the chauffeur. On the trip, they run out of gasoline and the party must push the automobile to a friendly inn. Flora's father learns the true identity of their driver and is about to attack Arthur, but he seeks protection in the cellar of the inn. Mr. Powell follows excitedly until he sees Arthur strike a match near a barrel labeled "gasoline." He retreats, then descends once again only to see Arthur dropping ashes from his cigar into the bunghole of the barrel. He flees. Arthur finds choice food in a refrigerator and proceeds to relieve his hunger. Meanwhile, upstairs, the innkeeper tells the guests that all the food is in the cellar. The minister tries to dislodge Arthur, but is frightened away. Then Flora, driven to distraction by hunger, descends and is warmly greeted by Arthur. The minister tries once more, but is seized by Arthur, who threatens to blow them all up unless the minister marries them at once. After he complies, Arthur reveals that the gasoline container is empty.

A Quarter After Two
IMP, 7/13/1911. 1000 ft. J157341.

Cast: Mary Pickford (Mrs. Warren), King Baggot (Dan Nolan).

Synopsis: Dan Nolan is a mechanic who has been without work for many weeks due to a strike. Hungry and in despair, he resolves to steal. He finds a likely house, climbs the trellis and cuts the telephone wires. He has entered the home of Homer Warren, where the family is saddened by the serious illness of their little daughter. He hides in the closet of the child's room and watches events unfold through the keyhole. A nurse tries to summon the doctor by telephone, not knowing that the lines have been cut. She rushes out and returns with the doctor, who gives instructions to give medicine to the child promptly at the hour specified. The nurse and mother are nearly exhausted and Nolan, waiting in the closet, sees the mother leave the room and the nurse fall asleep. He emerges from hiding and sees it is the hour to administer the medicine. He rouses the child, tenderly gives the medicine and leaves a note. He emerges from the house, connects the telephone wires and walks away satisfied that he did not steal and that he performed a valuable service to the family. When the family awakes, they realize they have missed the critical hour until they see the note that Dan has left. The child confirms this. They are mystified. The next morning, Dan learns that the strike is over and he is once more content that he did no wrong.

Notes: *Moving Picture News* lists the title as *At a Quarter to Two*. All other sources give title as above. Reissued by IMP, 8/31/1914, as *Mr. Burglar, M.D.*

Science
IMP, 7/24/1911. 750 ft.

Cast: Mary Pickford (Mrs. Crawford), King Baggot (Dr. Crawford), Lassie, the dog, Imp, the puppy.

Synopsis: Dr. and Mrs. Crawford are at home with their little daughter Elsie, playing with their Scotch collie puppy, Imp. Another doctor visits them and they show him a newspaper article about the rescue of their daughter by Lassie, the mother of Imp. Lassie comes in and is admired. Two more physicians arrive, needing help with an experiment using a newly discovered anesthetic. Dr. Crawford planned to use a guinea pig, but discovers the animal has died. They decide to use Imp for the experiment in spite of Elsie's protests. The puppy dies under the anesthetic. Both Lassie and Elsie are inconsolable. The gardener digs a grave and the sorrowful procession goes out to bury the dog. Lassie sees the grave dug as she follows the gardener about. She goes to the laboratory, then back to the garden where clods of earth are being placed over the body of her puppy. She trots sorrowfully to the grave and places her paws on it in an attitude of prayer, her grief being pitiful to witness.

Notes: From a short story by Mark Twain, *A Dog's Tale*, written for the Christmas number of *Harper's Magazine* in 1903 on behalf of the National Anti-Vivisection Society of London. Split-reel with *Won by a Foot*.

The Call of the Song
IMP, 8/3/1911. 1000 ft. J158243.

Cast: Mary Pickford (Amy Gordon), King Baggot (Hugh Norton).

Synopsis: Amy and Hugh are village sweethearts. He is a bright young man and she is the village schoolteacher. Hugh receives an offer to enter a business firm in the city. He finds Amy in her beloved rose garden and tells her of his good fortune. He promises to return to her with the last rose of summer. He goes to the city and plunges into dissipation. He becomes enamored of a young society woman. Amy sends him a pair of slippers she has embroidered with his initials. He receives them while entertaining his new companions. The gift is tossed about the room in derision. Amy waits for word of Hugh in vain. Then she hears of his engagement to the wealthy city woman, which so overwhelms her nerves that she loses her reason. Later, at a dinner, a street singer entertains Hugh and his companions. She sings the song "With the Last Rose of Summer I'll Come Back to You." Hearing it, Hugh looks around him and sees the sham of it all — his neglect of Amy, the condition of his half-tipsy fiancée. His better nature asserts itself. He rises half-crazed with remorse and hurries back to his home. He finds the demented Amy in her garden picking a rose. Sorrowfully, he plays a guitar and sings, "The Last Rose of Summer." Hearing that loved voice, Amy's reason gradually returns. She turns to him with a glad look of recognition and is clasped in his arms.

Notes: Included specially arranged

music with instructions to the pianist and the singer.

Battle of the Wills
IMP, 8/21/1911. 500 ft. J159003.

Cast: King Baggot (The Hero), William E. Shay (The Villain), Lucille Younge (The Girl).

Synopsis: A villain is attempting to come between two lovers. He uses hypnotism and seems to have subdued the girl's will so that she has the appearance of loving the dark-mustached, mysterious stranger. It seems his cunning plans will prevail, for when the hero leaves the girl to make preparations for the wedding, the villain appears. The girl is about to go away with him when the hero comes back. Now there is a battle of wills between the two men. The girl seems drawn one way and then the other, but at length the hero is victor.

Notes: Split-reel with *Love in a Teepee*.

The Brothers
IMP, 9/14/1911. 1000 ft. J159917.

Dir: George Loane Tucker, Joseph Smiley.
Scen: Herbert Brenon.
Cast: King Baggot (Patrick Curran), Robert Z. Leonard (Father Curran), Lucille Younge (Rose Grady).

Synopsis: The story is set in Ireland. Patrick has a rival for the affections of Rose, Dennis O'Day. Patrick's brother is Father Curran, who watches earnestly over his flock, which includes Shamus McCarty, the village drunkard. One day Dennis finds Patrick and Rose together and flies into a rage. Father Curran comes on the scene in time to keep a fight from breaking out. The two shake hands and are friends again. Proceeding on his way, the good Father finds Shamus under the influence. He takes away his bottle and lectures him. Returning home, he sits in front of the fire with his pipe and newspaper. He falls asleep and dreams that Patrick and Dennis fight and Dennis is thrown over a cliff. Patrick hides in the family house, but the villagers come looking for him. Father Curran tells them his brother is not there and they go away; however, Shamus believes he is lying. He comes back, and peeking through the window, sees Patrick. To get even with the priest, he tells the villagers and, returning to the house, sets it on fire. Father Curran awakes to find it was all a dream and his pipe has set the newspaper afire. Patrick and Rose come for his blessing.

The Rose's Story
IMP, 10/2/1911. 1000 ft. J160518.

Dir: George Loane Tucker, Joseph Smiley.
Scen: King Baggot.
Cast: King Baggot (Gerald Kinney), Lucille Younge (Myrtle Edgar), Robert Z. Leonard, Isabel Rea.

Synopsis: Gerald Kinney is a young man who travels with a fast set, but one day his better nature asserts itself. He leaves his club, where the wine is flowing and the tables are strewn with poker chips, to motor out into the country. In a pretty wooded dell, he meets Myrtle, a simple country maiden. She shyly gives him a drink of cool water. He tries to take liberties with her, but is gently but firmly rejected. Roses grow in profusion here and she plucks one and pins it to his lapel. He goes away, but the rose acts as a talisman. Whenever he is tempted to do wrong, he regards the flower and remembers the girl. His friends want to know his secret, but he guards it. At a society function one night, he suddenly thinks of her. Leaving his handsomely gowned partner, he walks out into the night. With the memory of the sweet country girl before him, he seeks her out and declares his honest love for her. He tells her of his past. For a time she puts him on probation, but eventually agrees to wed. After a few years, they have a child to gladden their lives. One night Myrtle is leafing through his old Bible and finds a withered rose. She questions him and he tells her it is the rose she gave him so long ago. The flower has made a man of him and brought him a true and trusting wife to complete his happiness.

Notes: Library of Congress record lists the title as *The Story of the Rose*. First known scenario credit for Baggot.

Through the Air
IMP, 10/5/1911. 1000 ft. J160519.

Cast: King Baggot (Jack Baldwin).

Synopsis: Flo Garret and her father go on a prospecting trip to the gold country. Her father's partner is Ned Bullard, who loves her, but his affections are unreturned. They meet an aviator, Jack Baldwin, who has his dirigible housed in a tent. Jack guides the party into the hills where they make camp; the father and Ned start to look for gold. Flo goes into town to get a bag of flour and is rescued by Jack when a drunk molests her. The aviator offers to help her any time she might need it. Back at camp, gold is found, but the partners, Ned and Flo's father, disagree about the claim. Flo's father is shot and Ned rushes off to register the claim in his own name. The father manages to write out another claim and sends Flo off to try to beat Ned to the claims office. At the railroad station, Ned finds he has missed the train and hijacks a car instead. Flo goes to the station and, finding out what has happened, enlists the help of the aviator, who takes the claim and flies to the registration office. The car owners overpower Ned in time to allow Jack to arrive there first. The daring young aviator wins the girl and the thanks of her prospector father.
Loc: BFI.

The Better Way
IMP, 10/12/1911. 1000 ft. J161181.

Dir: Thomas Ince.
Cast: Mary Pickford (A Salvation Army Lass), King Baggot (A Reformed Crook).

Synopsis: The hero is just out of prison. He marries a good little woman, but the undertow of his former life is very hard to contend with. A woman of the streets comes to his room and tells his wife that she is going to get him back to his old ways again. He is absent at the time, having gone for a doctor to help a child whom he has just rescued. The evil woman hides her purse and accuses him of theft. A policeman finds the purse and is about to arrest him when he discovers that the child is his own. The trouble is then straightened out.

Notes: Reissued by IMP in 1914 as *Mary's Convert* and in 1922 by Universal as a spoof, *Going Straight*.

King, the Detective
IMP, 11/2/1911. 1000 ft. J162089.

Cast: King Baggot (King), Frank W. Smith (Ashton).

Synopsis: Mr. Armstrong's chauffeur Ashton drives the banker home with a large sum of money. Armstrong's daughter Edna has a sweetheart, Walter Hoskins, who has been ordered to cease his attentions. In order to see her, he climbs the latticework on the piazza and is observed by Ashton. Armstrong is murdered in his den and Ashton accuses Hoskins of the crime, for which he is arrested. Edna calls in King, the detective. He searches the murder room and finds a thumb print on the collar of the murdered man. He also searches the grounds and the garage where he carefully inspects the tools. He examines the print in his laboratory and decides to conduct an experiment. Placing powder on his wrist, he goes to see Ashton. Shaking hands, he presses the driver's thumb into the powder. After comparing the prints again, he returns to the house and confronts Ashton. He also produces a wrench used as the murder weapon. Ashton is terrified and confesses the murder. Hoskins is released and rejoins a joyful Edna. Together they seek out King and thank him.

Tony and the Stork
IMP, 11/7/1911. 1000 ft. J163272.

Cast: King Baggot (Tony).

Synopsis: Tony, a young married Italian, is out of work just when money is most needed because his wife is expecting a child. He strives to find work, but there are difficulties because his English is imperfect and his curious garb and manner do not impress his possible employers. Finally a railroad crew takes him on, but he will have to be out of town. Months go by and at last he receives a letter telling him his wife has given birth and is in the hospital. He draws his pay and sets out for home, stopping first to buy a baby carriage and other toys to gladden the hearts of his wife and child. Arriving at the hospital, he is told that his wife has died. He is led to a sheeted figure and is wild in his grief. When the covering is removed, he shouts for joy, for it is not his wife. She is strong and well and further surprises him by telling him he is the father of twins. Tony starts out to exchange his go-cart for one with a larger carrying capacity.

The Wife's Awakening
IMP, 11/9/1911. 1000 ft. J162417.

Cast: King Baggot, Lucille Younge.

Synopsis: An inventor is blinded by an electric flash while working. He can no longer take his wife to dances and show her a good time as he formerly did and she is led into temptation. Packing up her things, she is about to leave with another man when she comes upon the dress of her baby who has died. This brings her to herself. She rushes to her blind husband and discovers him about to commit suicide. She begs his forgiveness and they are reconciled.

Executive Clemency
IMP, 11/22/1911. 1000 ft. J162975.

Cast: King Baggot (Dan Fuller), Isabel Rea (Mrs. Fuller), Mrs. Brenon (Governor's Daughter).

Synopsis: Dan Fuller is an honest mechanic. He is at home when the rent collector calls. The man is a masher and tries to force his attentions on Dan's wife. She screams and Dan rushes in to defend her, beating the man severely. A policeman hears the disturbance and, not listening to Dan's defense, arrests him. His wife's story is not believed and he is sent to prison. He becomes a model prisoner and the governor intends to release him on Thanksgiving Day. However, before the holiday, he receives a letter announcing that he is a father. Obsessed by a need to see his wife and child, he escapes and returns home late at night while they are sleeping. He tenderly kisses them and voluntarily returns to prison. Word of this gets to the governor, who rescinds his pardon. The governor's daughter reads of his escape and the reason for it, and pleads with her father to reinstates the pardon. He is released on Thanksgiving Day. The governor's daughter has gone before him with a bountiful dinner. The corned beef and cabbage his mother has prepared is laid aside and there is a joyful reunion.

Notes: "Mrs. Brenon" was probably Herbert Brenon's wife Helen Oberg Brenon. Her stage name had been Helen Downing.

Over the Hills (To the Poorhouse)
IMP, 11/30/1911. 1000 ft. J163138.

Dir: George Loane Tucker, Joseph Smiley.
Scen: Herbert Brenon.
Cast: King Baggot (Wayne Holland), Lucille Younge (Ethel Edgar), Robert Z. Leonard, Margarita Fischer, Isabel Rea, Anita Herndon, Violet Mersereau.

Synopsis: While her father is away on a prospecting trip, his pretty daughter Ethel dresses up as a boy and goes prospecting herself. She falls over a cliff and is rescued by a young miner, Wayne. He takes her to his cabin and soon realizes she is not what she seems. Leaving her in the cabin, he sleeps outdoors. A thief breaks into the cabin and her screams awake Wayne. He throws the thief down the mountainside. Ethel goes home where she dons suitable wearing apparel. Wayne comes to visit her wearing his best suit. He is smitten, but she will have nothing to do with him in his good clothes. He goes home crestfallen, but Ethel follows him and makes amends.

Notes: From the poem by Will Carlton.

The Girl and the Half-Back
IMP, 12/18/1911. 700 ft. J163638.

Cast: King Baggot (Victor Fisher), Margarita Fischer (Alice), William E. Shay (Dick Allison).

Synopsis: Two college chums love the same girl. She favors the football captain, Victor. Rival Dick sends the signals to the other team and, in a letter to Alice, blames Victor. He is banished from the game and is forced to watch from the sidelines, powerless to help his side. Alice finds she has been deceived by the letter, which is produced on the field. Dick is put out of the game and Victor scores the winning touchdown.

Notes: William E. Shay is not credited for this film, but in *Moving Picture World*, 12/16/1911, page 863, he is depicted with Baggot and Fischer. Football scenes were shot in Charleston, South Carolina.

A Lesson to Husbands
IMP, 12/30/1911. 400 ft. J163923.

Cast: King Baggot (Jack Armstrong), Margarita Fischer (Mrs. Aubrey).

Synopsis: A young businessman falls prey to a pretty woman who calls upon him and asks him to cash a check for her. She is so alluring that she entices him into further indiscretions. He lends her money to buy hats, calls at her house and leaves her flowers. His infatuation is so great that he grows cold toward his wife. A newspaper item recalls him to his senses. The girl with the checks is a notorious creature against whom the public is warned; her victims are businessmen. The paragraph has a salutary effect upon the young husband, who recalls himself to his duty and puts himself right with his wife.

Notes: Split-reel with *Broke ... or How Timothy Escaped*. 600 ft.

1912

The Trinity
IMP, 1/4/1912. 700 ft. J164089.

Cast: King Baggot (Henrick), Margarita Fischer ("Baby" Lena), William R. Daly (August).

Synopsis: August, an old taxidermist whose bachelor companion is the young artist Henrick, receives a letter from an old friend in Germany informing him that he is sending his baby daughter for a short stay. The two men are alarmed at the imminent invasion of their home by a baby. Nevertheless, they buy toys and go off to meet her train. "Baby Lena" proves to be a handsome young woman with whom the artist falls in love and she with him. The old taxidermist is fearful that he will lose the companionship of his friend. This is averted when, after much thought, he draws up plans to put an addition on the house. This is satisfactory to the trio and the old German is again happy, assured that they will all continue to be companions.

The Winning Miss
IMP, 1/8/1912. 1000 ft. J164368.

Cast: King Baggot.

Synopsis: This is a farcical situation in which a girl hides from an objecting parent in a wardrobe, delivered to the hero's room and

William E. Shay, Margarita Fischer, and King Baggot in the college romance *The Girl and the Half-Back,* IMP, 1911. Photograph courtesy of Wichita State University, Ablah Library.

then carried away without his knowing it, with the girl inside.

After Many Years

IMP, 1/18/1912. 1000 ft. J164578.

Cast: King Baggot (Harry and George Chilton), Edith Haldeman (Little Ethel).

Synopsis: Two brothers part and take different paths. One, Harry, makes a success in life; the other, George, is, if not a failure, at any rate, conspicuously not flourishing.

Both are residents of the same city, unknown to each other. The daughter of the wealthy brother, little Grace, gives a children's party. This attracts the attention of George's poorly dressed child Ethel, who peers longingly through the fence. She is taken in, but is snubbed by the other children. When they leave, Grace entertains her with great kindness. Ethel becomes ill and is carried home to her parents by Harry. When the two fathers meet, it is discovered that they are brothers. They are brought together again by the always-powerful influence of children.

Notes: Although no credit for Edith Haldeman has been found, a still from this film shows her in the cast. Baggot played both brothers.

The Kid and the Sleuth
IMP, 1/29/1912. 1000 ft. J165201.

Dir: Thomas Ince.
Cast: King Baggot (Nick Carter), Lucille Younge (The Villainess), William R. Daly (The Villain), Ethel Grandin (The Heroine), Thomas Barry (Red Gallagher).

Synopsis: Red Gallagher, a messenger boy, reading of the adventures of Nick Carter instead of delivering his messages, has a dream. In it, he obtains the services of the famous detective in order to foil a villain and villainess who conspire against the personal safety of the unhappy and helpless heroine. They subject her to a whole series of dastardly outrages in order to get her to "sign the papers." There is a spirited chase with the detective and the messenger kid pursuing the villains. It ends at a sawmill just as the heroine is about to be mangled by a huge saw. At last Red is a hero, but the detective puts the fair maid in his car and carries her off after giving Red only a nickel for the labor he has put into helping rescue the heroine. After the boy has followed the dramatis personae of his dreams to the bitter end, he awakens.

Notes: Story adapted by Thomas Barry from his own vaudeville sketch.

The Power of Conscience
IMP, 2/1/1912. 1000 ft. J165166.

Dir: King Baggot, William R. Daly.
Scen: R. Sayer.
Cast: King Baggot (Eric Masters), Lottie Brisco (Mrs. Masters), William E. Shay (Vernon Godfrey).

Synopsis: Eric Masters and his wife are leading the lives of society people on a limited income. Their friend Vernon Godfrey, who is interested in Mrs. Masters, holds a note of Eric's, which he is willing to renew, provided the wife would go away with him. She very nearly consents when he threatens to ruin her husband, but in the end, her love for her little child (whom she has been neglecting) and that of her husband triumphs and she remains true to him. Before this, at a fashionable ball, one of the guests, Mrs. Leslie, loses a valuable jewel, which is found by Eric. This means a way out of all his difficulties, as the jewel is worth $10,000. He is tempted to retain it, give his wife all that she desires and repay his friend. But after deliberation, he returns the jewel, preferring to be honest. With his repentant wife, he resolves to lead a happier and more economical life in the future.

Through the Flames
IMP, 2/15/1912. 1000 ft. J166373.

Dir: Thomas Ince.
Cast: King Baggot (John Allen), Lucille Younge (His Wife), William R. Daly (The Telegraph Operator).

Synopsis: The wife of John, a railroad engineer, is dangerously ill when a message comes announcing that a village is threatened with a forest fire. The telegraph office is on fire and the lives of the inhabitants are endangered. The telegraph operator alerts John. There is no one else to man the train and he goes, driving the engine, which rocks and sways at the high rate of speed through clouds of smoke and flame. He reaches the panic-stricken villagers and rescues them. When he returns from his perilous trip, he finds his wife much improved and receives the plaudits of his kind neighbors. He is presented with flowers and obliged with an impromptu speech of thanks.

The Tables Turned

IMP, 2/17/1912. 800 ft. J166701.

Cast: King Baggot (Mr. Despard), Miss Cummins (Rose Despard), William E. Shay (The Sanitarium Manager).

Synopsis: Rose suspects her husband of flirting. He does not, of course; he is only being interviewed by a lady client. At the instigation of her maid, the jealous young wife pretends to go mad. When hubby comes home he is mystified, but put wise by the maid, who wheedles a few dollars from him for the suggestion that he should also go mad. So mad does he go, despoiling the house and alarming his wife, who has him placed in a sanitarium. The attendants use him brutally and he ends up in a tub of ice guarded by an attendant with a most ferocious demeanor. All ends well when Rose is able to convince the sanitarium manager that it was all a mistake.

Notes: Split reel with *The Savannah Pushmobile Race*. 200 ft.

A Modern Highwayman

IMP, 2/19/1912. 1000 ft. J166503.

Dir: Otis Turner.
Scen: Otis Turner.
Cast: King Baggot (Noah Prescott), William R. Daly (William Steele), William E. Shay.

Synopsis: Old Noah Prescott, an inventor, has his ideas stolen from him by a modern highwayman, an unscrupulous manufacturer William Steele. Poetic justice is accomplished by the intervention of a little child, whose doll is stuffed with papers conclusively proving the guilt of the highwayman, who is made to disgorge a proportion of his ill-gotten gains.

The Lie

IMP, 2/22/1912. 1000 ft. J166596.

Dir: King Baggot, William R. Daly.
Scen: A. Castlebaum.
Cast: King Baggot (Capt. Robert Evans), Lottie Briscoe (Edith Hobson), William E. Shay (Lt. Hobson), William R. Daly (Mr. Hobson).

Synopsis: During the Civil War, brave Northern Capt. Robert Evans kisses his sweetheart Edith Hobson and rides off to take his place on the field. Victory after victory attends the Northerners. Edith's brother Lt. Hobson is fighting on the Confederate side and is a fugitive from Grant's men. He takes refuge in his own home, hidden by his father and sister, but Capt. Evans and his men come in search of him. Evans is admitted alone into the house where he sees the wounded brother of his fiancée. Should he arrest him, or should he not? He takes pity on the stricken family and decides on the latter course. Returning to his men, he lies that Hobson is not there. The poor hunted wretch escapes, presumably to recover and to interpose no barrier to the marriage of the victorious Northerner and Edith.

The Immigrant's Violin

IMP, 2/26/1912. 1000 ft. J166713.

Dir: Otis Turner.
Scen: Clay Mantley.
Cast: King Baggot (Albert Radley), Vivian Prescott (Mrs. Radley), Lena Loraine (Lora).

Synopsis: A young Italian violinist arrives in New York with her family. She is met at the pier by a friend, but becomes separated from them and is lost. She is taken under the protection of a society lady and her son, who soon begin to love her. The girl becomes a talented violinist, is invited to play for an East Side audience and there, meets her people. For a moment she is indifferent to them, then faints at the recognition. She is taken home, but filial duty asserts itself. She exchanges her fine clothes for her old Italian garments and returns to them. Finding her gone, Albert and Mrs. Radley are distressed. Albert traces her through the number on a taxi. Down in the tenement district he finds her and tells her he truly loves her. The story ends with the engagement of the poor but beautiful Italian girl to the son of her benefactress.

Far from the Beaten Track
IMP, 3/4/1912. 1000 ft. J166914.

Dir: Otis Turner.
Scen: Otis Turner.
Cast: King Baggot (A Trapper), Vivian Prescott (His Wife), William R. Daly (The Stranger).

Synopsis: Away in the lonely northern land of the Hudson Bay lives a trapper and his young wife. He goes about his occupation without noticing that his mate finds her life monotonous. Ennui sets in and they become tired of each other. A handsome young stranger becomes separated from his hunting party and meets with an accident. He is found by the trapper, who takes him to his cabin to be cared for by his wife. As days pass, they fall in love. The husband returns at a moment when a love avowal has been exchanged, but he conceals his knowledge. The couple decides to elope, but they have barely started away when the man is injured falling into a bear trap. The husband appears. He decides she cannot return to his home. Her lover is wounded. So he leaves them there and returns to his lonely hut. What becomes of the pair? How does the story end? It does not end. It concludes with a note of interrogation.

Shamus O'Brien
IMP, 3/14/1912. Two reels. J167144.

Dir: Otis Turner.
Scen: Herbert Brenon.
Cast: King Baggot (Shamus O'Brien), Vivian Prescott (Aileen Brennan), William R. Daly (Michael O'Farrel), Agustus Balfour (Father Malone), William E. Shay (Capt. R. MacDonald), Herbert Brenon (Tim Mooney), Rolinda Bainbridge (Mrs. O'Brien).

Synopsis: Shamus, a patriot with a price on his head, is fighting for Ireland during the uprising for Home Rule in 1789. He is hiding in the hills, but is anxious to attend a dance with his friends and his sweetheart Aileen. At the dance, he surprises the guests by appearing. Michael O'Farrel, his rival for Aileen, tells the Redcoats of his whereabouts. When they arrive, Shamus hides in the hayloft. When Capt. MacDonald begins insulting Aileen, Shamus jumps down, floors the officer and makes his escape. He visits his mother, but O'Farrel sees him there and betrays him to the British once again. Shamus is taken to prison and stands trial. He is convicted and the day of his execution is set. As this draws near, his mother makes a plea to the parish priest for help. Through a ruse on the part of the good priest, Shamus is saved. The picture closes as mother, son and sweetheart sail for "The Land of the Free"—America.

Notes: From the poem by Joseph Sheridan Le Fanu. Advertising copy in *The Implet*, 3/9/1912, has Samuel Lover as the poet. IMP's second and Baggot's first two-reel film.

Loc: LC, BFI.

The Man from the West
IMP, 3/18/1912. 1000 ft. J167279.

Dir: Otis Turner.
Scen: J.W. Culbertson of Indianapolis, Indiana.
Cast: King Baggot (Steve), Vivian Prescott (The Cook), William E. Shay (Steve's Friend), Violet Horner (The Society Woman), Agustus Balfour, Miss Krause.

Synopsis: Steve, a man of the West, comes to New York with much money and the intention of seeking a wife. His friends and relatives have a sophisticated young woman of their own kind in mind for him, but Steve has other ideas. He sees the plump and pretty cook and, after he has tasted her pies, he is (in the best sense of the term) a lost man. He loses his heart to the cook and defies the schemes of his relatives. His friend marries the girl Steve does not want.

The Romance of an Old Maid
IMP, 3/25/1912. 1000 ft. J167491.

Dir: Otis Turner.
Scen: R.H. Danforth of Berkeley, California.
Cast: King Baggot (Frank Rogers), Rolinda Bainbridge (Julia Dayton), Gladys Eagan (Little Lucille), William E. Shay (James Hopkins).

Synopsis: Julia Dayton, engaging in philanthropic work on New York's East Side, finds it her duty to help reform a workman who has an unfortunate addiction to alcohol. She also takes a liking to his little daughter, Lucille. However, it is a difficult matter to reform a man. Frank resents Julia's attentions to his daughter and forcibly insists on keeping possession of the girl. Undaunted, Julia perseveres and succeeds in obtaining a job for Frank through her brother-in-law James. He rises to the occasion, becoming a better man. During his regeneration, he discovers that he has a fondness for his benefactress and that she returns the sentiment. The final result is that they marry. By marrying, Julia surprises her friends and relatives, who had hardened to the conviction that she had passed the age or opportunity of sentiment.

Notes: Reviews give Rolinda Bainbridge's character name as "Julia Wharton" or "Ruth Dayton," but it appears as "Julia Dayton" in the viewed print.

Loc: LC.

Tempted but True
IMP, 3/28/1912. 1000 ft. J167584.

Dir: Otis Turner.
Scen: Otis Turner.

Cast: King Baggot (John), Vivian Prescott (Mary), William E. Shay (Mary's Employer), Mr. Welsh, Mrs. Hurley, Mr. Dillon.

Synopsis: John is a happy country blacksmith looking forward to marrying his sweetheart, Mary. However, she is lured to the big city by the prospects of earning her own living there. Once there, she tastes boarding house life and secures a job at a ribbon counter. Here, her good looks attract the attention of her employer. She is repulsed by his cafe manners, so he schemes to entrap her in a bogus marriage. Meanwhile, John becomes so concerned for Mary that he goes to the city to find her. He puts up at the very hotel where the plot is in progress to entrap Mary. He makes his way to her boarding house, but she rejects poor homely John in favor of her city admirer. John discovers the scheme of the bogus marriage. He finds the license is forged and before any mischief can be consummated, he finds a minister and they defeat the plot. John and Mary meet at the depot and return together. The girl has been sorely tempted, but she remained true and thus a happy marriage is in store for the honest blacksmith and his sweetheart.

The Loan Shark
IMP, 4/25/1912. 1000 ft. J168683.

Cast: King Baggot (The Doctor), Grace Lewis (His Fiancée), Rolinda Bainbridge (The Loan Shark's Secretary), William E. Shay (The Old Clerk).

Synopsis: An old clerk has financial difficulties and is compelled to raise money from a loan shark whose factotum, a woman, is particularly merciless. The old clerk is driven to steal money in order to pay his installment. His daughter is engaged to a young doctor who accidentally discovers the old man's plight through the loan shark's daughter. The doctor confronts the loan shark and demands in payment for his services the amount of the old clerk's loan. With the papers in his possession, the doctor arrives just in time to prevent the old clerk from taking his life and that of his daughter out of shame and disgrace.

Notes: The review in *Moving Picture World*, 5/20/1912, gives William E. Shay's role as "The Loan Shark," but illustrations in ads from various sources show he played "The Old Clerk."

Lady Audley's Secret

IMP, 5/16/1912. Two reels. J169341.

Dir: Otis Turner.
Cast: King Baggot (George Talboys), Jane Fearnley (Lady Audley), William E. Shay (Sir Robert Audley), Thomas Welsh (Sir Michael), William R. Daly (Luke Marks), Violet Horner (Clarice).

Synopsis: George Talboys marries a woman below him in the social scale and is disinherited by his father. Foreseeing his wife's fury when she hears of this calamity, he deserts her and departs for the gold fields of Australia. She pronounces herself dead through the press and assumes a new identity. She soon meets and marries Sir Michael Audley, a very rich but older man, and they go to live at Audley Hall. George Talboys returns from the gold fields with his fortune and looks for his wife. His search is unrewarded until he is invited to Audley Hall by his old friend Robert Audley. He recognizes her, but she rejoins him to silence and asks that he meet her that night at the old well. He wishes to reunite, but she wishes to kill him. When his back is turned, she pushes him down the well and leaves him for dead. However, Luke Marks, a poacher, rescues him and takes him to the inn. Robert Audley, anxious over his friend's failure to return, starts a search for him. When he hastens to the inn, Lady Audley follows. She locks Robert in a room and, realizing that both her enemies are beneath one roof, she sets fire to the building, watching the blaze with diabolical exultation. A heroic escape saves her intended victims. They confront her on the threshold of the castle, just as she fancied that all evidence against her had been consigned to the flames. Lady Audley collapses and insanity closes the portals of her distorted mind.

Notes: Based on the novel by Mary Ellen Braddon. Re-released 9/25/1916 as *The Bigamist*. Credits in the re-release give variant names to the cast members, i.e., "Jane Vernon" for Jane Fearnley and "William J. Welsh" for Thomas Welsh, and Herbert Brenon is credited as the producer. However, there is no mistaking this very distinctive story and its characters.

A Cave Man Wooing

IMP, 5/20/1912. 1000 ft. J169924.

Dir: Otis Turner.
Scen: B.M. Conners.
Cast: King Baggot (The "Sissy" Hero), Violet Horner (The Girl), William R. Daly (Prof. S. Trong), William E. Shay.

Synopsis: A good-looking young man is in love with a girl, but is no match for his rival, who displays the prowess of a young giant. He goes to Prof. S. Trong's Physical Culture School and, after three months of practice, he emerges a strong man. He makes a renewed play for the girl. He shows that he can lift the family piano and then he physically lifts the girl and carries her off. He is pursued by the girl's friends, but instead of wanting to be rescued, the girl chooses to marry her "cave man."

Loc: NF.

The Peril

IMP, 5/30/1912. 1000 ft. J169922.

Dir: Otis Turner.
Scen: Dr. S.W. French, U.S. Army.
Cast: King Baggot (The Lieutenant), Violet Horner (His Sweetheart), William R. Daly (The Japanese Spy), William E. Shay.

Synopsis: A young lieutenant is on duty at the fort and one night sits so late at the bottle that he becomes intoxicated. He is

Baggot as George Talboys in *Lady Audley's Secret*, IMP, 1912. Photograph courtesy of the Academy of Motion Picture Arts and Sciences.

discovered by his prospective father-in-law and threatened with court martial. While in the commandant's home, he discovers a disguised Japanese spy who has been acting as a butler, stealing papers that give information about U.S. military installations. The lieutenant catches him in the act and a struggle ensues. The spy is vanquished. The lieutenant is restored to the good graces of the commandant and given the hand of his daughter.

Up Against It

IMP, 6/1/1912. 600 ft. J69858.

Dir: Otis Turner, William R. Daly.
Scen: George Elmore.
Cast: King Baggot, Vivian Prescott, William R. Daly, William E. Shay.

Synopsis: A man finds himself in a crowded house one evening and is unable to do himself justice toward his hostess and fellow guests because he has torn his pants in a very conspicuous spot. His efforts to conceal the awkward rent are amusing to the well-dressed ladies and gentlemen, although they do not know the cause of it. The poor fellow finally obtains access to the bedroom of a girl and is about to ply the needle when he is discovered by the girl's father, who does not recognize him and mistakes him for a burglar. He is threatened with a gun and has a very bad time of it until he is rescued by his friends. He is given a dressing gown and the dear girl herself undertakes the repair of his torn garment. It is presumed this is practice for the future position of becoming the young man's wife.

Notes: Split-reel with *The Art of Silver Plate Making*.
Loc: NF.

The Breakdown

IMP, 6/3/1912. 1000 ft. J169879.

Dir: Otis Turner.
Scen: King Baggot.
Cast: King Baggot (Huntley Sharpe and Jim Simpkins, the double), Violet Horner (The Maid), William E. Shay (Robert Harmon), William R. Daly (John Hamilton).

Synopsis: Wall Street businessman Huntley Sharpe, president of the Mutual Constructing Company, has to find a large sum of money on a certain day in order to save the company from collapse. He himself collapses and has to be taken to Hot Springs for a rest. Luckily, a double is found so the stockholders do not know the company's president is ill. At the Springs, he is rejuvenated and meets several wealthy financiers who give him a check for half a million dollars. He is able to race back to the company in time to save it. He also discovers that while his double has been an ideal president, he is having a corking good time in the society of women and wine.

Notes: Some scenes shot at Grand Central Station and on Wall Street. Baggot played both roles.

Let No Man Put Asunder

Universal IMP, 6/13/1912. 1000 ft. J170220.

Cast: King Baggot (The Good Man), William R. Daly (The Reformed Worker), Violet Horner (His Wife), Joe Moore (Their Son), Edith Haldeman (Their Daughter).

Synopsis: A pretty woman with a drunken husband leaves him and secures a divorce. The husband reforms and goes to work for a good man. The good man meets the woman and her children and falls in love, not knowing of his workman's former relationship with them. One day they meet by accident. The good man stands aside on the grounds that, "What God hath joined together, let no man put asunder."
Loc: LC.

The Schemers

Universal IMP, 6/20/1912. 1000 ft.

Dir: Otis Turner.
Cast: King Baggot (Arthur Dennison), Harley Knowles (Alfred Dennison), Minnie Allen (Mrs. Montague), Violet Horner (Lucy), William E. Shay (Capt. Montresser).

Synopsis: An old man disinherits his stage-struck son. He goes away and joins a traveling company. An adventuress and her good-looking partner ensnare the old man and he agrees to convey the sum of $300,000 on her at the time of their marriage. Meanwhile, the actor son has an adopted sister, Lucy, who discovers the plot to trap her guardian. She and the son are actually lovers and she wires him of the danger. He finds the wicked woman and presents himself as an admirer. He wires the police and they arrive at a critical moment to arrest the scheming pair. The father forgives his son, who then marries the girl who has been instrumental in shielding her guardian from the schemers.

A Child's Influence
Universal IMP, 6/27/1912. 1000 ft. J170426.

Cast: King Baggot (Godfrey Clark), Jane Fearnley (Mrs. Clark), William E. Shay (Andron Sarto).

Synopsis: An old college chum, Andron Sarto, comes to visit the Clark's. He is immediately attracted to Mrs. Clark. Godfrey Clark's engineering business calls him away and Andron is left with Mrs. Clark and their daughter. He wastes no time trying to win her and even goes so far as to intercept a letter from Godfrey and forge one that says he has gone off with another woman. Mrs. Clark, heartbroken and bitter, is about go away with Andron when her daughter accidentally falls out of a window. Her maid reports this at a critical moment and she returns to the house. Mother love triumphs over jealousy. Meanwhile, Andron, while waiting for her, is thrown from his horse and killed. Godfrey returns to find his daughter not seriously injured and his wife contrite. In reporting the death of his friend, she keeps secret his attempt at dishonor.

His Other Self
Universal IMP, 6/29/1912. 600 ft. J170641.

Scen: King Baggot.
Cast: King Baggot (The Lover and His Other Self), Violet Horner (The Girl).

Synopsis: A lover has a quarrel with his sweetheart. She has received a box of American Beauty roses and a note and playfully refuses to tell him who sent them. They quarrel and he leaves the house in anger. Arriving home, he sits before the fire where he falls asleep and dreams he appears in another guise. He sees himself in evening attire leaving the room. The other self heads for the house of the girl. The lover picks up a pistol and follows. He arrives on the scene just in time to see the girl struggling in the arms of the other self. Unable to restrain himself, he fires at the other self who is mistreating his sweetheart. The other self is not injured. He smiles and leaves the room. The dreamer then awakes and rushes to the telephone to call his sweetheart to be sure his fears are unfounded. After many attempts, he reaches the girl. She tells him the flowers were a birthday gift from her father. He sighs with relief that it was all a dream.

Notes: Split-reel with *Portuguese Joe*. 400 ft. Baggot played both roles.

Caught in a Flash
Universal IMP, 7/11/1912. 1000 ft. J170755.

Dir: Otis Turner.
Cast: King Baggot (Jack Gayboy), Jane Fearnley (Dolly Varden), William R. Daly (Mr. Gayboy).

Synopsis: Jack Gayboy is in love with Dolly Varden, a famous Broadway actress. His father objects to his son's marriage with an actress, although it is shown as the situation develops that he, too, is an admirer of the fair sex. Jack, knowing of his father's weakness, arranges for his sweetheart to impersonate a maid in their home, and by a well-arranged plan, they succeed in securing Kodak evidence of the old man's penchant for those he professes to consider not in his sphere. When confronted with the proofs of his fondness for the girl, Mr. Gayboy relents and gives permission to the marriage.

Winning the Latonia Derby
Universal IMP, 7/18/1912. Two reels.

Dir: Otis Turner.
Cast: King Baggot (Howard Clews), Jane Fearnley (The Adventuress), Violet Horner (The Sweetheart), William R. Daly (The Father), William E. Shay (The Villain).

Synopsis: Young Howard makes a fool of himself. He gets into the hands of an adventuress, who steals the family jewels. He owns "Queen Bee," the favorite to win the Derby, but must sell her to an unscrupulous poolroom owner to pay his debt. This man also owns another horse that will be in the race. Just when it looks as if "Queen Bee" will be made to lose the race, Howard's sweetheart buys a half-interest in the animal and by this and other means, "Queen Bee" wins the race, the adventuress gives back the jewels, he is united with his sweetheart and his father forgives him. Everything ends happily.

Notes: Partially filmed in Kentucky at the stud farm of J.E. Madden and at the track during the running of the twenty-ninth annual Latonia Derby classic before a crowd of 30,000 people.

Loc: GEH.

Blood Is Thicker Than Water

Universal IMP, 8/8/1912. 1000 ft. J171890.

Cast: King Baggot (Officer of the Northwestern Mounted Police), Violet Horner (His Sister).

Synopsis: A gambler is in love with the sister of one of Canada's police. The girl's brother, knowing the wickedness of the gambler, warns her to stay away from him and to give her love to a young ranchman whose only fault is a tendency to drink. She refuses. A poker game is in progress at a local saloon where the gambler hides cards in his boot and is detected by the young ranchman. A fight follows. The gambler escapes after wounding the ranchman. The officer, arriving at the scene, hears the story and rides off to catch him. The gambler, weak from loss of blood, falls off his horse almost at the door of the officer and his sister. She takes the gambler in and hides him when her brother finds the riderless horse outside his home. The gambler escapes and rides his horse to the river. He tries to swim across and, in so doing, drowns. The officer arrives at the scene and witnesses his death. Returning home, he finds his sister in the arms of the ranchman who had been sent to look after her. The two are united and the officer of the Royal Mounted again assumes his lonely vigil with only his horse for a companion.

The Castaway

Universal IMP, 8/22/1912. One reel.

Cast: King Baggot (Joseph Lee), Violet Horner (Ruth Carew), William R. Daly (Stanley Carew).

Synopsis: Joe, a wealthy young man with wanderlust, leaves home for a long trip on a sailing vessel. The ship goes down in a storm and Joe and a sailor spend three days and nights without food or water. The sailor dies and Joe loses his mind. He is washed ashore and found by Ruth Carew, a wealthy young woman who takes charge of the situation. She takes Joe to a fisherman's cabin and pays for his care. Joe recovers his health, but not his memory. Ruth teaches him to read and write again, but he roams the village, the butt of jokes. Ruth's cousin Stanley pretends to be in love with Ruth, but it is really her uncle's fortune he wants. A letter from a lawyer in England reaches Stanley, telling him his uncle, recently deceased, has disinherited him. He is advised that his uncle's attorney has sailed for America with a second will. Stanley plots to get the new will and gets the help of fishermen who waylay the attorney on his arrival. He takes him to a secluded spot and there tries to get the wallet, which contains the will. In the struggle, one of the fishermen gets the wallet, but falls over a cliff to his death. Joe, walking below the cliff, discovers the dead man. He picks up the wallet and begins to understand the situation. Stanley, above on the cliff, sees Joe with the wallet and hurls a large rock over the cliff in an effort to kill him. He is struggling to kill the lawyer when Joe rushes up the incline and saves him. Stanley lunges for Joe but slips and falls to his death. Ruth learns that Joe has saved the lawyer and that his mind has returned. The friendship that has grown between them blossoms into the full-grown rose of love.

In Old Tennessee

Universal IMP, 8/25/1912. Two reels. J172203.

Dir: Otis Turner.
Scen: King Baggot.
Cast: King Baggot (Jim Howard), Jane Fearnley (Nell Gwinn), William E. Shay (A Moonshiner), Violet Horner (The Moonshiner's Sympathizer), William R. Daly (A Moonshiner), Joe Moore (Joe, the Crippled Brother).

Synopsis: Woodcutter Jim Howard has a crippled young brother whom he must help and cure. It will cost $300, which he does not have. He is approached by some moonshiners who invite him to make money by joining them. He reluctantly agrees. About that time, Washington authorities send beautiful spy Nell Gwinn down to root out the moonshiners. She poses as a dressmaker, and Jim, now a moonshiner, falls in love with her. She has no idea of his present trade. One day a woman sympathetic to the moonshiners spots Nell taking notes on the position of the stills. She is set upon by a group of furious women, but is saved by the intervention of the crippled boy. The story ends with Nell revealing her identity and Jim swearing off his evil work. After the destruction of the stills, peace is restored.

Notes: Shot on and around 210th Street, New York City.

A Happy Family

Universal IMP, 8/29/1912. One reel.

Cast: King Baggot, William R. Daly, Susanne Willis.

Synopsis: Mr. Black and Mrs. White were married to each other, then divorced. Mr. White and Mrs. Black were also man and wife, but divorced. The two ladies assumed their maiden names again and, each meeting the other's former husband, fall in love and marry. Mrs. Black becomes Mrs. White and Mrs. White becomes Mrs. Black. Neither of the couples tell their newly married partners they have been married before. The Whites have rented a house that is too large for their needs, so they advertise for a congenial couple to share it with them. The Blacks answer the ad and each former man and wife confronts each other separately; since neither is in a position to give away the other, they swear each other to secrecy. The mothers-in-law of both men make unexpected visits on their daughters-in-laws, precipitating the disclosure they have all been dreading. Mr. and Mrs. Black beat a hasty retreat, sadder but wiser, while Mr. and Mrs. White decide that no one will ever share their home again.

Human Hearts

Universal IMP, 9/12/1912. Two reels.

Dir: Otis Turner.
Scen: Hal Reid.
Cast: King Baggot (Tom Logan), Jane Fearnley (Jeanette LaTourre), Mayme Kelso (Mrs. Logan), Dick Lee (The Tramp).

Synopsis: Fred Armsdale, a man about town in New York, has a mistress, Jeanette LaTourre. They discover that on the farmlands of Arkansas, near the home of the Logan family, there are large iron deposits and plan to profit from the ignorance of the Blue Ridge people. They meet handsome young Tom, the town's blacksmith; Jeanette, after blinding Tom to her faults, consents to marry him. A year later, a child is born and later still, Armsdale returns and secretly renews his friendship with Jeanette. They fear reprisal from Tom and conclude to murder him, but accidentally kill Tom's father instead. A tramp sees the murder, but does not come forward. Tom is found leaning over his father's dead body and is accused of the crime by his erstwhile wife. Despite the efforts of his mother, his half-witted brother and his former sweetheart Ruth, he is condemned to serve five years. His mother's grief is such that she goes blind from excessive weeping. She goes to the Governor of the state, carrying with her a bunch of yellow roses. The Governor at first refuses to hear her, but after receiving the roses, he remembers his own old mother and grants the pardon. Logan, now liberated, searches for his child, who in the meantime has been stolen by the heartless mother. In a confrontation, Armsdale, endeavoring to kill Logan, kills Jeanette instead.

The Millionaire Cop

Universal IMP, 9/16/1912. One reel.

Cast: King Baggot (Jack Gardner), Violet Horner (Pauline White), William E. Shay (Justin Gardner), Mabel Horsley (Mrs. Sherry), Joseph Slayton (Boss McCoy).

Synopsis: Jack Gardner, son of wealthy Justin Gardner, wishes to pursue a political career. When the ward boss and his associates call at Jack's house, his father, meeting them, considers them bad companions and refuses to back Jack's campaign. Brokenhearted, Jack decides to become a motorcycle policeman. The father, a widower, has fallen in love with a charming widow, Pauline White. He has not told her about his son. While on duty one day, Jack stops a runaway horse and carriage, saving the widow's life, but he does not tell her who he is. The widow calls Justin, telling him of her near miss. In his hurry to be with her, Justin is speeding and is arrested by Jack. He is made to pay a fine, in spite of his angry protestations. Arriving at the widow's home, Justin finds her smiling and happy and proposes to her on the spot. Later, as Justin and the widow enter their auto, they accidentally meet Jack. The widow throws herself into Jack's arms, hailing him as her hero. The father is mad with jealousy until explanations are made, then reconciliation is effected.

The Parson and the Moonshiner

Universal IMP, 9/26/1912. 1000 ft.

Dir: James Kirkwood.
Cast: King Baggot (The Parson), Jane Fearnley (The Girl).

Synopsis: A parson comes to a small Tennessee mountain village as a circuit preacher. He comes to a cabin where a brother and sister live with their old father. The two men are engaged in the time-honored practice of moonshining. The brother takes an instant dislike to the parson and suspects him of being a revenue man, but his sister greets him with courtesy and faith. The brother attends the parson's first meeting and breaks it up. They come to blows and the parson wins. His hatred increases as his sister's admiration increases. One day, the parson comes upon the still where the men are working and is almost shot by the brother, but for the young woman's interference. A few days later, the parson goes back to the still to try to convince the men to give up their illegal practices. He is arrested by revenue offices who think he is a moonshiner. Rather than tell on the moonshiners, he submits to arrest and spends a year in prison. When his time expires, he returns to the village, this time entirely free of suspicion and for the very pleasant purpose of marrying the pretty sister of the moonshiner.

The Bridal Room

Universal IMP, 10/10/1912. One reel.

Dir: William R. Daly.
Cast: King Baggot (Tom Walsh), Violet Horner (Mary Carter), Ellen Walker (Sarah Walsh), William R. Daly (Pietro), Thomas McAvoy (Frank Stone).

Synopsis: Tom Walsh loves an office girl, Mary Carter and is engaged to marry her.

Unknown to her, he furnishes two rooms in the old homestead, intending to surprise her after their marriage. But she jilts him on the day set for their marriage and runs away with Frank Stone. Tom, almost insane with rage and grief, demolishes the contents of one room and rushes into the bridal chamber to destroy this also, but his old mother calms him and he locks the room, vowing never to enter again unless his bride returns. Time passes and Tom becomes wealthy while Mary and Frank become impoverished by Frank's drunkenness. Ruined in health, Mary returns to town and by a twist of fate she is staying in a boarding house when she overhears a plot to kill Tom. (Tom had caught one of his workers, Pietro, abusing a horse and fired him. Now Pietro has borrowed a pistol and vows to kill Tom.) Mary follows Pietro to Tom's home as fast as her frail health will allow and intercepts the bullet meant for Tom. He picks her up and carries her into the house. He recognizes her in spite of her ravaged appearance and sends for a doctor. Then he slowly moves to the door of the bridal room and unlocks it. He tenderly lifts her and places her upon the bridal bed. He talks to her and she faintly recognizes him and responds. Pietro is arrested.

Notes: Some sources list James Kirkwood in the cast as "the rival, James," but in the viewed print that role was played by Thomas McAvoy as "Frank Stone." William R. Daly commented that 650 feet of "good stuff" had to be cut to keep the film at one reel. The review in Universal Weekly, 10/12/1912, states that Mary lives, but in Moving Picture World, 10/12/1912, she dies. In the viewed print, the film ends as Tom carries Mary into the bridal room.

Loc: LC.

King, the Detective and the (Opium) Smugglers

Universal IMP, 10/24/1912. One reel

Cast: King Baggot (The Detective), Jane Fearnley (The Girl), Fred Kelsey (The Bully), Edith Haldeman (The Girl's Sister).

Synopsis: King is sent to capture some opium smugglers operating in a seaport town. Posing as a fisherman, he mingles with the townspeople. One day, while walking on the beach, he sees a brother and sister fighting. He separates them and meets their older sister. He accompanies them home and meets their old father and the bully who is in love with the girl. The bully is jealous of King at once and also suspects he is a spy. When they meet at a dance hall that evening, the bully starts a fight, which his friends break up. Later, the bully follows King and attacks him and knocks him down. The gang ties him up and puts him in a shed while they smuggle the opium. The little brother sees this and he and his sisters go to the shed where they untie King and help him escape in a rowboat. The gang discovers King is free and the bully goes after the boat where King is weak and exhausted. The bully chops a hole in the boat and leaves King for dead, but the girl and her brother and sister discover what has happened. They get a motorboat and rescue King just in time. The smugglers are arrested and King and the girl fall in love.

Notes: In some reviews, the word "opium" is omitted. Edith Haldeman's role was uncredited, but she was seen in the viewed print.

Loc: VID.

John Sterling, Alderman

Universal IMP, 10/31/1912. Two reels.

Dir: James Kirkwood.
Scen: King Baggot.
Cast: King Baggot (John Sterling), Jane Fearnley (John's Wife).

Synopsis: Young John Sterling, lives in the slums and is a crook. But one night, as he is robbing a house, he finds a little child in a crib. This arouses all his good instincts and he decides to reform. As he is returning the jewelry he has just stolen, he is captured by the homeowner, but he sees that John is repentant and lets him go. John becomes a storekeeper and a good citizen. He has a loving wife, a beautiful daughter and becomes an alderman. A streetcar franchise comes before the Board of Aldermen and two attorneys first try to bribe John. When he refuses, they threaten to reveal his past. John's wife stands by him and urges him to go to the district attorney, which he does. At a critical moment, the alderman feigns to take the bribe. The conspirators are caught red-handed and arrested and John is forgiven his past.

A Strange Case

Universal IMP, 11/4/1912. One reel.

Cast: King Baggot, Jane Fearnley, William E. Shay.

Synopsis: A girl's father and then her lover are accused of the theft of a necklace. Her father finally confesses after another crime has been fastened upon him.

Officer 174

Universal IMP, 11/14/1912. 1000 ft.

Dir: George Loane Tucker.
Cast: King Baggot (Officer 174), Jane Fearnley (His Wife), Joe Moore, Edith Haldeman.

Synopsis: Wearied from sitting up all night with his ailing wife, Officer 174 falls asleep on post and is discharged. He cannot find employment and faces poverty. He reads a news account of the escape of a well-known criminal who is one of the most desperate in police history. A large reward is offered. Ex-officer 174 decides to capture him. After careful detective work, he tracks him to a low tenement and after a terrific fight he takes him and his accomplice prisoners. He drags them to the police station and for this he is reinstated. Good times are ahead for Officer 174 and his little family.

Notes: Re-released 1/2/1913 as *The Bearer of Burdens.*

Mamma's (Baby) Boy

Universal IMP, 11/25/1912. 1000 ft.

Cast: King Baggot, Jane Fearnley.

Synopsis: No information found.

Through Shadowed Vales

Universal IMP, 12/5/1912. 1000 ft.

Cast: King Baggot (Roy Erlynne), Jane Fearnley (His Wife).

Synopsis: The young husband is a sport. His wife disapproves of his society butterfly friends who flock to his elaborate dinners. They have high stakes bridge games. They are not teetotalers like his wife, nor do the other wives mind all-night poker parties. He is displeased with her and tells her so. One night he gives a dinner party in her honor and insists that she take a drink, which she does, but with such bad grace he is even more displeased. That night he dreams that at the first glass he has made her a drunkard, that he has been caught embezzling at the bank and hurries home to her only to learn that she has eloped with his best friend. He disappears into the whirlpool of the city — a tattered, bearded outcast, begging for a drink. She is even more pitiable and is about to take refuge in the river when he finds her and is appalled at the wreck she has become. He then awakes and rushes to her room, telling her she was right and he will never drink again.

The World-Weary Man

Universal IMP, 12/9/1912. 1,000 ft.

Cast: King Baggot (A Millionaire), Edith Haldeman (A Waif), Agustus G. Balfour (The Waif's Father).

Synopsis: A young millionaire bachelor with all the treasures of the earth at his disposal finds his life empty. One night, after a brilliant reception at his home, he takes a stroll, finds himself at a waterfront dock and discovers a crying child. When questioned, she relates she had been sent out on the rough streets to sell newspapers and had been driven away by some street boys. Her day had been a failure and no papers had been sold. He accompanies her to her wretched room and leaves her. The next day, he tells his servants he is going away to another country. He speedily makes his way to the place where the waif lives and rents a room next door. He makes friends with the waif's father, a derelict, broken in health and ambition. The world-weary man has found the world still attractive and he becomes interested in the amusements of the poor. One day the wretched father dies. The once world-weary man goes to the room of the waif, where he finds her asleep. He puts her rag doll in her arms and brings her to his mansion, where ever after he is a father to her.

1913

She Slept Through It All

Universal IMP, 1/6/1913. 1000 ft.

Cast: King Baggot.

Synopsis: Mr. Newlywed devises a scheme to get out of the house and spend an evening with his pals at the Mutton Chop Club. He comes home intoxicated and retires in the wrong house. Two women, returning from a suffragette meeting, discover him and call the police. Newlywed escapes and goes home to his own bed safely. His wife sleeps through the whole performance and does not know of his night's adventures.

Gold Is Not All

Universal IMP, 1/30/1913. Two reels.

Dir: Wilfred Lucas.
Cast: King Baggot (Karl), Jane Gail (The Girl), Bess Meredyth (The Slavey), William Cavanagh (The Miser Uncle), Frank Russell (The Director), William Cowper (The Artist), Harry Fisher (The Writer), William Dunn (Mr. Rich).

Synopsis: A great opera singer ignores the advice of her physician and attempts one more concert in order to complete a trust fund for her little daughter. She overtaxes herself and dies on the stage. Her brother, who has been made guardian to the child, moves her to a tenement where he hides the money and keeps her a virtual prisoner. The girl's only friend is a little slavey who unlocks the door and visits her occasionally. A dozen years go by and three friends; a pianist-composer, an artist and a writer, rent the tenement over the rooms where the girl is held prisoner. Through the clever work of the slavey, Karl the pianist meets the girl, now budding into womanhood. One night, after the miser uncle has counted his money, he falls asleep and the wind blows a curtain against a candle, setting the tenement on fire. The uncle meets his death. The three friends adopt the girl and Karl discovers she has a wonderful singing voice. He finds a rich benefactor willing to pay for her lessons. He in turn introduces her to a great impresario who arranges for her debut. Just before her performance, she gives a little party for her guardians and an alcohol lamp explodes. Karl saves her but, in doing so, burns his hands so badly he can never play again. The girl's debut is a success and there is a party afterward where the rich man, in an inebriated state, tries to force himself on the girl. Karl and the man struggle. The two fall against the cupboard where the old miser had kept his hoard. As the bills fall upon the floor, Karl picks up a bunch of them and thrusts them into the hat of the drunken man and bids him leave. Karl wins the girl and the little party rejoices.

Dr. Bunion

Universal IMP, 2/1/1913. Half-reel.

Cast: King Baggot.

Synopsis: A light but very short farce. (No other information found.)

Notes: Split-reel with *A Winning Ruse*.

King Danforth Retires

Universal IMP, 2/27/1913. Half-reel.

Cast: King Baggot (King Danforth).

Synopsis: A gambler has a daughter, now grown, from whom he has concealed his occupation. She lives in a country house on the Hudson. A friend of his in the gambling business appears unexpectedly at the home and they become sweethearts. He insists on making the facts known to the girl. The picture ends with the father quitting his former life and the sweetheart forgiven by the girl.

Notes: Split-reel with *A Dead Town Beaux in Provence*.

Dr. Jekyll and Mr. Hyde

Universal IMP, 3/6/1913. Two reels.

Dir: Herbert Brenon.
Cast: King Baggot (Dr. Jekyll and Mr. Hyde), Jane Gail (Alice), Matt Snyder (Her Father), Howard Crampton (Dr. Lanyon), William Sorelle (The Attorney).

Synopsis: Dr. Jekyll, a kind and philanthropic man, is preoccupied with the problems of good and evil. He develops a drug that transforms him into the demonic Mr. Hyde, in whose person he exhausts all the latent evil in his nature. He also creates an antidote that will restore him to the respectable existence of Dr. Jekyll. Gradually, however, the unmitigated evil of his darker self predominates, until finally he performs an atrocious murder. His saner self tries to curb the alternative personality, but he finds he is losing control over his transformations and slips increasingly into the world of evil. Finally, unable to procure one of the ingredients for the mixture of redemption and on the verge of being discovered, he commits suicide.

Notes: From the novel *The Strange Case of Dr. Jekyll and Mr. Hyde* by Robert Louis Stevenson. Re-released 8/27/1915. Dissolve effects were used to show the transition from Jekyll to Hyde. Baggot played both roles.

Loc: LC, VID.

To Reno and Back

Universal IMP, 3/27/1913. One reel.

Cast: King Baggot, Jane Gail.

Synopsis: Jane and King, just returning from their honeymoon, are preparing to go to the opera. At the sight of Jane so beautifully dressed, King cannot resist taking her in his arms and completely disarranging her coiffure. She asks him to wait "a minute" while her maid repairs the damage. King nearly smokes himself to death waiting and after an hour gives Jane her ticket and sets out alone for the opera. Incensed, she sends her maid in her place, which humiliates King; they quarrel. Jane sends him a note saying she is off to Reno to get a divorce. King leaves quickly enough to get the same train and the berth above her, but she will not let him near her. However, once in Reno, a drunken janitor, a smoky fireplace, a fire escape to which the only access is through King's room, a cynical hotel clerk and the feminine instinct to rush to the man she loves when danger threatens enable Jane and King to come together after a trying experience.

The Wizard of the Jungle

World's Best Film Company. Ad. 4/5/1913. Two reels. LP469.

Dir: Howard Shaw.
Scen: King Baggot.
Cast: Jack Bonavita (Himself), Joe Graybill (Capt. Hanscombe), Nancy Avril (Pearl), William Cavanaugh (Daniel Bonavita), Brutus, the lion.

Synopsis: Abdullah, the wizard of the jungle, has just buried his only son when a party of white hunters arrive, led by Daniel Bonavita. He reprimands the wizard for bringing liquor into the jungle. Led by the wizard, the natives rebel and attack the party. During the fight, Jack, Daniel's young son, is left in the camp and is struck in the arm by a poisoned arrow. He wanders into the jungle and is found by the old wizard just in time to save him from being attacked by a lion. To save the boy's life, the wizard has to amputate his arm. Meanwhile, Daniel believes his son dead and returns to England. Abdullah treats Jack as his own son, teaching him the ways of the jungle and especially how to handle wild animals. Twenty years later, Daniel Bonavita stops at an army post in Africa with his young ward Pearl. Jack, grown to manhood, is now the wizard of the jungle, his adopted father having died. He meets Pearl when he saves her from being attacked by a lion and, later, when an officer, Capt. Hanscombe, tries to make love to her. In anger, the Captain orders Jack's arrest and goes into the jungle to see that his orders are carried out. Jack is arrested, but Hanscombe is killed by a lion. As Jack is brought into camp, he is thanked by Pearl and introduced to Daniel, who recognizes the arrested man as his son. There is a happy reunion and indications point to a union between Jack and Pearl.

Notes: Released on a states rights basis. Shot near Tampa, Florida. Capt. Jack Bonavita, a well known lion tamer, was mauled by his lion, Brutus, during the making of this film, but he recovered. However, he was later clawed by a bear at Los Angeles Animal Farm and died of his injuries March 19, 1917.

The Wanderer

Universal IMP, 4/7/1913. One reel.

Cast: King Baggot (The Shepherd).

Synopsis: An allegorical story in which a husband, a wife and "one who covets" are enacting the "eternal triangle." On the heights, the shepherd hears the call and becomes the wanderer whose gentle influence stops the maddened husband from murder and suicide. He exposes the wife to her own consideration and points out the consequences of her folly. Finally he takes "the one who covets" away from the born passions of the valley. Having averted the disaster, the wanderer returns to his peacefully grazing sheep.

Notes: Re-released under the Universal/Laemmle brand on 3/3/1917 as *Undoing Evil*.

The Leader of His Flock

Universal IMP, 4/17/1913. Two reels.
LU 631.

Scen: Ruth Baggot.
Cast: King Baggot (The Minister), Jane Gail (The Young Woman).

Synopsis: A young minister is popular with his congregation and all is well until a scandalous situation is discovered in a tenement owned by the president of the board of trustees. A young woman and her baby are deserted by her husband, leaving her penniless. The child dies and, after the funeral, she is snubbed on all sides. The husband had torn up the marriage certificate and the community believes she is unmarried. She determines to leave the city and gets as far as the minister's door where she collapses from lack of food. The minister and his old mother take her in, but the congregation objects and the minister is forced to resign. He takes a mission in the slums and preaches the gospel of good will and kindness to all. The wretched husband finds his way to the mission, fleeing from arrest after he has attempted to rob a saloon. The minister saves him from jail, only to find he is Jane's husband. Jane will have nothing to do with him and, incensed, he tells her it is because she is in love with the minister. He overhears this and silences him, then sends the wretch out into a terrible rainstorm, where lightning strikes a building and he is buried under a wall that collapses on him. Jane and the minister have in truth fallen in love. Meanwhile, the congregation has been unable to get along with their new minister and send after the old minister of the flock. He agrees, naming only the conditions that he keep his old mission and that they respect his new wife. When all the circumstances are heard, they gladly agree. The story concludes with the minister preaching a message of good will while Jane and his mother sit reunited with the congregation.

Notes: From a story by Robert and Frank Griffin. Ruth Baggot was King Baggot's wife.

The Rise of Officer 174
Universal IMP, 5/1/1913. Two reels. LU 659.

Scen: Walter MacNamara.
Cast: King Baggot (Officer 174), Jane Gail (His Sweetheart).

Synopsis: Officer 174 is in love with Jane, secretary to "the man higher up," who has the whole criminal element of the city in his grasp. The city is so alarmed that the mayor appoints a special squad headed by Officer 174 to clean it up. The criminals appeal to "the man higher up" to protect them. He sends an emissary, offering the officer a huge sum to go to Florida and manage an orange grove. But Officer 174 cannot be bought. Meanwhile, Levenstein, proprietor of the Nestor Gambling Club, defies the law. Officer 174 leads a sensational raid and arrests Levenstein, his operators and guests. Drastic measures are then taken by the underworld and two gunmen are sent to get Officer 174 out of the way. By a clever ruse, he puts a dummy in his place and foils them. Finally, "the man higher up" goes to the police commissioner and accuses Officer 174 of graft. He has the commissioner mark some bills and tells the commissioner to be in his office at three o'clock for proof. He then sends a message to Officer 174 to come to his office at three o'clock and he will make a confession and give evidence. Using the office dictaphone, Jane hears this but cannot reach her sweetheart in time to warn him. While he is in the office, the marked bills are secretly placed in his hat. The commissioner arrives, the bills are found and Officer 174 is arrested. Then Jane arrives in the office and compels the commissioner to listen to the voice on the dictaphone. The commissioner has "the man higher up" arrested and the city is relieved of the terror that had menaced it for so long.

Notes: Reissued by IMP 11/30/1916 retitled *The Heel of the Law* as a "Special Release." The reissue gives director credit to George Loane Tucker.)

The Heart That Sees
Universal IMP, 5/15/1913. One reel.

Cast: King Baggot (The Optician), Jane Gail (The Blind Girl).

Synopsis: The greatest optician in New York is a hunchback. Although he is very charitable to the poor, he is sensitive of his deformity, but with all his goodness no woman has ever loved him. He takes an interest in a poor blind girl and gives her and her brother a place in his home with himself and his mother. The oculist and the girl learn to love each other. He tries to keep his deformity from her but, unbeknownst to him she learns of it with her sense of touch. He finds a way to restore her sight with an operation and is about to leave the country so she will never see him as he is, but she tells him she has long known of his disfigurement and that it will make no difference to her. After all, "It is the heart that best sees."

The Comedian's Mask
Universal IMP, 6/7/1913. Two reels.

Dir: Herbert Brenon.
Cast: King Baggot (The Comedian), Little Mimi Yvonne (His Daughter).

Synopsis: An out-of-work comedian finally secures work with "The Girl from Wayback" company. He is devoted to his wife and child, but his wife is vain and accepts the attentions of the company's tenor, Basil Graham. This is done to such an extent it arouses the attentions of the stagehands with whom the comedian is a great favorite. One night, before his performance, he is in his dressing room using a poisonous salve to treat some old wounds. His little girl sees the jar and tries to play with it, but he stops her, explaining that it is poison. On stage, he scores a great triumph as a comedian, making the audience laugh and cry at his will. While he is on stage, the little girl plays with the button on the door of the wing, making it necessary for the comedian to exit behind the other wing, where he finds his wife in the arms of the tenor. They do not see him. Brokenhearted, he goes to his dressing room and takes the poison, determined to end it all. He rushes on stage for his last act while the tenor and the wife decide to elope. They are hastily leaving the theater when the comedian, at the finish of his last scene, drops with agony to the stage. The manager frantically calls for a doctor and milk is produced by the property man. The child meanwhile strays out looking for her mother, and finds her about to leave with the tenor and shows her the poison. When the mother realizes what she has done, she rushes to her recovering husband's side and begs forgiveness. The tenor is thrown out of the company and goes on his way to find another home to wreck.

Notes: Viewed print out of sequence.
Loc: MOMA.

The Stranger

Universal IMP, 7/28/1913. Two reels.

Cast: King Baggot (Elbert Havens), Violet Mersereau (Jen), Howard Crampton (John Howard), A.E. Walsh (Jack Nobel), Laura Lyman (Grace Howard), Matt Snyder (Jen's Father), Raymond Murray (Jen's Brother), William Cavanaugh (Lem).

Synopsis: John Howard and Jack Nobel are business partners, but the firm is in financial difficulties. Jack is in love with John's daughter, Grace. However, John wants Grace to marry Elbert Havens because he is a millionaire. Their engagement is announced at a reception given for Elbert and Grace. Jack takes Grace into the conservatory, where he begs her to elope with him. Elbert sees Grace in Jack's arms and leaves in anger. He wanders into a motion picture house where the song "The Trail of the Lonesome Pine" is sung and decides to go far away to the mountains. He packs his clothes, discharges his staff and sends Grace a note saying he is gone forever, which greatly displeases her father. The press finds out and it becomes a big story. Elbert takes a train for the mountains of Tennessee. On the train, he meets an old lady who gets off at Stumpville, as does he. She has the newspaper in her purse and recognizes him, but says nothing. He finds a hotel and settles in. He begins to take walks about the area and one day he sees Jen on a bridge. She notices him and their attraction is mutual; however, she runs away. This happens several times until she finally stops and they talk. She finds him very polite, but their actions are noted by Lem, Jen's sweetheart. He mocks the stranger and then grabs Jen, but she bites his hand and runs away. Elbert goes to Jen and she takes him home, where he meets the old lady from the train. After he leaves, the mother shows Jen the newspaper. Jen tears out the photograph and hides it in her bosom. Len becomes jealous of Elbert and starts a rumor that Elbert is a revenue officer. Jen's father and brother are moonshiners and a plot is hatched to do him harm. Jen overhears them and arrives just in time to tell the mob of moonshiners Elbert's real identity.

Ivanhoe

Universal IMP, 9/22/1913. Four reels.

Dir: Herbert Brenon.
Scen: Herbert Brenon and George Edwardes Hall.
Cam: Ernest G. Palmer and Stewart P. Kinder.

Cast: King Baggot (Wilfred of Ivanhoe), Evelyn Hope (Lady Rowena), Wallace Bosco (Cedric, Ivanhoe's Father), Herbert Brenon (Isaac of York), Leah Baird (Rebecca of York), Arthur Scott Craven (Richard, the Lion-Hearted), Jack Bates (Reginald Front-de Boeuf), Mr. Widdecombe (Sir Brian de Bois Guilbert), William Calvert (Gurth, the Swineherd), Walter Thomas (Robin Hood), H.M. Holles (Friar Tuck), George Courtenay (Prince John), A.J. Charlwood (Athelstane), Helen Downing (Elgitha), Maurice Norman (The Jester, Wamba).

Synopsis: In the days when Richard the Lion-Hearted was in the Holy Land, his brother King John ruled England and plotted to keep the throne. At Rotherwood, Cedric held to the claims of the Saxons against the invading Normans while his son favored King Richard and was awarded the barony of "Ivanhoe." Cedric had an adopted daughter of royal Saxon blood with whom Ivanhoe falls in love (over the objections of Cedric, for political reasons). Ivanhoe joins Richard in the Holy Land and no news of him is heard for many years. In his absence, King John bestows Ivanhoe's barony on Reginald de Boeuf, a Norman. Rowena refuses a marriage proposed by Cedric. Ivanhoe returns from the Holy Land disguised as a holy man to find out the feelings of Rowena and her father toward him. Isaac of York, a Jewish moneylender, with his daughter, Rebecca, seek shelter with Cedric. Isaac is in disguise as a poor peddler. Everyone shrinks from Isaac, who must eat apart, but the beautiful Rebecca receives unwanted attentions. Ivanhoe comes forward to offer her protection. The knights conspire to rob Isaac of his money. Ivanhoe hears of this and spirits the two out of the castle. The conspirators surround and attack Ivanhoe. When he revives, Isaac and Rowena have been carried off. Meanwhile, in Robin Hood's camp, Richard, the Lion-Hearted enters alone. He has been deprived of his throne. Robin and Friar Tuck revive his spirits and Ivanhoe hears their revelry. He rejoins King Richard, Robin Hood and his merry band. They form an army to attack de Bois Guilbert's castle where the captives are held. Ivanhoe and the Black Knight meet in combat. The Normans are forced back to their castle, while the Black Knight escapes with Rebecca as captive. He takes her to the Order of Good Templars on the grounds she is a sorceress. She must find a knight to defend her innocence in mortal combat with her accuser. She is tied to a stake with faggots piled around her feet when Ivanhoe bursts in, defeats the Black Knight, and rescues her. Richard reveals his identity as King. Ivanhoe is reconciled with his father and marries Rowena. Rebecca loves Ivanhoe too, but sacrifices her feelings and as she goes off with her father, she sees a vision of the happy couple.

Notes: Based on the novel by Sir Walter Scott. Filmed at Chepstow Castle, Monmouthshire, England. Helen Downing was the stage name of Herbert Brenon's wife.

Loc: MOMA, BFI, NF.

The Anarchist

Universal IMP, 10/23/1913. One reel.

Dir: Herbert Brenon.
Cast: King Baggot (The Anarchist), Leah Baird (His Sweetheart).

Synopsis: An anarchist has a sweetheart who is sought after by another man. The rival meets the girl in the park and makes violent love to her, but she rejects him. This is seen by the anarchist. He suspects her loyalty and casts her aside. The other man, seeking revenge, tells the police where the anarchist and his companions are hiding. The unhappy anarchist meets a little girl on his way home and he buys her a toy horn. She lives in the apartment immediately above where the anarchist has his studio. He enters his studio and his sweetheart comes to warn the band that the police are coming. When they arrive, the anarchist is standing with bombs in each hand, ready to blow everyone up, but before he can light them, from the rooms upstairs he hears the sound of the little girl playing on her horn. Realizing that an innocent will be killed along with the others, he surrenders and takes the hand of the girl, assured of her love.

Notes: Filmed in Paris. The film was shown to reviewers with no intertitles, but they could have been added later. Columnist George Blaisdell in *Motion Picture World*, 10/18/1913, remarked that when first seen, it ran 1,500 feet and was clearly understandable, but when it was reduced to 1,000 feet it was far less comprehensible. Re-released under the IMP brand, 11/7/1916, as *The Voice Upstairs*.

The Child Stealers of Paris

Universal IMP, 11/20/1913. One reel.

Dir: Herbert Brenon.
Cast: King Baggot, Leah Baird.

Synopsis: A husband and wife separate. A few years later, the husband becomes a successful financier. The wife come to Paris on a visit, bringing their little daughter, whom the husband has never seen. The little one is lost and falls into the clutches of a child stealer who rents her out as a beggar. On the street, the little vagrant attracts the attention of the financier. He buys her and takes her home to his lonely mansion. The distracted mother keeps up her quest. One day, looking through an iron fence, she sees her child. In a moment, she is with her. A reunion of the two parents follows.

Notes: Filmed in Paris. Views of the Arc De Triomphe, the Bourse, the Louvre and the Latin Quarter are incorporated into the story. Re-released 2/25/1917 as *Lost in the Streets of Paris* under the Rex brand.)

Love vs. Law

Universal IMP, 12/1/1913. Two reels.

Cast: King Baggot (Jack), Ethel Grandin (Ethel), Charles Eldridge (Ethel's Father).

Synopsis: Ethel's father, a war veteran, is constantly boasting of his prowess on the field of battle and telling what he would do if accosted by a bandit. A bandit comes along and the father flees. Jack, thinking to scare the old man again, disguises himself as a bandit, but gets arrested. Ethel finds the real bandit and asks his help. He appears in the courtroom, holds them all up and tells the truth. He then makes his escape. Jack is freed and married right then and there.

The Return of Tony

Universal IMP, 12/8/1913. One reel.

Dir: King Baggot.
Scen: King Baggot.
Cast: King Baggot (Tony), Howard Crampton (Doctor), Miss Marie Hall (Nurse), Master Willie Gibbons (Little Tony), Baby Katherine Lee (Little Rosa).

Synopsis: The story shows the overwhelming love a father can have for his two children. He risks getting caught and jailed for breaking into a house where his little ones have been quarantined during a diphtheria epidemic.

Notes: During the filming, there were several scenes that called for Baggot to walk through a rock quarry in very thin shoes, causing his feet to be bruised and swollen. For a time, he had to wear larger shoes.

Mr. and Mrs. Innocence Abroad

Universal IMP, 12/18/1913. One reel.

Dir: Herbert Brenon.
Cast: King Baggot, Leah Baird.

Notes: Filmed in London and Paris. A semi-documentary—part story, part travelogue. The reviews give no real plot. It featured views of their shipboard journey from London to Paris and showed the Cliffs of Dover, Calais, Notre Dame and the Eiffel Tower.

The Actor's Christmas

Universal IMP, 12/22/1913. One reel.

Cast: King Baggot, Jane Gail, Katherine Lee, Howard Crampton, Frank Smith.

Synopsis: A down-and-out actor is induced to play the part of Santa Claus in a rich man's home; while there, he is tempted to steal toys for his child. He is caught, but the spirit of the theft is recognized and the whole ends with much advantage all around.

King, the Detective in the Jarvis Case

Universal IMP, 12/29/1913. Two reels.

Dir: King Baggot.
Cast: King Baggot, Frank Smith, Ethel Grandin.

Synopsis: An old recluse wishes to get a poor girl into difficulty because her mother slighted him years before. He pretends death after having written to her, inviting her to visit him, in order that she may be accused of his murder. King the detective manages to ferret out the mystery of his seeming death and disappearance.

Notes: Some outdoor scenes filmed in Leonia Heights. A work crew was digging a tunnel in a hillside to connect the recluse's shack to a clump of bushes when it caved in due to recent heavy rains. Smith sustained a wrenched back and King a bruised hip in the accident. Reissued as a "Special Release," 11/5/1916, titled *The Secret Cellar*; Baggot's character is called "John Hardin" instead of "King, the Detective."

1914

Absinthe

Universal IMP, 1/22/1914. Four reels.

Dir: Herbert Brenon.
Scen: Herbert Brenon, George Edwardes Hall.
Ph: William Creevy Thompson.
Cast: King Baggot (Jean Dumas), Leah Baird (Mme Dumas).

Synopsis: Jean Dumas, a Parisian artist, is introduced to this addictive liquor by his mistress, a laundress, who also convinces him to rob his parents' house. Discovered and disowned, he marries his mistress, who eventually leaves him for a wealthy man. Jean begins to suffer from hallucinations and joins an Apache gang to support his habit. One night, disguised as a cabby, he attempts to rob a passenger who turns out to be his wife. In his anger, he drives her though the streets of Paris and a terrible struggle takes place. He strangles her in a forest and leaves her for dead. The next morning, he staggers back home to his sorrowful parents. They do not know what to do with him. Then, suddenly, a company of soldiers marches by, recruiting for the war. His father puts his old gun in his son's hands and sends him out. The picture closes with Jean, dragging his gun along, following the soldiers, determined to enlist and make a man of himself amid new surroundings.

Notes: Filmed in Paris. Purchased in 1916 by Baggot from Universal and re-released in 1917 in five reels on a states rights basis by Argosy Films, Inc., with added material pertinent to World War I. Suggested by the novel *Wormwood* by Marie Corelli.

King, the Detective in Formula 879

Universal IMP, 2/5/1914. Two reels.

Dir: King Baggot.
Scen: King Baggot.
Cast: King Baggot (Cecil Disney and King, the Detective), Jane Gail (Mrs. Disney), Frank Smith (District Attorney).

Synopsis: Cecil Disney, a noted chemist, is experimenting to discover how to manufacture artificial rubber. He mixes two toxins, the combustion of which creates deadly fumes. In order not to be overcome by the lethal gas, he throws the mixture into the laboratory sink and slams down the hood. At that moment, his wife, entertaining a mutual friend on their roof garden, leaves to get their friend a match for his cigar. The friend, seated near the standpipe that gives vent to the sink, inhales the fumes and is killed instantly. The chemist is arrested and is about to be convicted of murder when King, the detective, is called in and ultimately manages to solve the case.

Notes: Double exposure effects were used. Baggot played two roles. Partially filmed at the Screen Club on West 47th Street in New York City.

The Box Couch

Universal IMP, 2/16/1914. 1000 ft.

Cast: King Baggot, Ethel Grandin.

Synopsis: A jealous young husband believes his wife is being unfaithful to him. In order to spy on her, he hides himself in a new box couch and orders it shipped to his house. But the couch is not shipped. It is nailed up and then stolen by an undertaker and a piano mover who are mistaken for doctors, which causes some amusement at the denouement. The poor husband suffers much. He is finally found exhausted.

The Touch of a Child

Universal IMP, 2/23/1914. Two reels.

Cast: King Baggot (Paul Vivian), Howard Crampton (Maurice DeBray), David Lithgoe (Henri DeBray), Stuart Patton (DeFarge, the Thief).

Synopsis: Paul, a rich American artist, is visiting his sister Frances in Paris. One evening, while dining at a fashionable cafe, gambler Henri DeBray insults Frances. They settle the matter with rapiers and DeBray is killed. A thief, whose enmity Paul has incurred, is a witness to the duel, and gives the dead man's brother a wrong version of the quarrel. Paul flees to South America. Maurice DeBray is a physician and the brother of Henri. He has sworn that he will kill the man who killed his brother. Frances and Maurice meet, marry and move to New York. Frances does not know that her brother was the cause of Henri's death. After five years, Paul returns to New York, and on his way to visit his sister, by coincidence, he saves a little girl from being killed by an automobile. It is his sister's child. The family grows close, but the doctor cannot forget his brother's death. One day he shares his grief with Paul. Paul admits his involvement and tries to straighten out the chain of events, but Maurice will not listen. He challenges Paul to a duel. Paul agrees to a duel, but of a novel nature. Each man is to sit on the sofa, neither speaking, and have the little girl come into the room. Whomever little Mimi touches first, that one should take a gun and shoot himself. The child touches them both at the same time.

Notes: Review in *Motion Picture News*, 2/28/1914, suggests that at least some scenes may have been shot in Paris during IMP's visit there in 1913.

The Flaming Diagram

Universal IMP, 3/9/1914. Two reels.

Cast: King Baggot (Erickson, Jr.), Leah Baird (Lillian, the Inventor's Daughter), Frank Smith (Erickson), Charles Bainbridge (Of the War Department), Howard Crampton (Brack, the Foreign Spy).

Synopsis: An inventor has perfected a powerful explosive which he manufactures for the U.S. Government without revealing the secret of its composition. Spies of a foreign nation try vainly to discover the process. The inventor dies and the spies steal the sealed papers from the office of the Secretary of War. They find only a meaningless drawing of some bottles and a blank sheet of paper, with the instructions that the key is in the desk drawer at the home of the inventor. They try to break into the house but are captured by young Erickson. He is just as puzzled by the instructions. A tag on the key reads, "Burn diagram." While he and his sister puzzle over the mystery, his cigarette accidentally sets the blank paper aflame and, in a peculiar manner, leaves an intricate design which, when fitted over the diagram of the bottles, gives them the formula. The inventor had prepared the paper with chemicals so as to burn away a part and leave the words that counted untouched by the flames.

Notes: Re-released 4/21/1917 under the IMP brand as *The Blazing Secret*.

King, the Detective in the Marine Mystery
Universal IMP, 3/23/1914. Two reels.

Dir: King Baggot.
Scen: King Baggot.
Cast: King Baggot (The Detective), Frank Smith (Sergeant of Police), David Lithgoe (The Sailor and the Sailor's Brother), William Welsh (The Bank Manager), Howard Crampton (The Doctor), Miss Coffin (The Sweetheart).

Synopsis: The police pick up a sailor, wandering helplessly. A physician declares the man is under the influence of a strong opiate. King, the detective, unravels the mystery. The sailor's tan is actually a stain. His tattoo marks have been painted on. Until recently, the man had a mustache. His hands are too soft to be a sailor's. The sailor is actually a broker and a crime has been committed. King finds the man's sweetheart in New Jersey and learns that he also has a twin brother who is a sailor. He interviews the office manager of the man's firm and, after finding enough evidence, he arrests the manager and the twin brother for stealing money from the broker's safe and conspiring to change identities. The man comes to his senses and is reunited with his sweetheart. King retires, happy in the thought of another good work well done.

Notes: Re-released 3/11/1917 as *The Man of Mystery*.

The Blood Test
Universal IMP, 4/2/1914. Two reels.

Dir: King Baggot.
Scen: Harry G. Stafford.
Cast: King Baggot (Walter Ames), Ethel Grandin, Howard Crampton, Frank Smith, William Welsh, David Lithgoe.

Synopsis: Walter Ames is an inventor who is in danger of being swindled out of rights to his machine by the owner and the superintendent of the factory in which he is employed. They secure a draftsman to make blueprints of the invention. As it turns out, he is afflicted with "a strange oriental disease." He tries to blackmail the owner and, during a quarrel, he shoots him. The superintendent tries to make it appear that Ames is guilty, but the murderer left a bloodstain on the window pane. In it are germs of the strange disease. Walter's sweetheart has an uncle, a doctor who identifies the disease. Assured that King does not have it, the doctor inserts an advertisement in the newspaper to the effect that he will cure, free of charge, anyone afflicted with the disease. The murderer is apprehended and confesses. Ames is vindicated and wins the factory owner's daughter, who has always believed in him.

Notes: Re-released 4/7/1917 under the Universal Laemmle brand as *The Blue Print Mystery*.

Notoriety
Universal IMP, 4/18/1914. One reel.

Cast: King Baggot (King, the Actor), Frank Smith (His Friend), Howard Crampton (The Detective), Helen Field Gilmore (The Landlady).

Synopsis: King, a broken-down actor, attempts to get back into the limelight by pretending to be the instigator of a terrible murder that is baffling detectives around the country. He leaves proof of his innocence with a friend, but at a crucial moment the friend discovers that he has destroyed it.

King goes to the chair. As the electric current is turned on, he wakes up in his shabby little hall bedroom to find it has all been a horrible dream.

A Mexican Warrior

Universal IMP, 5/25/1914. One reel.

Cast: King Baggot (The Warrior), Arline Pretty (His Wife), Helen Field Gilmore (His Mother-in-Law), Frank Smith (A Friend), Howard Crampton (A Pal), John Powers (A Comrade), Mrs. Allan Walker (A Neighbor), Millie Liston (Another Neighbor).

Synopsis: One night, the "Warrior" and his friends are at a thirst emporium. In order to trick his meek wife and dominating mother-in-law into thinking he has business that will keep him away from home for some time, he and his friends rent a soldier's costume and an old horse. They go to his house and declare that he has enlisted in the army to fight the Mexicans. His wife is in tears, but the "Warrior" and his friends are gleeful that he can rejoin them and make a night of it. They get into an auto and give the steed a parting kick as they go off to diminish the town liquor supply. The horse returns to the "Warrior's" house and the wife thinks her dear one is already a casualty of the war. Later that night, his friends bring him to his door in a non compos mentis state. The mother-in-law comes to the door and, seeing him in that state, marches him down to the station and forces him to enlist.

Across the Atlantic

Universal IMP, 6/11/1914. Three reels.

Dir: Herbert Brenon.
Cast: King Baggot (Wilber Norton), Evelyn Hope (His Wife), Claude Graham White and Gustav Hammell, (Professional Aviators), Herbert Brenon (Oyama).

Synopsis: Wilber Norton, an inventor, has perfected a new aeroplane, but he is being followed by a Japanese spy who wants the plans. Wilber and a friend go out to celebrate because his plans have been accepted by the U.S. government. Wilber becomes intoxicated and his friend takes the plans for safekeeping. On the way home, the spy stabs the friend and takes the plans. Wilber, who had been in a drunken stupor, awakes on the sidewalk in the morning to find a knife stuck in his friend. He thinks he has murdered him. In shame and despair, he buries himself in a London slum selling newspapers. He has left his American wife and child, but the murdered man's fortune has been willed to her. Trying to find her husband, she comes to London where she meets the spy. Wilber is now working at a Punch and Judy show and sees his wife riding in a car. He tries to follow her, but loses her in the crowd at the Derby. The wife again meets the spy and, during the excitement of the race, succeeds in securing the papers. Wilber finds his wife and confronts the spy, who tries to escape in an aeroplane piloted by White. The flight is a short one and a chase follows. While being chased by Wilber across rooftops, the spy loses his footing and falls to his death. Wilber and his family are reunited.

Notes: British title: *The Secret of the Air*. Filmed in and around London. It included live coverage of the Derby Day race at Epsom Downs and location shooting at Hendon Aerodrome.

The Baited Trap

Universal IMP, 6/15/1914. Two reels.

Scen: Monte M. Katterjohn.
Cast: King Baggot (Dennis), Arline Pretty (Norah), Frank Smith (Black Louie), Howard Crampton (Craven), John Powers (Blondie).

Synopsis: Dennis, an Irish boy, leaves his sweetheart Norah and his family to make his fortune in America. He gets work in a saloon and innocently falls in with a gang of thieves. He is scrubbing floors and sleeping in a storeroom when one morning he awakes to find a wallet full of money on his chest. This is the "trap." Black Louie has seen Norah's photograph, which Dennis carries with him, and decides to capture her for their white slavery ring. He tells Dennis that it is a present from his employer to help him bring Norah to America. He sends for her, but when she arrives, Dennis is arrested on a "plant." Norah is kidnapped and taken to a house of ill repute where she is imprisoned. Dennis is cleared of all charges and discovers where the gang has taken Norah. He drops through a skylight into the room where Norah is being held and, after a gun battle, Norah is rescued.

Notes: This film was shown at the Republic Theatre, New York, the week of April 6, 1914, at 4 and 9 P.M. The entire cast enacted a stage play that began with the cast presumably waiting for Baggot, who had been delayed at the Screen Club. They ran the first part of the actual film as though they were in the projection room. When they came to the part where Dennis rescues Norah, they stop. Baggot appeared on stage and they did the ending on stage showing the audience how a film was acted and photographed; complete with mistakes and retakes. They then ran another film showing how a film was printed, dried and assembled. It was Baggot's first theatrical appearance since *The Wishing Ring* in which he supported Marguerite Clark in a touring company production during the 1908/1909 season. The film itself was not released until June 15, when the prologue and epilogue were added as part of the motion picture.

The One Best Bet

Universal IMP, 7/2/1914. One reel.

Cast: King Baggot (Jack), Arline Pretty (Arline).

Synopsis: Jack is engaged to be married, but he has one fault in the eyes of his stern prospective father-in-law. When the old man finds that Jack has been betting on the races, he forbids him the house. In the meantime, Jack, who has not abandoned his determination to win the girl, plays the races with success. At his club, the old man hears of nothing but the races and threatens to resign. Finally, his curiosity aroused, he visits a poolroom. While there, the poolroom is raided. He is captured and jailed. Through the influence of Jack, after consent has been given to the marriage, the prospective father-in-law is released.

The Great Universal Mystery

Universal Nestor, 7/10/1914. One reel.

Dir: Allan Dwan.
Cast: King Baggot, Pauline Bush, Ford Sterling, William Clifford, Lois Weber, Lee Moran, Ella Hall, Hobart Henley, William Welsh, Betty Schade, Leah Baird, Howard Crampton, Al Christie, Carl Laemmle, Maurice Fleckles, Herman Fichtenberg, Allen Curtis, Florence Lawrence, Francis Ford, Robert Z. Leonard, Cleo Madison, Victoria Forde, Murdock MacQuarrie, Ethel Grandin, Alexander Gaden, Rupert Julian, Edna Maison, Edmund Mortimer, Frank Crane, Lule Warrenton, Frank Lanning, Frank Lloyd, Anna Little, Gail Henry, Louise Fazenda, Bob Vernon, Max Asher, Wilfred Lucas, F.A. Van Husan, V.J. Bryson, Henry McRae, J. Warren Kerrigan, Grace Cunard, Herbert Rawlinson, Phillips Smalley, Eddie Lyons, William E. Shay, Irene Wallace, Matt Moore, Marie Walcamp, Frank Smith, Sherman Bainbridge, Louise Glaum, Bobby Fuehrer, Bess Meredyth, Harry Schumm, George Periolat, Vera Sisson, Ernest Shields, William Dowlan, Herbert Brenon, Isadore Bernstein, Otis Turner, Bob Thornby, David Horsley, Fred Balshofer, R.H. Cochrane, J.C. Graham, Joe Brandt.

Notes: A semi-documentary and a mystery story said to contain virtually every employee of the Universal Corporation. No synopsis has been found. It was filmed at Universal City in California, Imp Studios in New York, Coytesville Studios in New Jersey, Victor Studios in New Jersey and the Universal executive offices at 1600 Broadway in New York.

The Universal Boy
Universal IMP, 7/16/1914. Series #1.
One reel.

Cast: Matty Roubert, King Baggot, William E. Shay, Frank Crane, Annette Kellerman, John McGraw (Manager of the New York Giants), Jimmy Ford (New York Giants Mascot).

Synopsis: Little Matty is an IMP star. He is seen from the time he awakes in the morning, has his breakfast and goes to the studio. There he is greeted by stars Baggot, Shay and Crane. He makes up and rehearses a scene. Later, his father takes him to the Polo Grounds where, the Giants are warming up. Matty meets the team's manager John McGraw and team mascot Jimmy Ford. Leaving the ballpark, Matty is taken to the New York Globe Theatre and is introduced to swimming star Annette Kellerman. He ends his day in a theater where he sees himself on screen.

Jim Webb, Senator
Universal IMP, 8/24/1914. Three reels.

Dir: King Baggot.
Scen: King Baggot.
Cast: King Baggot (Jim Webb), Leah Baird (Marion), Howard Crampton (A Friend and Senator), William Welsh (A Lobbyist), Frank Smith (Minister), Mrs. Allan Walker (Jim's Mother).

Synopsis: An upright young country politician wins election to the U.S. Senate and goes to Washington, where a group of corrupt politicians try to buy his vote to get a bill passed. When their attempt fails, they employ a bewitching female lobbyist to ensnare him. Jim falls in love with her, but she never betrays him, as her heart is won by a visit to his old home where she meets his mother. In a last ditch stand to keep Jim from voting against the bill, the conspiring lobbyists try to stop him from getting to the capitol by riding ahead of the pair and throwing puncturing objects under the wheels of their car. They manage to stop the vehicle, but he and Marion jump into their pursuer's vehicle and get to the Senate floor in time to vote. Jim forgives Marion for her original deception and the story ends with the lovers looking forward to a happy future together.

The Silent Valley
Universal IMP, 9/7/1014. Two reels.

Dir: King Baggot.
Scen: George Edwardes Hall.
Cast: King Baggot, Arline Pretty, Frank Smith.

Synopsis: He grew from an incorrigible boy into a giant bully terrorizing the entire country district of Silent Valley. One day he breaks up a traveling show by carrying off the troupe's lovely young dancer. He takes her to his cabin, pursued by the angry villagers, but releases her unharmed. He falls in love with her, which changes his brutal nature, and he gradually turns into a good citizen. The girl returns to wed him.

The Man Who Was Misunderstood
Universal IMP, 9/17/1914. Two reels.

Dir: King Baggot, George Lessey.
Scen: George Edwardes Hall.
Cast: King Baggot (Ned Jackson), Arline Pretty (Betty Austin), Frank Smith (Col. Austin), Robert Hill (George), Ben Hall (The Jockey), Mrs. Allan Walker (Ned's Mother), Roger (A Dog).

Synopsis: An impoverished old street fiddler and his dog Roger are invited into a mansion by a little girl and her mother and encouraged to tell his life's story. The scene flashes back to his boyhood days when he was in love with Betty Austin, whose father, Col. Austin, owned a string of racehorses. The Colonel, in financial trouble, needs to win the Derby. George, Ned's rival, tricks him into betting against the Colonel's horse, which leads to a breach between Ned and his loved one. George then abducts the jockey who was to ride the Colonel's horse. Circumstantial evidence leads the Colonel to believe Ned is responsible. Betty rides in the jockey's place and wins. In spite of Ned's protestations, George manages to forge a note wherein Ned confesses his guilt. He loses the hand of his loved one and starts to decline. In his old age, alone and friendless, he saves the life of a puppy that becomes his companion. The last we see of the old misunderstood man is his form, accompanied by his faithful friend, silhouetted against the skies, waiting for a happier day.

Notes: A squib in *Universal Weekly*, 8/8/1914, announced George A. Lessey as director, but a profile and synopsis on 9/12/1914 showed Baggot as director. In the 9/12 profile, Robert Hill's character was called "Chester Smythe," but in the viewed print he was called "George." Also, according to the synopsis of 9/12, there is a scene late in the film where "Chester" and Ned had a chance meeting on a wharf. They struggled and "Chester" fell into the water and drowned. Ned was accused of the murder, but later exonerated. In the viewed print, "George," in a deathbed confession, told how he had wronged Ned.

Loc: LC.

Shadows

Universal IMP, 10/5/1914. Special Feature. Two reels.

Dir: King Baggot.
Cam: Mr. Schellinger.
Scen: George Edwardes Hall.
Cast: King Baggot.

Synopsis: Mr. and Mrs. Clark live alone in sorrow with their Chinese servant. Years before, their only son, a fun-loving boy, left them. As the story opens, the boy returns, but his father deems it best to give him money and send him away again. After he leaves, a thief breaks in. He robs the servant of his savings. The old father hears the commotion and confronts the thief, who kills him and flees. The police are summoned and King, the detective, is called in on the case. In search of clues, King visits a tavern where he overhears a quarrel between the thief and his sweetheart. She flings coins he has given her into the crook's face. One of the coins rolls in King's direction. When he picks it up, he discovers it is a Chinese coin. The son is arrested for the murder; however, King believes him to be innocent. He verifies that the coin belonged to the Chinese servant and hurries back to the tavern in time to trail the thief to his lodging house. He calls the police to assist in the arrest of the thief and they break down the door. After terrific fight, King pursues the thief up onto the roof where, a pistol duel takes place. The thief is winged and falls to the ground several floors below. He lives long enough to clear the son of any suspicion. The story closes with the son leaving the jail with his mother and King showing the satisfaction of a job well done.

Notes: This film was a motion picture "first." Baggot played ten different characters: the detective, a rich banker, his wife, her wayward son, a Chinese servant, a woman of the world, a crook, a German innkeeper, a police captain and a French jailer. It used both double and triple exposures with Baggot playing up to three roles on the screen at one time. In order to show the picture was not a "fake," and to prove that Baggot played all the parts, the film showed him putting on and taking off each different makeup as one scene dissolved into another. Many thousand feet of negative were edited down to just two reels. It was called *Shadows* because many exteriors were used in which the rays of a low sun played an important part. Shooting took six weeks.

The Turn of the Tide

Universal IMP, 11/2/1914. Two reels.

Dir: George A. Lessey
Cast: King Baggot (Tom Walters), Arline Pretty (Nell Brown, His Sweetheart), Frank Smith (James Brown, Her Father), Bessie Toner (Margaret Swithers, the City Girl), Ned Reardon (Clem Masters, a Lawyer).

Synopsis: Tom wishes to marry Nell, but her father refuses. The father needs to pay off a

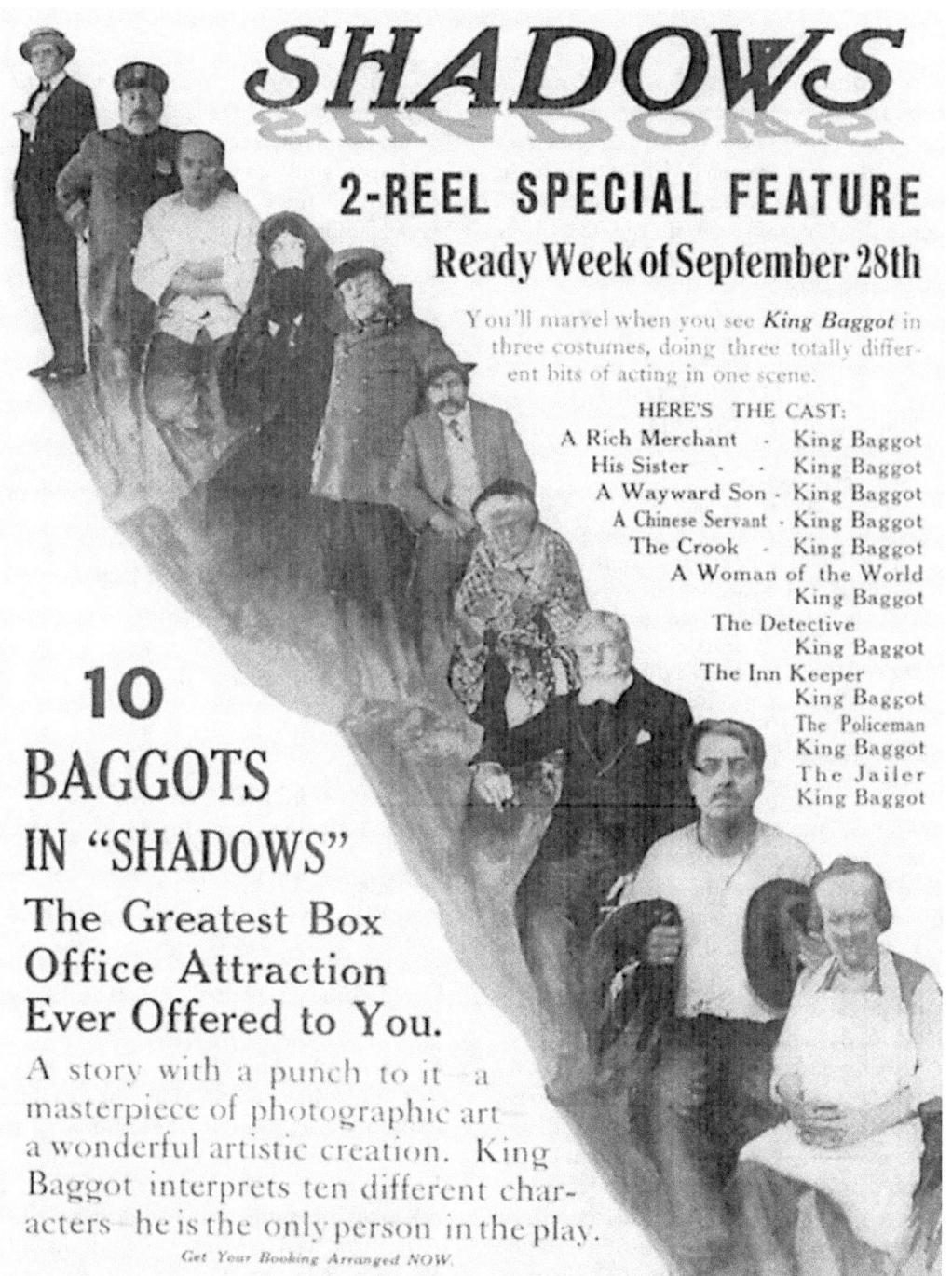

Advertisement for Baggot's famous *Shadows* in which he played 10 roles. IMP, 1914. *Montography*, 1914.

loan to Clem Masters, who is willing to wed Nell and forgive the note. Nell gives Tom the note and he secretly pays it. When he goes to Brown's house with the receipt, he finds no one home and hides the note in an old armchair. Brown sees him leave the house and, refused an explanation, he shoots Tom in the head, causing him amnesia. Tom falls for the wiles of a pretty girl and follows her to the city, where he learns she is only amusing herself with him. He settles down and becomes a successful businessman. By accident, he visits his old seaside town where he rescues Nell, who has been caught in a storm in an open boat. He carries her home and places her in the armchair when the old note drops out. This revives his memory and a joyful reunion takes place.

The Treasure Train

Universal IMP, 11/16/1914. Two reels.

Dir: George A. Lessey.
Scen: George Edwardes Hall.
Cast: King Baggot (John Armstrong), Arline Pretty (Nell Blythe), Frank Smith (Herbert Blythe), Ned Reardon (Jack Neill), Mr. Driscoll (Red Gube), Fred Herzog (Gummy McGaw), Mr. Wise (Caleb Durand), Mr. Leroy (James Bardell), William Burbridge (Oliver Starbuck), Joe Chialloe (Albert Winchell), Mr. Slattery (Fred Bonden), Mr. Bates (James Oldham the Railroad Boss), Nan Toner (Baelita Carmelita).

Synopsis: John Armstrong was once a tramp who sought shelter on a cold night in a railroad station. Thieves entered the station, tied up the tramp and the station master and planned not only to rob, but to wreck a train with passengers and gold on board. Armstrong managed to free his feet and used them to telegraph ahead to Lone Pine. A young girl there was taking the place of her sick father. She took a wild ride on a handcar to get the train flagged down, saving the train and the passengers. The tramp was eventually rewarded by being made superintendent of the railroad. Five years later, Armstrong hears that the girl operator of the Lone Pine Station is going to be replaced by a man of influence. His sense of justice is aroused and he goes before the railroad board of directors. He tells them how the girl helped save the train and helped him to land his present position. They agree to retain her. Then he tells them it is immaterial whether they keep her because she is soon to become his wife. The young lovers are seen together, happily married.

Notes: According to *The Dramatic Mirror*, arrangements were made with several orphanages for the services of 250 children supposedly going on a picnic. After climbing on, then off the train, they were guests of Universal for the day.

Human Hearts

Universal IMP, 11/26/1914. Three reels.

Dir: Otis Turner.
Scen: George Edwardes Hall.
Cast: King Baggot (Tom Logan), Arline Pretty (Ruth), Frank Smith (Sam Logan), Bertram Busby (Fred Armsdale), Ben Hall (Jimmy), Mr. Bates (Mose), Mrs. Allan Walker (Mrs. Logan), Bessie Toner (Jeanet Logan).

Notes: A remake of IMP's 1912 production. Some scenes were filmed at the New York State Prison. Based on the play by Hal Reid.

The Mill Stream

Universal IMP, 12/14/1914. Two reels.

Dir: George A. Lessey.
Scen: H.K. Brooks, King Baggot, George A. Lessey.
Cast: King Baggot (Jack Thornby), Arline Pretty (Mary Wheatley), Robert Hill (Tom Craven), Frank Smith (Dan Wheatley).

Synopsis: Jack Thornby, owner of a small grist mill, is in love with Mary, the daughter of his mill foreman. Jack finds Tom Craven, who had been fishing in a nearby stream, sitting on the bank nursing a sprained ankle. Jack takes him home and helps him recover. He is introduced to Mary, who finds his polished ways in contrast to Jack's hearty manners, and she begins to reject poor Jack. Jack becomes jealous and the two men have a fight, which is witnessed by the mill watchman. The next day, Tom's body is found in the stream with stab wounds to his back and neck. Jack is sentenced to 20 years in prison. Months later, Mary is rowing in the stream and comes upon the body of a tramp.

Protruding from his pocket is a pocketbook which belonged to Tom. Investigation discloses that the tramp killed Tom, then stumbled into the stream and drowned. Jack is released from prison and he and Mary are married.

Notes: The story was based on a true murder known as "The Carmen Case," which took place on Long Island. Most of the filming was done at Smithtown, Long Island.

1915

Three Times and Out

Universal IMP, 1/4/1915. One reel.

Cast: King Baggot (Jack), Ned Reardon (Ned), Arline Pretty (Ned's Wife).

Synopsis: Ned and Arline are a happily married couple. Ned receives a letter from his old friend Jack, who will be coming to town that day and will stop at Ned's office. Arline says she will be glad to meet him there. Jack arrives at the office but finds Ned is busy and decides to go out for a stroll. He starts to flirt with an attractive woman who turns out to be Arline. She does not know it is Ned's friend and has him arrested. Ned bails him out and takes him home for dinner, but Arline has not returned home yet. Ned leaves Jack in the library and goes back to some unfinished business at the office. When Arline returns and finds Jack in the library, she thinks he has followed her home. She calls the police and has him arrested again. Again, Ned is called and bails him out. Ned has to finish a business deal, but gives Jack a key to his office and asks him to wait there. Arline decides to go to the office to tell Ned what a bad day she has had. Once more Jack is arrested. Arline goes home and Ned, back in the office, gets another call. Again, Jack is bailed out, but when Ned suggests they go home for dinner, Jack knocks Ned to the ground and runs off. On the next street, a pretty girl tries to flirt with Jack, who with wild shrieks boards a passing trolley and is seen no more.

The Millionaire Engineer

Universal IMP, 1/29/1915. Two reels.

Dir: George A. Lessey.
Scen: Constance Brinsley.
Cast: King Baggot (Daniel Spencer), Arline Pretty (Maude Allyne), Frank Smith, Bessie Toner, Ned Reardon.

Synopsis: Daniel Spencer is a self-made man who came up through the ranks to become president of the railroad. On the eve of his engagement to Maude Allyn, a group of railroad employees hold a mass meeting in the village square to protest the greed of the president in his mansion while the workers starve in squalor. They appoint a committee to go to his house to present their grievances; however, their bullying manner angers him and he defies them. Maude pleads for them but he does not listen. She gives him back her ring and leaves. Time passes as the bitter strike continues until one day, while in the yard, Daniel hears of a forest fire that, if not checked, will destroy an orphan asylum. The workers refuse to run the engine to go to the rescue of the children. He jumps into the cab of the locomotive, charges through the flames and rescues the children. The strike is settled and he is reconciled with Maude.

Notes: Location shooting was done near Fort Lee, Leota Heights, Amboy and Coytesville, New Jersey. The 150-year-old Marks Mansion was purchased and burned to the ground. Five small houses were erected and several abandoned shacks were brought to the site, where they were drenched with oil and set aflame to produce the effects of the spectacular fire. In one scene, the heat was so intense that Baggot's clothing caught fire and had to be put out with blankets. A complete train with baggage and passenger coaches was used in the filming and the train's real engineer, Jack McGuire, taught Baggot how to operate it.

The Story the Silk Hats Told

Universal IMP, 2/1/1915. One reel.

Dir: George A. Lessey.
Scen: Curtis Benton
Cast: King Baggot.

Synopsis: An old second-hand clothing dealer sits in his shop near a section of shelves containing six silk hats. He falls asleep and has a dream in which the hats assume faces. Each hat has a price tag and description, and one by one the former owners tell their stories. The first has a price of $1.50. It says, "I have aided Big Business"—a business man. The second sells for $1.25 and says, "I have been Cupid's messenger"—a lover. The third, at $1.00 says, "I have been a political power"— a politician. The fourth, at 75 cents says, "I have made millions laugh"—a German burlesque comedian. The fifth, at 50 cents says, "I have ended lovers' quarrels"—a doctor. The sixth, at 25 cents says, "I have aided the needy"—a bank clerk.

Notes: Baggot played all seven of the parts.

An Oriental Romance

Universal IMP, 2/19/1915. Two reels.

Dir: George A. Lessey.
Cast: King Baggot (Hop Kung), Arline Pretty (Clara Fenton), Ned Reardon (Dick Fenton), Frank Smith (Lian Kung), Charles Burbridge (Clara's father), unnamed actor (Heapley, the Loan Shark).

Synopsis: Hop Kung, a young Chinese man attending an American college, makes friends with Dick Fenton, a classmate who has gotten himself into a large gambling debt. Hop Kung and his father help him out of the clutches of Heapley, the loan shark, and they win the unbounded admiration of Dick. Hop Kung is invited to the Fenton home and meets Dick's sister Clara. She falls in love with him and, over time, a romance develops which is pounced upon by the girl's father and brother. They reject the young man and overlook entirely the great service which Hop Kung has done for Dick. That night, at a formal gathering, in order to break off the affair, Hop Kung makes love to all the girls in turn in the presence of the woman he really loves. The Chinaman's heart is broken and so is Clara's.

Notes: For the scenes shot in Lian Kung's shop in Chinatown, no expense was spared. The arms of the chairs were set with tiny colored bulbs and the eyes of the carved dragon-head arms blinked on and off with "amazing realism." Baggot supplied his own gold and hand-painted Chinese gown. Chinese porcelain vases, rugs and tapestries were purchased or loaned from art dealers and exclusive Fifth Avenue stores.

Pressing His Suit

Universal IMP, 3/1/1915. One reel.

Dir: George A. Lessey.
Cast: King Baggot, Arline Pretty, Ned Reardon, Frank Smith, Ben Hall.

Synopsis: A man means to send his pants to the tailor and flowers to his girl, but the opposite occurs. The flowers go to the tailor and the girl gets the pants with a note saying "Wear these for my sake."

Notes: *Motion Picture News*, 3/6/1915, called this a "reissue"; however, it is more probable that was a remake of *Pressed Roses*, released 9/26/1910, with Florence Lawrence in the cast.

The Five Pound Note

Universal IMP, 3/12/1915. Two reels.

Dir: George A. Lessey.
Cast: King Baggot (Lord Avon Ledgard), Frank Smith (Jock Hawkins, a Costermonger), Arline Pretty (His Daughter, Nell), Ned Reardon (Haggard, a Sea Captain).

Synopsis: A dissolute young Englishman makes a bet that he can earn five pounds within ten days by real work. He obtains a donkey and a cart and poses as a costermonger; however, his friends come to taunt him and throw his green goods about. He is defended by a real coster and falls in love with the man's daughter. The girl is menaced by a drunken sea captain and is saved by Ledgard. Although his loses the bet, he wins the heart of girl.

Notes: Some scenes filmed under the Brooklyn Bridge and Garden City, Long Island, New York.

One Night

Universal IMP, 3/22/1915. One reel.
LP4681.

Dir: George A. Lessey.
Cast: King Baggot (The Crook), Arline Pretty (The Woman), Ned Reardon (The Husband), Frank Smith (The Banker), Mrs. Ward (The Housekeeper).

Synopsis: A burglar is in the act of robbing a house when a destitute widow leaves her baby on the stoop. The thief hears its cries and finds it. He is so touched by the innocent that he returns the loot and places the baby on a sofa with a note explaining that the sight of the child has reformed him. Leaving, he meets the mother who has come back for the child and recognizes her as an old sweetheart. They repair to the house to get the baby, but the owner surprises them and is about to call the police when the reformed burglar gets a chance to explain. All ends well and the rich gentleman gives them a large check to start a new life.

The City of Terrible Night

Universal IMP, 4/2/1915. Two reels.
LP4792.

Dir: George A. Lessey.
Scen: Mrs. George E. Hall.
Cast: King Baggot (Walter Herron), Arline Pretty (Tessa, Rudolph's Daughter), Ned Reardon (Seneti), Frank Smith (Luigi), Ed Duane (Jack's Valet).

Synopsis: Walter, a wealthy bachelor, is bored with his life. He heads for the meaner side of town and goes into an Italian dance hall where he finds a beautiful young girl being attacked by some jealous women. He escorts her home, but is rejected by the girl's father Seneti, an exiled nobleman, now impoverished. After an argument, Walter breaks the old man's cane over his knee and leaves. Later he goes back to try to explain his interest in Tessa. There he finds an old enemy of Seneti's in the act of stabbing and killing him. Walter struggles with the assassin and strikes a terrible blow to his head, but he gets away. Walter is arrested for the murder, but he escapes and returns home. However, he and his faithful valet are soon rearrested and jailed. Meanwhile, the assassin, suffering from the effects of the blow to the head, is thought to be drunk and is arrested and thrown into the same cell with Walter and his valet. Here, his delirious babbling reveal him to be the murderer. Exonerated, Walter marries Tessa.

Notes: *Universal Weekly*, 3/27/1915, lists the character names as above however, the synopsis filed with Library of Congress gives the names as Jack Van Rensselaer, Olga, Boris and Rudolph. Originally a poem by James Thompson, "The City of Dreadful Night," later a story by Rudyard Kipling.

The Streets of Make Believe

Universal IMP, 4/12/1915. One reel.
LP4890.

Dir: George A. Lessey.
Scen: Anthony P. Kelly.
Cast: King Baggot (Bert Wall), Jane Gail (Katherine Drew), Ned Reardon (Store Manager), Frank Smith (Laundry Manager).

Synopsis: Bert is a clerk in a dry goods store. One day, a wealthy man purchases some goods and gives Bert his card telling where to deliver them. He pockets the card. A clerk later tells him which articles will be marked down for the next day's sale. He has no paper and writes the information on his shirt cuff. That night, he sees Katherine getting out of a chauffeur-driven automobile belonging to a friend. Thinking her rich, Bert strikes up an acquaintance with her and gives her the rich man's card to impress her. The next day he drops his shirts off at the laundry. As it happens, Katherine works there, but he does not see her. She sees the note about the sale on the cuff and goes to the store. To her disgust, she finds that Bert is a clerk. She leaves without buying anything. When Bert goes to pick up his laundry, he finds Katherine bent over a tub. They exchange recriminations and accusations, which eventually lead to friendship and then love.

At the Banquet Table
Universal IMP, 4/30/1915. Two reels.
LP5123.

Dir: George A. Lessey.
Scen: Harvey Gates.
Cast: King Baggot (Sheerl Jones), Arline Pretty (Mrs. Jones), Ned Reardon (Bill Coles), Frank Smith (Robert), Ed Duane (Maurice).

Synopsis: Jones gives a bachelor dinner for some of his friends at the club. Much laughter and drinking ensue. He falls asleep and dreams that he meets Bill Cole, a young naval officer just returned to New York. He and his friends go out on the town and Bill forgets all about his wife and child waiting at home. Bill, very drunk, can't remember where he lives. His friends take him to a house they hope is his, put him through a back window and leave him. Mrs. Jones is up with her small child and hears a noise. She quietly takes a gun and fires it through the curtains where she thinks a burglar is hiding. She then goes next door to her friend Mrs. Cole, who calls the police and then joins Mrs. Jones at her house. She parts the curtains only to find her husband alive, but very drunk. In the meantime, Jones goes back to his club where he receives a call from his hysterical wife. In his hurry to leave, he takes the wrong overcoat. He is stopped by the police, who suspect he may be the burglar. They question his identity and take him to jail, where they give him the third degree. Having visions of going to the electric chair, he awakens to find himself still at the banquet table with all his friends. He receives a phone call from his patient wife and, bidding good night to his cronies, he rushes home to her.

Tony
Universal IMP. 5/7/1915, One reel.
LP5163.

Dir: George A. Lessey.
Scen: George A. Lessey.
Cast: King Baggot (Tony), Jane Gail (Giulia), Ned Reardon (Schuyler Armitage), Frank Smith (Guetanio Marco Arlani), Jane Lee (Rosa).

Synopsis: Tony, a poor Italian immigrant, comes to America to seek his fortune, leaving his wife and child behind. After a few years he has accumulated a tidy amount, but when he goes to the bank to withdraw it, he finds a notice on that door telling depositors that payment has been suspended. Armitage, a local millionaire, has volunteered to look at the books and see what he can do to help the bank, but when he comes outside, the crowd thinks he is responsible for the bank's possible failure. Tony follows him to his home and, from behind a hedge, sees him playing with his little girl. Tony is hoping for an opportunity to revenge himself on Armitage. Armitage goes into the house and the little girl wanders over to a place where workmen have just placed a fuse for a blast to excavate an artificial lake. All thoughts of revenge are banished when Tony thinks of his own little girl. Rushing to the spot, he picks her up just as the blast goes off. She is unharmed, but Tony is knocked unconscious. For days he is in a delirious state. When Armitage learns how Tony saved the child and how he misses his own family, he sends to Italy for them and they are Tony's first sight when he awakens from his delirium.
Loc: BFI.

The Corsican Brothers

Universal IMP, 5/14/1915. Three reels. LP5238.

Dir: George A. Lessey.
Scen: George A. Lessey.
Cast: King Baggot (Louis and Fabien Dei Franchi), Jane Gail (Emilie De Lesparre), Ned Reardon (Alfred Meynard), Hal Clarendon (Chateau Renard), Frank Smith (Montgerion), Mathilde Brundage (Madam De Franchi).

Synopsis: Louis and Fabian were Siamese twins joined at birth and separated by a surgeon hours later. They remained united by suggestive mentality. Whatever one experienced was reciprocated by the other. Louis falls in love with the daughter of a French officer, stationed in Corsica. The officer is transferred to Paris and takes his daughter with him. Louis decides to go to Paris to study law and to be near to Emilie, but the father almost immediately marries her to an old naval officer who sails on an extended cruise, leaving her at home. Louis, brokenhearted, watches over her, but she is ensnared into a compromising position by Chateau Renard, a duelist and libertine. While trying to save her, Louis is killed in a duel. At the moment of his death, Fabien, at his mountain home in Corsica, feels a sharp pain in his side and, placing his hand there, finds it covered with blood, although there is no trace of a wound. He hurries home to tell his mother of the occurrence and has a vision of the duel. He travels to Paris, meets Renard and kills him. He then returns to Corsica with his brother's body.

Notes: From the novel by Alexander Dumas *père*. Baggot played both brothers. The production featured a modern setting. It opened with a triple exposure as Baggot introduced himself and showed the book upon which the story was based. He bowed first to the right and Fabian appeared. He then bowed to the left and Louis, the other brother, made his formal entrance. Original release date was changed from 5/8/1914 to 5/14/1914.

Fifty-Fifty

Universal IMP, 5/24/1915. One reel.

Dir: George A. Lessey.
Cast: King Baggot (David Briggs), Jane Gail (Jennie Joyce), Ned Reardon (Hiram Quickly), Frank Smith (Algernon Trimmer), Bert Busby (Stiffen Stout), Jeanette Lawrence (Miss Astorocks).

Synopsis: Briggs has been transferred from the dry goods department to the management of the soda department where he must wear a white coat, which amuses Jennie, who teases him. Miss Astorocks, a wealthy society girl, is robbed while drinking a soda. Briggs manages to recover her property and takes it to her home. Before he can explain to the butler why he is there, he is mistaken for one of Miss Astorock's unwanted suitors and thrown into the street. He has no money and faces a long walk home. He passes the store and is permitted by the night watchman to sleep under a counter, but he finds a bed in the store window more comfortable. The next morning, the window dresser does not see David in the bed and raises the street curtain. Soon a large crowd has gathered, including Miss Astorocks. There is a sign in the window, which says, "Take me home for $4.50." After a hearty laugh, Miss Astorocks finds the store manager and tells him she wants what is in the window. When he sees what she is referring to, he bodily throws David out and fires him. Miss Astorocks pleads for him and David promises never to get into a scrape again. Miss Astorocks' jewelry is returned and Jennie asks David to forgive her for the teasing, which he does.

Notes: *Moving Picture World*, 5/22/1915, and *Universal Weekly*, 5/29/1915, called this film the second episode in *The Life of David Briggs*. No information on a first episode has been found.

A Life in the Balance

Universal IMP, 6/4/1915. Two reels. LP5397.

Dir: George A. Lessey.
Scen: Anthony P. Kelly.
Cast: King Baggot (Dr. Savage), Arline Pretty (Katherine Webb), Ned Reardon (Dr. Smiley), Frank Smith (Farmer Robbins), Mrs. Ward (Mrs. Robbins), Katherine Lee (Baby Robbins), Jane Lee (Baby Webb).

Synopsis: Farmer Brown's little daughter has a high fever. He calls in old Dr. Smiley, who diagnoses the illness as a severe case of appendicitis and orders an immediate operation. The farmer, noting the doctor's failing eyesight and enfeebled condition, refuses to allow him to perform it. He calls in a young doctor from another village. When the operation is successful, he decides to move from the little hamlet, as he can make no money there. Dr. Smiley dies of old age and discouragement and his daughter Katherine, a young widow, is now alone in the world. One day her little daughter receives a severe burn, but she will not allow the new doctor to attend her. She feels he is somehow responsible for her father's death. However, he realizes the seriousness of the child's injury. In order to save the child, he goes to the sick room, ejects the protesting mother and saves the child. In the days and months that follow, he continues to attend the child and he and Katherine fall in love and eventually marry.

A Strange Disappearance
Universal IMP, 6/11/1915. Three reels.
LP5472.

Dir: George A. Lessey.
Scen: Raymond L. Schrock.
Cast: King Baggot (Andrew Blake), Edna Hunter (Evelyn, His Sweetheart), Ned Reardon (Hoenmaker, a Scoundrel), Jane Gail (Luthia, His Daughter), Frank Smith (John Blake).

Synopsis: In the period just before the Mexican War, Andrew is told by his father, a rich merchant, that he must marry the daughter of the firm's partner. But Andrew is in love with Evelyn. They quarrel and Andrew goes to the Maine woods to consider the matter. He is taken in by Hoenmaker who, with his son, plot to rob and kill him. Hoenmaker's daughter Luthia overhears the plot and helps Andrew to escape. He takes her to a convent fearing that she will come to harm for her kind act. Back home, Andrew again quarrels with his father and the old man becomes so ill that Andrew fears he will die. Overcome with remorse, he promises not to marry Evelyn; his father urges him to marry someone else, as he would dearly like to see him married before he dies. Andrew goes to the convent and proposes to Luthia, who accepts and they marry. Shortly afterwards, she overhears Andrew confess to his father that he still loves Evelyn. In despair, she rushes to the lake intending to kill herself, but she is captured by her brother and father and taken away. Andrew thinks that she has drowned, but is told by a stranger that she has been kidnapped. He rushes to the Maine woods in the company of detectives. He goes inside the cabin to rescue Luthia, but is struck on the head by the son. To hide their crime they set fire to the cabin, but the detectives get there in time to rescue him. He is revived and immediately rushes back into the flames and saves Luthia. The Hoenmakers are arrested and Andrew and Luthia start on a postponed honeymoon.

Notes: Several scenes were filmed around an inn built in 1753. From the novel by Anna Katherine Green.

The Riddle of the Silk Stockings
Universal IMP, 6/14/1915. One reel.
LP5498.

Dir: George A. Lessey.
Scen: Raymond L. Schrock.
Cast: King Baggot (King Cole), Jane Gail (Jane Clark), Ned Reardon (Jefferson Spangler), Frank Smith (Frank Swartz).

Synopsis: King and Jane, clerks in a store, decide they need a vacation. They take a train to King's parents' house, but the parents are away. Back at the train station, they run into King's old friend, a traveling salesman in the hosiery trade, who finds himself stranded, as there will be no train in the little town until the next day. They repair to the local inn where Jane is given a room upstairs while the two men have first-floor quarters with a large window. To pass the time, the salesman unpacks his wares—of two or three dozen leg forms, fancy pumps and assorted hosiery in loud and wild colors. They decide to try to sell the goods and set them up in the window with the shade about three-quarters drawn. Children playing nearby see the collection of legs and men's hands smoothing out the wrinkles and decide something is going on. They alert an assortment of townspeople, who rush to see the scandalous scene. The deacon and others burst in to confront them and are embarrassed to find their activities have been harmless. The salesman takes advantage of their confusion and makes them buy enough of his hosiery so that the trio can afford to hire a rig to get home.

Notes: Synopsis and characters (submitted to the Library of Congress) give Ned Reardon's character name as "John Stanton"; however, *Moving Picture World*, 6/26/1915, gives his name as above.

Mismated

Universal IMP, 6/21/1915. One reel. LP5558.

Dir: George A. Lessey.
Scen: Raymond L. Schrock.
Cast: King Baggot (Shoe Clerk), Jane Gail (China Clerk), Ned Reardon (Floorwalker), Frank Smith (The Hack Driver).

Synopsis: King is a shoe clerk and his sweetheart Jane works in the china department. A dainty society woman comes to the shoe department and King decides to start a flirtation, which Jane observes. The lady is reading a newspaper, but King has to stop helping her to go to wrap some packages. The lady gets tired of waiting and departs. Jane decides to have some fun. She removes one of her slippers and takes the lady's place hiding behind the newspaper; however, some people come to the china counter and the floorwalker goes in search of Jane. Jane must go back to her counter, leaving the slipper and a customer card dropped by the lady. King returns to find the customer gone, but seeing the card and the slipper, he gives them to the package boy to deliver. An old hack driver comes in to buy shoes and the slipper is accidentally given to him by the package boy while his shoes go to the society lady. Jane must now find another shoe. She goes home at lunchtime and finds another to put on. Her slippers are now mismated. When the hack driver and the society lady discover the mix-up, they both go back to the store where they all try to settle matters, which eventually they do. The package boy disappears from sight and Jane asks King's forgiveness.

The Marble Heart

Universal IMP, 7/2/1915. Four reels. LP5670.

Dir: George A. Lessey.
Scen: George A. Lessey.
Cast: King Baggot (Raphael/Phidias), Jane Fearnley (Marco/Aphasia), Frank Smith (Volage/Diogenes), Ned Reardon (Viscount/Georgias), Edna Hunter (Marie/Thea), Marie Weirman (Clementine/Lais), Yona Landowska (Dancer).

Synopsis: A modern artist named Raphael dreams that he is the ancient Greek sculptor Phidias, who has been commissioned by the wealthy Georgias to carve three beautiful female statues. When Georgias comes to claim them, the sculptor refuses to give them up. Diogenes appears with his lantern looking for an honest man. He happens upon Phidias and learns of his predicament. He then urges Phidias to ask the statues themselves if they wish to stay with him or go with Georgias. The statues come to life and decide to go with the rich man, leaving Phidias brokenhearted. Awakening, Raphael continues to pursue the beautiful Marco, a society woman who has posed for him. She ultimately spurns his love for the wealthy viscount, leaving Raphael to seek happiness with the humble but loving Marie.

Notes: Based on the 1864 play by Charles Selby. The prologue followed the original Greek setting, but the rest of the film was done in modern dress. Most of the cast played dual roles. The Greek street scenes were filmed on Staten Island. During the chariot race, the winner was injured when his vehicle turned over and he broke his arm. Yona Landowska danced in two scenes. In the dream sequences, the Greek characters and their modern counterparts "dissolved" into one another to tell the story.

His New Automobile
Universal IMP, 7/13/1915. One reel. LP5748.

Dir: George A. Lessey.
Scen: George A. Lessey.
Cast: King Baggot (King Drake), Jane Gail (Jane Gallup), Ned Reardon (Ned Roarer, the Floorwalker).

Synopsis: King and Jane get the auto bug. In their boarding house, they practice driving an imaginary car until they disturb all their fellow boarders. Jane even dreams of prospective joy rides. King orders a new car on the installment plan. He mails off a new dollar bill and in a few days the car arrives. It is a one-cylinder insert, commonly known as a "road louse." He invites Jane to join him on a joy ride, but he has never driven a car before. The car starts off unexpectedly and he and Jane have to chase after it. He soon becomes too confident of his new driving skills. He speeds up and loses control of the car. It starts to skid backwards. They stop and try to find the cause of the reverse action. King inspects the fuel tank, but something goes wrong and there is a terrific explosion. King and Jane pick themselves up, the worse for wear, and find the remains of the auto smoldering in the branches of a tree. He and Jane sadly limp up the road toward home.

Notes: In one sequence, in King's imagination, the little roadster becomes a large touring car. Baggot is said to have done his own stunt work. The *Moving Picture World* review, 5/15/1915, lists the title as *His First Automobile*, but all other sources say "*New.*"

The New Jitney in Town
Universal IMP, 7/27/1915. One reel. LP5868.

Dir: George A. Lessey.
Scen: King Baggot.
Cast: King Baggot (Drake Salesman), Jane Gail (Jane Saleslady), Frank Smith (Store Manager), Ned Reardon (Floorwalker).

Synopsis: Drake gives up his job in the department store to start a jitney bus business. On his first day, he tells Jane to wait for him that evening outside the store. His first customer is a lady whose car has broken down. Jane sees her riding in the jitney and becomes jealous. The jitney soon breaks down and the lady gets out and leaves him in the lurch. Drake does not appear that evening so Jane asks the floorwalker to escort her home. Meanwhile, Drake is trying to fix the jitney, which starts up unexpectedly while he is underneath it and goes racing up the road. Presently he meets Jane with the floorwalker and offers her a ride home, which does not sit well with the floorwalker. Drake takes advantage of the opportunity and asks Jane to marry him. She accepts and they go to find a parson. After he marries them, they discover they have no money to pay him. They offer him the jitney as security, but he declines. They drive off, but soon it breaks down again. In disgust they leave it smoking in a field, but it apparently objects to this. It starts up and chases them up the road. They are forced to hide behind a tree and hug each other delightedly when it passes them as they are now rid of their ill-fated jitney.

The Only Child
Universal IMP, 8/31/1915. One reel. LP6172.

Dir: George A. Lessey.
Scen: George A. Lessey, from a story by King Baggot.
Cast: King Baggot (Papa), Marie Weirman (Wifey), Jane Lee (Baby), Ned Reardon (The Boss).

Synopsis: Wifey is addicted to matinees. After papa goes off to work, she and a neighbor decide to go, but must decide what to do with baby. They drop her off at papa's office and he is delighted to see her, but trouble begins. Baby punches holes in the hat of an important customer, pokes the head clerk with a letter opener and succeeds in upsetting the entire staff. Finally the little disturber wanders out into the street after dropping her hat by the time-lock safe. Papa misses his "dearest" and thinks she is locked in the safe. He runs out to find a safe opener, who proves to be a very slow one. While baby is wandering down the street, she is taken in charge by a policeman. Wifey and friend come out of the theater and see baby with the policeman. Wifey hugs her rapturously and exclaims how clever she is to come to meet them. Meanwhile, the safe is finally blown open and behold, there is no child inside. There is consternation on the part of the office staff and papa has to buy his boss a new safe.

Notes: Some basic elements of this plot are also found in *The Time-Lock Safe*, released 3/17/1910.

Crime's Triangle

Universal IMP, 9/10/1915. Two reels. LP6275.

Dir: King Baggot.
Scen: King Baggot.
Cast: King Baggot (John Small), Edna Hunter (Lillian Small), William Bailey (Harold Briar), Frank Smith (Stephen Kopf).

Synopsis: John Small, the assistant cashier of a bank, is married to an extravagant, pleasure-loving wife whose brother, Harold Briar, is an addicted gambler. Harold calls on John at the bank and manages to steal from his desk $5,000 left by a new depositor. John realizes the money is missing and knows that Harold is responsible. He rushes to confront Harold, but he has lost the money in a game of faro. John cannot repay the money and decides to end his life. He goes home and writes a note to his wife to explain, then enters the kitchen. He pours a whiskey glass of hydrocyantic acid and is about to drink it when he remembers an important note he must add to the letter. He puts down the drink and returns to his desk. As he is writing, Stephen Kopf, the bank's cashier, comes into the house with the intention of shooting John. He has embezzled large amounts from the bank and plans to frame John and make the shooting appear to be a suicide. He has a fake suicide note which he plans to try to pass off as John's writing. As he raises his hand to shoot, it trembles so badly he cannot complete the act. He sees the glass and thinking it is whiskey, downs it. Before he can fire, he falls to the floor, dead. John rushes in and, discovering the note, realizes what has almost occurred. He calls the police and when they arrive he shows them Stephen's note. They assume the confession was his and was genuine. They pronounce Stephen a suicide. Lillian helps John repay the lost money. He is promoted to the cashier's position and brother Harold moves to the Philippines, where he reforms.

The Suburban

Universal IMP, 9/17/1915. Four reels. LP6326.

Dir: George A. Lessey.
Scen: James Dayton.
Cast: King Baggot (Donald Gordon), Frank Smith (Robert Gordon), Iva Shephard (Alice Gordon), Little Sarajane Low (Little Florence Gordon), William Bailey (Jack Brambough, Donald's Chum), Brinsley Shaw (Ralph Fisher), Florence Malone (Helen Fisher), John Milton (Lee Thurston, a Horseman), Ned Reardon (Reddy Hyde), Harry Gripp (Hyde's Son), William Jardin (Tom Gegg), Bob Pansey (Joe Clayton), Mrs. Fanny Ward

(Maggie McGee, an Irish Servant), Harry Graff (Jockey Willen), Max Heine (Dietrich, a German Servant).

Synopsis: Robert Gordon is a wealthy stock owner who lives in a mansion near Sheepshead Bay. He wants his son Donald to marry Sir Ralph Fisher's daughter Helen, but Donald loves Alice, the lodge keeper's daughter. They wed in secret, but are discovered, and Donald is disowned. Before he leaves his family home, he takes from the safe some stocks left to him by his mother. Sir Ralph is deeply in debt and tries to steal money from Robert's open safe, but is caught by the butler, Hyde, who procures a confession and uses it for blackmail. While looking for work in another town, Donald hears that his father has entered his horse in the prestigious "Suburban," and has bet heavily on it. He returns and discovers that Sir Ralph and Tom, the Gordon's jockey, have conspired to throw the race. The jockey is replaced, the race is won and, after the butler is found murdered, Sir Ralph's confession is revealed. He commits suicide and the family is reunited.

Notes: Two hundred scenes were said to have been filmed in 50 different locations using a cast of over 200. The Belmont Handicap race was filmed. Other locations used were Long Island Sound and Lake Mahopac, Canada. A steam yacht, a schooner and a steam launch were used for various scenes. Based on the play by Charles Turner Dazey.

His Home Coming

Universal IMP, 9/21/1915. One reel. LP6372.

Dir: George A. Lessey.
Scen: George A. Lessey.
Cast: King Baggot (Will Move), Marie Weirman (Mrs. Move), Ned Reardon (Jim Newcomer), Miss Spencer (Mrs. Newcomer), Joe Daily (Mr. Quick), Jane Courtney (Mrs. Quick).

Synopsis: Mr. Move covets Mr. Quick's beautiful house next door, but the Quicks seem uninterested in moving out. One day he has to go out of town on business. As Mrs. Move returns home from dropping Mr. Move at the train station, she sees a "To Let" sign on the Quick house and immediately rents it. She puts an ad in the paper to sublet their old house and it is snapped up by Mr. and Mrs. Newcomer, who have been living in a very crowded flat in Harlem. She writes a letter to Mr. Move, but forgets to mail it. Mr. Move comes home on the midnight train not knowing that his old house is now occupied by the Newcomers. In order not to wake his wife, he takes off his shoes on his old porch. He goes upstairs in the semi-dark and begins to remove his clothing. Meanwhile, Mr. Newcomer has been working late and arrives to find a pair of men's shoes on his porch. A terrible scene ensues as Mrs. Newcomer screams and Mr. Newcomer throws Mr. Move out of the house and into the arms of Mrs. Move, who explains everything. Peace is restored.

An All Around Mistake

Universal IMP, 9/29/1915. Two reels. LP6436.

Dir: George A. Lessey.
Scen: King Baggot.
Cast: King Baggot (John Goody), Bessie Toner (Mrs. Goody), Arline Pretty (Mrs. Jones), William R. Sadler (Fred Dashing), Ned Reardon (Tom Rounder), Frank Smith (Gactano Arianie Colona, an Italian).

Synopsis: John Goody has a very jealous wife who keeps him close to home. He may not drink or look at other women and must do all that his wife commands. One day Mrs. Goody is called away by her mother, who believes she is very ill. On his way back from the train station, John runs into an old bachelor friend and they go out on the town. They get very drunk and behave very badly and are thrown out by a bouncer. They get into a fight with a peanut vendor, but finally make it home to John's house, where he collapses. He awakens the next morning with a severe hangover and has a few eye-openers to ease the pain. He picks up a newspaper and reads of an axe murderer who has just killed his mother-in-law and his entire family. Somehow he convinces himself that he has committed the crime. He leaves his wife a note confessing to the murders and goes to the police station to give himself up. Meanwhile, Mrs. Goody returns after finding her mother in better health and discovers John's friend asleep in her bed. She calls the police, then finds the note from John. They all end up at the police station where John is being given the "third degree." However, John shows them the newspaper and they discover it is over a year old. Everyone enjoys a good laugh and John is reconciled with his wife.

The Reward
Universal IMP, 11/5/1915. Three reels. LP6810.

Dir: Henry McRae Webster.
Scen: Mildred Considine.
Cast: King Baggot (Jack Hutchinson), Frank Smith (Perry Hutchinson), Mrs. Ford (Mrs. Hutchinson), Robert Fisher (Jasper Smythe), Edna Hunter (Claudia Smythe), Harry Spingler (Egbert Smythe), Lillian Beyers (Rhoda Dunbar).

Synopsis: The Cafe Bon Vivant is a notorious meeting place where persons from all classes and stations in life revel late into the night. Upstairs, games of chance entice in open defiance of the law. Jack Hutchinson is the manager, but a character called "Big Jim" is the real owner. No one knows his true identity, but he is actually Jasper Smythe, a retired banker and a highly regarded family man with two children. One night, Claudia and a group of young friends go slumming and visit the Cafe. They are recognized as newcomers and given personal attention by Jack. One of Claudia's escorts becomes drunk and Jack rescues Claudia from him. From that moment, he cannot forget her beautiful and unspoiled face. He becomes increasingly distant from Rhoda Dunbar, a prostitute who is in love with him. One day, Jack finds Claudia in the park and is invited to her home. Her father's picture hangs in the living room and he realizes that "Big Jim" is actually Jasper Smythe. He and Claudia fall in love, but Rhoda has hired a detective to find Jack's new love and also learns of Smythe's real identity. She taunts "Big Jim" and tells him of his daughter's involvement with Jack. In a fury, he discharges Jack. That night, Jack secretly visits Claudia and finds her brother Egbert stealing money from his father's safe. At first Jack is accused, but his lost father is found. He proves to be a good friend of Smythe's and he is welcomed into the family.

Man Or Money?
Universal IMP, 11/26/1915. Three reels. LP7008.

Dir: Henry McRae Webster.
Scen: William Lippert.
Cast: King Baggot (Donald Britt), Robert Fisher (George Ferris), Edna Hunter (Aime Ferris), Harry Spingler (Paul Ferris), Ned Reardon (Russell Hopkins).

Synopsis: Donald Britt and George Ferris are college classmates. At a lawn fete on the campus, Donald meets and falls in love with George's sister Aime. Aime's father opposes the match and Donald sets out for the West in order to establish himself. Aime agrees to wait. He takes a job as a civil engineer for a construction firm. Meanwhile, Russell Hopkins, a man of wealth but a notorious schemer, ingratiates himself into the good graces of the Ferris family in order to be near Aime. He proposes to her, but she refuses. Only after the persistent urging of her brother and father does she finally agree, but almost immediately after the wedding Hopkins must flee to escape the victims of his latest scheme. The couple moves to the Northwest and, by accident, settle in the very place where Donald is prospecting for virgin pine. The three meet and Donald soon finds that Hopkins is a crook. For a time he believes that Aime is his accomplice, but she tells him of her sad married life and they fall in love once more. Donald decides to do the honorable thing and leave; however, Hopkins, too, believes he should go. They fight and Hopkins jumps off a cliff into the river trying to end his life. Donald jumps in and rescues him, but the effort is so great that both men are unconscious when Aime finds them. Donald recovers first and sees Aime bending over her husband. Donald assists her in bringing him back to life. He then places their two hands together, wishes them happiness and bids them farewell.

Notes: Originally titled *The Turning Point*.

Almost a Papa

Universal IMP, 12/14/1915. One reel. LP7159.

Dir: Henry McRae Webster.
Scen: Raymond L. Schrock.
Cast: King Baggot (Tom Conley), Edna Hunter (His Wife), Hattie Delaro (Mother).

Synopsis: Tom Conley is a suspension bridge salesman who has not sold one in five years. He must go on the road for at least six months to try to make a sale. His wife has always wanted to own a dog and takes advantage of her husband's absence to purchase one. Being short of cash, she goes to Tom's closet and sells some of his suits to get the cash. She writes him a letter telling him there will soon be an addition to the family and Tom thinks it is a baby on the way. He rushes home, stopping at a toy store on the way to buy all manner of toys and furniture for the nursery. Arriving home, he finds his wife has gone to his mother's. He is setting up the nursery when he trips on a go-cart and injures his neck. A doctor is called and he suddenly remembers an insurance policy which he had kept in the pocket of his blue suit. His wife returns to find Tom injured. He inquires after the suit and she must tell him she sold it. He then wants to see the "new addition" and she brings in a large clothes basket lined with eiderdown and silk. She gently removes the covering and reveals a little puppy. With an agonized groan, the would-be papa falls backward into his chair. She is in tears realizing how her deception has affected him, but he comforts her and assures her he has not given up hope of one day being a real papa.

1916

The Law of Life

Universal IMP, 1/7/1916. Three reels LP7332.

Dir: Henry McRae Webster.
Scen: Maie B. Harvey.
Cast: King Baggot (Robert McKenzie), Edna Hunter (Helen Willoughby), Ned Reardon (Sid Powell), Elsie McLeod (Nan), Clara Beyers (La Carmona).

Synopsis: Robert and Sidney both love Helen. She prefers Robert and accepts his proposal because she thinks him to be good. Sidney has ruined a young girl, Nan, and she has become an outcast in the village. His hatred for Robert, leads him astray. In the city, he introduces him to a dancer, La Carmona, who immediately falls in love with him. He entices him to drink and puts him in a compromising position with La Carmona. Later, Robert is ashamed and confesses all to Helen, but she sadly turns him adrift and decides to become a nurse. One day, Robert meets Sidney, who tells him tauntingly that Helen has promised to marry him. For a time, Robert goes back to La Carmona, but he cannot forget about Helen. He goes to Sidney's apartment to find out the details of his engagement and finds him shot to death. Nan is also there, having been lured by Sidney who promised once more to marry her. When she arrives, he merely laughs at her and tries to take her in his arms. She shoots him and then turns the gun on herself and dies. Even though he knows she loves him, Robert leaves La Carmora and takes a job in a large mill where he tries to forget, but he begins to pity her and returns to find that she has a child, whom she claims is his. La Carmora becomes ill. He marries her and she dies happy. One day, the child becomes ill and a nurse is called. It is none other than Helen. The two forget the past and once more, by the side of the sleeping baby, they pledge their troth.

Notes: From a story by Carl Werner.

The Soul Man
Universal IMP, 2/4/1916. One reel.
LP7529.

Dir: Henry McRae Webster.
Scen: William Addison Lathrop.
Cast: King Baggot, Marie Weirman, Ned Reardon, William Bailey, Lois Alexander, Henry McRae Webster.

Synopsis: A wanderer returns home after ten years. He is unknown to anyone, including his former sweetheart, who fails to recognize him. She is now married and the wanderer saves her child.

The Hoax House
Universal IMP, 3/3/1916. Two reels.
LP7711.

Dir: Henry McRae Webster.
Scen: Raymond Schrock.
Cast: King Baggot (Frank King), Edna Hunter (Belle Adair), Joe Daly (Mr. Ryan), Nellie Slattery (Mrs. Ryan), Wallace Clark (Mr. Henry Stewart), Marie Weirman (Mrs. Stewart).

Synopsis: Frank King is a candy salesman and Belle Adair is a vaudeville actress. After they meet, they are fired from their respective jobs. To make money, they set up in a hotel to impersonate a mind reader and his assistant. They soon have many clients, one of whom is Mr. Stewart. He asks if his wife is cheating on him. Next comes Mrs. J.P. Ryan, who asks the same question about her husband. They are put off while Frank does some detective work. He disguises himself and learns that it is Mrs. Ryan who is being unfaithful and so is Mr. Stewart. When they return for their expensive answers, King somehow mixes the two up. He tells Mrs. Ryan that her husband is having an affair with "Frou Frou," and Mr. Stewart, that his wife is carrying on with the butler. Violent quarrels erupt in the two households. Frank and Belle have a premonition that something is about to happen and prepare to leave the hotel when a telegram arrives for Frank. He is being asked back to his old job with a splendid raise. Frank asks Belle to be his assistant for life.

Patterson of the News
Universal IMP, 3/17/1916. Two reels.
LP7806.

Dir: Henry McRae Webster.
Scen: Harry Dittmar.
Cast: King Baggot (Jack Patterson), Howard Crampton (Daniel Brennon), Edna Hunter (Phyllis Brennon), Joe Daly (Bertie Ralston), Bert Busby (City Editor).

Synopsis: Ace reporter Jack Patterson joins the police for a raid on a notorious gambling club, "The Tenderloin." Inside they find a group of socialites who have been slumming there. The party includes the rich but idle Bertie Ralston and his fiancée, Phyllis, who is terrified of this encounter with the police. Jack helps her escape and falls in love with her; however, she has promised her father, a wealthy but crooked banker, that she would marry Bertie. She refuses Jack, who is heartbroken. Jack then discovers that Daniel Brennon is attempting to embezzle bank funds. He threatens to expose him, but when Phyllis comes in and he learns that she is his daughter, he promises to keep the information to himself if Brennon makes restitution. He agrees and Phyllis, knowing that she can now follow her heart, agrees to marry Jack.

The Haunted Bell

Universal IMP, 4/20/1916. Two reels. LP8076.

Dir: Henry Otto.
Scen: J. Grubb Alexander.
Cast: King Baggot (John Lane), Edna Hunter (Mrs. Lane), Joseph Granby (Prof. Nassaib Haig), Sam Crane (His Servant), Frank Smith (The Butler), Joseph Smiley (The Curio Dealer).

Synopsis: John Lane is a novelist writing about India. He has acquired a large bell which he and his wife soon discover seems to ring on the hour of its own accord. They invite Prof. Haig to dinner and when he sees it he bows before it. Later he confides to a Hindu priest and a curio dealer that it is the lost sacred bell of the Taj Mahal Temple and offers a thousand dollars for it. The curio dealer tries to get John to sell, but John wants to solve the mystery. He discovers that it rings when the window is open, but not when it is closed. He deduces that vibrations from the church tower match those of the bell when the windows are open. The next morning, John finds the body of the curio dealer in his den. The butler is suspected, but when the police arrive they have the Hindu priest with them. He was picked up in the neighborhood and they suspect he might have some connection. After a third degree, he admits to the crime. John and his wife agree to get rid of the "haunted bell."

Notes: From a story by Jacques Futrelle.

Won with a Make-Up

Universal IMP, 5/4/1916. One reel. LP8159.

Dir: Henry Otto.
Cast: King Baggot (William King), Frank Smith (The Deacon), Edna Hunter (Josephine).

Synopsis: A moving picture company arrives in a small town to do some location shooting. Josephine has just returned from boarding school and is met by her father, the deacon, at the train station. She sees the acting company and is much taken with the leading man, William King. The director of the company, in search of a location, obtains Josephine's consent to take a scene in front of the deacon's gate. When the Deacon sees the rehearsal in progress, he rushes out to drive the actors away. However, Josephine and William have already fallen in love. Josephine feigns a sudden illness and insists on being seen by the "city doctor" staying at the hotel. This proves to be none other that William in disguise. He makes the house call accompanied by the company's leading lady, dressed at a nurse. They shoo the anxious parents out of the room and Josephine makes a speedy recovery. She pulls her already packed suitcase from under the bed and the three make their escape out the window. Finally the parents enter the room and find it empty except for the note left by Josephine begging their forgiveness for marrying an actor.

Notes: From a story by Elliott H. Robinson.

Half a Rogue

Universal Red Feather, 5/22/1916. Five reels. LP8207.

Dir: Henry Otto.
Scen: Henry Otto.
Cast: King Baggot (Richard Warrington), Leslie Ford (Anna Warrington, His Aunt), Clara Beyers (Katherine Challoner), Joseph Castellanos (John Bennington), Mathilda Brundage (John's Mother), Edna Hunter (Pattie), Howard Crampton (Daniel McQuade), Henry Otto (Ex-Senator Henderson).

Synopsis: New York playwright Richard Warrington returns to his hometown in the south to run for mayor on the Republican ticket. The Democrats decide to unearth a scandal that will ruin his chances and discover that actress Katherine Challoner once had spent a night in Richard's apartment. Although Katherine had merely had a fainting spell, the Democratic newspaper turns the overnight visit into an illicit rendezvous.

Richard quickly explains the true facts to Katherine's husband John Bennington, a longtime friend, and John's sister Pattie, with whom he has fallen in love. He then beats up the man who printed the lie. The public never believed the newspaper story and Richard is overwhelmingly elected.

Notes: From the novel by Harold Mac-Grath, who was paid $250 for the story. Partially filmed in Savannah, Georgia, and on Broadway in New York. Baggot's first five-reel film.

Jim Slocum, No. 46,393
Universal IMP, 6/2/1916. Two reels. LP8364.

Dir: Robert Cummings.
Scen: Robert F. Hill.
Cast: King Baggot (Jim Slocum), Edna Hunter (Kittie, His Wife), Charles Ogle (Dr. Turner), Norma Winslow (Mrs. Turner), Nellie Slattery (Mrs. Cassidy).

Synopsis: Jim Slocum is a taxi driver whose baby is taken ill. While he is at their tenement giving his wife Kittie a rest from her constant care of the child, another driver steals a wheel from his cab. He returns to the cab stand and falls asleep owing to his night's vigil. He is accused of drunkenness and discharged with no pay due to the loss of the wheel. He tries to have their baby examined by a noted specialist, Dr. Turner, who agrees to take the case without charge until a rich man takes the doctor out of the office to attend his own child, who is not really sick at all. Jim returns home to find his child has died and Kittie ill and half-mad with grief. Meanwhile, Mrs. Turner summons their colored chauffeur, Carter, and is driven to a fashionable reception. Later that evening, Jim, with his face disguised, enters Dr. Turner's house to steal money, partly for revenge and partly because he and Kittie have nothing to eat. Mrs. Turner returns and Jim hides in the library. Carter has been drinking and thinks he has made a conquest of Mrs. Turner. As Carter advances on her, she screams. Jim repulses him and throws him into the street just as Dr. Turner returns. The doctor eventually discovers the identity of the gallant burglar and employs him as his new driver. Kittie is restored to health by Dr. Turner and the couple is given a cottage near his house to be their new home.

The Man from Nowhere
Universal Red Feather. 6/19/1916. Five reels. LP8372.

Dir: Henry Otto.
Scen: William H. Clifford.
Cast: King Baggot (James Herron), Irene Hunt (Betty Herron), Joseph W. Girard (Governor Dudley Ward), Helen Marten (Ruth Ward), Johnny Walker (Larry Ward), Joseph Granby (Dorenzo), Frank Smith (The Warden).

Synopsis: James is sentenced to life in prison on a charge of killing his sister, when in reality she was shot by Dorenzo, a slaver. During a prison revolt, James saves the governor's life and is made a trustee. He falls in love with Ruth, although they have yet to meet. Larry, the governor's son, complains to his father that a card sharp has cheated him. The governor sends James to try to expose the cheater. He introduces himself to Ruth at the card game as " Barrs, the man from nowhere," and skillfully reveals that the villain is Dorenzo masquerading as an Italian count trying to win the affections of Ruth. The two men fight a duel with swords and Dorenzo is mortally wounded. As he is dying, he confesses to the murder of Betty Herron. Freed from prison, James begins a romance with Ruth.

The Man Across the Street
Universal IMP, 7/6/1916. Two reels. LP8594.

Dir: Henry Otto.
Scen: Henry Otto.
Cast: King Baggot (John Warren and Dr. Carl), Edna Hunter (Mrs. Warren), Nellie Slattery (The New Maid), Henry Otto (Himself).

Synopsis: John Warren is a traveling salesman with a vain and frivolous wife. He comes home from a trip to find a new maid, just hired by his wife, and furs and gowns she has purchased without telling him. He soon discovers she is having an affair with Dr. Carl, the man across the street. After breakfast one day, he announces that he must go on a long business trip. Instead, he rents a room across the street and observes Dr. Carl and his wife in their affair. One night Dr. Carl brings Mrs. Warren home and, soon after, he leaves. The maid sees them arrive but does not know Dr. Carl has gone home. John makes himself up to look like the doctor and even manages to steal some clothes from Dr. Carl. He enters his own house, leaving Dr. Carl's overcoat and gloves in the library before turning out the light. He goes into the bedroom where his wife, in the darkness, believes it is Dr. Carl and warmly embraces him. He then strangles her and leaves. The police are called and they find the doctor's belongings in the library. At the trial, the maid accuses Dr. Carl and he is led off to prison. The picture now fades into the next scene where Baggot is observed reading the manuscript with director Henry Otto. Baggot tells Otto that the story is a fine one. Otto agrees and tells Baggot he will be playing the husband as well as the doctor.

Notes: Baggot played both parts. Originally titled *A Borrowed Identity*, it was based on a Robert Thomas Hardy short story published in *Snappy Stories Magazine*.

His Own Story

Universal Big U, 7/20/1916. One reel
LP8668.

Dir: George A. Lessey.
Scen: George A. Lessey.
Cast: King Baggot (Himself), William Bailey (Bill Harding), Jane Courtney (Mag).

Synopsis: One day at the Screen Club, director Dan Clayton offers $50 for a good one-reel story. Baggot recounts a story that is then visualized on the screen. He and his friend Bill Harding have been shipwrecked and held captive by smugglers on a deserted island. Mag, a girl the smugglers have captured, decides to help them. She digs a hole in the rear of a hut where the two men are being held and assists in their escape. They overpower the guard and sight a ship, which they signal with an improvised flag. The ship is an American yacht sent to search for King and Bill. It comes in time to save them and the girl who has risked her life to help them. In the next scene we see Clayton handing King a check for $50, declaring that the adventure should prove very effective when thrown onto the screen.

Notes: Some scenes shot at the Screen Club in New York.

The Captain of the Typhoon

Universal Big U, 8/6/1916. Two reels
LP8775.

Dir: Henry McRae Webster.
Scen: Harry Dittmar.
Cast: King Baggot (Angus Steele), Wallace Clark (Tom Steele), Howard Crampton (Capt. Morton), Edna Hunter (Bess Morton), Beatrice Allen (The Girl).

Synopsis: Angus Steele is captain of the *Typhoon*. One day he hears a disturbance on deck and finds a destitute girl shivering under a tarpaulin. He takes her below and is prompted to tell her his story. As a young man, Angus falls in love with Bess, the skipper's daughter. When her father dies, Bess turns to Angus, although she does not love him. Then Tom, Angus' brother, returns from a drunken brawl and Bess falls in love with him. They marry and Tom sinks lower and lower, finally abandoning Bess. She commits suicide. Having told the story, it is time for Angus to make his ship ready to leave. Suddenly Tom returns, demanding money. The girl recognizes Tom's voice and says she once knew him and knew he would return. Tom flings her aside, which so angers Angus that he throws Tom overboard. Then the girl turns on Angus and says she hates him. As the ship sails to sea, Angus is standing on the bridge looking wistfully out at the disappearing lights of the city.

The Silent Stranger

Universal Big U, 8/18/1916. One reel. LP8813.

Dir: King Baggot.
Scen: Frank Smith.
Cast: King Baggot (The Silent Stranger), Irene Hunt (The Dance Hall Girl), Frank Smith (The Doctor).

Synopsis: A man of mystery comes to a little town. He lives in a cabin and will not talk to his neighbors. However, one night he agrees to tell his story. He had been a prosperous lawyer in an Eastern town and was engaged to be married to the sweetest of girls. The night before the wedding day, she died, and in his anguish he called upon the Devil. The Devil said he would bring back the departed one, but if the man smiled or laughed he would lose his love again. And in the man's joy at seeing his sweetheart's recovery, he forgot — and laughed. Straight away, the girl died once more. Having told the story, the stranger says, "Here is Satan now," and he falls over dead.

Notes: *Moving Picture World* gave the title as *The Silent Man*.

The Chance Market

Universal Gold Seal, 8/29/1916. Three reels. LP8961.

Dir: King Baggot.
Scen: King Baggot.
Cast: King Baggot (John Marmaduke and Jim Fowler), Irene Hunt (Mary Cullen), Jack Ridgeway (Tim Cullen, Her Father), Frank Smith (Buxton), Howard Crampton (John Coyle).

Synopsis: Mary is engaged to be married to Jim Fowler, a crook. He and his pals go out to commit a burglary despite Mary's protestations. The house they pick belongs to John Marmaduke, a rich, world-weary young bachelor. When he hears them enter, a struggle ensues. Jim's pals run outside, but John kills Jim. John's butler Buxton comes in and remarks that the two men look exactly the same. John decides to take on Jim's identity and exchanges clothes with him, swearing Buxton to secrecy. Outside the house, the crooks are waiting. They beat Jim/John and take the loot. Mary finds him and takes him home. Except for his improved table manners, she does not notice the difference. The next day he attends his own funeral and notes that his former fiancée seems unmoved by his death. John is warned by Buxton that Jim's friends are looking for him. Mary wants him to escape, but he will not leave without her. The men arrive and a fight takes place. Buxton helps John rout the crooks and Mary is rushed to a waiting auto. As the picture fades out, the two are seen in the tonneau of the car embracing each other.

Notes: John Marmaduke was the name of one of King Baggot's brothers. In this dual role, double exposure photography was used to achieve the effects.

The Lie Sublime

Universal Big U, 9/28/1916. Two reels LP9116.

Dir: King Baggot, Bennett Molter.
Scen: Harry Dittmar.
Cast: King Baggot (Julian Ormond), Frank Smith (Mr. Morton), Nellie Slattery (Mrs. Morton), Enda Hunter (Mollie Morton), A. Von Haussen (Jim Wilson), Joseph Granby (Pietro Bonelli), Jane Courtney (Mildred, The Girl Who Waited).

Synopsis: Julian Ormond is a professional actor and musician. Tired after a long season of performing, he asks his manager for a rest and goes to a small town where he boards with the Morton family. That evening,

Mollie Morton is asked to sing for the family and Julian realizes she has a remarkably fine voice. Her sweetheart Jim is concerned that she will become famous and forget about him, but she kisses away his fears. Julian sends for impresario Pietro Bonelli to hear her sing, but before he arrives, Julian has second thoughts. He remembers his love for Mildred, the girl he left behind in order to pursue his career. When Bonelli comes to the house, Julian takes him aside and tells him not to let the family know of Mollie's great gift. Bonelli does as Julian asks and tells them that, although Mollie has a pleasing voice, she will never be a great star. Afterwards, he asks Julian why and Julian responds that he sacrificed his own love on the altar of art. Julian now makes a resolution. He goes to Mildred, who has waited so patiently for him, and the two are reunited.

Notes: The Library of Congress record lists Henry Otto as director and omits Jane Courtney's name in the cast; however, the viewed print credits show Baggot and Molter as directors and includes Jane Courtney.

Are You an Elk?

Universal Laemmle, "Special Release," 10/16/1916. One reel LP9324.

Dir: Henry McRae Webster.
Scen: King Baggot.
Cast: King Baggot (Stewart King), Edna Hunter (His Wife), Jack Ridgeway (His Pal).

Synopsis: King is a salesman for the Kewt-Kut Clothing Company. His pal Jack, other salesmen and his boss are all Elks. He is persuaded to join. His wife is told that it is a serious thing to become an Elk, and that she should have his insurance policy ready and also the address of a trustworthy undertaker. In bed that night, she dreams that King has his head cut off trying to become an Elk. Meanwhile, King goes to the meeting and becomes royally tight. On his way home, he thinks everyone he meets is an Elk. At home he falls on the bed and begins to dream of meeting all sorts of animals, some of whom are wearing the antlers of elks. The scene shifts to the Bronx Zoo, where a parade of cows pass by, but they are not wearing horns. After that, there is a close-up of an elk that appears very friendly to King, who feeds him. Suddenly King is being chased by a goat that butts him over a wall. Presently we see King fall into his wife's bed, which startles her awake. King jumps back into his own bed and gives his wife the mysterious sign of the Order. The scene dissolves into the head of an enormous elk.

So This Is Paris

Universal Victor, "Special Release," 12/19/1916. One reel. LP10014.

Dir.: Herbert Brenon.
Cast: King Baggot, Leah Baird.

Synopsis: A young couple crosses the English Channel to Paris for a visit to many of the sights, including the Eiffel Tower. They are followed about Paris by a Frenchman whom they believe is a Customs House inspector, but they discover their mistake when he comes up to them and requests their autographs.

Notes: This is a semi-documentary which may be comprised of outtakes of films shot by the IMP Company in Europe in 1913, or perhaps is a re-release of *Mr. and Mrs. Innocence Abroad*.

1917

The Boonton Affair

Universal Bison, 2/3/1917. Two reels. LP 10015.

Dir: King Baggot.
Scen: King Baggot.
Cast: King Baggot (Jack Walton), Irene Hunt (Mary Hatfield), Frank Smith (Bill Hatfield), Jack Newton (Jim Calahan).

Synopsis: Mary, a moonshiner's daughter, who resents the attentions of Jim Calahan. Jim is stopped by the arrival of Jack Walton, a revenue officer. Mary becomes attracted to Jack, and Jim swears revenge. The moonshiners attack Jack, beat and bind him and lock Mary in an adjoining room. Doby, a friend, sees Jack's horse and becomes suspicious. He returns to town for help. Mary continues to pound on the door. Finally, she hears the men planning to lynch Jack. Her father, who attempts to interfere, is struck on the head with a pitcher. Doby returns and, while holding the men at gunpoint, frees Mary, who then frees Jack. They discover that her father is seriously hurt. Jack offers to go to town to get a doctor. As he rides over the hills, he is once again attacked by the moonshiners, but he repels them. When he returns with the doctor, he has fallen in love with Mary. Because her father was implicated in the moonshine activity, he decides to forget his duty for once. Jack and Mary become engaged and the old man promises to have nothing more to do with the gang.

1918

The Eagle's Eye

Wharton for Foursquare Pictures, 2/25 — 8/1918. 20 Chapter Serial. Two reels each.

Dir: George A. Lessey, Wellington Player.
Scen: Courtenay Ryley Cooper.
Cast: King Baggot, Marguerite Snow, William N. Bailey, Florence Short, Bertram Marburgh, Paul Everton, John P. Wade, Fred Jones, Wellington Player, Louise Hotelling.

Notes: From a story by William J. Flynn, former chief of the U.S. Secret Service. Each episode focused on a particular plot by German agents against the United States during World War I. This was Baggot's first role in a serial. Chapter titles: *Hidden Death*; *The Naval Ball Conspiracy*; *The Plot Against the Fleet*; *Von Rintelen, the Destroyer*; *The Strike Breeders*; *The Plot Against Organized Labor*; *The Brown Portfolio*; *The Kaiser's Death Messenger*; *The Munitions Campaign*; *The Invasion of Canada*; *The Burning of Hopewell*; *The Canal Conspirators*; *The Reign of Terror*; *The Infantile Paralysis Epidemic*; *The Campaign Against Cotton*; *The Raid of the U-53*; *Germany's U-Base in America*; *The Great Hindu Conspiracy*; *The Menace of the I.W.W.*; *The Great Decision*. Filming began in late November 1917. Some scenes filmed in New York City, Ithaca, New York, and Washington DC.

I'll Fix It

Universal Nestor, 3/18/1918. One reel.

Dir: King Baggot.
Scen: King Baggot.
Cast: King Baggot, Paul Porcasi, Virginia Dare, Alice Mann.

Synopsis: A genial busybody seeks to assist a lady in distress.

Notes: A notice for this film appeared in *Moving Picture World*, 3/9/1918, p.1393. It was billed as a "reissue," and stated that Baggot "returns to the Universal program," and "has been seen in but few roles of a comedy nature ... when he was a Universal star." The plot is too incomplete to compare with an earlier film. It cannot be documented that the other players ever worked with Baggot, or necessarily worked in Universal films, although Porcasi and Mann can be verified as film performers. This is a strange and puzzling credit.

The Mission of the War Chest

Wharton. "A Liberty Loan Special," 6/1918. Length undetermined.

Dir: Theodore and Leopold D. Wharton.
Cast: King Baggot, Marguerite Snow.

Synopsis: A father would not give to the war effort until he began receiving letters from his son serving at the front. The son described the work of the Red Cross, YMCA, Knights of Columbus and the Salvation Army — all of which derive their money from the war chest, but it is with his son's description of the death of a chum that the father begins to see that while he has been giving nothing, his son has been giving his all — including his life. The father finally sees the light and becomes a subscriber.

Notes: Large numbers of U.S. troops were used in the battle scenes, in which a reproduction of the explosion on Vimy Ridge was shown. Production on *The Eagle's Eye* was halted for one week while the cast made this film. LC copyright is entered under the title *The Missionary*, LU12994. No length given. No release date found. It was officially presented to the Chamber of Commerce of the city of Rochester, New York, in May or June 1918.

Building for Democracy

Metro Pictures. "A Liberty Loan Special," 8/1918. Length undetermined.

Cast: King Baggot, Emily Stevens, Christine Mayo.

Synopsis: The wife's one ambition is to save enough money to build a home like the model her husband has built. The fourth Liberty Loan drive starts and everyone is investing. A vision of Democracy comes before the wife, presenting the crimes of autocracy — then she is glad to use her savings to buy Liberty Bonds.

Notes: No length given. No release date known. Completed in July or August 1918 by Metro in cooperation with the Treasury Department to help boost the fourth Liberty Loan drive.

Kildare of Storm

Metro Pictures. "All-Star Series," 9/16/1918. Five reels. LP12858.

Dir: Henry L. Franklin.
Scen: Jere Looney and June Mathis.
Cast: Emily Stevens (Kate Kildare), King Baggot (Basil Kildare), Crauford Kent (Dr. Jacques Benoix), Florence Short (Mahaly), Edwards Davis (Gov. Claiborne), Helen Lindroth (Mrs. Leigh), Maggie Breyer (Mrs. Benoix), Fred H. Warren.

Synopsis: Kate marries Basil Kildare, the wealthy owner of a southern plantation called Storm. His female servant Mahaly is the mother of his illegitimate son. She protests his infidelity so bitterly that he takes the child away from her. Kate soon learns that he is a cad and an alcoholic and finds solace in the company of Dr. Benoix and his mother. Basil is jealous of their friendship and engages him in a fierce fight. Later, Basil is found dead and the doctor goes to prison for his murder, although he is innocent. Kate works tirelessly to free him and he is finally granted a pardon. On her deathbed, Mahaly confesses that it was she who killed Basil, and Jacques and Kate begin a new life together.

Notes: From the novel *Kildares of Storm* by Eleanor Mercein Kelly.

1919

The Man Who Stayed at Home

Screen Classics for Metro Pictures, 7/6/1919. Six reels. LP13930.

Dir: Herbert Blanché.
Scen: June Mathis.
Cast: King Baggot (Christopher Brent), Claire Whitney (Molly Preston), Robert Whittier (Fritz), Alexandre Herbert (Norman Preston), Lilie Leslie (Miriam Lee), Frank Fisher Bennett (Carl Sanderson), Ricca Allen (Miss Myrtle), Robert Paton Gibbs (Judge Preston), Julie Calhoun (Fräulein Schroeder), Ida Darling (Mrs. Sanderson), A. Lloyd Lack (Gaston Letour), Betty Hutchinson.

Synopsis: In 1918, in a small Virginia town, Christopher Brent is considered a slacker for not enlisting in the war. He and Miriam Lee are actually working for the Secret Service. His fiancée Molly is concerned by the talk about him and because he is spending time with Miriam Lee. Molly's brother Norman finds a German code book in Miriam's room and both are suspected of being spies. However, Christopher saves the hotel when the real spies ignite a bomb to signal a German U-boat. He captures a list of the spies and, with the aid of a U.S. destroyer, sinks the U-boat. He is honored by the town and Molly asks to be forgiven.

Notes: Based on the play by Lechmere Worrall and J.E. Harold Terry.

The Hawk's Trail

Burston Films, 12/13/1919–4/1920. A States Rights Release. 15 Chapter Serial. Two reels each.

Dir: W.S. Van Dyke.
Scen: Louis and George Burston.
Cast: King Baggot, Grace Darmond, Reah Mitchell, Harry Lorraine, Fred Windermere, Stanton Heck, George Siegmann, Alfred Hollingsworth.

Notes: From a story by Nan Blair. Baggot's first film produced in California. He disguised himself as a different character in each episode. Episode titles: *False Faces*; *The Superman*; *Yellow Shadows*; *Stained Hands*; *The House of Fear*; *The Room Above*; *The Bargain*; *The Phantom Melody*; *The Lure*; *The Swoop*; *One Fatal Step*; *Tides That Tell*; *Face to Face*; *The Substitute*; *The Showdown*.

Loc: LC.

1920

Note: From 1920 on, due to modern scholarship, the documentation of films becomes easier to obtain. Entries have been shortened to exclude synopses and character names with the exception of Baggot's roles while he was still working as an actor.

The Thirtieth Piece of Silver

American Film Co., Inc., Flying "A" Special for Pathé, 5/15/1920. Six reels. LP14931.

Dir: George Cox.
Scen: Daniel Whitcomb.
Cast: Margarita Fischer, King Baggot (Tyler Cole), Lillian Leighton, Forrest Stanley.

Notes: Based on the story by Albert Payson Terhune.

The Cheater

Screen Classics for Metro Pictures Corp., 6/7/1920. Six reels. LP15289.

Dir: Henry Otto.
Scen: Lois Zellner.
Cast: May Allison, King Baggot (Lord Asgarby), Frank Currier, Harry Von Meter, May Geraci, Percy Challenger, Lucille Ward, P. Dempsey Tabler, Alberta Lee, Rudolph Valentino.

Notes: Based on the play *Judah* by Henry Arthur Jones. Valentino played a small part as a villain in this film.

Life's Twist

B.B. Features for Robertson-Cole, 8/11/1920. Six reels.

Dir: William Christy Cabanne.
Scen: Harvey Gates.
Cast: Bessie Barriscale, Walter McGrail, King Baggot (Jim Sargent), Claire Dubrey, George Periolat, Truly Shattuck, William V. Mong, Marcia Manon.

Notes: Based on the short story by Thomas Edgelow.

The Dwelling Place of Light

Benjamin B. Hampton Productions for Hodkinson Corp., 9/12/1920. LP15686. Seven reels.

Margarita Fischer gives King Baggot a quizzical look in *The Thirtieth Piece of Silver*. American Film Company, 1920. Collection of the author.

Dir: Jack Conway.
Scen: William H. Clifford.
Cast: Claire Adams, King Baggot (Brooks Insall), Robert McKim, Ogden Crane, Lassie Young, Lydia Knott, George Berrell, Beulah Booker, William V. Mong, Aggie Herring, Nigel de Brulier, C.B. Murphy.

Notes: Based on the 1917 novel by the American writer Winston Churchill.

The Forbidden Thing
Allan Dwan Productions for Associated Producers, Inc., 11/27/1920. Six reels. LP15761.

Dir: Allan Dwan.
Scen: Allan Dwan.
Cam: Tony Gaudio.
Cast: James Kirkwood, Helen Jerome Eddy, Marcia Manon, King Baggot (Dave), Gertrude Claire, Jack Roseleigh, Arthur Thalasso, Newton Hall, Harry Griffith, Katherine Norton, J. Montgomery Carlyle.

Notes: Based on the short story by Mary Mears. Cameraman Tony Gaudio worked with Baggot and IMP as early as 1911. Some scenes shot near Oxnard and Port Hueneme, California.

1921

The Girl in the Taxi
Carter DeHaven Productions for First National, 4/1921. Six reels. LP16424.

Dir: Lloyd Ingraham.
Adapt: Bob McGowan.

Cast: Flora Parker DeHaven, Carter DeHaven, King Baggot (Frederick Smith), Grace Cunard, Otis Harlan, Tom McGuire, Margaret Campbell, Lincoln Plummer, Freya Sterling, John Gough.

Notes: From the play by Stanislaus Strange. Production was said to have taken four months. It was filmed at the Chaplin Studios by the DeHavens on a rental basis.
Loc: BFI.

Cheated Love
Universal, 5/16/1921. Five reels. LP16494.

Dir: King Baggot.
Scen: Lucien Hubbard, Doris Schroeder, Sonya Levien.
Cast: Carmel Myers, George B. Williams, Allan Forrest, John Davidson, Ed Brady, Snitz Edwards, Smoke Turner, Virginia Harris, Inez Gomez, Clara Greenwood, Meyer Ouhayou, Laura Pollard, Rose Dione, Theresa Gray, Fred Becker.

Notes: Working title: *Thou Art With Me*. A remake of *The Heart of the Jewess*. Story by Lucien Hubbard and Doris Schroder from an idea by John Colton. Baggot's first work in California as a director.

The Butterfly Girl
Playgoers Pictures for Pathé, 6/12/1921. Five reels. LU16533.

Dir: John Gorman.
Scen: John Gorman.
Cast: Marjorie Daw, Fritzie Brunette, King Baggot (H.H. Van Horn), Jean DeBriac, Ned Whitney Warren, Leslie Darnell.

Notes: Working title: *The Soul of the Butterfly*.

Luring Lips
Universal, 7/25/1921. Five reels. LP16771.

Dir: King Baggot.
Scen: George Hively.

Cast: Edith Roberts, Darrell Foss, Ramsey Wallace, William Welsh, Carlton King, M.E. Stimpson.

Notes: Based on *The Gossamer Web* by John A. Moroso.

Moonlight Follies
Universal, 9/26/1921. Five reels. LP16962

Dir: King Baggot.
Scen: A.P. Younger.
Cast: Marie Prevost, Lionel Belmore, Marie Crisp, George Fisher, Clyde Fillmore.

Notes: Working titles: *The Butterfly* and *Touch Me Not*. Marie Prevost's first starring role for Universal. She and King Baggot appeared together in a specially written prologue at Tally's Theatre in Los Angeles twice nightly during the run of the film.

Nobody's Fool
Universal, 10/31/1921. Five reels. LP17099.

Dir: King Baggot.
Scen: Doris Schroeder.
Cast: Marie Prevost, Helen Harris, Vernon Snively, R. Henry Guy, Percy Challenger, Harry Myers, George Kuwa, Lucretia Harris, Lydia Titus.

Notes: From a story by Roy Clements. Working title: *The Girl Who Knew All About Men*. Some scenes filmed at Big Bear Lake and at the Cofin Estate in Pasadena, California.

Screen Snapshots
Pathé/Federated Exchanges. Series 2, #13F, 12/10/1921.

Notes: King Baggot directed a bathing girl scene for a Marie Prevost film. Other segments featured various stars and personalities in promotional activities.

1922

Kissed

Universal, 5/22/1922. Five reels. LP17891.

Dir: King Baggot.
Scen: Doris Schroeder.
Cast: Marie Prevost, Lloyd Whitlock, Lillian Langdon, J. Frank Glendon, Arthur Hoyt, Percy Challenger, Harold Miller, Marie Crisp, Harold Goodwin.

Notes: Based on the story by Arthur Somers Roche. There is an animation sequence which occurred near the end of the film when Prevost is being kissed by the man she had originally thought to be less romantic (an animated thermometer registered the warmth of the kiss).
Loc: MOMA, NF.

Human Hearts

Universal-Jewel, 8/5/1922. Seven reels.

Dir: King Baggot.
Scen: Lucien Hubbard, Marc Robbins.
Cast: House Peters, Russell Simpson, Gertrude Claire, George Hackathorne, George West, Lucretia Harris, Edith Hallor, Ramsey Wallace, Mary Philbin, H.S. Karr, Snitz Edwards, Gene Dawson, Emmett King, Wilton Taylor.

Notes: Based on the play by Hal Reid. Baggot played the lead in IMP versions in 1912 and 1914. This time he directed. Some scenes shot near the Owens Valley, California.
Loc: GEH, VID.

The Lavender Bath Lady

Universal, 11/13/1922. Five reels. LP18341.

Dir: King Baggot.
Scen: George Randolph Chester, Doris Schroeder.

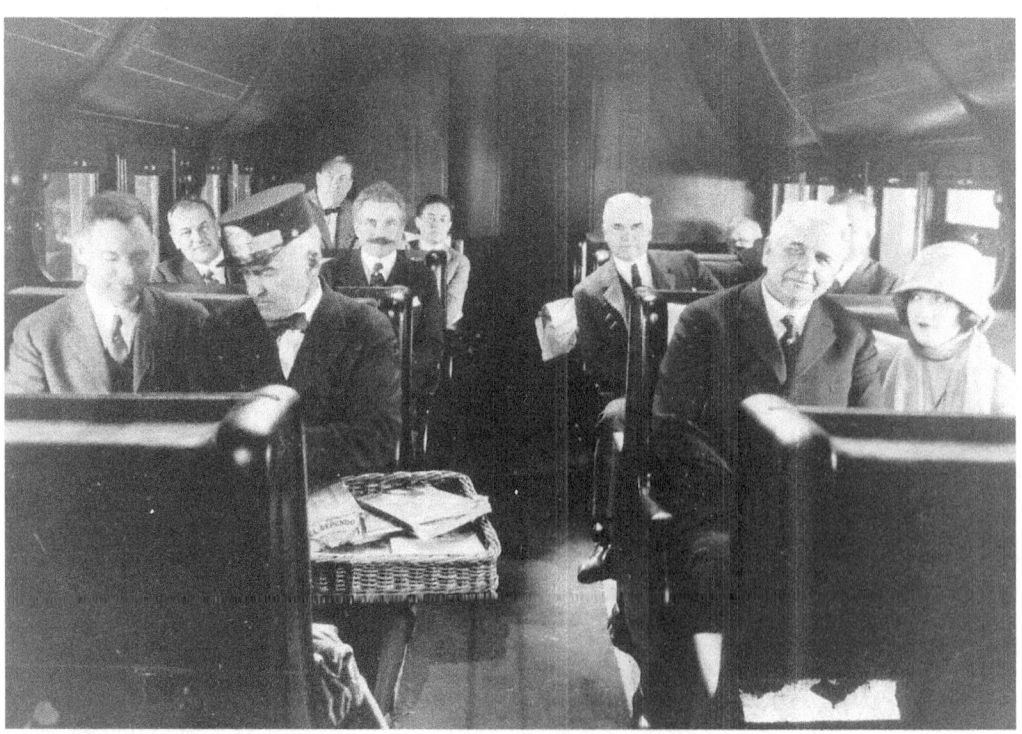

Publicity photograph in the railroad car from *Kissed*, Universal, 1922. Marie Prevost, front row right. King Baggot and Irving Thalberg in last row on the left. Collection of the author.

Cast: Gladys Walton, Charlotte Pierce, Edward Burns, Tom Ricketts, Lydia Yeamans Titus, Mary Winston, Al MacQuarrie, Harry Lorraine, Earl Crain.

Notes: Adapted by George Randolph Chester from a story by Shannon Fife.

The Kentucky Derby
Universal-Jewel, 12/4/1922. Six reels. LP18337.

Dir: King Baggot.
Scen: George C. Hull.
Cast: Reginald Denny, Lillian Rich, Emmett King, Walter McGrail, Gertrude Astor, Lionel Belmore, Kingsley Benedict, Bert Woodruff, Bert Tracy, Harry Carter, Wilfred Lucas, Pat Harmon, Anna Hernandez, Vern Winter.

Notes: Based on the play *The Suburban* by Charles T. Dazey. Location shooting in Louisville and Lexington, Kentucky, and around Southern California. Baggot starred in IMP's 1915 version titled *The Suburban*.

A Dangerous Game
Universal, 12/17/1922. Five reels. LP18466.

Dir: King Baggot.
Scen: Hugh Hoffman.
Cast: Gladys Walton, Spottiswoode Aitken, Otto Hoffman, Rosa Gore, William R. Daly, Robert Agnew, Edward Jobson, Anne Schaefer, Christine Mayo, Harry Carter, Bill Gibbs.

Notes: Based on the story *Gert'n Ann* by Louis Dodge.

1923

The Love Letter
Universal, 2/9/1923. Five reels. LP18634.

Dir: King Baggot.
Scen: Hugh Hoffman.

Cast: Gladys Walton, Fontaine LeRue, George Cooper, Edward Herne, Walt Whitman, Alberta Lee, Lucy Donohue.

Notes: From a story by Bradley King.

Gossip
Universal, 3/12/1923. Five reels. LP18710.

Dir: King Baggot.
Scen: Hugh Hoffman.
Cast: Gladys Walton, Ramsey Wallace, Albert Prisco, Freeman S. Wood, Carol Halloway.

Notes: Based on a story by Edith Barnard Delano.

The Town Scandal
Universal, 4/16/1923. Five reels. LP18832.

Dir: King Baggot.
Scen: Hugh Hoffman.
Cast: Gladys Walton, Edward McWade, Edward Hearne, Charles Hill Mailes, William Welsh, William Franey, Anna Hernandez, Virginia True Boardman, Nadine Beresford, Louise Reming Barnes, Rosa Gore, Margaret Morris.

Notes: Based on a story by Frederic Arnold Kummer. Working titles: *The Chicken* and *The Chicken That Came Home to Roost*.

Crossed Wires
Universal, 5/14/1923. Five reels. LP18931.

Dir: King Baggot.
Scen: Hugh Hoffman.
Cast: Gladys Walton, George Stewart, Tom S. Guise, Lillian Langdon, William R. Daly, Kate Price, Eddie Gribbon, Marie Crisp, Eloise Nesbit, Helen Broneau, Lewis Mason.

Notes: From a story by King Baggot.

Screen Snapshots
Pathé/Federated Exchanges. Series 4, # 3, 9/18/1923.

Notes: King Baggot with Baby Peggy Montgomery.

The Thrill Chaser

Universal, 11/26/1923. Six reels. LP19549.

Dir: Edward Sedgwick.
Scen: E. Richard Schayer.
Cast: Hoot Gibson, James Neill, Billie Dove, William E. Lawrence, Bob Reeves, Gino Gerrado, Lloyd Whitlock, Mary Philbin, Norman Kerry, Reginald Denny, Hobart Henley, King Baggot, Edward Sedgwick, Laura LaPlante

Notes: From a story by Edward Sedgwick and Raymond L. Schrock.

The Darling of New York

Universal-Jewel, 12/3/1923. Six reels. LP19546.

Dir: King Baggot.
Scen: Raymond L. Schrock.
Cast: Baby Peggy Montgomery, Sheldon Lewis, Gladys Brockwell, Pat Hartigan, Frank Currier, Junior (Frank) Coghlan, Dorothy Hagan, Estelle Goulder, Carl Stockdale, William H. Turner, Jose Devere, William Jack Quinn, Max Davidson, Emma Steele, Walter "Spec" O'Donnell, Frederick Esmelton, Betty Francisco, Anderson Smith.

Notes: Working titles: *Wanted, A Home,* and *Whose Baby Are You?* Story by Raymond L. Schrock and King Baggot. Some scenes shot on shipboard between Los Angeles and San Francisco, at Ellis Island and in New York City. This was five-year-old Baby Peggy's first feature film for Universal.

1924

The Whispered Name

Universal, 1/21/1924. Five reels. LP19701.

Dir: King Baggot.
Scen: Lois Zellner or Raymond L. Schrock.
Cast: Ruth Clifford, Niles Welsh, Jane Starr, Buddy Messinger, Carl Stockdale, Hayden Stevenson, William E. Lawrence, May Mersch, John Merkyl, Charles Clary, Herbert Fortier, Joseph North, Emily Fitzroy.

Notes: Working title: *Blackmail.* Studio reports in October and November 1923 credit Raymond L. Schrock as scenario writer with continuity by Lois Zellner.

The Gaiety Girl

Universal-Jewel, 7/31/1924. Eight reels. LP20214.

Dir: King Baggot.
Scen: Bernard McConville
Cast: Mary Philbin, William Haines, Joseph J. Dowling, Grace Darmond, Otto Hoffman, James O. Barrows, DeWitt Jennings, Lydia Yeamans Titus, Freeman S. Wood, William Turner, Duke R. Lee, George B. Williams, Tom Ricketts, Roy Laidlaw.

Notes: Adaptation by Frank Beresford and Melville Brown from the story *The Inheritors* by Ida Alexa Ross Wylie.

The Tornado

Universal-Jewel, 12/13/1924. Seven reels. LP20733.

Dir: King Baggot.
Adapt: Grant Carpenter.
Cast: House Peters, Ruth Clifford, Richard Tucker, Snitz Edwards, Dick Sutherland, Jackie Morgan, Kate Price, Charlotte Stevens, Fred Gamble, Caroline Irwin, James Welsh.

Notes: Based on Lincoln J. Carter's play *The Tornado; A Spectacular Comedy Drama in Five Acts.* Location shooting done in June, 1924 in and around St. Maries in Northern Idaho.
Loc: MOMA, BSU, NF.

1925

Raffles, the Amateur Cracksman

Universal-Jewel, 5/24/1925. Six reels. LP21350.

Dir: King Baggot.
Scen: Harvey Thew.
Cast: House Peters, Miss Dupont, Hedda Hopper, Frederick Esmelton, Walter Long, Winter Hall, Kate Lester, Freeman S. Wood, Roland Bottomley, Lillian Langdon, Robert Bolder.

Notes: Adapted for the screen from the works of Earnest William Hornung and Eugene W. Presbrey.

The Home Maker

Universal-Jewel, 7/26/1925. Eight reels. LP21671.

Dir: King Baggot.
Scen: Mary O'Hara.
Cast: Alice Joyce, Clive Brook, Billy Kent Schaeffer, Maurice Murphy, Jacqueline Wells, Frank Newburg, George Fawcett, Margaret Campbell, Martha Mattox, Alfred Fisher, Alice Flower, Virginia True Boardman, Elaine Ellis, Mary Gordon, Lloyd Whitlock.

Notes: From the novel by Dorothy Canfield. *AFI Catalog* gives release date as 11/22/1925, but *Film Daily* gives 7/26/1925. Other reviews support this date.
Loc: UCLA.

Tumbleweeds

William S. Hart for United Artists, 12/20/1925. Seven reels. LP21988.

Dir: King Baggot.
Adapt: C. Gardner Sullivan.
Cast: William S. Hart, Barbara Bedford, Lucien Littlefield, J. Gordon Russell, Richard R. Neill, Jack Murphy, Lillian Leighton, Gertrude Claire, George F. Marion, Capt. T.E. Duncan, James Gordon, Fred Gamble, Turner Savage, Monte Collins.

Notes: From the story by Hal G. Evarts. Partially filmed at La Aguerro Rancho, California. William S. Hart's last screen role.
Loc: GEH, LC, UCLA, VID.

1926

Lovey Mary

MGM, 5/31/1926. Seven reels. LP22936.

Dir: King Baggot.
Scen: Agnes Christine Johnson.
Cast: Bessie Love, William Haines, Mary Alden, Vivia Ogden, Martha Mattox, Jackie Combs, Freddie Cox, Gloria Holt, Mary Jane Irving, Annabelle Magnus, Eileen Percy, Russell Simpson, Rosa Gore, Sunshine Hart.

Notes: Adapted by Charles Maigne from the story by Alice Hegan Rice. A sequel to *Mrs. Wiggs of the Cabbage Patch*.
Loc: VID.

Life in Hollywood

L.M. BeDell/Goodwill Pictures. Series circa 1926/1927. One reel each.

Cast: Max Davidson, Neely Edwards, King Baggot, Hobart Henley, Hoot Gibson, Lon Chaney, Reginald Denny, Harry A. Pollard, Baby Peggy Montgomery and others.

Notes: This was a series of one-reel films shot in and around Hollywood, meant to be shown in theaters to accompany feature films. Reel 3 featured the Universal lot and its personnel. Exact time of release is not known.
Loc: VID.

1927

Perch of the Devil

Universal-Jewel, 3/6/1927. Seven reels. LP23106.

Dir: King Baggot.
Adapt: Mary O'Hara.
Cast: Mae Busch, Pat O'Malley, Jane Winton, Theodore Von Eltz, Mario Carillo, Lincoln

Stedman, Martha Franklin, George Kuwa, Gertrude Oakman.

Notes: From the novel by Gertrude Franklin Atherton.

The Notorious Lady
Sam E. Rork for First National, 3/27/1927. Seven reels. LP23755.

Dir: King Baggot.
Adapt: Jane Murfin.
Cast: Lewis Stone, Barbara Bedford, Ann Rork, Earl Metcalfe, Francis McDonald, Grace Carlyle, E.J. Ratcliffe, J. Gunnis Davis.

Notes: From the play *The River* by Sir Patrick Hastings.
Loc: VID.

Down the Stretch
Universal-Jewel, 5/29/1927. Seven reels. LP23430.

Dir: King Baggot.
Adapt: Curtis Benton.
Cast: Robert Agnew, Marian Nixon, Jack Daugherty, Otis Harlan, Ward Crane, Virginia True Boardman, Lincoln Plummer, Ena Gregory.

Notes: From a story by Gerald Beaumont, *The Money Rider*. Racing scenes shot on location at Aura, Illinois. Baggot's last known film as a director for Universal.
Loc: LC.

1928

The House of Scandal
Tiffany-Stahl Productions, 4/1/1928. Six reels. LP25154.

Dir: King Baggot.
Scen: Frances Hyland.
Cast: Pat O'Malley, Dorothy Sebastian, Harry Murray, Gino Corrado, Lee Shumway, Jack Singleton, Ida Darling, Lydia Knott.

Notes: Based on a story by E. Morton Hough.

The Romance of a Rogue
A. Carlos/Quality Distributing, circa 8/27/1928. Six reels.

Dir: King Baggot.
Scen: Adrian Johnson.
Cast: H.B. Warner, Anita Stewart, Alfred Fisher, Charles Gerrard, Frederick Esmelton, Billy Franey.

Notes: Based on a story by Ruby Mildred Ayres. Baggot's last known credit as a director.

1930

The Czar of Broadway
Universal, 5/25/1930. Eight reels. Sound. LP1291.

Dir: William James Craft.
Story-Cont.: Gene Towne.
Cast: John Wray, Betty Compson, John Harron, Claude Allister, King Baggot (Dane Harper), Wilbur Mack, Edmund Breese.

Notes: Based on the life of Arnold Rothstein. A silent version was also produced. Baggot's first known sound film.
Loc: LC.

Once a Gentleman
James Cruze for Sono Art-World Wide, 9/1/1930. Nine reels. LP1474.

Dir: James Cruze.
Scen: Walter Woods and Maude Fulton.
Cast: Edward Everett Horton, Lois Wilson,

Francis X. Bushman, King Baggot (Van Warner), Emerson Treacy, George Fawcett.

Notes: From the story *A Private Engagement* by George E. Worts.

1931

Sweepstakes

RKO Pathé, 7/10/1931. Eight reels. Sound. LP2344.

Dir: Albert Rogell.
Scen: Lew Lipton, Ralph Murphy.
Cast: Eddie Quillan, Lew Cody, ... King Baggot (Weber's trainer).

Notes: Working title: *The Whoop-Ta-Do Kid*. With this film, and for most subsequent films, Baggot began spelling his last name, when used professionally, with two ts.
Loc: LC, UCLA.

Scareheads

Richard Talmadge Productions. States Rights, Mercury Corporation, 10/1931. Six reels. Sound.

Dir: Noel Mason.
Cast: Richard Talmadge, Gareth Hughes, Jacqueline Wells, Joseph Girard, Virginia True Boardman, ... King Baggot (The Policeman, "King Bailey").

Loc: LC.

Sporting Chance

Peerless Productions, 11/21/1931. Six reels. Sound.

Story: King Baggot.
Dir: Albert Herman.
Cast: Buster Collier, Jr., Claudia Dell, James Hall.

Notes: Publicity claimed this featured the first steeplechase ever shot for a sound film.

1932

Girl of the Rio

Herbert Brenon Productions for RKO, 1/15/1932. Eight reels. Sound. LP2760.

Dir: Herbert Brenon.
Cast: Dolores Del Rio, Leo Carrillo, Norman Foster, ... King Baggot (Maitre d'Hôtel).

Notes: *AFI Catalog* points out that although the film is announced as a "Herbert Brenon Production," his name as director was omitted from the screen credits. Baggot's unbilled role was as the maitre d'hôtel in the Purple Pigeon café scenes.
Loc: VID.

Police Court

Monogram, 2/15 or 3/1/1932. 60-65 min. Sound.

Dir: Louis King.
Cast: Henry B. Walthall, Leon Janney, Eileen Pringle, ... King Baggot (Harry Field).

Notes: Working title: *Fame Street*.
Loc: VID.

What Price Hollywood?

RKO Pathé, 6/24/1932. 88 min. Sound. LP3114.

Dir: George Cukor.
Cast: Constance Bennett, Lowell Sherman, Neil Hamilton ... King Baggot (department head).

Notes: Working titles: *The Truth About Hollywood*, *Hollywood Madness* and *Hollywood Merry-Go-Round*.

Hello Trouble

Columbia, 7/15/1932. Seven reels. Sound. LP3111.

Dir: Lambert Hillyer.

Cast: Buck Jones, Lina Basquette, Wallace MacDonald.

Notes: Working title: *Born to Trouble*. Baggot's exact participation in this film is not known; however, a blurb in the *L.A. Record*, 9/27/1931, notes that he was signed to appear in Buck Jones' new picture, *Born to Trouble*.
Loc: LC, VID.

The Big Flash

Educational Film Exchanges, Inc., 11/1932. 22 min. Sound. LP3590.

Dir: Arvid E. Gillstrom.
Scen: Robert Vernon, Frank Griffin.
Cast: Harry Langdon, Vernon Dent, Ruth Hiatt, Lita Chevret, Mathew Betz, King Baggot (Mr. Hinkle, Managing Editor), Jack Grey, Helen Foster.

Notes: From this point onward, Baggot played parts so small that he had very few (if any) lines and seldom a specific character name.
Loc: VID.

Afraid to Talk

Universal, 12/20/1932. Eight reels. Sound. LP3380

Dir: Edward L. Cahn.
Cast: Eric Linden, Sidney Fox, Tully Marshall, ... King Baggot as a police officer.

1933

The Death Kiss

KBS Productions, 1/8/1933. Eight reels. Sound. LP3964.

Dir: Edwin L. Marin.
Cast: David Manners, Adrienne Ames, Bela Lugosi, John Wray, ... King Baggot (Al Payne, Chief Electrician).
Loc: VID.

Secrets

The Pickford Company for United Artists, 4/16/1933 Nine reels. Sound. LP3749.

Dir: Frank Borzage.
Cast: Mary Pickford, Leslie Howard, C. Aubrey Smith, ... King Baggot as a bit player.

Notes: Other bit players included Florence Lawrence, Francis Ford, and Paul Panzer.
Loc: UCLA.

Only Yesterday

Universal, 11/6/1933. Eleven reels. Sound. LP4227.

Dir: John M. Stahl.
Cast: Margaret Sullavan, John Boles, Edna Mae Oliver, Billie Burke, ... King Baggot (Bit Player).

Loc: LC.

1934

Beloved

B.F. Zeidman Productions for Universal, 1/22/1934. Nine reels. Sound. LP4407.

Dir: Victor Schertzinger.
Cast: John Boles, Gloria Stuart, Morgan Farley, ... King Baggot (Second Doctor).
Loc: LC.

The Black Cat

Universal, 5/7/1934. Seven reels. Sound. LP4664.

Dir: Edgar G. Ulmer.
Cast: Boris Karloff, Bela Lugosi, David Manners, ... King Baggot (Cultist).

Loc: LC, VID.

The Love Captive
Universal, 5/21/1934. Seven reels. Sound. LP4704.

Dir: Max Marcin.
Cast: Gloria Stuart, Nils Asther, Paul Kelly, ... King Baggot as a policeman.

Loc: LC.

The Red Rider
Universal, 7/1934. 15 episode serial. Two reels each. Sound. LP4815 (first episode).

Dir: Louis Friedlander (Lew Landers).
Cast: Buck Jones, Marion Shilling, ... King Baggot.

Loc: VID

Romance in the Rain
Universal, 8/13/1934. Eight reels. Sound. LP4886.

Dir: Stuart Walker.
Cast: Roger Pryor, Heather Angel, Esther Ralston, ... King Baggot (Milton McGillicuddy).

Loc: LC.

Cheating Cheaters
Universal, 11/5/1934. Seven reels. Sound. LP5059.

Dir: Richard Thorpe.
Cast: Fay Wray, Cesar Romero, Minna Gombell, ... King Baggot (Official).

Loc: LC.

Father Brown, Detective
Paramount, 12/14/1934. Sound. LP5187.

Dir: Edward Sedgwick.
Cast: Walter Connolly, Paul Lukas, Gertrude Michael, ... King Baggot (Priest).

Loc: UCLA.

I've Been Around
Universal, 12/31/1934. Seven reels. Sound. LP5210.

Dir: Phil Cahn.
Cast: Chester Morris, Rochelle Hudson, Gene Lockhart, ... King Baggot (Doorman).

Tailspin Tommy
Universal, 1934/1935. 12 episode serial. Two reels each, except Episode 1 in three reels. Sound. LP5226 (first episode).

Dir: Louis Friedlander (Lew Landers).
Cast: Maurice Murphy, Patricia Farr, ... King Baggot (Airplane Inspector).

Loc: VID.

1935

Call of the Savage
Universal, 1/15/1935. 12 episode serial. Two reels each. Sound. LP5405 (first episode).

Dir: Louis Friedlander (Lew Landers).
Cast: Noah Beery, Jr., Dorothy Short, ... King Baggot.

Loc: VID.

A Notorious Gentleman
Universal, 1/21/1935. Eight reels. Sound. LP5257.

Dir: Edward Laemmle.
Cast: Charles Bickford, Helen Vinson, Onslow Stevens, ... King Baggot (Police Sergeant).

Night Life of the Gods
Universal, 3/11/1935. Eight reels. Sound. LP5331.

Dir: Lowell Sherman.

Cast: Alan Mobray, Florine McKinney, Peggy Shannon, ... King Baggot as an unbilled extra in the lobby.

It Happened in New York
Universal, 3/18/1935. Seven reels. Sound. LP5404.

Dir: Alan Crosland.
Cast: Lyle Talbot, Gertrude Michael, Heather Angel, ... King Baggot as the policeman.

Mississippi
Paramount, 3/22/1935. Eight reels. Sound. LP5417.

Dir: A. Edward Sutherland.
Cast: Bing Crosby, W.C. Fields, Joan Bennett, ... King Baggot (Gambler).

Loc: UCLA.

Chinatown Squad
Universal, 5/20/1935. Seven reels. Sound. LP5540.

Dir: Murray Roth.
Cast: Lyle Talbot, Valerie Hobson, Hugh O'Connell, ... King Baggot (Bit Player).

She Gets Her Man
Universal, 8/19/1935. Seven reels. Sound. LP5724.

Dir: William Nigh.
Cast: ZaSu Pitts, Hugh O'Connell, Helen Twelvetrees, ... King Baggot (Businessman).

Diamond Jim
Universal, 9/2/1935. Ten reels. Sound. LP5720.

Dir: A. Edward Sutherland.
Cast: Edward Arnold, Jean Arthur, Binnie Barnes, ... King Baggot (Bit player).

Loc: LC.

Three Kids and a Queen
Universal, 10/21/1935. Ten reels. Sound. LP5897.

Dir: Edward Ludwig.
Cast: May Robson, Henry Armetta, Herman Bing, Frankie Darro, ... King Baggot (Druggist).

A Night at the Opera
MGM/Loew's, Inc., 11/15/1935. Ten reels. Sound. LP59261.

Dir: Sam Wood.
Cast: The Marx Brothers (Groucho, Chico and Harpo), ... King Baggot (Dignitary).

Notes: Unbilled, King is in the scene where the Marx Brothers impersonated aviators and wore beards at the docks in New York. King is one of the dignitaries on the platform, wearing a top hat and glasses at their arrival.

Loc: VID.

The Adventures of Frank Merriwell
Universal, 1935/1936. 12 episode serial. Two reels each. Sound. LP6001.

Dir: Louis Friedlander (Lew Landers) and Clifford Smith.
Cast: Donald Briggs, Jean Rogers, ... King Baggot (Chemistry Professor in Chapter 3 "Death at the Crossroads").

Loc: VID

1936

Next Time We Love
Universal, 1/27/1936. Nine reels. Sound. LP6116.

Dir: Edward H. Griffith.
Cast: Margaret Sullavan, James Stewart, Ray Milland, ... King Baggot (Character Man).

We Went to College

MGM/Loew's, Inc., 6/19/1936. Seven reels. Sound. LP6485.

Dir: Joseph Santley.
Cast: Charles Butterworth, Walter Abel, Hugh Herbert.

Notes: *AFI Catalog* notes that "news items and production charts list Baggot in the cast, but he was not seen in the viewed print."

The Devil Doll

MGM/Loew's, Inc., 1/10/1936. Eight reels. Sound. LP6486.

Dir: Todd Browning.
Cast: Lionel Barrymore, Maureen O'Sullivan, Frank Lawton, ... King Baggot.

Loc: GEH.

San Francisco

MGM/Loew's, Inc., 6/36/1936. Twelve reels. Sound. LP6457.

Dir: W.S. Van Dyke.
Cast: Clark Gable, Jeanette MacDonald, Spencer Tracy.

Notes: An announcement was made in the MGM press book that Baggot, Flora Finch, Mahlon Hamilton and many other silent stars were to have roles in this film.
Loc: VID.

Mad Holiday

MGM/Loew's, Inc., 11/13/1936. Eight reels. Sound. LP6863.

Dir: George B. Seitz.
Cast: Edmund Lowe, Elissa Landi, ZaSu Pitts, ... King Baggot (Director).

Notes: Working Titles: *The Cock-Eyed Cruise* and *The White Dragon*. A news item in *Hollywood Reporter*, 8/31/1936, included Baggot in the cast as "a director." *AFI Catalog* notes he was not seen in the viewed print.

1937

Torture Money

MGM/Loew's, Inc., 1/2/1937. Two reels. Sound. LP6887.

Dir: Harold S. Bucquet.
Scen: John C. Higgins.
Cast: Edwin Maxwell, Herbert Meyerling, George Lynn, Larry Martin, Raymond Hatton, John Hamilton, Mary Howard, Murray Alper, Jason Robards, Bernadene Hayes, Charles Trowbridge, Joe Young, ... King Baggot (Witness).

Notes: Number 9 in the series *Crime Does Not Pay*. It won an Academy Award for Best Short Film of 1937.

A Day at the Races

MGM/Loew's, Inc., 6/11/1937. Twelve reels. Sound. LP7207.

Dir: Sam Wood.
Cast: The Marx Brothers (Groucho, Chico and Harpo), ... King Baggot (Race Track Official).

Loc: VID.

The Emperor's Candlesticks

MGM/Loew's, Inc., 7/2/1937. Ten reels. Sound. LP7250.

Dir: George Fitzmaurice.
Cast: William Powell, Luise Rainer, Robert Young, ... King Baggot (Customs Official).

Loc: VID.

1941

Come Live with Me

MGM/Loew's, Inc., 1/21/1941. Nine reels. Sound. LP10217.

Even when playing a bit part like "a man in a crowd," Baggot (in the light hat) still evoked that star quality. Production still from "Torture Money," episode 19 of *Crime Does Not Pay* series, MGM, 1937. Collection of the author.

Dir: Clarence Brown.
Cast: James Stewart, Hedy Lamarr, Ian Hunter, ... King Baggot (Doorman).

    Loc: GEH.

A Woman's Face

MGM/Loew's, Inc., 5/23/1941. Twelve reels. Sound. LP104621.

Dir: George Cukor.
Cast: Joan Crawford, Melvyn Douglas, Conrad Veidt.

    Notes: A 5/4/41 *New York Times* article stated that Baggot, Naomi Childers, William Farnum and Mahlon Hamilton were working in this film.

1942

Babes on Broadway

MGM/Loew's, Inc., 1/1942. Thirteen reels. Sound. LP11315.

Dir: Busby Berkeley.
Cast: Mickey Rooney, Judy Garland, Fay Bainter, ... King Baggot (Extra in Several Audience Scenes).

    Loc: VID.

Grand Central Murder

MCM/Loew's, Inc., 5/1942. Six reels. Sound. LP11273.

Dir: S. Sylvan Simon.

Cast: Van Heflin, Patricia Dane, Cecilia Parker, ... King Baggot (unbilled extra).

Her Cardboard Lover

MGM/Loew's, Inc., 6/1942. Nine reels. Sound. LP11416.

Dir: George Cukor.
Cast: Norma Shearer, Robert Taylor, George Sanders, ... King Baggot (unbilled police officer in the court scene).

Tish

MGM/Loew's, Inc., 7/16/1942. 84 min. Sound. LP11545.

Dir: S. Sylvan Simon.
Cast: Marjorie Main, ZaSu Pitts, Aline MacMahon, ... King Baggot (Man on the Street).

1944

Barbary Coast Gent

MGM/Loew's, Inc., 9/1944. Nine reels. Sound. LP1811.

Dir: Roy Del Ruth.
Cast: Wallace Beery, Binnie Barnes, John Carradine, ... King Baggot .

Notes: *AFI Catalog* notes Baggot's name in production charts for this film.

1945

Abbott and Costello in Hollywood

MGM/Loew's, Inc., 6/1945. Eight reels. Sound. LP2901.

Dir: S. Sylvan Simon
Cast: Bud Abbott, Lou Costello, Francis Rafferty, Robert Z. Leonard, ... King Baggot (Barbershop Patron).

Loc: VID.

1946

Holiday in Mexico

MGM/Loew's, Inc., 9/1946. 127 min. Sound. LP482.

Dir: George Sidney.
Cast: Walter Pidgeon, Jose Iturbi, Roddy McDowall, Ilona Massey, ... King Baggot (Dress Extra).

Notes: Although no documented credit has been found, Roddy McDowall stated that Baggot was in the film as a dress extra. McDowall recognized him and asked for his autograph, which Baggot gave him.

Loc: VID.

The Yearling

MGM/Loew's, Inc., 12/18/1946. Thirteen reels. Sound. LP743.

Dir: Clarence Brown.
Cast: Gregory Peck, Jane Wyman, Claude Jarman, Jr.

Notes: According to notes in the *AFI Catalog*, production began in 1941 when an undated publicity item indicated that Wyman and Peck were to be joined by Baggot, making his "comeback" in the role of Pa Weatherby. But when the film was finally released in 1946, he did not appear in the completed film.

Loc: VID.

Appendix

Films Wrongly Attributed

Snowy Baker (as a film title), 1921.
The Shadow of Lightning Ridge, 1921.
The Fighting Breed, 1921.
The Better Man, 1922.
His Last Race, 1923.

In the *Film Daily Yearbooks* for 1926 and 1927, typographical errors occurred that confused the credits of Snowy (Rex L.) Baker with Baggot's films. In 1926, Baggot's films were omitted, although his name appeared in bold type. Directly below it appeared "Snowy Baker" as though it was a film title and went on to list four other titles actually made by Baker. In 1927, the publication dropped Baker's name altogether and listed his credits under Baggot's name. These erroneous titles continue to be listed in some sources as Baggot's credits, but they are not.

Films Never Released or Abandoned Before Completion

It Is Never Too Late to Mend, Universal IMP, 1912. Mentioned in *Moving Picture World*, 6/15/1912. Based on a story by Charles Reade with an Anglo-Australian setting. Slated for release "in the near future," but it was unrealized.

Othello, Universal IMP, 1912. First announced in *Universal Weekly* August 31, 1912, as being in production and in the trade press into October; however, it was never released.

Detective Lawrence Rand Series, written by Broughton Brandenberg and bought by Universal in June, 1914 to star Baggot. Reported by the *New York Dramatic Mirror*, 7/1/1914, but never produced.

The Adventures of Francois Villon. This title was originally announced by *Blue Book Magazine*, 7/14/1914. A photograph showed Baggot in the costume of Villon; however, later that year it was produced by 101 Bison in four episodes between August and November and starred Murdock MacQuarrie.

One Was a Man. Announced in *Moving Picture Weekly*, 4/15/1916. The article said, "...soon to be released, wherein ... Baggot played as a 'Canuck,' and a bad one. It has the distinction of being a 'stag' picture ... without a suspicion of a woman in the whole thousand feet of it." Baggot was to have directed it with the assistance of Henry Otto's assistant director, Ben Molter. No trace of the title or the plot can be found.

Films Credited to Others, but in Which He May Have Participated

The Tragedy of Youth. Tiffany-Stahl, released 3/1928. Baggot was listed as the director of this film in *The Standard Casting Directory* each month from January through December 1928 and, although Baggot *was* working for Tiffany-Stahl in the early months of 1928, the director of record was George Archainbaud.

Notes

Prologue

1. "King Baggot Home Again," *Universal Weekly*, 30 September 1913, p. 4.

Chapter 1

1. Encyclopedia Americana. 17th ed., s.v. "*St. Louis*." (New York: Americana Corporation, 1944), p. 148.
2. Information on the Baggot family was found in: John W. Leonard, *The Book of St. Louisans: A Biographical Dictionary of Leading Men of St. Louis* (St. Louis, Missouri: The St. Louis Republic, 1906), pp. 32–33; Floyd Calvin Shoemaker, *Missouri and Missourians: Land of Contrasts and People of Achievements*, v. 5. (Chicago, Illinois: Lewis Publishing Company, 1943), pp. 123–124; U.S. Census. City and County of St. Louis, 1870, 1880, 1900, 1910 (the 1890 census was destroyed by fire.); and St. Louis City Directories: 1859, 1860, 1871, 1874, 1878, 1881, 1884, 1886, 1889–1911. Thanks to David Stielow for his remarkable help with the genealogical aspects of this research.
3. Brothers of the Christian Schools. Christian Brothers of the Midwest, Memphis, Tennessee. Archives of registration books of the Christian Brothers Colleges, St. Louis, 1890–1899. Thanks to Brother Robert Werle, FSC, for his compilation.
4. IHA Online. Chicago Irish Families Database, 1830–1900.
5. "Associated Football League: A Complete Roster of the Officers and Players," *St. Louis Post-Dispatch*, 9 November 1899, p. 12.
6. "King Baggot Rated Great Soccer Star by Old Time Coach," *Universal Weekly*, 6 October 1925, p. 23.

Chapter 2

1. Hugh Hoffman, "As King Baggot Sees Himself," *Picture-Play Weekly*, 28 August 1915 [clipping], New York, Lincoln Center Collection.
2. Janet Barry, "King Baggot — Chronic President," *Photoplay*, November 1913, p. 53.
3. Hoffman, *ibid*.
4. Thornton Fisher, "King Baggot the First," *Moving Picture World*, 5 September 1914, p. 1354.
5. *New York Clipper*, (*Queen of the Highway*), September 1903 through May 1904. The tour was followed from week to week by consulting this source. Many thanks to Bruce Long for this compilation and other information he found in the *Clipper*.
6. Fisher, *ibid*.
7. *New York Dramatic Mirror*, "Dates Ahead" section (*More to Be Pitied Than Scorned*), August 1904 through May 1905.
8. Burns Mantle and Garrison Sherwood, eds., *Best Plays of 1899–1909* (New York: Dodd & Co., 1947), p. 463.

9. *New York Dramatic Mirror*, "Dates Ahead" section (*Mrs. Wiggs of the Cabbage Patch*), September through November 1906.

10. *Ibid.*, March through May, 1907. Thanks to Bob Birchard for his serendipitous find of the Mason Opera House playbill.

Chapter 3

1. "Real Estate Man Whose Body Was Found in River," *St. Louis Globe-Democrat*, 24 April 1909, p. 2.

2. St. Louis Metropolitan Police Department. Report dated 23 April 1909 and Coroner's Office. City of St. Louis, Case #90. "Inquest Upon the Body of William Baggot," dated 9 A.M. 24 April 1909.

3. Playbills for the entire 1909 season at the Suburban Garden Theatre can be found at the Missouri Historical Society, St. Louis, Missouri.

4. William Curtis Nunn, *Marguerite Clark: America's Darling of Broadway and the Silent Screen* (Fort Worth, Texas: Texas Christian University Press, 1981), p. 22.

5. *New York Clipper*. "Our Chicago Letter" section, 20 November 1909, "She will remain a fortnight longer…," 4 November 1909, "…another extension of her time here and will stay next week…" These extensions of her appearance at the Great Northern Theatre caused the play to close November 27, 1909. Thanks again to Bruce Long for providing this information.

6. Nunn, p. 23.

7. Gladys Roosevelt, "King Baggot of the IMP Company," *Motion Pictures*, November 1912 [clipping], New York, Lincoln Center Collection.

8. Donald Hayne, ed., *The Autobiography of Cecil B. De Mille* (Englewood Cliffs, New Jersey: Prentice-Hall, 1959), p. 63.

9. John Drinkwater, *The Life and Adventures of Carl Laemmle* (New York: G.P. Putnam's Sons, 1931), p. 139.

10. Burns Mantle and Garrison Sherwood, eds. *Best Plays of 1909–1919* (New York: Dodd, 1947), p. 451.

11. Selwyn A. Standhope, "The Jekyll and Hyde of the Photoplay," *Motion Picture Supplement*, October 1915, pp. 54–55.

Chapter 4

1. John Drinkwater, *The Life and Adventures of Carl Laemmle* (New York: G.P. Putman's Sons, 1931), p. 60.

2. *Ibid.*, p. 65.

3. *Ibid.*, p. 66.

4. *Ibid.*, p. 82.

5. *Ibid.*, p. 73.

6. Julius Stern, "Reminiscences of a Studio Manager," *Moving Picture World*, Part 1, 5 June 1915, p. 1592.

7. Bernard Dick, *City of Dreams: The Making and Remaking of Universal Pictures* (Lexington, Kentucky: University of Kentucky Press, 1997), p. 24.

8. *Moving Picture World*. List of film releases. 8 January 1910, p. 35.

9. Kelly R. Brown, *Florence Lawrence, the Biograph Girl: America's First Movie Star* (Jefferson, North Carolina: McFarland and Company, 1999), pp. 40–41. This is the most detailed and well-researched source published to date on Florence Lawrence. Thanks to Kelly for all her personal help.

10. Selwyn A. Standhope, "The Jekyll and Hyde of the Photoplay," *Motion Picture Supplement*, October 1915, pp. 54–55.

11. Peter Pepper, "The Dean of the Screen: An Interview With King Baggot, *Moving Picture Weekly*, 6 November 1915, p. 28.

12. Standhope, p. *54.*

13. "The IMP Films: The Laemmle Company Establishes a Record," *Moving Picture World*, 8 January 1910, p. 20.

Chapter 5

1. "Photographs of Moving Picture Actors: A New Method of Advertising," *Moving Picture World*, 15 January 1910, p. 50.

2. Ben Turpin might be considered to be the first film performer mentioned in the press in *Moving Picture World*, 3 April 1909, p. 105, but this was only a trade paper.

3. Researchers have made many attempts to find an article stating that Florence Lawrence died in an automobile or street car accident, in any newspaper from the time the event supposedly happened. To date no such article has ever been found. The searches have

only turned up articles published after the fact, denying the rumors. This provides a strong supposition that IMP supplied this information to the press in order to call more attention to Lawrence. After that, "she died" and "he died" rumors about the stars popped up in fan magazines on a weekly or monthly basis with great regularity.

4. " Dame Rumor Hands a Hot One, Ingenious Minds Busy," *The Billboard*, 5 March 1910, p. 17.

5. "St. Louis To the Fore," *Moving Picture World*, 26 February 1910, p. 289. The original article was titled "The Moving Picture Theatre Now a Permanent Factor In Public Entertainment," and appeared in the *St. Louis Republic* 6 February 1910, pt. II, p. 1.

6. "We Nail the Lie," *Moving Picture World*, 12 March 1910, p. 365.

7. "The Girl of a Thousand Faces," *St. Louis Post-Dispatch*, 20 March 1910, pp. 1–3.

Chapter 6

1. "Appearing At a Reception Tomorrow At Union Station and Appearing At the Grand, Too," *St. Louis Star*, 25 March 1910, p. 10.

2. [Advertisement] *St. Louis Times*, 25 March 1910 Sunday Magazine, unpaged.

3. "Ovation for Film Star at Union Station," *St. Louis Times,* 26 March 1910, p. 3.

4. John Drinkwater, *The Life and Adventures of Carl Laemmle* (New York: G.P. Putnam's Sons, 1931), p. 141.

5. "Vitagraph Girl Feted," *Moving Picture World*, 23 April 1910, p. 644, and "A Vitagraph Night," 31 December 1910, p. 1521.

6. [Advertisement] *St. Louis Past Dispatch*, 27 March 1910, p. unknown.

Chapter 7

1. John Drinkwater, *The Life and Adventures of Carl Laemmle* (New York: G.P. Putnam's Sons, 1931) p. 110.

2. *Moving Picture World*, 26 August 1911, p. 523, and *Moving Picture World*, 18 November 1911, p. 548.

3. Drinkwater, p. 84. A count of IMP films released that year found in Paul Spehr's *American Film Personnel and Company Credits, 1908–1920,* shows a total of 101. Baggot's known credits for that year amount to only 15 films. Many of the roles he played during this period were uncredited.

4. Drinkwater, *ibid*.

5. [Advertisement] *Moving Picture World*, 25 June 1910, p. 1080.

6. Florence Lawrence's husband, Harry Solter, in an undated letter to her. From the Natural History Museum of Los Angeles County, Seaver Center for Western Historical Research. The Florence Lawrence Collection, Box 1, Folder 3.

7. Kelly R. Brown, *Florence Lawrence, the Biograph Girl: America's First Movie Star* (Jefferson, North Carolina: McFarland and Company, 1999), chapter six, pp. 59–72 has a well-documented discussion of the Solters' break with IMP.

8. "The IMP Has a Birthday Party," *Moving Picture World*, 5 November 1910, p. 1048. Although the actor was identified as "Robert Miles," it is likely that he was David Miles, who was working for IMP in 1911.

9. Einar Lauritzen and Gunnar Lundquist, *American Film-Index, 1908–1915* (Stockholm, Sweden: Film-Index, 1976). Their work was arranged alphabetically by film title. There was no name index until Paul Spehr's work was published in 1996. Also see Eileen Whitfield, *Pickford, the Woman Who Made Hollywood* (Lexington, Kentucky, University Press of Kentucky, 1997) p. 106.

10. "Owen Moore Sues," *New York Dramatic Mirror*, 15 April 1914, p. 33.

11. "Miss Florence Lawrence ... Miss Pickford," *Moving Picture World*, 7 January 1911, p. 26.

Chapter 8

1. Eileen Bowser, *The Transformation of Cinema, 1907–1915,* Volume 2 of the History of the American Cinema series (New York: Charles Scribner's Sons, 1990), p. 157.

2. Mary Pickford, "My Own Story," *Ladies' Home Journal*, August 1923, p. 118.

3. Mary Pickford, *Sunshine and Shadow* (Garden City, New York: Doubleday, 1955), p. 137.

4. [Advertisement] "Imps in Cuba!" *Moving Picture World*, 28 January 1911, p. 168, and

"The Imp Company Invades Cuba," *Moving Picture World*, 21 January 1911, p. 146.

5. "Making American Pictures in Cuba," *Universal Weekly*, 6 March 1926, p. 4.

6. John Drinkwater, *The Life and Adventures of Carl Laemmle* (New York: G.P. Putnam's Sons, 1931), p. 154.

7. Brownlow conducted his interview with Irvin Willat, C.A. "Doc" Willat's brother, in 1969. Many thanks to Brownlow for providing the author with this information.

8. *Dario De La Marina* (Havana, Cuba), 16 January 1911, p. 8. Many thanks to Mirta Diaz Dominguez of the Biblioteca National Jose Marti for finding these sources.

9. *El Mundo* [Havana, Cuba], 17 January 1911, p. 7.

10. Pickford, *Sunshine and Shadow*, p. 138.

11. Terry Ramsaye, *A Million and One Nights: a History of the Motion Picture* (New York: Simon and Schuster, 1926), p. 541.

12. Henry E. Daugherty, "Baggot Tells of Pioneering Days In Pictures," *Los Angeles Express*, 1 October 1921, p. 11.

13. *"Pictureland"* [review], *Moving Picture News*, 11 February 1911, p. 17.

14. Ramsaye, *ibid*.

15. Drinkwater, pp. 157–58.

16. Drinkwater, p. 159.

17. Brownlow, *ibid*.

18. Pickford, pp. 138–39.

19. "Making American Pictures in Cuba," *The Motion Picture Director*, 6 March 1926, p. 26.

Chapter 9

1. [Advertisement] *Moving Picture World*, 13 May 1911, p. 1049.

2. "That IMP Book," *Moving Picture World*, 20 April 1911, p. 13.

3. Jack Lodge, "The Career of Herbert Brenon," *Griffithiana*, #57/58, October 1996, p. 9.

4. *Moving Picture News*, 20 May 1911, p. 12.

5. "Owen Moore and Little Mary at Majestic," *Moving Picture World*, 21 October 1911, p. 217. The defections were noted in Terry Ramsaye, *"A Million and One Nights: A History of the Motion Picture Through 1925* (New York: Simon and Schuster, 1926), p. 576.

6. "Future IMP Releases," *Moving Picture World*, 6 January 1912, p. 30.

7. "The Thursday IMPS," *The Implet*, 17 February 1912, p. 4.

8. Eileen Bowser, *The Transformation of Cinema, 1907–1915*, Volume 2 of the History of the American Cinema series (New York: Charles Scribner's Sons, 1990), p. 151.

9. "Doings In Los Angeles" [column], *Moving Picture World*, 29 June 1912, p. 1218.

10. "Stern Back From California," *Moving Picture World*, 13 April 1912, p. 141.

11. "Doings In Los Angeles" [column], *Moving Picture World*, 22 June 1912, p. 1110.

12. "Doings At the IMP," *Moving Picture News*, 16 December 1911, pp. 16–18 and "IMP Changes Corporate Name," *Moving Picture World*, 23 December 1911, p. 995.

Chapter 10

1. *The Implet* was published from January 20 through June 8, 1912, Volume 1–21. In August 1912, it was replaced by *Universal Weekly*. A bound copy is owned by the Library of Congress, Motion Picture and Television Division. Thanks to research librarian Madeline Matz at the Library of Congress for all her help.

2. "IMP Players," *The Implet*, 20 January 1912, p. 4.

3. Eileen Bowser, *The Transformation of Cinema, 1907–1915*, Volume 2 of the History of the American Cinema series (New York: Charles Scribner's Sons, 1990). She gave a clear and concise discussion of the major players in the formation of the Sales Company, pp. 80–81, and further enlightenment about the complicated subject of the formation of Universal Film Manufacturing Company, pp. 221–22.

4. Anthony Slide, *The American Film Industry* (New York: Greenwood Press, 1985), p. 365. This is an excellent source for information on each of these early companies, their founders and their fortunes. A new edition was published in 2001 as *The New Historical Dictionary of the American Film Industry*.

5. "Universal Adding Features," *New York Dramatic Mirror*, 25 September 1912, p. 24.

6. John Chapman and Garrison Sherwood, eds., *Best Plays of 1894–1899* (New York: Dodd Mead and Company,1955), pp. 136–37.

7. Hugh Hoffman, "Human Hearts" [review], *Moving Picture World*, 7 September 1912, p. 958. Hoffman later became Baggot's publicist.

8. "Human Hearts, Great Two-Reel IMP Drama, September 12," *Universal Weekly*, 7 September 1912, p. 14.

9. "Otis Turner," *Universal Weekly*, 31 August 1912, p. 22.

10. *Universal Weekly*, 25 September 1912, p. 4.

11. "King Baggot as Author — Actor," *Moving Picture World*, 24 August 1912, p. 776.

12. M.I. MacDonald, "Personalities of the Players," *Motion Picture News*, 26 October 1912, p. 19.

13. "King Baggot," *Photoplay*, October 1912 [clipping] and Gladys Roosevelt, "King Baggot of the IMP Company," *Motion Pictures*, November 1912 [clipping], New York, Lincoln Center Collection.

Chapter 11

1. Joseph W. Farnham, *The Screen Club: Printed on the Occasion of the Club's First Annual Ball at the Terrace Garden, N.Y.* (New York: American Press, 1913), pp. 3–6. A copy of this book is owned by the Academy of Motion Picture Arts and Sciences Library, Beverly Hills, California.

2. "The Screen Club," *Blue Book of the Screen*, August 1914, unpaged. New York, Lincoln Center Collection.

3. "Screen Club Elects Officers," *Moving Picture World*, 12 October 1912, p. 131.

4. Farnham, p. 2.

5. "Screeners Settled in New Home," *Moving Picture World*, 4 November 1916, p. 675.

6. Hugh Hoffman, "As King Baggot Sees Himself," *Picture-Play Weekly*, 28 August 1915, p. 1.

7. City of Boston. Births Registered in the City of Boston, 1889, #11244.

8. "King Baggot, IMP's Leading Man, Weds," *New York Telegraph*, 8 December 1912 [clipping], New York, Lincoln Center Collection.

9. Paul C. Spehr, *The Movies Begin: Making Movies In New Jersey, 1887–1920* (Newark, New Jersey: The Newark Museum, 1977), pp. 48–50.

10. *New York Telegraph*, 8 December 1912, *ibid*.

Chapter 12

1. "Screen Club Dinner," *New York Clipper*, 22 February 1913, p. 10.

2. "Screen Club Dinner: King Baggot Is Honored at Function in Hotel Astor," *New York Dramatic Mirror*, 19 February 1913, p. 27.

3. "Dinner to King Baggot: Members of the Screen Club Give Testimonial To Their President At the Astor Hotel," *Moving Picture World*, 22, February 1913, p. 762. Although the mahogany chest was later lost, the silver is still held by the Baggot family. The pattern is "Madam Jumel."

4. Michael B. Druxman, *Make It Again, Sam: A Survey of Movie Remakes* (New York: A.S. Barnes and Company, 1975), p. 50.

5. "Dr. Jekyll and Mr. Hyde," *Moving Picture World*, 1 March 1913, p. 899.

6. *Moving Picture World*, 13 August 1911, p. 278.

7. "Royal Send-Off For Baggot," *New York Dramatic Mirror*, 28 May 1913 [clipping], New York, Lincoln Center Collection.

Chapter 13

1. "British See Invasion By American Picture Stars, By the Special Correspondent To the Morning Telegraph." Dateline: London, May 29 [1913]. Frances Howard Goldwyn, Hollywood Library, Special Collections, Herbert Brenon Papers.

2. George Blaisedell, "At the Sign of the Flaming Arcs" [column], *Moving Picture World*, 28 June 1913, p. 1350.

3. "Exciting Derby Race Film," *Moving Picture World*, 12 July 1913, p. 189.

4. *Cinematograph Exhibitors Mail* (London), 9 July 1913, p. 153. Herbert Brenon Papers.

5. Alan Reid, *The Castles of Wales* (London: George Philip and Son, Ltd., 1973), pp. 57–60.

6. "Chepstow Castle Stormed, From Our Special Correspondent," *The Daily News and Reader* (London), 28, June 1913. Herbert Brenon Papers.

7. "Film Sham Fight," *Daily Express* (London), 28, June 1913. Herbert Brenon Papers.
8. "Filming *Ivanhoe*, by Our Special Correspondent," *Cinematograph Exhibitors Mail* (London), 2 July 1913, p. 71. Herbert Brenon Papers.
9. *Cinematograph Exhibitors Mail* (London), 2 July 1913, p. 70. Herbert Brenon Papers.
10. "The Taking of Chepstow Castle," by Arthur Scott Craven [clipping], Herbert Brenon Papers.
11. Jack Lodge, "The Career of Herbert Brenon," *Griffithiana*, #57/58, October 1996, p. 13.
12. "Historical Novels on the Film" [clipping], Herbert Brenon Papers.

Chapter 14

1. [Photo] *Motion Picture News* 16 November 1913, p. 38.
2. *Moving Picture World*, 18 October 1913, p. 265.
3. "King Baggot Essays Greatest Role," *Universal Weekly*, 17 January 1914, p. 12.
4. Frances Howard Goldwyn, Hollywood Library. Special Collections. Herbert Brenon Papers. Correspondence, William Laidlaw.
5. Ibid.
6. George Blaisdell, "The Child Stealers of Paris; the European Imp Company Produces a Single Reel of Deep Human Interest..." *Moving Picture World*, 15 November 1913, p. 721.
7. Terry Ramsaye, *A Million and One Nights: A History of the Motion Picture* (New York: Simon and Schuster, 1926), p. 617. Ramsaye also mentioned that Baggot, George Loane Tucker, Herbert Brenon, film editor Jack Cohen and William Robert "Bob" Daly each put up $1000 toward the making of *Traffic in Souls*, p. 614. Perhaps they did, but if so, Baggot's participation in the film would have been limited as he and Brenon were in Europe during its production.
8. "King Baggot's Plays," *Universal Weekly*, 27 September 1913, p. 5.

Chapter 15

1. "IMP European Company Back," *Motion Picture News*, 16 November 1913, p. 42.

2. "King Baggot and Company in Kentucky," *Universal Weekly*, 4 October 1913, p. 9.
3. *Moving Picture World*, 13 December 1913, p. 1280.
4. Jack Lodge, "First of the Immortals: The Career of George Loane Tucker," *Griffithiana*, #37, December 1989, pp. 37–68. Lodge's article is one of the best and most comprehensive to date on this pioneer filmmaker.
5. *New York Dramatic Mirror*, 14 January 1914, p. 72.
6. "King Baggot Buried Alive When Bank Caves In," *Universal Weekly*, 6 December 1913, p. 17.
7. "Actors' Equity Association," *New York Dramatic Mirror*, 5 November 1913, p. 7. Thanks to Valerie Yaros of Screen Actors Guild for this citation.

Chapter 16

1. Robert Grau, *The Theatre of Science: A Volume of Progress and Achievement in the Motion Picture Industry* (New York: Broadway Publishing Company, 1914), p. 207.
2. "King Baggot of the IMP Company" [clipping, no source], Wisconsin Center for Film and Theatre Research, Madison, Wisconsin.
3. "Photoplayers' Popularity Contest," *Photoplay*, January 1914, p. 103.
4. *Photoplay*, June 1914, pp. 140–41.
5. "Ladies World Contest," *Moving Picture World*, 3 January 1914, p. 56.
6. "Bushman Wins Big Contest," *Moving Picture World*, 23 May 1914, pp. 1121–22.
7. "First Universal Ball a Gala Affair," *Motion Picture News*, 17 January 1914, p. 17.
8. "The Universal Ball," *Moving Picture World*, 17 January 1914, p. 293.
9. "Cinema Club's First Annual Ball," *Motion Picture News*, 31 January 1914, p. 22.
10. "Screen Club's Jolly Ball," *New York Dramatic Mirror*, 11 February 1914, p. 30.
11. "Screen Club Ball a Brilliant Affair," *Motion Picture News*, 14 February 1914, p. 21.
12. *New York Dramatic Mirror*, ibid.
13. *The Baited Trap* received a great deal of press coverage, but the best details were found in: "Seeing King Baggot at the Republic," *New York Star*, 4 April, 1914 [clipping], New

York, Lincoln Center Collection, "King Baggot & Co. in a New Species of Silent Drama at Republic," *New York Clipper*, 18 April, 1914, p. 3, and George Blaisdell, "At the Sign of the Flaming Arcs" [column], *Moving Picture World*, 18 April, 1914, p. 363.

14. "An Heir to the Throne," *New York Daily Mirror*, 15 July 1914, p. 25.

15. "A Matinee Idol of the Screen," *Blue Book Magazine*, July 1914, pp. 469–473.

16. George Blaisdell, "At the Sign of the Flaming Arcs" [column], *Moving Picture World*, 1 August 1914, p. 710.

17. "Lessey Leaves Edison to Direct Baggot for Big U," *Universal Weekly*, 1 August 1914, p. 8.

18. "George A. Lessey," *Moving Picture World*, 22 August 1914, p. 1089.

19. "Universal Growth," *Moving Picture World*, 21 November 1914, p. 1050.

Chapter 17

1. "King Baggot Featured in *The Suburban*," *Moving Picture Weekly*, 11 September 1915, p. 41 and 44.

2. Richard Koszarski, *An Evening's Entertainment: The Age of the Silent Feature Picture, 1915–1928*, Volume 3 of the History of the American Cinema series (Berkeley, California: University of California Press, first paperback edition, 1994), p. 87.

3. "Hugh Hoffman Branches Out," *Moving Picture World*, 13 February 1915, p. 1002.

4. "Tabloid Tales" [column], *New York Clipper*, 31 July 1915, p. 13.

5. Karl K. Kitchen, "What They Really Get," *Photoplay*, October 1915, p. 139.

6. "Big U Stars Entertain the Century Club," *Universal Weekly*, 3 April 1915, p. 16 and 28.

7. "King Baggot Visits Sing Sing Prison," *Universal Weekly*, 20 March 1915, p. 31.

8. "Billy Quirk Screeners New Head," *Moving Picture World*, 16 October 1915, p. 424.

9. "Screen Club Squabble," *Variety*, 15 October 1915, p. 18.

10. "Screen Club Holds Annual Meeting," *Moving Picture World*, 6 November 1915, p. 1122.

11. "King Baggot Under Charges by Four Screen Club Members," *Variety*, 26 November 1915, p. 20.

12. *New York Dramatic Mirror*, 15 January 1913, p. 49.

13. "Screen Club Wins Suit," *Motion Picture News*, 5 April 1919, p. 2100. The Club had been sued for $2,500 in back rent. Their former landlords claimed that since the Club had been dispossessed, they had not been able to rent to anyone else. The Club defended on the grounds that the dispossession proceeding terminated the lease. The Club won the judgment.

14. "Just Gossip by the Mahoney" [column], *Moving Picture News* 12 April 1913, p. 22.

Chapter 18

1. "Baggot Has New Director," *Moving Picture Weekly*, 18 September 1915, p. 44.

2. Peter Pepper, "Dean of the Screen," *Moving Picture Weekly*, 6 November 1915, pp. 28–29.

3. *Ibid.*, p. 28.

4. "Amateur Notes" [column], *New York Dramatic Mirror*, 29 March 1902, p. 15 and 30 August 1902, p. 25.

5. "Henry Otto, Director, Universal," *Motion Picture News*, 29 January 1916, p. 97.

6. "Red Feather Productions Name for 'U Broadway,'" *Motion Picture News* 15 January 1916, p. 213.

7. Ingvald C. Oes, "Growth of the Feature Film," *Moving Picture World*, 23 November 1912, p. 759. There is an excellent discussion of the development of the length of the feature film in Eileen Bowser, *The Transformation of Cinema, 1907–1915*, Volume 2 of the History of the American Cinema series (New York: Charles Scribner's Sons, 1990), chapter 12, pp. 191–215.

8. "The Feature Has a Future," *Moving Picture World*, 14 August 1915, p. 1166.

9. W. Stephen Bush, "Are Short Subjects Coming Back?" *Moving Picture World*, 23 September 1916, p. 1947.

10. *Motion Picture News*, 25 December 1915, p. 54.

11. Richard Koszarski, *An Evening's Entertainment: The Age of the Silent Feature Picture, 1915–1928*, Volume 3 of the History of the American Cinema series (Berkeley, California:

University of California Press, first paperback edition, 1994), p. 87.

12. "Universal Program," *Moving Picture World*, 20 May 1916, p. 1344.

13. "King Baggot in *Half a Rogue*," *Moving Picture World*, 10 June 1916, p. 1909.

14. Peter Milne, *Motion Picture News*, "*The Man from Nowhere*" [review], 17 June 1916, p. 3766.

15. "Convenient Melo With Good and Bad Moments" [review], *Wid's Weekly*, 8 June 1916, p. 629.

16. *Moving Picture World*, 3 June 1916, p. 33.

17. "Removal of 'U' Studio To West Definitely Decided," *Motion Picture News*, 10 June 1916, p. 3585.

Chapter 19

1. "Mary Pickford Announcement Misleading," *Moving Picture World*, 8 August 1914, p. 818, and "Concerning 'Little Mary,'" *Moving Picture World*, 29 August 1914, p. 1244.

2. "Fuller and Baggot Leave 'U,'" *Variety*, 18 August 1916, p. 19.

3. "King Baggot and Mary Fuller Leave Universal," *Motion Picture News*, 26 August 1916, p. 1200.

4. Julian Johnson, "A Year's Acting: A Review of Personal Performers," *Photoplay*, September 1916, p. 128.

5. "King Baggot in *Absinthe*," *Moving Picture World*, 9 December 1916, p. 1478.

6. "King Baggot Closing Tour," *Moving Picture World*, 28 April 1917, p. 594.

7. "King Baggot on Tour," *New York Dramatic Mirror*, 24 March 1917 [clipping], New York, Lincoln Center Collection.

Chapter 20

1. "Baggot Has Lead in Serial," *New York Dramatic Mirror*, 24 November 1917, p. 14.

2. Some controversy arose in the 1970s about whether the *Lusitania* was carrying concealed munitions. See bibliography under Colin Simpson for the pro view and Thomas Bailey and Paul Ryan for the argument against that theory. Other prominent people to die in the disaster were wealthy Alfred Vanderbilt, philosopher-writer Elbert Hubbard and producer Charles Frohman.

3. "*Eagle's Eye* to Expose Menace," *Motion Picture News*, 19 January 1918, p. 438.

4. "Electrical Power Diverted to Wharton Studio," *Theatrical News*, Buffalo, New York, 20 January 1918, p. 1.

5. "Officials Applaud *Eagle's Eye* Serial," *New York Dramatic Mirror*, 9 February 1918, p. 20.

6. "Special Showing For *Eagle's Eye*," *New York Dramatic Mirror*, 23 February 1918, p. 25.

7. *Ibid.*

8. "Facts and Comments" [column], *Moving Picture World*, 9 March 1918, p. 1340.

9. "Serial to Test Value of the Press," *New York Dramatic Mirror*, 2 March 1918, p. 20.

10. "Only Newspaper Advertising for Serial," *Moving Picture World*, 29 June 1918, p. 1382.

11. "Whartons Make Picture for War Charity," *Moving Picture World*, 29 June 1918, p. 1830.

12. "Assembling and Cutting of the *Eagle's Eye* Finished," *Moving Picture World*, 29 June 1918, p. 1875.

13. "Metro Completes Contribution for Fourth Liberty Loan Drive," *New York Dramatic Mirror*, 31 August 1918, p. 327.

14. "Rolfe Makes Deal with Fiske," *Moving Picture World*, 26 December 1914, p. 1858, and "Fiske Not to Produce Pictures," *Moving Picture World*, 2 January 1915, p. 52. Mrs. Fiske made only two films, *Tess of the D'Urbervilles* for Famous Players in 1913 and *Vanity Fair* for Edison in 1915.

Chapter 21

1. "Metro Obtains Screen Rights to Successful *Man Who Stayed at Home*," *New York Dramatic Mirror*, 17 August 1918, p. 248.

2. "*Kildare of Storm*" [review], *Variety Film Reviews, 1907–1980*, Debra Handy, ed. (New York: Garland Publishing, Inc., 1985), 27 September 1918.

3. "Emily Stevens in Hospital," *Moving Picture World*, 30 October 1920, p. 1285.

4. "Producers Decide to Close Up Shop,"

Moving Picture World, 26 October 1918, pp. 491–93.

5. "Influenza Epidemic on the Wane," *Moving Picture World*, 9 November 1918, p. 647.

6. "Sleuthing as a Fine Art," *Photoplay*, July 1918, pp. 59–60.

7. "Baggot and Claire Whitney Head Strong Metro Cast, *Moving Picture World*, 26 October, 1918, p. 532.

8. "Metro Gets Rights To *The Man Who Stayed at Home*," *Moving Picture World*, 17 August 1918, p. 101.

9. "Picture News of the Week" [column], *New York Dramatic Mirror*, 11 May 1918, p. 653.

10. "Metro Building West Coast Studio," *Moving Picture World*, 30 November 1918, p. 964.

11. "Farnham President of Screen Club," *Moving Picture World*, 10 November 1917, p. 847.

12. "Without Fear or Favor — By an Old Exhibitor" [column], *New York Dramatic Mirror*, 16 February 1918, p. 8.

13. "Screen Club Wins Suit," *Motion Picture News*, 5 April 1919, p. 2100.

14. "King Baggot in Vaudeville," 9, January 1919 [clipping, no source], New York, Lincoln Center Collection.

15. "King Baggot Returns to Stage," *Moving Picture World*, 15 March 1919, p. 148.

Chapter 22

1. *Ohio State Journal* (Columbus, Ohio), 7 March 1919 [clipping], New York, Lincoln Center Collection.

2. "Baggot's New Play Rapped," Dateline Cincinnati, Ohio, 12 March [clipping, no source], New York, Lincoln Center Collection.

3. "King Baggot Ill," *Variety* [clipping], New York, Lincoln Center Collection.

4. From an oral interview with Frank Blount by Kevin Brownlow in 1967. Thanks to Kevin Brownlow for making this information available to the author.

5. "The Passing of Sidney Drew," *Moving Picture World*, 26 April 1919, pp. 511–12.

6. Frances Howard Goldwyn Hollywood Library, Special Collections. Herbert Brenon Papers. Correspondence, William Laidlaw.

Chapter 23

1. Robert C. Connom, *Van Dyke and the Mythical Hollywood* (Culver City, California: Murray and Gee, 1948), pp. 93–94.

2. "Louis Burston's New Serial *Hawk's Trail* Completed," *Moving Picture World*, 6 December 1919, p. 683.

3. *Moving Picture World* [Obituary], 7 April 1923, p. 618.

4. "King Baggot Plays Lead in *Thirtieth Piece of Silver*," *Moving Picture World*, 10 April 1920, p. 234.

5. *Moving Picture World* [Obituary], 2 November 1918, p. 575 (Lockwood died 19 October 1918).

6. "*The Cheater*" [review], 26 June 1920 (no source). Academy of Motion Picture Arts and Sciences Library, Production Files.

7. "Jack Conway Is Back With Metro Pictures," *Moving Picture World*, 26 July 1919, p. 527.

8. "*The Dwelling Place of Light*" [review], *Harrison's Reports*, 11 September 1920, p. 111.

9. Julian Johnson, "Mark Pickford and Her Career," *Photoplay*, Part 3, January 1916, pp. 37–38, and the Marriages Book for 1915, San Juan Capistrano Archives. Thanks to archivist Father William Krekelberg for his assistance.

10. "*The Forbidden Thing*" [review], *Motion Picture News*, 27, November 1920, p. 4153.

11. "De Havens Sign With First National," *Moving Picture World*, 2 October 1920, p. 626.

Chapter 24

1. "Who'll Be Who in 1921?" *Picture-Play Magazine*, January 1921, pp. 17–20, 86, 99–102.

2. *Ibid.*, p. 17.

3. *Ibid.*, pp. 89 and 99.

4. *Variety*, 3 June 1921, p. 42.

5. "The Matinee Idol of the Screen," *Blue Book Magazine*, July 1914, p. 472.

6. "King Baggot Directing," *Variety*, 11 February 1921, p. 44.

7. "The Director's Work," *New York Dramatic Mirror*, 10 June 1914, p. 28.

8. Clive Hirschhorn, *The Universal Story*

(New York: Crown Publishers, Inc., 1983), p. 37.

9. "*Cheated Love*" [review], *Moving Picture World*, 28 May 1921. Academy of Motion Picture Arts and Sciences Library, Production Files.

10. "*Cheated Love*" [review], 28 May 1921 [clipping, no source]. New York, Museum of Modern Art.

11. "*Luring Lips*" [review], *Variety Film Reviews, 1907–1980*, Debra Handy, ed., (New York: Garland Publishing, Inc., 1985), 29 July 1921.

12. *Universal Weekly*, 11 June 1921, p. 10.

13. *Universal Weekly*, 23 July 1921, p. 16.

14. Screen Snapshots, Pathé/Federated Exchanges, series 2 #13F, 10 December 1921 and Grace Kingsley, "Marie in Clothes," *Los Angeles Times*, 20 September 1921, pt. III, p. 5.

15. *Ibid.*

16. "The Screen" [column], *New York Times*, 19 September 1921, p. 12.

17. "*Nobody's Fool*" [review], *Motion Picture News*, 29 October 1921. Academy of Motion Picture Arts and Sciences Library, Production Files

Chapter 25

1. Baggot's whereabouts have been compiled from city directories and telephone books for New York City, where the first address was found in 1911, and in the Los Angeles area, until his death in 1948. Unlike so many celebrities, he seemed not to have needed the anonymity often prized by famous people. He was listed for almost every year.

2. Hazel Simpson Naylor, "Cabbages and Kings," *Motion Picture Supplement*, October 1921, p. 26 and 85.

3. Roland Flamini, *Thalberg, the Last Tycoon and the World of M-G-M* (New York: Crown Publishers, Inc., 1994), pp. 30–35.

4. "*Human Hearts*" [review], *Variety Film Reviews, 1907–1980*, Debra Handy, ed. (New York: Garland Publishing, Inc., 1985), 4 August 1922.

5. "*Human Hearts*" [review], *Universal Weekly*, 2 September 1922, p. 24.

6. "Universal to Do *Ivanhoe*," *Universal Weekly*, 10 June 1922, p. 13.

7. *Universal Weekly*, 3 June 1922, p. 13 and 24 June 1922, p. 17.

8. *Ibid.*, 20 May 1922, p. 24.

9. *Ibid.*, 22 July 1922, p. 11.

10. "*A Dangerous Game*" [review], *Variety Film Reviews*, 22 December 1922.

Chapter 26

1. Roland Flamini, *Thalberg: The Last Tycoon and the World of MGM* (New York: Crown Publishers, 1994), p. 47.

2. William S. Hart, *My Life East and West* (Boston: Houghton Mifflin, 1929), p. 183.

3. "King Baggot to Appear in Skit," *Los Angeles Examiner*, April 8, 1923, pt. IX, p. 7 and "Baggot a Hit in His Playlet," April 10, 1923, pt. I, p. 5.

4. Special thanks to Diana Serra Cary for her personal commentary as an eyewitness to this scene.

5. Frances Agnew, "King Baggot on Vacation," *New York [Morning] Telegraph*, "Happenings in Hollywood" [column], 22 July 1923, unpaged.

6. "King Baggot Rated Great Soccer Star by Old Time Coach," *Universal Weekly*, 6 October 1923, p. 23.

7. "*The Whispered Name*" [review], *Variety Film Reviews, 1907–1980*, Debra Handy, ed. (New York: Garland Publishing, Inc., 1985), 14 February 1924.

8. Oran M. Donaldson, "The Biltmore Dance Episode," *Holly Leaves* (Hollywood, California), 7 December 1923, p. 1 and 14, December 1923, p. 59.

9. "Screen Guild Votes to Lift Dance Curb," *Los Angeles Examiner*, 12/5/1923, p. 1.

10. Donaldson, *ibid.*

Chapter 27

1. I.G. Edmonds, *Big U: Universal in the Silent Days* (South Brunswick, New Jersey: A.S. Barnes, 1977), p. 136.

2. "*The Gaiety Girl*" [review], *Variety Film Reviews, 1907–1980*. Debra Handy, ed. (New York: Garland Publishing, Inc., 1985), 6 August 1924.

3. "*Tornado* Will Be Filmed Here," *St.

Maries Gazette-Record (Idaho), 12 June 1924, p. 1. Thanks to Tom Trusky, Boise State University, Hemingway Center for Western Studies, for making these articles available.

4. "Movie Players Here to Start Work," *St. Maries Gazette-Record* (Idaho), 19 June 1924, p. 1.

5. "Expect to Finish Outdoor Scenes of the *Tornado* Today," *St. Maries Gazette-Record* (Idaho), 3 July 1924, p. 1.

6. "King Baggot Out to Trap Real Tornado For His 'Reel' *Tornado*," *Moving Picture World*, 23 August 1924, p. 636.

7. "Universal Director to Risk Life to Provide New Thrills for Screen," *Universal Weekly*, 30 August 1924, p. 15.

8. "Exhibitors Report *Tornado* as Greater Than *The Storm*," *Moving Picture World*, 3 January 1925, p. 84.

9. "*Raffles, the Amateur Cracksman*" [review], *Variety Film Reviews*, 29 April 1925.

10. "Tragedies of Hollywood." *Picture-Play*, May 1925, p. 86. Thanks to Kevin Brownlow for providing this information.

Chapter 28

1. "*The Homemaker*" [review], *New York Times*, 10 August 1925, p. 8, and *Variety Film Reviews*, 1907–1980. Debra Handy, ed. (New York: Garland Publishing, Inc., 1985), 12 August 1925.

2. "Bill Hart to Start for United Artists Corporation," *Moving Picture World*, 15 August 1925, p, 763.

3. William K. Everson, *A Pictorial History of the Western Film* (New York: Citadel Press, 1969), p. 43.

4. William S. Hart, *My Life East and West* (Boston: Houghton Mifflin, 1929), p. 341.

5. Kevin Brownlow, *The War, the West and the Wilderness* (New York: Alfred A. Knopf, 1978), p. 271.

6. *Photoplay*, December 1925, p. 113.

7. Hart, pp. 341–42.

8. Hart, p. 342.

9. Everson, p. 44.

10. "Grand Revival of Bill Hart Classic in Which Old Western Star Speaks," *Film Daily*, 9 May 1939. Academy of Motion Picture Arts and Sciences Library, Production Files.

Chapter 29

1. "Universal Signs Director Baggot for Long Period," *Universal Weekly*, 26 September 1925, p. 14.

2. *Universal Weekly*, 20 March 1926, p. 12 and 14.

3. *Ibid.*, 6 March 1922, p. 22.

4. The Academy of Motion Picture Arts and Sciences has a short run of MGM payroll records from 1925 and 1926. Baggot's name does not appear with the regular salaried personnel on this picture; however, all of the technical personnel and actors were listed week by week for production #262, together with their weekly salaries. Bessie Love received $1,500 per week. Louis B. Mayer got $2,000 and Irving Thalberg $1,000.

5. "To Direct Bessie Love," *Moving Picture World*, 20 March 1926, p. 170.

6. "*Lovey Mary*" [review], *New York Times*, 21 June 1926, p. 17.

7. Lisa Mitchell, "Willard's Way" (Willard Sheldon), *DGA Magazine* (Directors Guild of America), March 1999, p. 83. Many thanks to Lisa Mitchell for this and many other helpful bits of information she gave the author.

8. Interview with Willard Sheldon by the author in June 1997.

9. "King Baggot Preparing for Next Jackie Coogan Picture," *The Motion Picture Director*, June 1926, unpaged.

10. "Webb Starts on Coogan Film," *Moving Picture World*, 31 July 1926, p. 278.

11. "2 Directors Now on Coogan Picture," *Variety*, 25 August 1926, p. 8.

12. "*Perch of the Devil*" [review], *Motion Picture News* [clipping, undated], Academy of Motion Picture Arts and Sciences, Production Files.

13. *Universal Weekly*, 23 October 1926, p. 31, and 13 November 1926, p. 11.

14. "*Down the Stretch*" [review], *Variety*, 4 May 1927 [clipping], Academy of Motion Picture Arts and Sciences Library, Production Files.

Chapter 30

1. "Baggot to Direct," *Moving Picture World*, 20 November 1926, p. 143.

2. "Laemmle Rallies After Operation," *Moving Picture World*, 10 July 1926, p. 1, and 13 November 1926, p. 11.

3. *Motion Picture News* [clipping, undated], Academy of Motion Picture Arts and Sciences, Production Files and *New York Times*, 11 April 1927, p. 18.

4. Copies of some of the Masquers' early records are held by the Screen Actors Guild Archives. Thanks to Valerie Yaros, Archivist, for her considerable help with these materials.

5. "Tiffany's Staff," *Moving Picture World*, 22 October 1927, p. 497.

6. "*The House of Scandal*" [review], *Variety Film Reviews, 1907–1980*. Debra Handy, ed. (New York: Garland Publishing, Inc., 1985), 6 June 1928.

7. "Vitagraph Wins Suit," *Moving Picture World*, 6 April 1918, p. 58.

8. "*Romance of a Rogue*" [review], *Variety Film Reviews*, 29 August 1929.

Chapter 31

1. Kevin Brownlow, *The Parade's Gone By...* (New York: Alfred A. Knopf, 1968), p. 566.

2. Alexander Walker, *The Shattered Silents: How the Talkies Came to Stay* (New York: William Morrow and Company, 1979), p. 41.

3. *Photoplay*, October 1928, p. 28. Thanks to Kevin Brownlow for providing this quote.

4. Peter Pepper, "The Dean of the Screen," *Moving Picture Weekly*, 6 November 1915, p. 28.

5. *Los Angeles Times*, 5 May 1930. Los Angeles Public Library, History Department, Index to the *Los Angeles Times*.

6. "Movie Director Divorced on Coast," *New York World*, 18 September 1930 [clipping], New York, Lincoln Center Collection.

7. County of Los Angeles. Superior Court, Case D-86371, 28 June 1930 and 17 September 1930.

8. *Los Angeles Times*, 14 July 1932. Los Angeles Public Library, History Department, Index to the *Los Angeles Times*.

9. "Everything Set for N.Y.M.P.E.L. Affair," *New York Clipper*, 21 August 1915, p. 20.

Chapter 32

1. "Carl Laemmle — 30th Anniversary," *Universal Weekly*, 7 March 1936, pp. 9, 21 and 23.

2. "Favorite Stars of Silent Days Make Comeback," MGM press book for *San Francisco*, 1936. Thanks to John Cocchi for providing this information.

3. Some details surrounding Ruth Baggot's death were related to the author by Mimi Baggot Landberg, King Baggot's daughter-in-law. Other details were found in Ruth Baggot's death certificate and records at the Hollywood Forever Cemetery. Thanks to Annette D'Agostino Lloyd for her assistance.

4. Information concerning Ruth Baggot's will, dated 22 May, 1930, and the disposition of her estate were found in Superior Court records, County of Los Angeles, California, between 27 February, 1937, and 23 January, 1940. Thanks to David Stielow for his diligent search to provide this information. John Musso's daughter Rose Keegel was interviewed by the author in 1997 and provided the information about the status of the Franklin Avenue property.

5. "Miriam Cornely Elopes," *Burlingame* (California) *Times and Daily Leader*, 7 July 1937, p. 15. Thanks to Mimi Baggot Landberg for providing this clipping.

6. Kelly R. Brown, *Florence Lawrence, the Biograph Girl: America's First Movie Star* (Jefferson, North Carolina: McFarland & Company, 1999), p. 146.

7. "Keep Pitching, Baggot's Advice," *Los Angeles Examiner*, 2 January, 1939, pt. I, p. 16.

8. "Do Unto Others" [column], *Official Bulletin of the Screen Actors Guild*, September 1939, p. 8.

9. Thomas Brady, "Stars of the Silent Screen Still Active," 4 May 1941, *New York Times Encyclopedia of Film*, unpaged.

10. The information about *Holiday In Mexico* was related to the author by Roddy McDowall in a series of telephone conversations in 1997.

11. "King Baggot Gets Final Cue," *Los Angeles Examiner*, 12 July 1948 [clipping], New York, Lincoln Center Collection.

Bibliography

Books and Serials

Adams, Les. *Shoot-Em-Ups: The Complete Reference Guide to Westerns of the Sound Era*. New Rochelle, NY: Arlington House, 1978.

Anbinder, Paul, editor. *Before Hollywood: Turn of the Century American Film*. New York: Hudson Hills Press in Association With the American Federation of the Arts, 1987.

Arvidson, Linda (Mrs. D.W. Griffith). *When the Movies Were Young*. New York: Benjamin Blom, 1925.

Bailey, Thomas A. and Paul B. Ryan. *The Lusitania Disaster*. New York: Free Press, 1975.

Barbour, Alan G. *The Serial*. Kew Gardens, NY: Screen Facts, 1967.

Blum, Daniel. *A Pictorial History of the American Theatre, 1900–1951*. New York: Greenberg, 1951.

_____. *A Pictorial History of the Silent Screen*. New York: G.P. Putnam's Sons, 1953.

Bowser, Eileen. *The Transformation of the Cinema, 1907–1915*. Volume 2 of the History of American Cinema series. New York: Charles Scribner's Sons, 1990.

Braff, Richard E. *The Universal Silents: A Filmography of the Universal Motion Picture Manufacturing Company, 1912–1929*. Jefferson, NC: McFarland, 1998.

Brown, Kelly. *Florence Lawrence, the Biograph Girl*. Jefferson, NC: McFarland, 1999.

Brownlow, Kevin. *Behind the Mask of Innocence*. New York: Alfred A. Knopf, 1990.

_____. *Hollywood, the Pioneers*. New York: Alfred A. Knopf, 1979.

_____. *The Parade's Gone By...* New York: Alfred A. Knopf, 1968.

_____. *The War, the West, and the Wilderness*. New York: Alfred A. Knopf, 1978.

Campbell, Craig W. *Reel America and World War I: A Comprehensive Filmography and History of Motion Pictures in the U.S., 1914–1920*. Jefferson, NC: McFarland, 1985.

Cary, Diana Serra. *Hollywood's Children: An Inside Account of the Child Star Era*. Paper edition. Dallas, TX: Southern Methodist University Press, 1997.

_____. *What Ever Happened to Baby Peggy: The Autobiography of Hollywood's Pioneer Child Star*. New York: St. Martin's, 1996.

_____. *The World of Boy King: The Life and Career of Jackie Coogan*. Not yet published.

Cary, Gary. *All the Stars in Heaven: Louis B. Mayer's MGM*. New York: E.P. Dutton, 1981.

Chapman, John and Garrison Sherwood, editors. *Best Plays of 1894–1899*. New York: Dodd Mead, 1955.

Connom, Robert C. *Van Dyke and the Mythical Hollywood*. Culver City, CA: Murray and Gee, 1948.

D'Agostino, Annette M. *An Index to Short and Feature Films in Moving Picture World: The Early Years, 1907–1915*. Westport, CT: Greenwood, 1995.

_____. *Filmmakers in the Moving Picture World: An Index of Articles, 1907–1927*. Jefferson, NC: McFarland, 1997.

deMille, William Churchill. *Hollywood Saga.* New York: E.P. Dutton, 1939.

Dick, Bernard F. *City of Dreams: The Making and Remaking of Universal Pictures.* Lexington: University of Kentucky Press, 1997.

Drinkwater, John. *The Life and Adventures of Carl Laemmle.* New York: G.P. Putnam's Sons, 1931.

Druxman, Michael B. *Make It Again, Sam: A Survey of Movie Remakes.* South Brunswick, NJ and New York: A.S. Barnes, 1975.

Edmonds, I.G. *Big U: Universal in the Silent Days.* South Brunswick, NJ and New York: A.S. Barnes, 1977.

Everson, William K. *A Pictorial History of the Western Film.* New York: Citadel, 1969.

Eyman, Scott. *Ernst Lubitsch: Laughter in Paradise.* New York: Simon and Schuster, 1993.

_____. *Mary Pickford: America's Sweetheart.* New York: Donald I. Fine, 1990.

Farnham, Joseph W. *The Screen Club: Printed on the Occasion of the Club's First Annual Ball at the Terrace Garden, New York.* New York: American Press, 1913.

Film Daily Year Book. New York: Film Daily, 1922–1927.

Flamini, Roland. *Thalberg: The Last Tycoon and the World of MGM.* New York: Crown, 1994.

Gomery, Douglas. *The Hollywood Studio System.* New York: St. Martin's, 1986.

Grant, H. Roger, Don L. Hofsommer and Osmund Overby. *St. Louis Station: A Place for People, a Place for Trains.* St. Louis, MO: St. Louis Mercantile Library, 1994.

Grau, Robert. *The Theatre of Science: A Volume of Progress and Achievement in the Motion Picture Industry.* New York: Broadway Publishing, 1914.

Handy, Debra, editor. *Variety Film Reviews, 1907–1980.* New York: Garland, 1985.

Harding, Alfred. *The Revolt of the Actors.* New York: William Morrow, 1929.

Harmon, Jim and Donald F. Glut. *Great Movie Serials.* New York: Doubleday, 1972.

Hart, William S. *My Life East and West.* Boston: Houghton Mifflin, 1929.

Hayne, Donald, editor. *The Autobiography of Cecil B. DeMille.* Englewood Cliffs, NJ: Prentice-Hall, 1959.

Hirschhorn, Clive. *The Universal Story: The Complete History of the Studio and Its 2,641 Films.* New York: Crown, 1983.

Jacobs, Lewis. *The Rise of the American Film.* New York: Harcourt, Brace, 1939.

Koszarski, Richard. *An Evening's Entertainment: The Age of the Silent Feature Picture, 1915–1928.* Volume 3 of the American Cinema series. New York: Charles Scribner's Sons, 1990.

Lahue, Kalton C. *Gentlemen to the Rescue: The Heroes of the Silent Screen.* South Brunswick, NJ and New York: A.S. Barnes, 1972.

Lauritzen, Einar and Gunnar Lundquist. *American Film Index.* Volume 1: 1908–1915 and Volume 2: 1916–1920. Stockholm: Film Index, 1976 and 1984.

Leonard, John W. *The Book of St. Louisans: A Biographical Dictionary of Leading Men of St. Louis.* St. Louis, MO: The St. Louis Republic, 1906.

Liebfried, Philip. *Rudyard Kipling and Sir Henry Rider Haggard On Screen, Stage, Radio and Television.* Jefferson, NC: McFarland, 2000.

Liebman, Roy. *Silent Film Performers: An Annotated Bibliography of Published, Unpublished, and Archival Sources for Over 350 Actors and Actresses.* Jefferson, NC: McFarland, 1996.

Magliozzi, Ronald S., editor. *Treasures from the Film Archives: A Catalog of Short Silent Films Held by FIAF (Federation of Film) Archives.* Metuchen, NJ: Scarecrow, 1988.

Mann, William J. *Wisecracker: The Life and Times of William Haines, the First Openly Gay Star.* New York: Viking, 1998.

Mantle, Burns and Garrison Sherwood, editors. *Best Plays of 1899–1909.* New York: Dodd Mead, 1947.

Marx, Samuel. *Mayer and Thalberg: The Make-Believe Saints.* New York: Random House, 1975.

Musser, Charles. *The Emergence of Cinema: The American Screen to 1907.* Volume 1 of the History of the American Cinema series. New York: Charles Scribner's Sons, 1991.

New York Times Directory of the Film. New York: Arno Press/Random House, 1971.

New York Times Film Reviews, 1913–1968. 6 vols. New York: New York Times, 1969.

Nunn, William Curtis. *Marguerite Clark: America's Darling of Broadway and the Silent Screen.* Fort Worth, TX: Texas Christian University Press, 1981.

Palmer, Edwin O. *The History of Hollywood.* 2 vols. Hollywood, CA: A.H. Cawston, 1937.

Pickford, Mary. *Sunshine and Shadow.* Garden City, NY: Doubleday, 1955.

Pratt, George C. *Spellbound in Darkness: A History of the Silent Film.* Greenwich, CT: New York Graphic Society, 1973.

Ramsaye, Terry. *A Million and One Nights: A History of the Motion Pictures Through 1925.* New York: Simon and Schuster, 1926. Reprinted New York: Simon and Schuster/Touchstone, 1986.

Reid, Alan. *The Castles of Wales.* London: George Philip and Sons, 1973.

Schutz, Wayne. *The Motion Picture Serial: An Annotated Bibliography.* Metuchen, NJ: Scarecrow, 1992.

Shoemaker, Floyd Calvin. *Land of Contrasts and People of Achievement.* Chicago, IL: Lewis Publishing, 1943.

Simpson, Colin. *Lusitania.* London: Longmans, 1972.

Slide, Anthony. *Aspects of American Film History Prior to 1920.* Metuchen, NJ: Scarecrow, 1978.

_____. *Early American Cinema.* Revised ed., Metuchen, NJ: Scarecrow, 1994.

_____. *International Film, Radio, and Television Journals.* Westport, CT: Scarecrow, 1985.

_____. *The New Historical Dictionary of the American Film Industry.* Metuchen, NJ: Scarecrow, 2001.

Spehr, Paul C., with Gunnar Lundquist. *American Film Personnel and Company Credits, 1908–1920: Filmographies Reordered by Authoritative Organizational and Personal Names From Lauritzen and Lundquist's American Film Index.* Jefferson, NC: McFarland, 1996.

_____. *The Movies Begin: Making Movies in New Jersey, 1887–1920.* Newark, NJ: Newark Museum, 1977.

Stedman, Raymond W. *The Serials.* Norman: University of Oklahoma Press, 1971.

Thrasher, Frederick. *Okay for Sound.* New York: Duell, Sloan and Pearce, 1946.

Variety Obituaries, 1905–1986. New York: Garland, 1985.

Truitt, Evelyn M. *Who Was Who On Screen.* New York: R.R. Bowker, 1985.

Vazzana, Eugene. *Silent Film Necrology.* Jefferson, NC: McFarland, 1995.

Wagenknecht, Edward. *The Movies in the Age of Innocence.* Norman, OK: University of Oklahoma Press, 1962.

Walker, Alexander. *The Shattered Silents: How the Talkies Came to Stay.* New York: William Morrow, 1979.

_____. *Stardom: The Hollywood Phenomenon.* New York: Stein and Day, 1970.

Whitfield, Eileen. *Pickford, the Woman Who Made Hollywood.* Lexington: University Press of Kentucky, 1997.

Windeler, Robert. *Sweetheart: The Story of Mark Pickford.* New York: Praeger, 1974.

Wing, Ruth, editor. *The Blue Book of the Screen.* Hollywood, CA: Blue Book, 1923.

Periodicals and Newspapers

This section is included to give the reader a sense of the broad array of possible sources that might be checked for information on film history for this period. Many are held by large libraries with substantial film research collections, but other titles appear here only because they came from clipping files of voluminous archival collections such as Lincoln Center in New York. Some no longer exist — not even on microfilm. The documentation of periodical and serial publications for inclusive dates is so daunting that even the Library of Congress has not been able to do a thorough job. Open entries, i.e., "The Billboard, NY, 1894–" means the title is still in publication. Closed entries, i.e., Holly Leaves, Hollywood, CA, 1918–1926, show when the publication began and ceased. When the extent of the run cannot be determined, it has sometimes been necessary to express the dates as only those which have been found for the purposes of the book. Those dates have been enclosed in brackets, i.e., "The Morning Telegraph, London, [1913]."

The Billboard, NY, 1894–
The Burlingame (California) *Times & Daily Reader*, [1937].
Cinematograph Exhibitors Mail, London, [1913].
Classic Images, Muscatine, IA, 1962–
The Daily Express, London, [1913].
The Daily News and Reader, London, [1913].
Dario De La Marina, Havana, Cuba, [1911].
DGA Magazine (Directors Guild of America), Hollywood, CA, [1999].

Film Daily, NY, 1922–1968.
Griffithiana, Pordenone, Italy, 1978–
Harrison's Reports, NY, 1919–1962.
Holly Leaves, Hollywood, CA, 1918–1926.
The Implet, NY, 1/20–6/8, 1912.
Ladies' Home Journal, Philadelphia, PA, 1889–
Los Angeles Examiner, Los Angeles, CA, 1903–1962.
Los Angeles Express, Los Angeles, CA, [1921].
Los Angeles Times, Los Angeles, CA, 1886–
Morning Telegraph, London, [1913].
The Motion Picture Director, Hollywood, CA, [1926].
Motion Picture News, NY, 1908–1913.
Motion Picture Supplement, NY, [1915].
Motion Pictures, NY, [1912].
Moving Picture Weekly, NY. Published by Universal, 1915–1922.
Moving Picture World, NY, 1907–1927.
El Mundo, Havana, Cuba, [1911].
New York Clipper, NY, 1853–1923.
New York Daily Mirror NY, 1924–1957.
New York Dramatic Mirror, NY, 1879–1922.
New York Morning Telegraph, NY, 1879–1972.
New York Star, NY, [1914].
New York World, NY, 1883–1931.
Ohio State Journal, Columbus, OH, 1897–1959.
Photoplay, Chicago, IL, 1911–1940.
Picture-Play, NY, 1915–1941.
St. Louis Globe-Democrat, St. Louis, MO, 1875–1986.
St. Louis Post-Dispatch, St. Louis, MO, 1879–
St. Louis Republic, St. Louis, MO, 1889–1919.
St. Louis Star, St. Louis, MO, [1910].
St. Louis Times, St. Louis, MO, [1910].
St. Maries Gazette-Record, St. Maries, ID, [1924].
Screen Guild Magazine, Official Bulletin, Hollywood, CA, 1934–1938.
The Standard Casting Directory, Hollywood, CA, 1922–1933.
Theatrical News, Buffalo, NY, [1918].
Universal Weekly, NY, 1912–1936.
Variety, NY, 1905–
Wid's Weekly, Hollywood, CA, [1916].

Index

Numbers in **bold** refer to photographs.
References to King Baggot in association with
family members are abbreviated KB.

Abbott and Costello in Hollywood [1945] 171, 259
Aberdeen Hotel, Venice, CA 171
Absinthe [1914] 66, 68, 71, 97–98, 120, 216
Academy Awards 158
Academy of Motion Picture Arts and Sciences Library 52
The Academy Players Directory 161
Acker, Jean 166
Across the Atlantic [1914] 60–61, 219
The Actor's Christmas [1913] 71–73, 216
Actors Equity Assoc. 73
Actors in film 18, 21–22, 28
Adams, Claire 116
Adams, Maude 14
The Adventures of Frank Merriwell [1935/36] 165, 256
Advertising actor's names 21–22, 27, 29, 40, 49
Advertising films 21, 23, 40
The Affairs of Anatol [1921] 128
Afraid to Talk [1932] 163, 254
After Many Years [1912] 78, 195–196
After the Ball [play] 137
Agnew, Robert 154
Ainslee's Magazine 129
Aitken, Harry E. 91
Albert, Dr. Heinrich 100
Alcoholism 111; see also Social drinking
Alcoholism in film 85, 111, 162–163
Alden, Mary 152
Alex Theatre, Glendale, CA 141

Alice Through the Looking Glass [novel] 127
An All Around Mistake [1915] 84–85 234–235
All Dolled Up [1921] 131
Allison, May 115, **116**
All-Star Feature Corp. 107
Almost a Papa [1915] 236
Ambassador Hotel, Los Angeles 137, 150
Ambrosio Co. 47
The American Film-Index 31
American Film Institute 163, 167
American Film Manufacturing Co. 75, 113, 117
American Film Personnel and Company Credits, 1908–1920 31
American Mutoscope and Biograph Co. see Biograph Film Co.
American Society of Cinematographers 137
American Theatre, NY 133
American Tobacco Co. 84
The Anarchist [1913] 65, 70, 96, 214–215
Anderson, Gilbert M. (Broncho Billy) 22, 51
Ansonia Hotel, NY 100
Apache Rifles [1964] 157
Apfel, Oscar C. 52
Arc de Triomphe, Paris 68
Archainbaud, George 157
Are You an Elk? [1916] 242
Argonne Forest, France 102
Argosy Films 98
Army Maneuvers in Cuba [1911] 37
Artcraft Pictures Corp. 117

Artful Kate [1911] 37
The Aspirations of Gerald and Percy [1910] 180
Assistant Directors Society 137
Associated Producers 117
Association Football League, St. Louis 9
Astor Hotel, NY 56, 84
Astor Pictures 148
Astor Theatre, NY 15
Astra/Pathé 166
At a Quarter to Two see A Quarter After Two
At the Banquet Table [1915] 228
At the Duke's Command [1911] 181–182
Atherton, Gertrude 149
Atwell, Roy 145
August, Joseph 147
Aurora, IL 154
The Awakening of Bess [1909] 16, 19, 177
Ayres, Ruby M. 158

Babes on Broadway [1942] 258
Baby Peggy Montgomery 133–134, 136; see also Cary, Diana Serra
Back to the Soil [1911] 37, 186, 188
Badger, Clarence 157
Baggot, Amos Taylor [KB brother] 7, 173
Baggot, Arthur Lee [KB brother] 7, 173
Baggot, Bruce [KB grandson] 141, 173
Baggot, Edward [KB uncle] 7, 8
Baggot, Edward [KB cousin] 8–9
Baggot, Harriet [KB sister] 173

Baggot, Harriet (Hattie) [KB mother] 7, 70, 163
Baggot, John Marmaduke [KB brother] 8, **142**, 173
Baggot, King Robert [KB son] 78, 113, 127, **142**, 155, 161, 162, 167, 168, 169, 170, 171, 173
Baggot, King Stephen [KB grandson] 173
Baggot, King William: acting technique 48, 50, 57, 59, 63, 78–79, 81, 117, 120; arrests 160, 162; birth 7; birth of son 16; changes of residence 126, 136, 149, 160, 161, 164, 169, 171; character actor 90, 160, 161 162–164, 165–171; control of work 42, 70, 72, 79, 120, 129–130, 132, 134; death 171; detective films 42, 73, 79; director 46, 70, 72, 97, 121, 131, 134, 139, 141, 143, 144, 148, 150, 152, 153, 158; divorce 160–161; drinking problems 87, 110–111, 152, 155, 160–161, 170; driving 152, 162; first five-reel film 90; first named as a star 25, 27; first seven-reel film 128; first two-reel film 46; in Calif. 12, 112, 120; in Chicago 8; in Cuba 33–39; in England 60–64; in France 65–69; injuries 62, 69, 73; interviews 9, 10, 11, 49–50, 53, 78–79, 83, 90, 99, 120, 127–128, 169–170; "King Baggot cigar" 84; *Ladies World* contest 75; leading man with IMP 15, 19, 42, 53, 93; left Universal 96–97, 155; loaned out 145, 150, 152; marriage 53–55; multiple roles 30, 78, 79–80, 81–82; personal appearances 25–27, 83, 84–85, 92, 98; *Photoplay* contest 74–75; physical appearance 14, 45–46, 115, 120, 127–128, 136, 169–170, 174; popularity 45, 70, 74, 80, 84–85; publicity photos 43, **47, 49, 71, 72, 88, 116, 118, 124, 147, 151, 153 163, 167, 187, 195, 201, 223, 246**; real estate career 9; re-releases of earlier films 95–96; return from Europe 5, 70; salary 10, 74, 84, 120, 156–157, 162, 170; scenarist 42, 49, 72, 97, 132, 133, 162; Screen Club 51–52, 56–57, 76, 80, 85–87, 121; separation from RB 155; serial roles 99, 112, 165; soccer 8, 9, 136; speaking voice 160; spelling of name 7, 161; "Tantalizing Eyes contest" 83–84; theatrical career 10–12, 14–16, 77, 108, 109–111, 120, 133; tour with *Absinthe* 19
Baggot, Marion Loretta [KB sister] 8, 13, 173

Baggot, Patrick [KB uncle] 7
Baggot, Ruth [KB wife] 63, 111, 113, 126, 127, **142**, 171, 173; and birth of son 78; changes of residence 126, 160, 162, 168; death 168; divorce 160; in Europe 5, 59, 63; marriage 53–55; separation from KB 155; will 168
Baggot, Thomas Gantt [KB brother] 8, 174
Baggot, Tom [KB nephew] 174
Baggot, William [KB father] 7, 9, 11, 53 and Suicide 13–14
Baggot & Brothers 7
Bailey, William 93
Bainbridge, Rolinda 46
Baird, Leah 59, 61, 65, 68, 69, 96, 106, 170
The Baited Trap [1914] 77–78, 91, 219–220
Baker, Friend 140, 141
Balfour, Agustus 46
Balshofer, Fred J 43, 112
Bank of America 168
Barbary Coast Gent [1944] 170, 259
The Bargain [play] 146
Barnes, Binnie 170
Barrett Towing Co. 5
The Barrier [play] 133
Barrington, Eugene 14
Barriscale, Bessie 115, 116, 164
Barry, Joseph 140
Barrymore, Ethel 106, 110
Barrymore, John 110, 119, 142, 152
Barrymore, Lionel 110
Barthelmess, Richard 119
Battle of the Thames [War of 1812] 70
Battle of the Wills [1911] 191
Baumann, Charles O. 76, 112
Bayonne, NJ 80
B.B. Features 115
Bear Ye One Another's Burdens [1910] 179
The Bearer of Burdens see *Officer 174*
Beaudine, William 137, 157
Beauford [duke] 61
Beaumont, Gerald 154
Beauty Co. 113–114
Bedding, Thomas 45
Bedford, Barbara 146, 156, 170
Beery, Wallace 170
Behind the Door [1920] 110
Behind the Stockade [1911] 37
Belasco, Arthur 166
Belasco, David 8, 16
Bell Hotel, Chepstow, Eng. 61
Belmont Handicap [race] 83
Belmont Racetrack, NY 130
Belmore, Lionel 162
Beloved [1934] **163**, 164, 254
Below the Surface [1920] 110
Benedict, Kingsley 133

Benham, Henry 57, 93
Bennett, Joan 165
Bermuda 54
The Better Way [1911] 192
The Big Flash [1932] 163, 254
The Big Parade [1925] 148
The Bigamist see *Lady Audley's Secret*
Billboard 22, 30, 31
Biltmore Hotel, Los Angeles 137
Bingham, Amelia 12, 14
Biograph Film Co 18–19, 27, 30, 32, 33, 43, 51, 55, 106, 117, 163
Bison Co. 43, 49, 112; see also New York Motion Picture Co.
Bitter Root Mountains, ID 140
Blaché, Herbert 105, 106
The Black Cat [1934] 254
Blackmail see *The Whispered Name*
Blackton, J. Stuart 27
Blackwell, Carlyle 75, 84, 97, 120
Blair, Nan 112
Blaisdell, George F. 51, 56, 57, 69
Blaney, Charles 11
The Blazing Secret see *The Flaming Diagram*
Blind Husbands [1919] 128
Blinkhorn, Arthur 56
"Blister Jones" [story] 154
Blood Is Thicker Than Water [1912] 204
The Blood Test [1914] 218
Blount, Frank 110
Blue Book Magazine 78
The Blue Print Mystery see *The Blood Test*
Boble, Bob 140
Boggs, Francis 43
Boise State University, ID 141
Boles, John 164
Bonavita, Jack 57
The Boonton Affair [1917] 242–243
Born to Trouble see *Hello Trouble*
A Borrowed Identity see *The Man Across the Street*
Borzage, Frank 157
Bosco, Wallace 61
Bostwick, Edith 33
Boulder Creek, ID 140
Bourse, Paris 68
The Box Couch [1914] 217
Boy-Ed, Capt. Karl 100
Boylan, Michael 123
Boyle Heights, CA 43
Brabin, Charles 157
Braddon, Mary Ellen 46
Bradford, James 148
Brandt, Joe 90
The Breakdown [1912] 49, 78, 202
Breese, Edmund 162, 164
Brenon, Helen 41, 59, 61,
Brenon, Herbert 41, 46, 49 51, 52, 56, 57, 58, 59, **64, 67**, 70, 91, 96, 111, 157; and in England 60–64; in France 65–69

Bretton Hall Hotel, NY 126
The Bridal Room [1912] 206–207
Brighton Beach, NY 126, 162
British Columbia, Canada 140
British Film Institute 46
Brockliss, Frank 60
Brockwell, Gladys 134
Broman, Ernie 140
Broncho Motion Picture Co. 116
Brook, Clive 144, 145
Brooklyn Heights, Los Angeles 43
The Brothers [1911] 191
Brown, Clarence 160, 170
Brownie, the Wonder Dog 133
Browning, Todd 121, 157
Brownlow, Kevin 33, 36, 110, 147, 159
Brundage, Mathilda 92, 143
Brunette, Fritzi 120, 166
Buckingham Palace 61
Buff: A Collie [novel] 114
Building for Democracy [1918] 103, 244
Bunny, John 22, 51, 56, 166
Burk, Frank J. 11
Burkhart, Addison 156
Burston, George 112
Burston, Louis B. 112, 113
Burston Films 112
Burton [photographer, *St. Louis Times*] 25
Busch, Mae 153, 164
Bush, Pauline 117
Bush, W. Stephen 91
Bushman, Francis X. 46, 56, 75, 84, 106, 161, 165
Butterfield Theatre Circuit 98
The Butterfly see *Moonlight Follies*
The Butterfly Girl [1921] 120, 121, 247

Cabanne, William Christie 115
"Cabbages and Kings" [poem] 127
Cahill, Thomas W. 9, 136
The Call of the Savage [1935] 165, 255
The Call of the Song [1911] 190–191
Calvary Cemetery, Los Angeles 171
Calvary Cemetery, St. Louis 14
Camp, William 51
Canfield, Dorothy 144
Cap'n Eri [1915] 89
Captain January [1924] 133
The Captain of the Typhoon [1916] 240–241
Carey, Harry 128
Carlos, A. Co. 157
Carlton, Lloyd 121
The Carmen Case [murder] 81
Carroll, J.P. 51
Carroll, Louis 127
Carter, Lincoln J. 139

Cary, Diana Serra 134–135; *see also* Baby Peggy Montgomery
The Castaway [1912] 204–205
Catalina Island, CA 135
Catholic Actors Guild 137
Caught in a Flash [1912] 203
A Cave Man Wooing [1912] 200
Cella, Peter 54
Cella's Park Hotel, NJ 53, 54, 54
Central Casting Office, Los Angeles 161
Century Studios 133
Century Theatre Club, NY 84
Chadwick, Helen 166
Chalmers, James Petrie 19–20
Chamber of Commerce, Rochester, NY 102
Champion Film Co. 47
Champs Elysées, Paris 68, 69
The Chance Market [1916] 93, 95, 121, 241
Chaney, Lon 115
Chaplin, Charlie 84, 113, 119
Chaplin Studios 118
Chase, Charley (Charlie) 137, 145
Château-Thierry, France 102
Cheated Love [1921] 121–122, 247
The Cheater [1920] 115, **116**, 245
Cheating Cheaters [1934] 255
Chepstow, Monmouthshire, Eng. 61, 62, 63
Cherokee Strip, OK. 146, 148
The Chicken That Came Home to Roost see *The Town Scandal*
The Child Stealers of Paris [1913] 68 70, 96, 215
Childers, Naomi 166, 170
A Child's Influence [1912] 203
Chinatown, Los Angeles, CA 112
Chinatown Squad [1935] 165, 256
The Christian [1923] 153
Christian Brothers College, St. Louis 8, 9, 136
Christie Hotel, Los Angeles 126, 164
Churchill Downs racetrack, KY 130
Cincinnati Enquirer 109
Cinecon 34, Los Angeles 141
Cinema Club of the Bronx 76
Cinematograph Exibitors Mail 61, 63
The City of Terrible Night [1915] 227
Clair, Pete 140
Claire, Gertrude 128, **130**
Clark, Marguerite 12, 14, 77, 84
Clary, Charles 136
"Cleek" [detective stories] 80
Clemens, Katherine Boland 30
Clements, Roy 124
Cleveland Theatre, OH 11
Clifford, Ruth 136, 139, 141
Clifford, William H. 92
Cline, Eddie 137

Cochrane, Robert H. 18, 22, 25, 27, 28, 40
Cochrane, Thomas D. 29, 42
The Cock-Eyed Cruise see *Mad Holiday*
Coeur d'Alene, ID 140
Cofin Estate, Pasadena, CA 123
Coghlan, Frank "Junior" 135
Cohn, Jack 39
Cohn, Ralph J. 14
Cole, Cornelius 106
Collier, Buster, Jr. 162
Collins, William 160
Columbia Pictures 163
Columbia Theatre, Chicago 8
Columbian Exposition [1893] 8
Combs, Jackie 150
Come Live With Me [1941] 170, 257–258
The Comedian's Mask [1913] 58–59, 212–213
Committee on Public Information 101
Compson, Betty 115, 160
Coney Island, NY 123
Connom, Robert 113
Constantine, Ann (Annie) [KB mother-in-law] 53, 54, 59, 168, 169
Constantine, Charles 53
Constantine, Fenwick 53
Constantine, Ruth see Baggot, Ruth
Continental Clothing Store, Oshkosh, WI 17, 18
Conway, Jack 116, 121
Coogan, Jack, Sr. 152–153
Coogan, Jackie 133, 152, **153**
Cook, Maude Carr 12
Cooper, Courtney Ryley 100
Cooper-Hewitt lamps 77
Cornely, Miriam see Landberg, Mimi Baggot
The Corsican Brothers [1915] 82, **83**, 84, 229
Costello, Maurice 22, 46, 75, 83, 84 120, 165
Cotton Club, Culver City, CA 173
The Count of Montebello [1910] 29, 180
Cowen, William H. 107
Coytesville, NJ 18, 80
Crampton, Howard 92
Craven, Arthur Scott 61, 63
Crescent Film Co. 43
Crime Does Not Pay [1937] 169, 257
Crime's Triangle [1915] 233
Crisp, Donald 157
Crolius, Louise 43
Cromwell, Oliver 61
Crosby, Bing 165
Crossed Wires [1923] 132, 133, 249
Cruze, James 57, 157, 161
Crystal Film Co. 47

Cuba 32–39
Cukor, George 163
Culver City, CA 169
Cummings, Irving 120, 157, 160
Cunard, Grace 80
Curtain [1921] 155
The Czar of Broadway [1930] 160, 252

Daeheel, Frank 26
Daly, Joe 33
Daly, William R. 33, 46, 49, 51, 52, 54 56, 78, 88, 106, 111, 131, 132
Dana, Viola 106
A Dangerous Game [1922] 131, 132, 249
Daniel Boone [1907] 18
Dario de la Marina [Havana] 33
The Darling of New York [1923] 133–135, 250
Darmond, Grace 112, 113, 133
Darnell, Lisle 120
Davidson, Emily 60
Davidson, Max 135
Davis, Howard O. 93–94, 95
Davis, Owen 14
Davis, Robert H. 107
Daw, Marjorie 120
Dawn, Norman 121
A Day at the Races [1937] 169, 257
Dazey, Charles Turner 82
Deakin, Dorthea 14
deAngelis, Jefferson 14
The Death Kiss [1933] 254
De Haven, Carter 118
De Haven, Flora Parker 118
DeMille, Cecil B. 15, 116, 158
deMille, Henry C. 8
DeMille, Matilda Beatrice 15
DeMille, William C. 15–16
Dempster, Robert 15
Dennis, E. 140
Denny, Reginald 130–131, 135
Depression (economic) 160, 164, 169
Deshler Hotel, Columbus, OH 109
Detroit, MI 98, 110
The Devil Doll [1936] 166, 257
The Devil's Pass Key [1920] 128
Diamond Jim [1935] 165, 256
Dillon, Edward 51
Dintenfass, Mark 5
Directors Guild of America 137, 152, 169
Dr. Bunyon [1913] 209–210
Dr. Jekyll and Mr. Hyde [1913] 57, 58, 71, 78, 210
Dodge, Louise 131
A Doll's House [1922] 128
Dolly Sisters 106
Domino Motion Picture Corp. 116
The Double [1910] 29–30, 78, 180
Double exposure in film 17

Down Home [1919] 110
Down the Stretch [1927] 150, 152, 154, 156, 252
Downing, Helen see Brenon, Helen
Draft 258 [1917] 105
Dramatic Mirror see *New York Dramatic Mirror*
Dream Theatre, St. Maries, ID 142
Drew, Sidney 110
Drinkwater, John 15, 26, 29, 33, 35
The Duality of Man [1910] 57
du Briac, Jean 120
Dumas, Alexander, père 82
Dun Laoghaire, Ireland 46
Du Pont, Miss 143
Dwan, Allan 117, 157
The Dwelling Place of Light [1920] 116–117, 245–246
Dyer, William 133

*The **E**agle's Eye* [1918] 99–102, **102**, 104, 105, 243
Earle, Edward 120
Eason, Reaves 121, 137, 153
Eastern Film Corp. 89
Eastman, George Co. 18
Eclair Film Co. 47
Eddy, Helen Jerome 117, **118**
Edendale, CA 43
Edeson, Robert 145
Edgelow, Thomas 115
Edgewater, NJ 53–54
Edison, Thomas A. 18
Edison Film Co 18, 32, 76, 80, 81, 96, 97, 121, 157
Edith's Victory [1918] 103
Educational Film Exchange 163
Edwards, Snitz 128, 139, 140
Eiffel Tower, Paris 65
El Mundo, Havana 33
Eldridge, Charles 71
Ellis Island, NY 134
The Emperor's Candlesticks [1937] 169, 257
Epsom Downs, Eng. 60
Equitable Films 112
Esmelton, Frederick 135, 143 145
Essanay Film Manufacturing Co. 18–19, 32, 52, 75, 157
The Eternal Triangle [1910] 178
Evarts, Hal G. 146
An Evening's Entertainment 91
Everson, William 68, 148
Everton, Paul 100
Executive Clemency [1911] 193
The Exploits of Elaine [1915] 99

*The **F**air Dentist* [1911] 37, 39, 186, 187
Fairbanks, Douglas 117, 119
Fame Street see *Police Court*
Family Secret [1924] 133
Family Theatre, Chicago 17
Famous Players 91, 121, 158

Far from the Beaten Track [1912] 198
Farnham, Joseph W. 56, 86, 107
Farnum, Dustin 135
Farnum, William 170
Father Brown, Detective [1934] 255
Fawcett, George 161
Fearnley, Jane 47, 96
Feature films see Film length
Federated Exchanges 123
Fields, W.C. 165
Fifty-Fifty [1915] 229
Figuhr, Harry 140
Fillmore, Clyde 133
Film length 69, 83, 91–91
Film Reports 30
Film Supply Co. 56
Finch, Flora 166
First National Exhibitors 106, 117, 155
Fischer, Margarita 43, 75, 84, 101, 113–114, **195**, **246**
Fisher, George 123
The Fisher-Maid [1911] 37
Fiske, Minnie Maddern 103
Fitzgerald, Dallas 85–87, 121
Fitzgerald, James 105
Fitzmaurice, George 157, 169
Fitz Osbern, William 61
Fitzpatrick, Loretta 161
The Five Pound Note [1915] 226–227
Flaherty, Robert J. 128
The Flaming Diagram [1914] 96, 217–218
Fleet Street, London 61
Fleming, Victor 157
Flexner, Anne Crawford 12
Floradora Shows 166
Flying A Films see American Film Manufacturing Co.
Flynn, William J. 99, 100, 101
Foolish Wives [1922] 131, 153
Fool's Highway [1924] 138
Foote, Courtenay 97
Foote, John Tainter 154
Foquet, Pierre de la Motte 90
For the Queen's Honor [1911] 42, 189
The Forbidden Thing [1920] 117, **118**, 156, 246
Ford, Francis 97, 112, 163
Ford, John 121, 157, 160
Fort Lee, NJ 18, 53, 54 80, 93, 96, 104, 157
Foss, Darrel 122
Four Square Distributors 100, 101
Frances Howard Goldwyn Hollywood Library 68
Francis, David R. 7
Franklin, Harry L. 104
Franklin, Sidney 157
Freulich, Henry 140
Freulich, Jack 140
Friars Club, NY 52, 107

Frohman, Charles 12
Frohman Amusement Corp. 107
From the Bottom of the Sea [1911] 91
Frontier Film Co. 47
Frou Frou [play] 14
Fuller, Mary 76, 83, 84, 93, 96–97
Futrelle, Jacques 90

Gable, Clark 166
Gade, Svend 30
The Gaiety Girl [1924] 138–139, 250
Gail, Jane 58, 73, 93, 106
A Game for Two [1910] 31, 179
Garrick Theatre, Chicago 10
Garwood, William 93
A Gasoline Engagement [1911] 42, 189
Gaston, Mae 112
Gates, Harvey 115
Gaudio, Eugene 115, 116
Gaudio, Tony 33, 36, 93, 115, 117, 156
Gaumont Co. 60
Gauntier, Gene 76
Geltzer, George 68
Gem Motion Picture Co. 69
Gem Theatre, St. Louis 26, 27
General Film Co. 28
George V [king] 60
German espionage *see* World War I
Gibson, Hoot 128, 135
The Girl and the Half-Back [1911] 114, 194, **195**
The Girl in the Taxi [1920] 118, 121, 246–247
Girl of the Rio [1932] 163, 253
The Girl Who Knew All About Men see Nobody's Fool
Gish, Lillian 170
Glendon, J. Frank 129
Going Straight see The Better Way
Gold Is Not All [1913] 209
The Golden Garter [play] 14
Goldsmith, Oliver 89
A Good Cigar [1911] 37
Good Housekeeping 138
The Good Little Devil [play] 57
Goodhall, Grace 15
Gorman, John 120
"The Gossamer Web" [story] 122
Gossip [1923] 132, 249
Goulding, Edmund 157
Graft [1915] 89
Graham J.C. 75
Grand Central Murder [1942] 258–259
Grand Central Palace, NY 76
Grand Opera House, St. Louis 10, 26, 27
Grand Theatre, Cincinnati, OH 109
Grandin, Ethel 70, 71, 106

Grandon, Francis J. 93
Granville, Fred LeRoy 121
Granville, Taylor 133
Grau, Robert 74
Grauman, Sid 133
Grauman's Million Dollar Theatre, Los Angeles 133
Great Northern Film Co. 91
Great Northern Theatre, Chicago 15
The Great Reward [1921] 113
The Great Universal Mystery [1914] 29, 92, 220
Greene, Charles H. 98
"Gret'n Ann" [story] 131
Grey, Zane 135
Griffith, David Wark (D.W.) 32, 121
The Grim Game [1919] 110
Gutman, Arthur 148

Hackathorne, George 128, **130**
Hackett Players, San Francisco 169
Haines, William 138, 152
Haley, William M. 8, 13
Half a Rogue [1916] 90, 92, 238–239
Hall, Donald 166
Hall, George Edwardes 66, 79, 81
Hall, Mordaunt 144, 152
Hallor (Halleran) Edith 128
Hamburg [ship] 33
Hamilton, Mahlon 133, 162, 166, 170
Hamlet [play] 10
Hammell, Gustave 61
Hammerstein, Elaine 136
Hampton, Benjamin B. 116
Hanley, Lawrence Stock Co. 11
A Happy Family [1912] 205
Harned, Virginia 12
Harrison's Reports 116–117
Harron, Anna 105
Harron, Robert (Bobby) 105
Hart, Joseph 108
Hart, William S. 133, 145–148, **147**, 149
Harte, Bret 14
Hartigan, Pat 135
Hartman Theatre, Columbus, OH 109
Hastings, Patrick 155
The Haunted Bell [1916] 90, 238
Havana [ship] 33
Havlin's Theatre, St. Louis 10, 27
The Hawk's Trail [1919] 112–113, 114, 166, 245
Hays, Jack 140
Hearn, Eddie 166
Heart of a Jewess see Cheated Love
The Heart That Sees [1913] 212
Hedlund, Guy 85–86
The Heel of the Law see The Rise of Officer 174

Held, Anna 166
Hello Trouble [1932] 163, 253–254
Hemingway Western Studies Center, Boise, ID 141
Henderson, Bert 113
Henderson, Dell 51
Hendon Aerodrome, Eng. 61
Hendrick Hudson Apartments, NY 126
Henley, Hobart 90, 93, 135, 157
Her Boy [1918] 105
Her Cardboard Lover [1942] 259
Herman, Albert 162
Herndon, Anita 42
Herne, Julia 14
Hiawatha [1909] 18
High Heels [1921] 131
Hill, Robert 93
Hillyer, Lambert 163
His First Automobile see His New Automobile
His Home Coming [1915] 234
His New Automobile [1915] 232
His Other Self [1912] 49, 78, 203
His Own Story [1916] 240
His Second Wife [1910] 178
The Hoax House [1916] 237
Hodkinson, W.W. 110
Hoffman, Hugh 83–84, 131, 132, 162
The Hold-Up [play], 133, 145
Holiday in Mexico [1946] 171, 259
Hollywood [Forever] Cemetery 167
Hollywood High School 162, 167
Hollywood Hotel, Los Angeles 113, 126
Hollywood Madness see What Price Holywood?
Hollywood Merry-Go-Round see What Price Holywood?
The Home Maker [1925] 144–145, 251
Hooley's Theatre, Chicago 8
Hope, Evelyn 61,
Hopper, De Wolfe 14
Hopper, Hedda 143
Hopwood, Avery 15
Horning, Ben 43
Horning, E.W. 142
Horsley, David 43
Horton, Edward Everett 161
Hotel Biltmore, Wash., DC 101
Hough, E. Morton 157
House of Scandal [1928] 157, 252
Howe, Herbert 119
Hubbard, Lucien 122, 128
Hulette, Gladys 18
Human Hearts [1912] 46, 48, 55, 128, 205–206
Human Hearts [1914] 128, 224
Human Hearts [1922] 128–129, **130**, 150, 169, 248

The Hunchback of Notre Dame [1923] 132, 133
Hunt, Irene 93
Hunter, Edna 89, 93
Hunter, Harry 109
Hunters Point Palace, Bronx, NY 76
Hyclass Producing Co. 142

Ideal Studios 60
I'll Fix It [1918] 243
An Imaginary Elopement [1911] 181
The Immigrant's Violin [1912] 197–198
The IMP Book 40–41
IMP Co. (Independent Moving Pictures Company of America), NY 15,17–20, 47, 50, 77, 81, 89, 92, 93, 110, 163, 170, 171; and advertising stars 29, 40; films in Europe 60–69; first birthday party 30; first company photograph 34; first studio 18, **19**; first three-reel film 49; growth 28–29, 44; in California 42, 43; in Cuba 32–38; lawsuits 28; name change to "IMP Films Co." 44; new plants 29, 80; publicity in St. Louis 25; re-releases of earlier films 95–96; "We Nail the Lie" 23; with Universal 47, 80; *see also* Universal Film Manufacturing Co.
Imperial Theatre, Chicago 10, 11
The Implet 45
Improved Order of Red Men [organization] 70
In Old Madrid [1911] 37
In Old Tennessee [1912] 49, 205
In the Bishop's Carriage [play] 12
"In the Evening by the Moonlight in Dear Old Tennessee" [song] 77
In the Sultan's Garden [1911] 42, 188–189
Ince, Thomas 33, 34, 35, 36, **37**, 38, 39, 46, 91, 96, 106, 115, 116, 146
Independent film companies 28
Independent Moving Pictures Company of America *see* IMP
Influenza epidemic [1918] 104–105
Ingersoll, Bob 166
"The Inheritors" [story] 138
Irish in St. Louis 7
The Irony of Fate [1910] 31, 179
It Happened in New York [1935] 165, 256
Italia Co. 47
Ithaca, NY 99, 100
Ithaca Light and Power Co., NY 100

Ivanhoe [1913] 61–64, **64**, 65, 66, 68, 70, 129, 213–214
I've Been Around [1934] 255

Jacksonville, FL 112
Jane and the Stranger [1910] 177
The Jazz Singer [1927] 159
Jenny [play] 14, 16
Jim Slocum, No. 46,393 [1916] 239
Jim Webb, Senator [1914] 121, 221
John Sterling, Alderman [1912] 55, 207–208
Johnny Get Your Hair Cut [1927] 152
Johnson, Adrian 158
Johnson, Arthur 46, 51, 56, 75, 87–88
Johnson, Bill 165
Johnson, Col. Richard M. 70
Johnson, Tefft 52, 56
Johnstone, Calder 51, 56
Johnstown, PA 41
Jones, Buck 163
Jones, Frederick 100
Jones, Henry Arthur 115
Joyce, Alice 144
Judah [play] 115
Judson, H.C. 51
Julian, Rupert 157

Kaiser Wilhelm der Gross [ship] 59
Kalem Film Manufacturing Co. 21–22, 41, 59, 75, 116, 157
Kalisch, Shaindel 165
Keith's Broadway Theatre, NY 158
Kelly, Eleanor Mercein 104
Kelly, Eugene 43
Kelsey, Fred 164
Kennedy, Edgar 113
Kenton, Erle 137
The Kentucky Derby [1922] 130–131, 148, 249
The Kentucky Derby [race] 25
Kentucky National Guard 70
Kerrigan, J. Warren 74, 75, 77, 84, 91, 165
Kerry, Norman 135
Kessel, Adam 76, 112
Key, Kathleen 166
Keystone Film Co. 74
The Kid and the Sleuth [1912] 46, 196
Kildare of Storm [1918] 104, 105, 244
Kimball, Beulah 10
Kimball Sanitarium, La Crescenta, CA 170
Kinder, Stewart 62
King, Ella [KB aunt] 8
King, Henry 157
King, John [KB grandfather] 7
King, Margaret [KB aunt] 8

King, Mary O'Brian [KB grandmother] 7
"The King Baggot Rag" [music] 77
King-Bee Comedy Films Corp. 112
King Danforth Retires [1913] 210
King Edward Hotel, NY 50, 126
King of Kings [1927] 158
King, the Detective [1911] 42, 73, 192
King, the Detective and the Opium Smugglers [1912] 42, 207
King, the Detective in Formula 879 [1914] 42, 216–217
King, the Detective in the Jarvis Case [1913] 42, 73, 96, 216
King, the Detective in the Marine Mystery [1914] 42, 218
Kingsley, Grace 123
Kingsley, Pierce 51, 52
Kinsler, George 54
Kirkwood, James 55, 85, 86 106, 117, 121
Kissed [1922] 123, 129, 248
Kitchen, Karl K. 84
Koerner's Garden Theatre, St. Louis 11, 14
Kohl and Middleton Theatre, Chicago 8
Kohner, Paul 156–157
Koszarski, Richard 91, 156–157
Kurland, Gilbert 140

La Aguerro Rancho, CA 147
Lackaye, Wilton 8, 12, 14
Lad: A Dog [novel] 114
Ladies' Home Journal 30, 130
Ladies World Magazine 75
Lady Audley's Secret [1912] 46, 47, 96, 200, **201**
Laemmle, Carl 17–18, 20, 25, 26, 27, 42, 56, 57, 68, 90, 95, 121, 127, 129, 130, 133, 142–143, 156; advertising practices 22; anniversary celebrations 30, 150, 165 **167**; birth 17; Cuban films 32–39; early career 17; first film 18; first theatre 17; formed Universal 47; founded Universal City 80; illness 150, 155; in St. Louis 26; lawsuits 28, 29; loving cup 75; re-release of earlier IMP films 95–96; resistance to feature films 83, 91–92
Laemmle, Carl, Jr. 164
Laemmle, Recha 17
Laemmle, Rosabell 155
Laemmle Film Exchange 17, 22
Laidlaw, William 68
Lamarr, Hedy 170
Lambs Club, NY 52, 106, 107, 110
Landberg, Mimi Baggot [KB daughter-in-law] 162, 169, 170, 173
Landowska, Yona 82
Lang, Philip 105

Langdon, Lillian 129, 132, 143
La Plante, Laura 135, 136
LaSaint, Edward, J. 43, 44
Lasky, Jesse L. 116
Lassie, the dog 41
Lauphein, Germany 17
Lauritzen, Einar 31
The Lavender Bath Lady [1922] 131, 132, 248–249
The Law of Life [1916] 236–237
Lawrence, Florence 16, 28, 31, 84, 85 92, 163, 166; at Biograph 18; death 169–170; dismissed from Biograph 19; early career 18; "Girl of a thousand faces" 23–24; IMP leading lady 18–19; leaves IMP 29, 31; neighbor of KB 29; personal appearance, St. Louis 25–27; rumors of death 22–23
Lawrence, William E. 136
The Leader of His Flock [1913] 57, 211–212
Leah, the Forsaken [1912] 49
The Leather-Pushers [1923] 130
LeDue, E. 140
The Legion of Death [1918] 105
Leonard, Robert Z. 41, 171
Leonia Heights, NJ 73
Leslie, Arthur 86
Lessey, George A. 80, 81, 82, 89, 100
A Lesson to Husbands [1911] 114, 194
Lest We Forget [1917] 105
Lester, Kate 143
L'Estrange, Julian L. 105
Let No Man Put Asunder [1912] 202
Lewis, Sheldon 134
Liberty Loan Drives 102, 103
Liberty Loan Jimmy [1918] 103
Library of Congress 46, 77, 81, 112, 154
Lichtman, Al 138
The Lie [1912] 197
The Lie Sublime [1916] 241–242
Liebler Organization 12
Lt. Robin Crusoe, U.S.N. [1966] 173
The Life and Adventures of Carl Laemmle 15, 26
Life in Hollywood [1926/27] 251
A Life in the Balance [1915] 229–230
Life's Twist [1928] 115–116, 245
Lighting effects in film 46
Lincoln, Joseph 89
Lincoln Theatre, Chicago 8
Lloyd, Harold 77, 119, 142
The Loan Shark [1912] 199–200
Lockwood, Harold 103, 105, 136
Loew, Marcus 101, 108
Logan's Luck [play] 48
London Film Co. 59, 73, 96

Long, Walter 105
Long Island Sound, NY 83
The Long Trail [1917] 97
Longacre Bldg., NY 112
Longacre Hotel, NY 76
Los Angeles Examiner 169–170, 171
Los Angeles Express 35
Los Angeles Police Dept. 137
Los Angeles Record 163
Los Angeles Times 123, 160
Lost Horizon [1937] 158
Lost in the Streets of Paris see *The Child Stealers of Paris*
Louisville, KY 131
Louvre, Paris 68
Love, Bessie 150, 152
Love, Montagu(e) 120, 145
The Love Captive [1934] 255
The Love Letter [1923] 131, 132, 249
Love vs. Law [1913] 71, 215
The Lover's Signal [1911] 37, 184
Love's Stratagem [1909] 19
Lovey Mary [1926] 149, 150, 151, 152, 156, 162, 251
Lovey Mary [novel] 12
Lowe, G.W. 77
Lubin, Siegmund 29
Lubin Co. 29, 32, 41, 52, 75, 87, 121
Lubitsch, Ernst 157
Lundquist, Gunnar 31
Luring Lips [1921] 122–123, 247
Lusitania [ship] 100
Lyceum Theatre, London 61, 63–64
Lyons, Edward (Eddie) 43
Lytell, Burt 145

McAvoy, May 170
McAvoy, Thomas 70
McChesney, Hortense [KB sister-in-law] 173
McClure Co. 75
MacDermott, Marc 120
McDermott, Tom 140
MacDonald, J. Farrell 41
MacDonald, Jeanette 166
MacDonald, M.I. 49–50
McDowall, Roddy 171
Mace, Fred 43–44
McGill, Lawrence B. 51, 52
McGowan, Archie 140
McGowan, Helen 11
McGrath, Harold 92
McIntyre, Elmer 140
Mack, Hayward 33
Mack, Willard 166
MacLaren, Mary 166
MacNamara, Walter 57
MacQuarrie, Murdock 33
MacRae, Henry A. 149, 150
McVey, Lucille 110
Mad Holiday [1936] 166, 257
Magic Castle, Los Angeles 126
Majestic Motion Picture Co. 41
Malloy, Thomas 51

Mama's (Baby) Boy [1912] 208
The Man Across the Street [1916] 95, 239–240
The Man from Nowhere [1916] 92–93, 239
The Man from the West [1912] 198–199
Man of Mystery see *King, the Detective and the Marine Mystery*
Man or Money? [1915] 89, 235–236
The Man Who Stayed at Home [1919] 104, 105, 107, 244–245
The Man Who Was Misunderstood [1914] 81, 221–222
A Manly Man [1911] 37
Manning, James 140
Mansfield, Richard 57
Mantell, Robert 97
Manufacturing Bldg., Chicago 8
Marberg, Bertram 100
Marble Creek, ID 140
The Marble Heart [1915] 82, 231–232
Marion, George F. 155
Marmaduke, John 7
Marshall, George 137
Martin, Al W. 27
Marx Brothers 165, 169
Mary's Convert see *The Better Way*
Mary's Duke [1915] 84
Mary's Patients see *The Fair Dentist*
Mason Opera House, Los Angeles 12
Masquers Club, Los Angeles 145, 156
The Master and the Man [1911] 37, **38**, 186
Maupassant, Guy de 41
Mayer, Louis B. 105, 106, 107, 132, 137, 166
Mayo, Archie 153
Mayo, Frank 128, 166
Mears, Mary 117
Mecca Film Co. 47
Meighan, Thomas 115, 119
The Merchant of Venice [play] 11
The Merry-Go-Round [1923] 138
Mersereau, Violet 93
The Message in the Bottle [1911] 37
Metro-Goldwyn-Mayer 149, 150, 152, 165–171
Metro-Goldwyn Pictures 27
Metro Pictures 93, 100, 103, 104, 105, 106, 110, 115; and Screen Classics 106, 115, 116; sold to Marcus Loew 108
Metropolitan Magazine 117
A Mexican Warrior [1914] 219
Meyer, Edwin H. 13
Meyer, Fred S. **167**
The Midnight Guest [1923] 133
Miles, David 33, 42

The Mill Stream [1914] 81, 224–225
The Million Dollar Mystery [1914] 100
The Millionaire Cop [1912] 206
The Millionaire Engineer [1915] 225
Milne, Peter 92
The Minister [1915] 89
Minneapolis, MN 18
The Miracle Man [1919] 115
The Miser's Daughter [1910] 178
Mismated [1915] 231
The Mission of the War Chest [1918] 101–102, 243–244
The Missionary see *The Mission of the War Chest*
Mississippi [1935] 165, 256
Mississippi Valley Kennel Club 27
Missouri Historical Society 11
Mr. and Mrs. Innocence Abroad [1913] 65, 70, 96, 215
Mr. Burglar, M.D. see *A Quarter After Two*
Mitchell, Rhea 112, 113, 166
A Modern Highway Man [1912] 197
Moffat, Edward 162
"The Money Rider" [story] 154
Monogram Pictures 162
Montgomery, Baby Peggy see Baby Peggy Montgomery
Montgomery, Jack 133, 134
Moonlight Follies [1921] 123–124, 124, 247
Moore, Mary 105
Moore, Matt 93, 105
Moore, Owen 31, 56, 88, 96, 105; at Biograph 31; at IMP 31, 40; at Victor Company 51; departed for Majestic 42; in Cuba 33, 35, 39; lawsuit against IMP 31; marriage in the Catholic Church 117; marriage to Mary Pickford 34, 117; Screen Club 51, 88
Moore, Tom 105
Moorehouse, A.P. 7
More to Be Pitied Than Scorned [play] 11–12
Moreno, Antonio 119
Morgan, Jackie 139
Moroso, John 122
Morvich, the Wonder Colt 131
Mother Love [1910] 22
The Motion Picture Director 152
Motion Picture Directors 37
Motion Picture Directors Assoc. 137, 145
Motion Picture Distributing and Sales Co. 47
Motion Picture Exhibitors League of America 91
Motion Picture Magazine 50
Motion Picture Men's Association, St. Louis 26

Motion Picture News 30, 39, 76, 90, 92, 93, 97, 117, 124, 153
Motion Picture Patents Company 17, 18, 28–29, 32, 35–36, 40, 47
Motion Picture Producers of America 137
Motion Picture Supplement 16, 83, 126
Movietone sound system 160
Moving Picture News 49, 87–88, 93, 117, 124, 153
Moving Picture Weekly 89
Moving Picture World 17, 18, 19, 28, 30, 31, 33, 39, 43, 45, 48, 49, 57, 60, 69 71, 73, 75, 82, 83, 86, 91, 97, 101, 102, 108, 113, 114, 115, 122, 140–141, 145, 150, 152, 155; advertising 21, 29, 40; influenza epidemic 105; length of feature film 91; naming actors 28; "St. Louis to the Fore" 23; Screen Club elections 85, 86; "We Nail the Lie" 23
Mrs. Wiggs of the Cabbage Patch [play] 12, 150
Muni, Paul 80
Murfin, Jane 156
Murphy, Frank T. 165
Museum of Modern Art, NY 58, 62, 129, 141
Musso, John 169
Musso & Frank's Restaurant, Los Angeles 169
Mutual Film Corp. 121
My Life East and West 133, 146
My Own United States [1918] 105
Myers, Carmel 121, 122, 128, 131
Myers, Harry 124, 166
The Mystery of Thirteen [1919] 112

Nanook of the North [1922] 128
National Association of the Motion Picture Industry 105
National Press Club 101
The Naval Ball Conspiracy [1918] 100
Naylor, Hazel Simpson 126
Nazimova, Alla 106, 128
Nederlands Filmmuseum 62, 69, 129, 141
Neilan, Marshall A. 157
Neill, Richard R. 146
Neptune's Daughter [1914] 91
Nestor Film Co 43, 47, 92, 116
Never Again [1910] 177
The New Jitney in Town [1915] 232
New York Clipper 15, 56, 84
New York Dramatic Mirror 59, 73, 76, 78, 87, 98, 99, 191, 104, 106, 107, 121
New York Evening World 114
New York Motion Picture Co. 43, 47, 76, 91, 146; see also Bison Films

New York Motion Picture Exhibitors League 52, 162
New York Sun 84
New York Telegram 15
New York Telegraph 53, 54
New York Times 124, 132, 144, 152, 170
The New York Theatre, NY 12
New York World 160
Newhall, CA 147, 148
Next Time We Love [1936] 165, 256
Niblo, Fred 137
A Night at the Opera [1935] 165, 256
Night Life of the Gods [1935] 165, 255–256
Nobody's Fool [1921] 124–125, 247
Nordisk Film Co. 57, 91
Normand, Mabel 74, 75
Notoriety [1914] 218–219
A Notorious Gentleman [1935] 165, 255
The Notorious Lady [1927] 156, 252

Oberg, Helen see Brenon, Helen
Oes, Ingvald C. 91
Officer 174 [1912] 208
Ogden, Vivia 151, **151**
O'Hara, Mary 144
Ohio State Journal 109
Olympic [ship] 59
Olympic Theatre, Chicago 10
O'Malley, Pat 157
Once a Gentleman [1930] 161, 252–253
The One Best Bet [1914] 220
One Night [1915] 227
One Wonderful Night [1914] 75
The Only Child [1915] 232–233
Only Yesterday [1933] 254
An Oriental Romance [1915] 81, 226
Oshkosh, WI 17
Othello [1912] 49, 50
Otto, Henry 90, 92–93, 95, 115
Over the Hills (To the Poorhouse) [1911] 193–194
Owens Valley, CA 129
Oxnard, CA 117

Paddington Station, London 61
Palacio del Carneado, Cuba 33, 34
Palmer, Ernest 62
Panzer, Paul 93, 163
The Parade's Gone By... 159
Paramount Pictures 19, 110, 115, 128, 165
Parrott, Charles see Chase, Charley
The Parson and the Moonshiner [1912] 117, 206
Partners of the Tide [1915] 89

The Passing of Hans Dippel [play] 109
Pathé Co. 16, 23, 123, 128
Paton, Stuart 121
Patterson of the News [1916] 237
Peacock Feathers [1925] 145
Peerless Productions 162
The Penniless Prince [1911] 37, 39, 183
Peoria, IL 110
Pepper, Peter 90
Perch of the Devil [1927] 149, 153–154, 156, 157, 164, 251–252
Percy, Eileen 151
The Peril [1912] 200–201
The Perils of Pauline [1915] 99
Pershing, Gen. John Joseph 102
Peter Pan [play] 14
Peters, House 128, 140, 141, 142, 143
The Phantom of the Opera [1925] 139, 148, 165
Philbin, Mary 128, **130**, 135, 136, 138, 139
Philharmonic Auditorium, Los Angeles 137
Phillips, Dorothy 93
Phillips, Norma 84
Phone 1707 Chester [1911] 181
Photoplay 18, 50, 83, 97, 105, 159–160; contests 74–75, 83–84; star salaries 84
Picadilly Theatre, NY 142
Pickford, Charlotte (Smith) 30, 33, 36
Pickford, Jack 31, 33, 34, 115
Pickford, Lottie 31, 33, 34, 96
Pickford, Mary 57, 85, 95–96, 115, 163; at Biograph 18, 30–31; at IMP 30–31, **38**, 40, 41, 84, **187**; "The Biograph Girl" 18; departed for Majestic 42; "The Girl with the Curls" 30; in Cuba 32–39; marriage in the Catholic Church 117; marriage to Owen Moore 34, 117; *Photoplay* contest 75; re-releases of IMP films 95–96; salary 30, 84
Pickford, the Woman Who Made Hollywood 31
Picture-Play Weekly 83, 119, 143
Pictureland [1911] 35, 37, 182
A Piece of String [1911] 41, 188
Pierre, Jacques 156
Planters Hotel, St. Louis 26
Players Club of St. Louis 10, 90
Playgoers Pictures 120
Plummer, Lincoln 145
Police Court [1932] 162, 253
Pollard, Harry A. 43, 113, 114
Port Hueneme, CA 117
Powell, Frank 51
Powell, William 169
The Power of Conscience [1912] 196

Powers, Patrick A. (Pat) 75, 76
Powers Co. 47
Presbrey, Eugene Wiley 142
Prescott, Vivian 49, 111
Pressed Roses [1910] 179
Pressing His Suit [1915] 226
Pretty, Arline 77, 106
Prevost, Marie 123–125, **124**, 129, 131
Price, Kate 131, 132, 139
Princess Theatre, Montreal 15
Prior, Herbert 42
The Prisoner of Zenda [play] 8
Proctor, Thomas 70
Proctor's Theatre, New York 11
Prohibition (law) 87, 145, 163–164

A Quarter After Two [1911] 189–190
Queen of the Highway [play] 11
Quinn, William, J. 135
Quirk, Billy 56, 85–86, 106

Raffles, the Amateur Cracksman [1925] 142, 250–251
Rainer, Luise 169
Ramsaye, Terry 34, 35
Rankin, Sidney 110
Ranous, William V. 18, 19
Rau, W. "Bill" J. 139
Raver, Harry R. 51, 56
Rawlinson, Herbert 128
Ray, Charles 119
Raymond, Ned Whitney 120
Rea, Isabel 37, 39, **187**
Reardon, Ned 82, 89
Rebecca the Jewess [1913] 64
The Red Cross 101, 105
The Red Rider [1934] 255
Redbook Magazine 154
Reeves, Billy 97
Rehan, Ada 8
Reid, Hal 48, 128
Reid, Wallace 48, 119
Reliance-Majestic Films 91
Reliance Motion Picture Co. 31
Republic Theatre, NY 77, 78
The Return of Tony [1913] 71, 215
Revier Motion Picture Co. 33
The Reward [1915] 89, 235
Rex Co. 47
Rice, Helen Hegan 12, 150
Rich, Lillian 166
Richardson, F.H. 28
The Riddle of the Silk Stockings [1915] 230–231
Rinehart, Mary Roberts 15
The Rise of Officer 174 [1913] 57–58, 96, 212
Rising, Will, 10
The River [novel] 155
RKO/ Pathé 161, 163
RKO Radio Pictures, Inc. 163
Roach, Bert 163
Roach, Hal 135

Robbins, Marc 128
Robert Palmer [ship] 5
Roberts, Edith 93, 121, 122, 128
Robertson-Cole Productions 115
Robinson, Ann *see* Constantine, Ann
Robson, May 165
Roche, Arthur Somers 123, 129
Rogers, Will 119
Roland, Gilbert 156
Rolfe, Benjamin A. 103
Rolfe Photoplays 103
Romance in the Rain [1934] 255
Romance of a Rogue [1928] 157, 252
The Romance of an Old Maid [1912] 199
Roosevelt, Gladys 50
Root, Frank K. & Co. 77
Rork, Ann 156
Rork, Sam E. 155–156
The Rosary [1922] 155
The Rose of California [1912] 42
Rose of the Rancho [1914] 116
Rosen, Philip 137
The Rose's Story [1911] 42, 191–192
Ross, Nat 123
Rothstein, Arnold 160
Rowland, Richard 106, 107
The Royal Mounted [play] 16
Russell, Frank 51
Russell, Gordon 146

Sadler, William J. 86
St. Joe, ID 140
St. John, Al 162
St. Louis, MO, 7, 18
St. Louis Dispatch 23
St. Louis Globe-Democrat 13
St. Louis Post-Dispatch 23, 27
St. Louis Star 14, 25
St. Louis Times 25, 30
St. Maries, ID 140, 142
St. Maries Gazette-Record 140
St. Paul [ship] 5, 70
St. Paul's Cathedral, London 61
The "Sales Co." *see* Motion Picture Distributing and Sales Co.
Salomy Jane [play] 12, 14
"Salomy Jane's Kiss" [story] 14
The Salvation Army 101
Samson [1914] 77, 91
San Francisco [1936] 166, 257
San Juan Capistrano Mission 117
San Mateo Junior College, CA 169
Santell, Al 137
Saratoga Moving Picture Park, Brooklyn 27
Savannah, GA 92
Scardon, Paul 86–87, 121, 145
Scareheads [1931] 161, 253
The Scarlet Letter [1911] 184–185
Scheff, Fritzi 166
Schellinger, Rial B. 79
The Schemers [1912] 202–203

Schenck, Joseph M. 101, 149
Schiller Theatre, Chicago 8
Schrock, Raymond 132, 133, 135, 149
Schroeder, Doris 122, 124, 129
Science [1911] 41, 190
Scott, Sir Walter 61
Screen Actors Guild 169
Screen Classics *see* Metro Pictures
Screen Club 50, 51–53, 55, 56–57, 59, 70 76–77, 99, 110, 115, 117, 132, 137, 145; anthem 52; demise 106–107; elections 85–87 founded 51–52; social drinking 111
Screen Snapshots [1921] 123, 247
Screen Snapshots [1923] 249
Screen Writers Guild 137
The Sea Beast [1925] 152
Sebastian, Dorothy 157
Second Sight [1911] 37, 185
The Secret Cellar see King, the Detective in the Jarvis Case
The Secret of the Air see Across the Atlantic
The Secret of the Palm [1911] 37, 39, 183
Secret Service *see* U.S. Secret Service
Secrets [1933] 29, 163, 254
Sedgwick, Edward 135
Selby, Charles 82
Selig, William N. 46, 155
Selig Polyscope Film Manufacturing Co. 33, 43, 48, 57, 75, 128
Selznick Picture Corp. 117
Sennett, Mack 123
Seven Days [play] 15
Seven Faces [1929] 80
Severson, Charlotte 11
Shadows [1914] 79–80, 81, 222, **223**
Shadur, Arthur 141
Shamrocks [soccer team] 9, 10, 136
Shamus O'Brien [1912] 46, 198
The Shattered Silents 159
Shaw, Harold 57, 59, 137
Shay, William E. 33, 46, 49, 51, 68, 111, **195**
She Gets Her Man [1935] 165, 256
She Slept Through It All [1913] 209
Shean, Al 166
Sheely, Elmer 139
The Sheik [1921] 128
Shelbourne Hotel, NY 126
Sheldon, H.S. 108, 109
Sheldon, Willard 152, 162
Short Skirts [1921] 131
Shriners Ball, Los Angeles 137
Shubert, Lee 12, 14
Shubert, Sam 12, 14
The Silent Man see The Silent Stranger

The Silent Mystery [1918] 112
Silent Mystery Corp. 112
The Silent Stranger [1916] 241
The Silent Valley [1914] 221
Simpson, Russell 130, 151, 166
Sing Sing Prison, NY 84
The Slacker [1917] 105
Smalley, Phillips 121
Smiley, Joseph 33, 34, 39, 41
Smith, A. Victor 52
Smith, Albert A. 27
Smith, Charlotte *see* Pickford, Charlotte
Smith, Frank 70, 73, 77, 82
Snow, Marguerite 99–100, 102
Snyder, Matt 56
So This Is Paris [1916] 19, 242
Soccer 8, 136
Social drinking 85, 87, 145
Society for Cinephiles 141
Society of Motion Picture Engineers 137
Solax Co. 21
Solter, Harry 16, 18; departs for Lubin 29; dismissed by Biograph 19
Sothern, E.H. 8
The Soul Man [1916] 237
The Soul of the Butterfly see The Butterfly Girl
Sound era in film 159–160, 165
Spedon, Sam 86
Spehr, Paul, 31
Sporting Chance [1931] 162, 253
The Squaw Man [play] 146
Stagecoach [1939] 148
Standard Casting Directory 161
Star Theatre, NY 11
Starr, Jimmy 156
Staten Island, NY 82
Statue of Liberty, NY 134
Stedman, Myrtle 166
Steele, Minnie 135
Stella Dallas [1925] 148
Sterling, Ford 84
Stern, Abe 133
Stern, Julius 43, 68, 133
Stern, Sam 17
Sterne, Elaine 84
Stevens, Emily 103, 104, 106
Stevenson, Robert Louis 57
Stewart, Anita 84, 157
Stewart, James 165, 170
Stewart, Roy 120
Stockdale, Carl 135
Stone, Louis 156
Storey, Edith 103
The Story of the Rose see The Rose's Story
The Story the Silk Hats Told [1915] 81–82, 226
The Strand, London 61
Strand Theatre, Lexington, KY 130
Strange, Stanislaus 118

A Strange Case [1912] 208
A Strange Disappearance [1915] 230
The Stranger [1913] 213
The Streets of Make Believe [1915] 84, 227–228
Stuart, Gloria 164
Stumar, John 140, 154
Sturgeon, Rollin 121
The Suburban [1915] 82, 89, 130, 233–234
Suburban Garden Theatre, St. Louis 14, 16
The Suffragette's Revenge [1913] 60
Sullavan, Margaret 165
Sullivan, C. Gardner 146
The Sultan's Garden see In the Sultan's Garden
Sunshine and Shadow 32
Swanson, Gloria 128, 170
Swanson, William H. (Bill) 75, 76
Sweepstakes [1931] 161, 253
Sweet, Blanche 84
Sweet Memories [1911] 37, 184
Sweetheart Days see Sweet Memories

*The **T**ables Turned* [1912] 197
Tailspin Tommy [1934/35] 165, 255
Talbot, Frank 26, 27
Talent, Jane 166
Taliaferro, Mabel 106
Tally's Theatre, Los Angeles 123
Talmadge, Norma 117, 136
Talmadge, Richard 161
The Taming of the Shrew [play] 11
Tampa, FL 57
Tantalizing Eyes Contest 83–84
Taylor, Charles 11
Tellegen, Lou 97
Temple, Shirley 133
Tempted but True [1912] 199
The Temptress [1911] 37, 185–186
Terhune, Albert Payson 114
Terrace Garden, NY 52
Terry, J.E. Harold 105
Thalberg, Irving, 121, 123, 124, 129, 132, 149
Thanhauser Co. 57 100
The Theatre of Science 74
Theatrical News [Buffalo, NY] 100
Theby, Rosemary 112, 166
The Thirtieth Piece of Silver [1920] 113–115, 129, 245, **246**
Thomas, Clifford 61
Thomas, J.H. 61
Thomas, Walter 61
Thompson, Paul 153
Thornby, Robert 121
Thou Art with Me see Cheated Love
Three Kids and a Queen [1935] 165, 256
Three Times and Out [1915] 225

The Thrill Chaser [1923] 135, 250
Through Shadowed Vales [1912] 208
Through the Air [1911] 192
Through the Flames [1912] 46, 196–197
Thurman, J. Herman 109, 110
Tidden, Fritz 122
Tiffany-Stahl Productions 157
The Time-Lock Safe [1910] 31, 177
Tish [1942] 259
To Hell with the Kaiser [1918] 105
To Reno and Back [1913] 210
Tony [1915] 228
Tony and the Stork [1911] 42, 71, 193
The Tornado [1926] 139–142, 145, 148, 250
Torture Money [1937] 169, 257
Touch Me Not see *Moonlight Follies*
The Touch of a Child [1914] 217
Tourneur, Maurice 157
Tower of London 63–64
The Town Scandal [1923] 132, 249
Tracked [1911] 37, 182–183
Tracy, Louis 75
Traffic in Souls [1913] 69, 73, 77, 91
Transfusion [1910] 178
The Treasure Train [1914] 224
Triangle Film Corp. 117
Trilby [play] 8
The Trinity [1911] 114, 194
Trusky, Tom 141
The Trust see Motion Picture Patents Company
Tucker, George Loane 33, 39, 41, 42, 73, 96, 106, 115
Tucker, Richard 139, 141
Tumbleweeds [1925] 145–148, 149, 156, 251
The Turn of the Tide [1914] 222–224
Turner, Florence 27, 56
Turner, Otis 46, 48–49, 96, 111
Turner's Society 70
The Turning Point see *Man or Money?*
Turpin, Ben 22
Twain, Mark 9
The Twin's Double [1914] 80

*U*ncle Tom's Cabin [play] 27
Undine [1916] 90
Undoing Evil see *The Wanderer*
The Unholy Three [1925] 153
Union Station, St. Louis 25–27
United Artists 128, 145, 146, 148
U.S. Secret Service 99, 100, 101
U.S. Soccer Football Assoc. 136
The Universal Boy [1914] 221
Universal City 80, 93, 96 136, 140, 141 145, 165
Universal Film Manufacturing Co. (later Universal Pictures Corp.) 29, 43, 47, 60, 63 69, 70, 71, 72, 75, 77, 82, 84 89, 115, 117, 120, 121, 126, 133, 157, 160, 163, 165; Big U brand 95; Bluebird brand 136; Broadway Features 82–83, 90, 91; East Coast plants 80, 93; films in the 1920s 87, 121, 128–129, 132, 149, 152; Gold Seal brand 80, 95; move to California 70, 93–94; Red Feather Productions 90–91, 92, 93; re-release of IMP films 95–96; Rex brand 96; Universal "Jewels" 128, 131, 133, 138, 139, 142, 152 154; *see also* IMP Co.
Universal Weekly 48, 49, 70, 93, 126, 129, 136, 138, 140, 141, 149, 150, 153, 154, 155, 165
University of California Los Angeles Film Archive 31, 144
Unreasonable Jealousy [1910] 181
Up Against It [1912] [202

*V*alentino, Rudolph 115, 128, 166
Valli, Virginia 145
Van, Wally 137
Van Dyke, W.S. (Woody) 113, 32–33, 166
Van Dyke, Zina 113
Variety 85, 86, 104, 121, 120, 122–123, 131, 136, 138–139, 142–143, 144, 154, 157, 158
Venturini [Countess] 14
Verdun, France 102
The Vicar of Wakefield [novel] 89
Victor Film Co. 29, 47, 51, 74, 84, 121
Vidor, King 157, 160
Vilmy Ridge, France 102
The Violation [play] 108, 109–111
The Virginian [play] 146
Vitagraph Co. of America 18, 19, 27, 59, 75, 86, 96, 97, 157–158, 166
Vitagraph sound system 159
The Voice Upstairs see *The Anarchist*
Von Bernsdorff, Count 100
von Papen, Franz 100
von Stroheim, Erich 128, 131, 138, 157

*W*ade, John 100
Waldorf Hotel, NY 11
Walker, Alexander 159
Wallace, Ramsey 122
Wallick, James H. 12
"The Walrus and the Carpenter" [poem] 127
Walsh, Raoul 157, 160
Walt Disney Pictures 173
Walthall, Henry 97, 162
Walton, Gladys 128, 131, 132
The Wanderer [1913] 96, 211
Wanted, a Home see *The Darling of New York*

War bonds 103
Warner, H.B. 158
Warner, Sam 159
Warner Bros. 159, 170
Warner's Features Film Co. 76
Warwick, Robert 97
We Went to College [1936] 166, 257
Webb, Millard 152–153
Weber, Lois 121, 150, 166
Webster, Henry McRae 89
Wehlen, Emily (Emmy) 106
Wehrenberg, Fred 26
Weiman, Rita 136
Weiner, Philip 75
Welch, Niles 136
Welsh, Thomas 96
West, Billy 112
Westbrook, Bertha Belle 48
Western Associated Motion Picture Advertisers [WAMPAS] 137
Western Electric Co. 159
Westminster Abbey, Eng. 61
Weston, Charlie 35
Wharton, Leopold 99–102
Wharton, Theodore 99–102
Wharton, Inc. 99–102
What Happened to Mary? [1912] 97
What Price Hollywood? [1932] 163, 253
The Whispered Name [1924] 136, 250
White, Claude Graham 61
White, Leo 33
White, Pearl 99
The White Dragon see *Mad Holiday*
The White Feather see *The Man Who Stayed at Home*
White Front Theatre, Chicago 17, 165
Whitfield, Eileen 31
Whitlock, Lloyd 129
Whitney, Claire 105–106
Who Will Marry Mary? [1913] 97
Whose Baby are You? see *The Darling of New York*
Wid's 93
The Wife [play] 8
The Wife's Awakening [1911] 193
Wilber, Crane 75, 97
Wilde, Percival 123
Willard, Edward Smith 115
Willat, C.A. (Doc) 33, 34, 35, 36, 51, 52 76, 110, 111
Willat, Irvin 36, 110, 157
Williams, C. Jay 52, 121
Williams, Kathlyn 75
Wilson, Ben 86
Wilson, Bob 140
Wilson, Woodrow 99
The Winning Miss [1912] 194–195
Winning the Latonia Derby [1912] 203–204
Winton, Jane 153

The Wishing Ring [play] 14–16, 77
Witzel Photographers 169
The Wizard of the Jungle [1913] 57, 210–211
The Woman [play] 16
A Woman's Face [1941] 170, 258
Won with a Make-Up [1916] 90 238
Wood, Freeman 138, 143
Wood, Sam 157
Woodward [Judge] 162

World War I 62–63, 66, 97, 99–103, 104; films of 66, 97, 99, 105
The World-Weary Man [1912] 208–209
The World's Best Film Co. 57
Worrall, Lechmore 105
Worthington, William 121
Wray, John 160
Writers Club, Los Angeles 137
Wylie, Ida Alexa Ross 138

Yankee Film Co. 47, 166
The Yearling [1946] 259
YMCA 101
Young, Clara Kimball 84
Young, Robert 189
Younge, Lucille 41

Zellner, Lois 115
Zenith Film Co. 63
Zukor, Adolph 76, 91

www.ingramcontent.com/pod-product-compliance
Lightning Source LLC
Chambersburg PA
CBHW081542300426
44116CB00015B/2720